ROGER BACON

The Art and Science of Logic

A translation of the *Summulae dialectices*
with notes and introduction
by
Thomas S. Maloney

Early in the 1240s the University of Paris hired a recent graduate from Oxford, Roger Bacon by name, to teach the arts and introduce Aristotle to its curriculum. Along with eight sets of questions on Aristotle's natural works and the *Metaphysics* he claims to have authored another eight books before he returned to Oxford around 1247. Within the prodigious output of this period we find a treatise on logic titled *Summulae dialectices*, and it is this that is here annotated and presented in translation.

The book is unique in several respects. First, there is the breadth of its sources. Not only do we find explicit reference to the usual authors such as Aristotle, Plato, Boethius, Porphyry, Cicero, and Priscian, we also find unexpected reference to Augustine, Bernardus Silvestris, Donatus, Terence, and Themistius, along with mention of the Muslim philosophers Algazel and Ibn Rushd. Second, it is clear that Bacon is drawing on or reacting to an extraordinarily wide variety of medieval sources: Garland the Computist, Hugh of St. Victor, Master Hugo, Hugutius of Pisa, Isidore of Seville, Nicholas of Damas, Nicholas of Paris, Richard of Cornwall, Robert Kilwardby, Robert of Lincoln, and Robert the Englishman. Third, it unexpectedly presents a full-blown treatment of Aristotle's theory of demonstration. And finally, Bacon reveals a highly unorthodox view of the signification of common terms.

Bacon, here, takes his students and us deeper into medieval sources and controversy than any of his rivals do.

MEDIAEVAL SOURCES IN TRANSLATION 47

ROGER BACON

The Art and Science of Logic

A translation of the *Summulae dialectices*
with notes and introduction

by

THOMAS S. MALONEY

PONTIFICAL INSTITUTE OF MEDIAEVAL STUDIES

Library and Archives Canada Cataloguing in Publication

Bacon, Roger, 1214?–1294
The art and science of logic : a translation of the Summulae dialectices with notes and introduction / by Thomas S. Maloney.

(Mediaeval sources in translation 0316–0874 47)

Text used for the translation of the Summulae dialectices: Les summulae dialectices de Roger Bacon. Parts 1–2: De termino, De enuntiatione; Part 3: De argumentatione. Edited by Alain de Libera. Archives d'histoire doctrinale et littéraire du moyen age 53 (1986); 139–289; 54 (1987): 171–278.

Includes bibliographical references and index.
ISBN 978–0–88844–297–0

1. Logic – Early works to 1800. I. Maloney, Thomas S. II. Pontifical Institute of Mediaeval Studies III. Title. IV. Series: Mediaeval sources in translation ; 47

B765.B23S8413 2009 160 C2009–901233–2

Pontifical Institute of Mediaeval Studies
59 Queen's Park Crescent East
Toronto, Ontario, Canada M5S 2C4
www.pims.ca

MANUFACTURED IN CANADA

To my wife Stephanie,

the wind in my sails.

"Indeed, thinking itself is sometimes injurious to health."
Aristotle
Nicomachean Ethics 1153a20

Contents

Roger Bacon: The Art and Science of Logic

Part Three: Argumentation

Preface

Early in the 1240s the University of Paris hired a recent graduate from Oxford, Roger Bacon by name, to teach the arts and introduce Aristotle to its curriculum. Along with eight sets of questions on Aristotle's natural works and the *Metaphysics* he claims to have authored another eight books before he returned to Oxford around 1247. Within the prodigious output of this period we find a treatise on logic titled *Summulae dialectices*, and it is this that is here annotated and presented in translation.

The book is unique in several respects. First, there is the breadth of its sources. Not only do we find explicit reference to the usual authors such as Aristotle, Plato, Boethius, Porphyry, Cicero, and Priscian, we also find unexpected reference to Augustine, Bernardus Silvestris, Donatus, Terence, and Themistius, along with mention of the Muslim philosophers Algazel and Ibn Rushd. Second, it is clear that Bacon is drawing on or reacting to an extraordinarily wide variety of medieval sources: Garland the Computist, Hugh of St. Victor, Master Hugo, Hugutius of Pisa, Isidore of Seville, Nicholas of Damas, Nicholas of Paris, Richard of Cornwall, Robert Kilwardby, Robert of Lincoln, and Robert the Englishman. Third, it unexpectedly presents a full-blown treatment of Aristotle's theory of demonstration. And finally, Bacon reveals a highly unorthodox view of the signification of common terms.

Bacon, here, takes his students and us deeper into medieval sources and controversy than any of his rivals do.

* * *

This book has been long in the making, and I am especially grateful to all for their encouragement along the way. But I owe a special debt of gratitude to Paul Spade and Simo Knuuttila for their patience in going over with me all too numerous texts that proved to be especially troublesome. The tedious task of checking references and proof reading was parceled out to relatives, who, because of blood, had no noble way out: John and Martha Maloney, Mary Zena, and Mariam Ballantine. Their invaluable contribution is immensely appreciated. And finally I wish to thank Ms. Jean Hoff of the PIMS Press. It is simply hard to imagine a more competent, efficient, and graceful person with whom to work in smoothing out the last wrinkles of the text: *inspiciens qua acutior cogitari nequit.*

Abbreviations

CHLMP Kretzmann, Norman, Anthony Kenny, and Jan Pinborg, eds. *The Cambridge History of Later Medieval Philosophy: From the Rediscovery of Aristotle to the Disintegration of Scholasticism 1100–1600*. Cambridge, London, New York, New Rochelle, Melbourne, Sydney: Cambridge University Press, 1982.

Cn Steele, Robert, ed. *Opera hactenus inedita Rogeri Bacon*. 16 vols. Oxford: Clarendon Press, 1905?–1941. Vol. 2: *Liber primus communium naturalium Fratris Rogeri* (Parts 1–2), 1905?

Cst Maloney, Thomas S., ed. and trans. *Compendium studii theologiae. Roger Bacon: Compendium of the Study of Theology*. Studien und Texte zur Geistesgeschichte des Mittelalters, vol. 20. Leiden, New York, Copenhagen, Cologne: E. J. Brill, 1988.

CTMPT Kretzmann, Norman and Eleonore Stump, trans. *The Cambridge Translations of Medieval Philosophical Texts*. Vol. 1: *Logic and the Philosophy of Language*. New York: Cambridge University Press, 1988.

CWA *The Complete Works of Aristotle: The Revised Oxford Translation*. 2 vols. Edited by Jonathan Barnes. Bollingen Series, vol. 71, pt. 2. Princeton, NJ: Princeton University Press, 1984.

"*Ds*" Fredborg, Margareta, Lauge Nielsen, and Jan Pinborg, eds. "An Unedited Part of Roger Bacon's *Opus Maius*: '*De signis*'." *Traditio* 34 (1978): 75–136.

GL Keil, Heinrich, ed. *Grammatici Latini*. 8 vols. Vols. 2–3: Priscian. *Institutiones grammaticae*. Edited by Martin Hertz. Vol. 4: Donatus. *De arte grammatica libri*. Edited by Martin Hertz. 1855–1880. Reprint, Hildesheim: Georg Olms, 1961.

Introductiones William of Sherwood. *Introductiones in logicam. Einführung in die Logik*. Edited and translated into German by Hartmut Brands and Christoph Kann. Philosophische Bibliothek, vol. 469. Hamburg: Felix Meiner Verlag, 1995.

William of Sherwood. *Introductiones in logicam*. Translated by Norman Kretzmann. *William of Sherwood's Introduction to Logic*. [Based on Grabmann's emended text.] Westport, CT: Greenwood Press, 1966.

Logica	Alessio, Franco, ed. *Logica* (*Summa Lamberti*). Pubblicazioni della facoltà di lettere di filosofia dell'università di Milano, vol. 59. Florence: La Nuova Italia Editrice, 1971.
LM	Rijk, L. M. de. *Logica Modernorum: A Contribution to the History of Early Terminist Logic*. 2 vols. Vol. 1: *On the Twelfth-Century Theories of Fallacy*. Vol. 2, pt. 1: *The Origin and Early Development of the Theory of Supposition*. Vol. 2, pt. 2: *The Origins and Early Development of the Theory of Supposition: Texts and Indices*. Assen: Van Gorcum, 1962 and 1967.
Mullally	Mullally, Joseph P., ed. and trans. *The Summulae logicales of Peter of Spain*. (Only the treatises on supposition, relatives, ampliation, appellation, restriction, distribution, and exponibles.) Publications in Mediaeval Studies, vol. 8. Notre Dame, IN: University of Notre Dame, 1945.
Ohi	Steele, Robert, ed. *Opera hactenus inedita Rogeri Bacon*. 16 vols. Oxford: Clarendon Press, 1905?–1941.
Sd	Libera, Alain de, ed. "Les Summulae dialectices de Roger Bacon." Parts 1–2: *De termino, De enuntiatione*. Part 3: *De argumentatione*. *Archives d'histoire doctrinale et littéraire du Moyen Age* 53 (1986): 139–289; 54 (1987): 171–278.
Tractatus	Rijk, L. M. de. *Tractatus, Called Afterwards Summule Logicales*. Assen: Van Gorcum, 1972.
"Le traité"	Libera, Alain de, ed. "Le traité *De appellatione* de Lambert de Lagny (Lambert d'Auxerre)." *Archives d'histoire doctrinale et littéraire du Moyen Age* 48 (1981): 227–285.

Introduction

I. INTRODUCTORY COMMENTS

During the 1240s at the University of Paris higher education in the liberal arts was undergoing one of its periodic revolutions. Since 1210 there had been a papal ban on lecturing on (and reading) the so-called natural works of Aristotle, the *Metaphysics*, and commentaries on these by Islamic authors. This left students and masters there extremely envious of their peers at other universities where the ban was not in effect. But at some point early in the 1240s a young Oxford-trained master by the name of Roger Bacon was invited to teach there and with him came a knowledge of and interest in the new Aristotle that was to result in a recognition of this master as a true pioneer in the study of Aristotle.

Before his return to Oxford, Bacon seems to have written eight sets of questions on Aristotle's natural works and the *Metaphysics* as well as one commentary. He speaks of eight other books, and Ferdinand M. Delorme thinks of these as other questions, whereas one of Bacon's recent biographers, Stewart Easton, suggests they may have been commentaries.[1] Whatever the case, this all represents a prodigious amount of work for so short a time and serves to give us our first indication of the kind of person Bacon was.

Among the works certainly ascribable to him from this period or immediately afterwards are a treatise on grammar (*Summa grammatica*) and one on logic (*Summulae dialectices*). Such labors are certainly in keeping with the duties of a master of arts at a university, so what distinguishes Bacon is not the mere fact that he wrote a treatise on grammar and one on logic but the range of sources they utilize and the evidence they supply for an author who is very much in touch with the cutting-edge of intellectual developments in his time. More to our purposes here, they portray Bacon as one who views the study of logic and language in a considerably more scientific setting than do other important teachers of this

1 For Delorme's list of the disputed books see *Opera hactenus inedita Rogeri Bacon*, ed. Robert Steele, vol. 13: *Questiones supra octo Physicorum Aristotelis*, ed. Ferdinand Delorme with Robert Steele (Oxford: Clarendon Press, 1935), pp. xx and xxi (henceforth, *Ohi* plus volume title); and for a discussion of this issue see Stewart C. Easton, *Roger Bacon and His Search for a Universal Science: A Reconsideration of the Life and Work of Roger Bacon in the Light of His Own Stated Purposes* (1952; reprint, New York: Russell and Russell, 1971), pp. 59–61.

period whose works have survived, like William of Sherwood, Peter of Spain, and Lambert of Auxerre.

Up to the present Bacon's grammar has not received the attention it deserves but his textbook on logic has come into its own in the last two decades or so, especially the section on semantics in Part 2. This was provoked principally by the discovery and editing of a missing chapter of his *Opus maius* of 1267 entitled "*De signis*," which caused a flurry of interest in Bacon's semiotics and semantics. The publishing of the "*De signis*" also ultimately inspired a new edition and English translation of Bacon's *Compendium studii theologiae* of 1292, all of whose Part 2 was a re-working of the material in the "*De signis*," and an English translation of three treatments by him of the problem of universals, two of which were written during the Parisian period already mentioned.[2]

In 1987–1988 another significant step in Bacon studies was taken with the appearance of a new edition of Bacon's *Summulae dialectices*, by Alain de Libera.[3] The first printed edition was published in 1940 by Robert Steele, but was based on only one of the two extant manuscripts and turned out to have some serious flaws.[4] The continuing interest in Bacon studies, the centrality of the *Summulae dialectices* to contemporary interest in medieval logic, and the specific interest in Bacon's semantics moved de Libera, then, to collate the two known manuscripts and the result is the Latin text that serves as the basis for the present translation.

The above considerations serve equally well as a motive for a translation of Bacon's treatise on logic. There is a special need for the translation and it devolves from the more general interest these days in the study of the history of logic, especially semantics and the theory of argument. Yet to those who do not enjoy facility in the Latin language the medieval period is effectively closed to direct inspection. And I suspect this is more true in the field of logic than in any of the other traditional branches of philosophy. The works of many of the great theologians of the thirteenth century

2 See *Compendium studii theologiae. Roger Bacon: Compendium of the Study of Theology*, ed. and trans. Thomas S. Maloney, Studien und Texte zur Geistesgeschichte des Mittelalters, vol. 20 (Leiden, New York, Copenhagen, Cologne: E. J. Brill, 1988; henceforth, *Cst*) and *Three Treatments of Universals by Roger Bacon*, trans. Thomas S. Maloney, Medieval & Renaissance Texts & Studies, vol. 66 (Binghamton, NY: Medieval & Renaissance Texts & Studies, 1989).

3 See Alain de Libera, ed., "Les Summulae dialectices de Roger Bacon," parts 1–2: *De termino, De enuntiatione*; part 3: *De argumentatione. Archives d'histoire doctrinale et littéraire du Moyen Age* 53 (1986): 139–289; 54 (1987): 171–278 (henceforth, *Sd*).

4 See *Ohi*, vol. 15: *Summa grammatica necnon Sumule dialectices Magistri Rogeri Bacon* (Oxford: Clarendon Press, 1940). For comment on the manuscripts see below, Section III: The Latin Text.

have long been accessible through translations, but only much more recently has interest shifted to the lesser masters of arts. So, the general interest in the history of logic, the significance of the masters of arts, and a very vibrant specific interest in Roger Bacon all support the labor entailed in such a translation.

II. THE AUTHOR, DATE, AND PLACE OF COMPOSITION

While at one time there was some question as to whether the *Summulae dialectices* was written by (the yet to be Franciscan) Roger Bacon or by the Dominican Robert Bacon, it seems now agreed that it is the work of the former. Among the considerations that support this view is the fact that its author has to be someone with an incredibly broad range of intellectual interests and a willingness not to be bound by tradition in deciding what sorts of sources are appropriate for a textbook on logic. The work reveals itself as a kind of synthesis between speculative and applied knowledge in that it draws on works beyond the expected Aristotelian *Organon* and Boethius' commentaries on those works. In support of this one could note the following.

(1) There are references, among others, to Aristotle's *Physics* and *Meteorology*, to Boethius' *De arithmetica*, Isidore of Seville's *Etymologiae*, the *Liber de causis*, Alfred of Sareshel's *De mineralibus* and his commentary on Aristotle's *Metaphysics*, Nicholas of Damas' *De plantis*, Bernardus Silvestris' *De mundi universitate* (*Cosmographia*), and Robert Kilwardby's commentary on Aristotle's *On Sophistical Refutations*. In addition it shows complete familiarity with Algazel's *Logica* and *Metaphysica*, Ibn Sina's *De congelatione et conglutinatione lapidum*, and Ibn Rushd's *De substantia orbis* along with his commentary on Aristotle's *Metaphysics*.

(2) It presents Aristotle's theory of demonstration, and this, in turn, reveals complete familiarization with that author's *Posterior Analytics*, a work only slightly known in the 1250s and almost never referenced, granted Peter of Spain points to it twice. Even as late as 1292 Bacon is lamenting the fact that the logical treatises of Aristotle were only "lately received and lectured on" and that (a now unknown) Master Hugo was the first to lecture on the *Posterior Analytics*. So extraordinary is familiarity with this work that Bacon goes out of his way to tell us that he met the man and read his book.[5]

(3) Apropos of the dispute over authorship there is the fact that the work espouses the semantic theory that names are originally imposed to signify (appellate) only existing things, a minority opinion in mid-thirteenth-century logic but one clearly adopted by

5 See *Cst* 1.14.

> Roger Bacon in his 1267 *Opus maius*, "*De signis*." Roger Bacon announces this theory in the present work (241) and holds fast to it to the end of his life, as is evidenced in his last work, the 1292 *Compendium studii theologiae*.

When one takes all of these things into consideration one can see why de Libera would say of this work: "It is not a dialectician, it is a philosopher who is speaking here, someone familiar with Greco-Arabic knowledge, doubtless already a scientist, soon perhaps an experimenter, in any case certainly a pupil of Robert of Lincoln and a continuer of Alfred of Sareshel."[6] The author has to be a master of arts, says de Libera, and the whole picture rules out anyone prior to 1245–1250 and Robert Bacon.[7]

But the date and place of the composition of the work are considerably more problematical. Robert Steele, the work's first editor, speaks of the *Summulae dialectices* as "the last work of his University career," and Easton agrees. Neither gives a clear reason for this belief, but I suspect that it is rooted in the recognition that it would have taken Bacon some years to acquire familiarity with the works cited above that ordinarily find no mention in a logic textbook. Easton does grant it could have been composed earlier in the 1240s.[8] Indeed, it would have been quite natural for a beginning teacher in the arts to include such a work in his earliest writings. Easton and Theodore Crowley both agree that Bacon probably left Paris for Oxford in 1247 and both (Easton explicitly, Crowley by inference) agree that it seems very improbable that he continued to teach in an arts faculty once he returned to Oxford.[9] In addition there is a practice within the work itself that supports a Parisian setting for its composition. In a work clearly written at Paris, and possibly before the *Summulae dialectices*, Bacon's *Questiones supra libros octo Physicorum Aristotelis*, he draws on the Seine river (not the Thames) for an example: "... as if my palm would touch the Seine."[10] Then in our work, when discussing supposition, Bacon proposes two propositions to analyze, "The Seine runs" and "England is a good land" (227) and goes on to give extended analysis only of the former. "The Seine runs" is used a third time as an example in this work, in a syllogism involving equivocation (387), and Montmartre is mentioned in yet another example (386). Twice he gives examples of the category Place. In

6 *Sd* 1–2, p. 147.

7 Ibid., p. 151.

8 *Ohi*, vol. 15, p. xx, and Easton, p. 61.

9 Easton, p. 70, and Theodore Crowley, *Roger Bacon and the Problem of the Soul in His Philosophical Commentaries* (Louvain: Editions de l'Institut Supérieur de Philosophie; Dublin: James Duffy, 1950), pp. 27–34. Easton (p. 87) says the return to Oxford could not have been later than 1250.

10 *Ohi*, vol. 13, p. 226.5–6.

the first he mentions Paris and England (not Oxford) (24); in the second he cites Vernon three times and Paris once, whereas London (not Oxford) and Rome get mentioned once (105). In another context, when he has cause to be speaking of languages, he mentions French, Greek, and Latin, but not English (118). And, finally, in Part Three, he chooses the French town Troisvaux for an example (442). Clearly, there is a pattern here. It is hard to imagine an English author's proclivity for French place names as examples if he were writing for students in an English locale. There was, after all, considerable rivalry between those two universities. So, these tend to support a Parisian site for the composition of the work and a date in the 1240s prior to 1247, both favored by Steele and Easton. Crowley, whose interests are elsewhere in his book, does not address the date of the *Summulae dialectices*.

The editors of the "*De signis*," on the other hand, point to a statement in Bacon's 1292 *Compendium of the Study of Theology* in which he says that he had aired the solution to the problem of the appellation of privative and negative terms forty years earlier, and our work is the principal one of his writings which does indeed discuss that problem.[11] Thus they speak of a date of 1250 for the composition and place it at Oxford. Neither Crowley nor Easton comments on this particular text and its significance for dating our work.

Alain de Libera, however, says that it is "probable" that the work was given a final redaction in Oxford around 1250, and mention of a redaction implies an earlier and initial composition at Paris.[12] It is, for him, a work that, while fundamentally in the Oxfordian tradition, has elements from the Parisian tradition: "The *Summulae dialectices* owes much to the Oxfordian tradition. Nothing, however, prevents thinking that it also reflects Bacon's teaching at Paris, the culture of the masters at the University of Paris, his discussions with the Parisian masters of arts of 1245 to 1250."[13]

11 "But this objection is reasonable which I came across forty [years] ago when I aired [the solution] to this difficulty." (*Cst* 2.106.) For the editors of the "*De signis*" see Margareta Fredborg, Lauge Nielsen, and Jan Pinborg, eds., "An Unedited Part of Roger Bacon's *Opus Maius*: '*De Signis*'," *Traditio* 34 (1978): 79, n. 7 (henceforth "*Ds*"). The "objection" he refers to is taken to be the theory held by Richard of Cornwall that terms like 'dead man' have univocal appellation, such that Christ can be said to be a man during the three days he was in the tomb. For Richard's position see Franz Pelster, "Der Oxforder Theologe Richardus Rufus O.F.M. über die Frage: '*Utrum Christus in triduo mortis fuerit homo*'," *Recherches de théologie ancienne et médiévale* 16 (1949): 258–280.

12 *Sd* 1–2, p. 152. See also p. 141.

13 Ibid., p. 154. Elsewhere (p. 152) he speaks of the Parisian influence as "very probable."

Support for an Oxford setting could, perhaps, come as a corollary to the answer to a further question: Does the work stand in the Oxfordian or the Parisian tradition?[14] Because of the work's link with, among others, the logic treatises *Cum sit nostra* and *Ut dicit* and the complete familiarity it shows with the *Fallaciae ad modum Oxoniae* (even if on several points it disagrees with it), those looking at the issue from this point of view, then, could be seen to be suggesting that the work was written in Oxford or that the influence entered principally through a redaction made there around 1250.

Now the hypothesis of a Parisian site in the 1240s for the composition cannot account for the Oxfordian tone of the work nor for the current interpretation of the words "forty [years] ago when I aired [the solution] to this difficulty." On the other hand the hypothesis of an Oxfordian site in 1250 cannot account for the consistent reference to Parisian or French place names, nor for the fact that such a book is not surprising for one who is writing profusely and teaching logic at Paris in the 1240s, nor for one who will not be teaching the arts after 1247. So, it is exceedingly difficult to say which of these two hypotheses is the more plausible since both stand on solid but mutually exclusive historical considerations. To accept the Parisian hypothesis it seems we must ignore the Oxfordian tenor of the work and a date of 1252 as plausibly inferred by Bacon's own words. To accept the Oxfordian hypothesis it seems we must ignore the Parisian place examples and the fact that Bacon would have had no real reason for either writing or redacting this work after 1247 since he is consumed by scientific interests and is no longer teaching in the arts. We are left with an urgent need for some third hypothesis about its composition, one that will reconcile all the data that ground such apparently well-founded historical considerations.

To that end I propose that we clarify one point and rethink one of the persuasions that ground the hypothesis that the work was composed at Oxford around 1250. The clarification pertains to the temptation to think that a work in the Oxford tradition must have been composed in Oxford and to the reinterpretation of the claim that Bacon's words in 1292 "forty [years] ago when I aired" refer to our work.

Does it follow that a book in the Oxfordian tradition has to have been composed in Oxford? Surely not. Bacon was educated in that tradition as a student before he left Oxford for Paris and it was that mind-set that he took with him to Paris. Then he developed it against his Parisian challengers, adopted some of their tradition when persuaded, and crafted the amalgamation we now call the *Summulae dialectices* during some seven

14 For a delineation of the issues that constitute these two traditions see Alain de Libera, "The Oxford and Parisian Traditions in Logic," in *CHLMP*, pp. 174–187, esp. 176–177. For a description of the Parisian and Oxfordian influences on this work see *Sd* 1–2, pp. 151–154.

years at Paris. De Libera speaks of this work as "a complex original of premises and themes where the Parisian magisterial element coexists often along side the usual authoritative data of the Oxford tradition."[15] Given Bacon's thorough foundation in that tradition as a student at Oxford it seems there is every good reason for thinking that whatever he composed in his early career would reflect that training. So, I do not think that anyone should be tempted by the mere fact that the work is predominantly in that tradition to overemphasize its significance for establishing the place of the work's composition.

The reinterpretation requires one to take another look at Bacon's claim in 1292 to have aired a solution to a problem of appellation forty years earlier, that is, in 1252. Easton recounts in his biography of Bacon that Adam Marsh writes in a letter of 1248 that Richard of Cornwall received permission to go to Paris to lecture on the *Sentences* but changed his mind "because of poor health" and remained in Oxford.[16] In letters of 1252 or 1253 Adam again requests the Minister General to allow Richard to act on the earlier invitation, but this time the reason given is "because of the more overwhelming situations of the disturbances."[17] Richard, he says, tells him that it is "very urgent" that he go. Easton suggests that Richard may have been mixed up in the disturbances or that they were directed against him (since no one else is urgently leaving Oxford at this time). At this point Easton notes that A. G. Little once suggested, without pursuing the point, that Bacon may have been involved in the disturbances.[18] Easton then proceeds to hypothesize that Bacon, who was a skilled debater and who disliked theologians in principle and Richard of Cornwall specifically, may have confronted Richard publicly and was thereby the cause of the disturbances. We know Richard was lecturing at Oxford in 1252, that Bacon knew him then, and that Bacon detested his teaching on the appellation of privative and negative terms. This would explain why Richard wanted out of Oxford and wanted out quickly, namely, to escape the harassment. Easton concludes: "All these facts are consistent with a public challenge about the year

15 *Sd* 1–2, p. 154.

16 For this and what follows in this paragraph see Easton, pp. 95–97.

17 The Latin for this phrase is somewhat obscure and reads: "*ob vehementiores perturbationum occasiones.*" One could translate it more literally by 'because of the more vehement occasions of the disturbances'. What is very curious is the use of the comparative degree of '*vehemens*'. Situations/occasions more overwhelming/vehement than what? The use could suggest that there was more than one situation/occasion that was overwhelming/vehement and Adam is referring to the worse of the two.

18 A. G. Little, "The Franciscan School at Oxford in the Thirteenth Century," *Archivum Franciscanum Historicum* 19 (1926): 842.

1252."[19] And, I would add, we know from Bacon's later writings just how obnoxious he could be. Such a public altercation with Richard would have been completely in character for him.

Now, if we – Easton does not do this – connect Richard's public harassment in 1252 with Bacon's comment "forty [years] ago when I aired," we have a way to resolve the conflicting data as to the place and date of our work. The airing mentioned in the *Compendium of the Study of Theology* would be reinterpreted to be referring, not to the *Summulae dialectices* and its composition, as the editors of the "*De signis*" suggest, nor to the redaction proposed by de Libera, but to the public confrontation with Richard in Oxford in 1252 over an issue on which he had done his homework earlier. This reinterpretation would provide a referent for the remark in 1292 and at the same time allow our work to have been composed in Paris before he left in 1247.

In this new hypothesis the scenario would be as follows. Bacon as a student, well educated in the tradition in logic at Oxford, is called to Paris around 1240 to teach the arts, logic among them, and writes a textbook on logic that reflects the Oxfordian tradition. In 1247 having become more and more familiar with the sciences through his reading of people like Isidore of Seville, the *Liber de causis*, Alfred of Sareshel, Nicholas of Damas, and Bernardus Silvestris, he becomes totally consumed by a new vision of a universal science, and gives up his position in Paris to be able to return to Oxford so he can associate with a group inspired by Robert Grosseteste who have similar interests in the sciences and languages, all the while prevailing on his wealthy brother to give him a huge sum of money for secret books and instruments and tables. While at Oxford he pays attention to what is going on in the University (though not teaching there) and in 1252 he becomes infuriated with Richard of Cornwall, then lecturing on the *Sentences* at Oxford, and begins to publicly harass him over the issue of the appellation of privative and negative terms – Christ may not be called a man during the three days in the tomb! – causing Richard to prevail upon Adam Marsh to intercede for him with the Minister General for permission to accept a deferred invitation to lecture in Paris. Richard goes to Paris and does not return to Oxford until 1256, and then to serve as regent master in theology for the Franciscans, and around 1257 Bacon enters the Order. This puts Richard in a position to repay Bacon for past offenses, and Easton speculates, "Richard's influence may have been one of many that prevented [Bacon] from rising to any degree of dignity within this Order in spite of his intellectual attainments."[20] It might also

19 Easton, p. 96. The hypothesis is somewhat reminiscent of the twelfth-century story of William of Champeaux being driven to a monastery by his public humiliations at the hands of Peter Abelard.

20 Ibid., p. 97.

explain the hostility Bacon reserved for Richard even forty years later and which finds expression in one of his final references to him: "And I knew well the worst and most foolish [author] of these errors, who was called Richard of Cornwall, a very famous one among the foolish multitude. But to those who knew, he was insane and [had been] reproved at Paris for the errors which he had invented [and] promulgated when lecturing upon the *Sentences* there, and after he had lectured on the *Sentences* at Oxford from the year of our Lord 1250. From that [year of] 1250 up till now the multitude has remained in the errors of this master, i.e., for forty years or more, and it is currently gaining strength at Oxford, just where this unlimited madness began."[21]

Just how plausible is this reinterpretation of the referent of Bacon's remarks in 1292? It has two major weaknesses. First, the case for it is circumstantial; there is simply no evidence in the historical record of a public altercation between Bacon and Richard at Oxford around 1252. Second, the current interpretation of the disturbances mentioned by Adam Marsh focuses on a conflict that arose when Adam, in February of 1253, insisted to the Chancellor and masters of the University that Thomas of York be appointed to take Richard of Cornwall's place in lecturing on the *Sentences* at Oxford.[22] The seculars were much opposed because Thomas was not a master of arts, was less qualified than Richard, since Thomas had never lectured on the *Sentences*, and indeed, the very request for any Franciscan to do such was most exceptional. The University finally agreed to Adam's request but only on the grounds that it would never happen again. One is left to speculate why Richard took deep offense in this struggle, for that is not part of the historical record. Whatever the reason, we have here a documented historical event that offers a possible understanding of what the disturbances could have been about.[23]

So where does this leave us? I am not prepared to say that Little's suggestion has no plausibility in it, (a) given what we know about Bacon's per-

21 *Cst* 2.86.

22 I am indebted to Rega Wood for the background to what appears in this paragraph. For a brief description of the debate over the inception of Thomas of York in theology at Oxford and the role Adam Marsh played in it see A. G. Little, *The Grey Friars in Oxford* (Oxford: Clarendon Press, 1892), pp. 37–39, and I credit Wood for the reference.

23 Ironically, the introduction of the York affair into the discussion could be taken in a way that accommodates Little's intuition about Bacon's trouble-making, namely, by clarifying Marsh's use of the comparative degree in his "because of the *more* overwhelming situations of the disturbances." He would be thinking of *both* the York and the Bacon situations and describing one of them as the more compelling. One could easily think of Bacon's public harassment as more painful than some hurt endured in the York affair. For the quotation see above, n. 17.

sonality and the contempt in which he held Richard; (b) given a strong consensus (Steele, Easton, Crowley, and presumably de Libera) that Bacon most probably was not teaching in an arts faculty after 1247, in consequence of which he would have no reason for composing a treatise on logic around 1250, and very little, if any, for redacting an earlier composition; (c) given the lack of a sufficiently plausible explanation of why the York affair would have been so painful to Richard that it would inspire such a sense of urgency in him to take up the invitation to go to Paris which he had so recently turned down; and (d) given the way in which the theory can settle the date and place of the composition of the *Summulae dialectices* in a way that conflicts with no historical data. Nevertheless, it must be stated again that there is no historical evidence of a public conflict between Richard and Bacon at Oxford around 1252. The upshot seems to be that now we have three hypotheses to account for the place and date this work, and all three of them have serious problems.

III. THE LATIN TEXT

The original printed edition of the *Summulae dialectices* was edited in 1940 by Robert Steele in the fifteenth volume of the *Opera hactenus inedita Rogeri Baconi*, comprising chiefly works written by Bacon during his first sojourn in Paris, i.e., during the 1240s.[24] Because it was based on only one manuscript, Oxford, Bodleian, Digby 204 (identified in the notes as O.), and because of numerous problems within the text, Alain de Libera has taken the pains to collate a second manuscript, Seville, Biblioteca Capitular Columbina 5–2–40 (identified as S.), with the former to produce the edition on which the translation is based. The existence of the second manuscript was announced by E. Longpré in 1938, too late for Steele's use, but no printed text was ever made from it.[25] De Libera lists the contents of each manuscript and gives an analysis of the quality of the two (both are seriously faulty), indicates his choice of the Digby manuscript as the principal text, and then proceeds to articulate his method of editing.[26]

Both manuscripts are highly contracted and the variations and lacunae present serious and numerous difficulties in producing a reasonable facsimile of the original text. Those familiar with the art of editing such texts, therefore, will not be surprised to find that de Libera's edition stands in need of not a few corrections. Where it is necessary to emend the Latin text

24 Robert Steele, ed. *Opera hactenus inedita Rogeri Bacon*. 16 vols. Oxford: Clarendon Press, 1905?–1941.

25 E. Longpré, "La *Summula dialectica* de Roger Bacon," *Archivum Franciscanum Historicum* 13 (1938): 204–205.

26 See *Sd* 1–2, respectively, pp. 139–140, 167, and 167–170.

in order to be faithful to the manuscripts or secure a coherent translation, I call attention to this in the notes.

In contrast to the recent editions of Peter of Spain's *Tractatus*, William of Sherwood's *Introductiones in logicam*, and Lambert of Auxerre's *Logica* de Libera has decided, more often than not, not to divide the contents of Bacon's *Summulae dialectices* into paragraphs in the logical sense, but rather into much smaller units, employing a rubric not always apparent. This results in unnecessary fragmentation and makes the larger logical moves within the text less apparent. In three instances it has even produced the anomaly of incomplete sentences. For this reason the translation abandons his format and re-structures the text along lines that give a much more clear indication of the major and minor breaks that Bacon himself intended. The result is, however, that now the paragraph numbers in the Latin text and in the translation do not agree. To facilitate cross referencing these two texts, de Libera's paragraph numbers are placed in brackets at the end of each of the paragraphs in the translation, and one may find in an appendix a table of correlations that matches up the paragraph numbers in the two works.

One who reads the Latin text of de Libera's edition will notice several anomalies. In Part Two the paragraph number 166 appears twice; the enumeration jumps from 329 to 340 and from 483 to 494; and 496 appears twice. In Part Three where 506 should be, one finds 596. But perhaps more bothersome is the numbering system itself. Instead of a simple, continuous enumeration from beginning to end, or at minimum within each of the three Parts and the Prologue, one finds that the enumeration begins anew after the Prologue at the beginning of two subdivisions of Part One: 1.1 (Predicables) and 1.2 (Predicaments). Parts Two and Three are numbered separately but at least continuously within each Part. De Libera's method makes referencing the text more troublesome than is necessary. For this reason in the translation all the paragraphs are numbered successively from beginning to end, thus providing a one-number basis for referencing any part of the translation, a process employed with success by Albert G. Judy in his edition of Kilwardby's *De ortu scientiarum*.

IV. TRANSLATION

The first question a translator of a Latin text like the *Summulae dialectices* must ask pertains to the audience for whom one is writing. Do they read Latin? How much do they know about medieval philosophical discourse? Should references to Latin sources by the Latin text's editor be reproduced? Surely no one will pick up this translation for a little casual reading, and hence one thing is certain: the translation need not be of such literary quality that the language itself would recommend the reading. Those who consult this work will be looking to understand the technical points made by Bacon about logic and semantics, his position in the thirteenth-century controversies. The translation has in mind principally three groups: (1) those who can read no Latin at all; (2) those who have a facility in Latin but who, having come upon an especially problematical text in Latin, wish to see how someone who has pondered the text at even greater length and is deeply familiar with the work as a whole has managed to make sense out of it; and (3) those who have a facility in Latin, but who often find much value in using a translation first and then proceeding to the original version when the translation gives evidence that the translator is having difficulty rendering the author's thought with complete confidence. This has brought me to the following considerations which guided the execution of various features of the present translation.

In the (French) Introductions to Parts 1–2 and Part 3 of his edition of the *Summulae dialectices* Alain de Libera has provided a wealth of material on the twelfth-and thirteenth-century influences on Bacon's position in the logic controversies of his time. Since these are then available to the reader, and for reasons of economy, they are not re-presented here. What are, however, noted are his occasional comments on the significance of what Bacon is saying.

Some translations leave the reader with an unwarranted level of confidence. To avoid this I have determined to present a more or less literal translation and to follow the custom that places the troublesome Latin terms and phrases in parentheses in the text itself. (See, e.g., the unusual use of '*demonstratio*' in the opening line of the Prologue.) The reader is immediately alerted to the fact that the meaning of the original needs close scrutiny even though an interpretation is presented in the form of the translation provided. It seems to me that the field of medieval philosophical literature is in rather desperate need of a greater standardization in the translation of what is already standardized terminology in Latin. To this end I have kept a ready eye on Kretzmann's translation of William of Sherwood's *Introductiones* and on those of Kretzmann and Stump in *The Cambridge Translations of Medieval Philosophical Texts*, sacrificing on occasion preference to harmony, without doing damage to the meaning to be conveyed. Much of their terminology and phrasing will be found in this translation. There is one notable exception, the term '*ad placitum*'. In the "Introduction" to my edition and translation of Bacon's *Compendium studii theologiae* (pp. 26–29) I argued at length, based on the research of J. Engels, that translation by "conventionally" or "arbitrarily" does not really do justice to the notion that the Medievals wanted to convey and that the more literal "at one's own pleasure" or simply "at pleasure" does just that.[27] Were

27 See J. Engels, "La doctrine du signe chez saint Augustin," ed. F. Cross, in *Studia Patristica*, vol. 6, pp. 366–373, Texte und Untersuchungen, vol. 81 (Berlin: Akademie-Verlag, 1962), and his "Origine, sens et survie du term boécien '*secundum placitum*'," *Vivarium* 1 (1963): 87–113.

Augustine the prevailing influence in this matter the case might be different; but (against others) I think it is more probable that Boethius is.[28] The paradigm for Bacon for the way in which words get attached to things is, after all, the naming of infants at Baptism and the naming of pets.

Apposition will often be used where '*sive*' is found in Latin and is obviously meant to convey true apposition; otherwise it will be translated by 'or', and the reader will be left to determine whether apposition or disjunction is intended. Similarly, '*vel*' and '*aut*' are often used by Bacon interchangeably, and cannot be relied on to signify, respectively, a soft or hard disjunction. (See, e.g., *Sd* 2.151, 157, 159 in the Latin text.) He also uses '*ei*' when the reflexive '*sibi*' is needed. When this is significant, attention is called to it in the notes.

The identification of the precise referent of pronouns (especially when subjects of verbs) is as problematical in Medieval Latin syntax as it is in modern English. Where such referents are too far removed to be easily remembered, or where they need to be disentangled from alternative candidates, I will use the convention of placing them in brackets. Thus, for example, what would otherwise appear as "it applies here" becomes "[the first meaning of the term] applies here." More often than not, however, bracketed words are supplied simply to make the text more understandable. The price, of course, is a less than aesthetically pleasing page, but scholars, I think, are willing to pay it in exchange for being alerted to the places where caution is due.

On those occasions when internal cross-references appear, often in the form of something like "as has already been said," I insert in parentheses the number of the paragraph in the translation to which reference is made. A clause such as "as was just said" refers one to a prior remark within the same paragraph.

With considerable reluctance I conceded to the removal of all third-level headings. Because, however, there are some noticeable shifts within the lengthy sections as now headed, I have inserted additional spacing between some paragraphs to indicate Bacon is moving to an issue different from the one just discussed but still covered by the prior heading. See, e.g., the break between paragraphs 23 and 24. When that extra spacing appears at the top of a page it is, of course, less noticeable.

Finally, when quoting from Sherwood's *Introductiones* I use the Brands and Kann edition of the Latin text and Kretzmann's translation of Grabmann's Latin edition. Because of the particular texts involved, this presents

28 That Augustine is the principal source of Bacon's semantics is a claim on which I have attempted to cast reasonable doubt. See Thomas S. Maloney, "Is the *De doctrina christiana* the Source for Bacon's Semiotics?" in Edward D. English, ed., *Reading and Wisdom: The* De doctrina christiana *of Augustine in the Middle Ages* (Notre Dame, IN, and London: University of Notre Dame Press, 1995), pp. 126–142.

no problem. In quoting from Peter of Spain's *Tractatus* I use de Rijk's edition of the Latin text and the selective translations by Kretzmann and Stump found in *The Cambridge Translations of Medieval Philosophical Texts*. For those parts of the *Tractatus* not translated by Kretzmann and Stump I have provided my own translation. This enables me to achieve a higher degree of standardization in terminology than had I used Francis P. Dinneen's translation of the *Tractatus*, a work to be used with considerable caution. For those parts of the *Tractatus* also translated by Joseph Mullally I provide reference so that the reader may consult his translation, even though all translations of that work are my own. For references to Lambert of Auxerre's *Logica* I use Alessio's edition of the Latin text (except for the section in Chapter Eight "On Appellation," for which I use de Libera's more recent edition) and the translation of the chapter called "Properties of Terms" by Kretzmann and Stump found in *The Cambridge Translations of Medieval Texts*; all other translations of this work are mine. Finally, when Aristotle is quoted in English the translation will be that provided in Jonathan Barnes' edition of *The Complete Works of Aristotle*, unless otherwise noted. On occasion the translation will be my own from the Latin version found in the series *Aristoteles Latinus*.[29]

Where reference to various works is required over and over again, abbreviations and full bibliographical data are supplied in the list of Abbreviations given above.

V. CONCLUDING REMARKS

The value of such a work as this is, obviously, entirely tied up with its use. Hopefully, the appearance of this translation will have a result that is

29 Translations in English now available are: William of Sherwood's *Introductiones in logicam*: *William of Sherwood's Introduction to Logic*, trans. Norman Kretzmann (Westport, CT: Greenwood Press, 1966; henceforth *Introductiones*); Peter of Spain's *Tractatus*: *Peter of Spain*: *Language in Dispute*, trans. Francis P. Dinneen, Amsterdam Studies in the Theory and History of Linguistic Science, Series III: Studies in the History of the Language Sciences, vol. 39 (Amsterdam and Philadelphia: John Benjamins, 1990) – note, however, that this translation has been severely criticized by E. J. Ashworth (*Vivarium* 30 [1992]: 277–281) and should be used with great caution; for tract 7 (On Properties of Terms): *The Summulae logicales of Peter of Spain*, ed. and trans. Joseph P. Mullally (Notre Dame, IN: University of Notre Dame Press, 1945; henceforth Mullally); and for tracts 2 (Categories), 3 (Predicables), 4 (Syllogisms), 5 (Topics), and 7 (selections: fallacies of Composition and Division): *The Cambridge Translations of Medieval Texts*, vol. 1: *Logic and the Philosophy of Language* (trans. Norman Kretzmann and Eleonore Stump (New York: Cambridge University Press, 1988), respectively, pp. 80–88, 88–101, 217–226, 226–245, and 245–261; and Lambert of Auxerre's *Logica* (selection: the Properties of Terms): trans. Kretzmann and Stump, ibid., pp. 104–162.

more than the sum of its parts, for with it, and for the first time, scholars competent in English but unable to read Latin will be able to compare three extremely rich sources for our understanding of thirteenth-century logic and semantics: William of Sherwood, Peter of Spain (in part or in Dinneens's sometimes idiosyncratic translation), and Roger Bacon. Shortly I hope to be able to provide a translation with explanatory notes of Lambert of Auxerre's complete *Logica* so that English readers can get at the comprehensive comparisons they need. Until then, at least Lambert's discussion of the property of terms can be approached fruitfully through the translation of the appropriate chapter by Kretzmann and Stump in *The Cambridge Translations of Medieval Philosophical Texts*. There is still much valuable work to be done simply in discovering where these four major figures of the mid-thirteenth century agree and disagree, to say nothing of all the work needed to uncover their various sources, few, if any, of which have been translated into any modern language. Much work is needed on a comparative study of their theories of categories, supposition, demonstration, modal argument, syllogistic, topics, and the fallacies, to say nothing of the pedagogical qualities of their works as textbooks on logic.

ROGER BACON

The Art and Science of Logic

Prologue

[1] An introduction is a short and straightforward lead-in (*aperta demonstratio*) to an art or a science.[1] An art is a collection of many principles leading to one end. For example, there are many rules or precepts for composing verses, and a collection of these is said to be the art of composing verses. And '*ars*' (art) is derived from '*arcere*' (prevent) or '*artare*' (prohibit) because it prohibits and keeps us from error. Science is the possession of a noble mind which, shared, receives increment, but refused, [creates] a possessor with an excessive desire, and which quickly perishes if not shared.[2] And art differs from science in that science is the very knowledge that rests in the mind and informs it,[3] whereas art is that same knowledge but as related to some task which it regulates. [P.1–4]

[2] There are two kinds of art, mechanical and liberal, and likewise two kinds of science. A mechanical art is one through which the subject matter takes a desired shape and is ordered to a fitting end by the work of hands in the open court of the senses, like the shoemaker's and the builder's. And they are said to be mechanical from '*moechari*' because they cause the intellect of man to be *moechus*, that is, adulterous, inclining it totally to temporal and inferior things when it ought to inquire after things perpetual and superior and thus finally arrive at a knowledge of the Creator. The liberal arts are those through which the intellect of man is perfected when it discovers and judges without manual labor what is true in signs, e.g., grammar, logic, and rhetoric, which are the parts of the Trivium, and arithmetic, geometry, music, and astrology, which are the parts of the Quadrivium.[4] Or, according to others, grammar, logic, and rhetoric are the parts of the Trivium and accidental modes of philosophy that treat of the

1 The *Cum sit nostra* also presents Bacon's wording of this definition of 'introduction' up to the phrase "or a science." (For this and comment by L. M. de Rijk see *LM*, vol. 2, pt. 1, pp. 442–446 and 417.8.) Alain de Libera points to the discussion of art and science in 1–2 as evidence of Parisian influence on this work, which book, however, he says, is basically in the Oxford tradition. See *Sd* 1–2, pp. 152–154.

2 For the sources of this definition of 'science', its various formulations, and its relevance for the hypothesis that the present work received its final redaction in Oxford see *Sd* 1–2, pp. 151–154. De Libera's references are to Hugh of St. Victor and Hugutius of Pisa.

3 For this notion of science see Aristotle *Physics* 7.3.247b18.

4 For an interesting study of the ways in which 'logic' and 'dialectics' came to be used in naming the branch of knowledge covered by *summulae* such as the

signs of things like discourse, whereas natural [philosophy], mathematics, mechanics, and moral [philosophy] are essential ones, because they treat of things and are the principal parts of the Quadrivium. These arts are said to be liberal either because they liberate man from the cares of this world, or because they make man free (since temporal things promote the servitude of those who seek them), or because only freemen or nobles were accustomed to learn them. Within the mechanical arts one supports another, as carpentry supports navigation, for it prepares a ship for the latter's use, and one supports all, as does the art of crafting. Likewise within the liberal arts one supports another, as the art of declining [a word] supports the art of forming patronymics, and geometry supports astrology, and one supports all, as does logic. [P.5–10]

[3] Logic, as a science, is the habit of distinguishing what is true from what is false by means of rules or maxims or dignities by which we comprehend the truth of a locution through our own efforts or with the help of others. And logic is so-called from '*logos*', which means discourse, and '*lexis*', which means reason or understanding – as it were, the science either of reason joined to discourse or of discourse joined to reason. [P.11–12]

[4] Logic, in as much as it is a science, requires four things, just as every science does, namely, a subject that it treats, parts of the subject, characteristics of the parts that are proven about the parts, and rules or dignities or maxims or principles or precepts by which the characteristics of the parts are proven. Its subject, moreover, is argumentation, i.e., syllogism, because every argument is a syllogism or is reduced to a syllogism.[5] A syllogism is a statement in which, certain things having been posited, necessarily something else comes about because of the things that were posited, as in 'Every man runs, Socrates is a man; therefore Socrates runs'. Syllogisms have integral parts, like a term and a proposition: a term, e.g., 'man', 'Socrates', 'runs'; a proposition, e.g., 'Every man runs'. In another sense syllogisms have subjective parts, like the demonstrative syllogism, the dialectical syllogism, and the sophistical syllogism. The syllogism that examines, however, is not an essential part of syllogism, but accidental to it, as will later become clear (372).[6] The characteristics of the parts are,

Summulae dialectices see Pierre Michaud-Quantin, "L'Emploi des termes *logica* et *dialectica* au Moyen Age," in *Arts libéraux et philosophie au Moyen Age*, Actes du quatrième congrès international de philosophie médiévale, Université de Montréal, Canada, 27 August–2 September 1967 (Montréal: Institut d'études médiévales; Paris: Librairie philosophique J. Vrin, 1969), pp. 855–862.

5 While Aristotle acknowledged a difference between inductive and deductive inference, in his formal logic he does attempt to show that induction can be reduced to syllogistic form. See *Prior Analytics* 2.23.68b15–36.

6 See also 5.

e.g., universal and singular, and finite and infinite, which pertain to a term; modal and assertoric (*de inesse*), and true and false, which pertain to a proposition; and perfect and imperfect, which pertain to the others. Dignities are common and *per se* known propositions that a logician uses when he constructs his proofs, like 'Of whatever a definition is predicated the thing defined is also predicated', and 'Of whatever a species is predicated its genus is also predicated', and the like. [P.13–17]

[5] Logic contains at least five parts,[7] namely, the book *Categories* which is on terms; the book *On Interpretation* which is on propositions, i.e., statements; the book *Posterior Analytics* which is on demonstrative syllogism; the book *Topics* which is on dialectical syllogism; the book *On Sophistical Refutations* which treats of sophistical syllogism; and some speak of a sixth book which is on syllogism that examines. But it can be better said that a science can be formulated about disputation that examines, since "that examines" is an essential differentia of *disputation* in that it directs one to something else just as disputation does.[8] But this science is not primarily and principally a part of logic, but secondarily and in a sense subordinated to it, because logic treats of syllogism and the differentiae of syllogism. [Science] that examines does not do this but rather pertains to disputation. Besides these there is the book *Prior Analytics*, which is on syllogism considered by itself and absolutely. But the book of Porphyry and the books of Boethius do not pertain to the substance of the art or its being, but to the well being of logic, and similarly [the book] *Six Principles*.[9] [P.18]

[6] Logic as an art is reason attentively discerning, that is, the careful science of disputing. In every art seven things are investigated, namely, the task, the work, the goal, the subject matter, the parts of the art, the instrument of the art, and the parts of the instrument. The task of logic is to dispute, and from this task it is called dialectics, i.e., from '*dia*' which means two, and '*logos*' which means discourse, and '*lexis*' which means reason, because it is an exchange between two, namely, between an opponent and a respondent, i.e., one who judges. And dialectics is three-fold. In one way it is said to be all of logic in as much as it is defined in this way: "Dialectics is the art of arts, the science of sciences, which alone knows

7 MS. O. reads "six parts." See *Sd* 1–2, p. 173, n. 61.

8 For Bacon's treatment of disputation that examines see below, 371–373. For comment on 'to something else' (*ad aliud*) see 3. n. 112.

9 The book that goes by the name *Six Principles* is in fragmentary form, treats principally of the *Categories* of Aristotle, and has often been attributed to Gilbert of Poitiers. For a discussion of its authorship see *Aristoteles Latinus*, ed. Lorenzo Minio-Paluello, vol. 1, pts. 6–7, *Porphyrii Isagoge, translatio Boethii, et Anonymi Fragmentum Vulgo Vocatum "Liber Sex Principiorum,"* (Bruges and Paris: Desclée de Brouwer, 1906), pp. xliii–lv, and for the text, ibid., pp. 35–59.

how to know, which alone knows how to make people know, that from which all and without which no science [is perfectly understood]."[10] In another way it is said to be the science of disputing and discerning based on probable things taken absolutely, that are set forth in the book *Topics*, which is on dialectical syllogism. Dialectics is given a third name, whether it proceed from probabilities taken absolutely or [from opinions probable] to someone, namely, to a respondent, and because of this, disputation that examines is said to be a kind of dialectical disputation. The work of this art is to not-lie about things it knows and to be able to expose those who do lie.[11] The goal is to bring to light or investigate what is true and destroy what is false. Its subject matter is every proposed question of which the truth or falsity is sought. A question containing a doubt is a proposition like 'Does Socrates run or not?' Logic has two parts: the art of discovering and the art of judging. The art of discovering is what teaches how to discover terms, propositions, and syllogisms; the art of judging is the correct analysis (*discretio*) of these as to whether they have been well discovered or not. The instrument of this art is argumentation. And the parts of the instrument are terms and propositions, about which mention has already been made (4). [P.19–27]

[7] One should know, therefore, that in one sense logic is part of philosophy, in the sense in which it has just been discussed. In another sense it is an instrument of philosophy, in as much as philosophy itself uses logic and the subject matter of logic and all its other parts, because every other science uses syllogism and argumentation and proves something about something else, and this with the help of logic. In connection with this one should know that in one sense logic is said to be the science of sciences in as much as it ensures that all the other sciences operate correctly, just as the hand ensures that it and all the other members operate correctly. And just as the hand is said to be the organ of organs, so logic is said to be the science of sciences, and thus is nobler than all the others. But in another sense and in as much as it is directed *per se* to other sciences, serving them, it is more base and more ignoble. [P.28–29]

10 The quotation is not exact. Cf. Augustine *De ordine* 2.13.18, ed. R. P. H. Green, Corpus Christianorum Series Latina, vol. 29 (Turnholt: Brepols, 1953), p. 128.5–11: "When, therefore, would one move to construct other things, unless one would first distinguish, note, set out, and project the discipline of disciplines, which they call dialectics, as one's very own sort of device and instrument? This teaches one to teach, this teaches one to distinguish; in this very [discipline] reason demonstrates and makes known what it is, what it desires, for what it is useful. It knows how to know; it alone not only desires but is able to make people know."

11 This is a paraphrase of what Aristotle says in *Sophistical Refutations* 1.165a24–27. I am indebted to Sten Ebbesen (University of Copenhagen) for pointing this out.

[8] The first part of logic, therefore, is the book *Categories* because it is on terms, as has been mentioned (5); they are the origin and starting point. Because of this one should diligently consider the whole nature of terms since "a small error in the beginning is large in the end," as Aristotle says in the beginning of *Heaven and Earth*,[12] because when those things that stand at the beginning are unknown, those things that come after them are also unknown. To this end Boethius offers an invitation to the teachers of boys in the book *On the Training of Scholars* when he says, "In this order is one to reach the heights of such a regal body, namely, logic: first, there must be acquired an integral knowledge of terms and their unhidden relation to one another in a proposition."[13] But a knowledge of the five universals comes first, because, as Porphyry says, this is very useful in understanding the categories.[14] And so we must first treat of these. [P.30]

12 Aristotle *On the Heavens* 1.5.271b8–9, 12–13.

13 Pseudo-Boethius *De disciplina scholarium* 1.11, ed. Olga Weijers, Studien und Geistesgeschichte des Mittelalters, vol. 12 (Leiden: E. J. Brill, 1976), p. 97.3–6.

14 Porphyry *Isagoge*, in *Porphyry the Phoenician: Isagoge*, trans. Edward W. Warren (Toronto: Pontifical Institute of Mediaeval Studies, 1975), p. 27.

Part One

Terms

PREDICABLES

[9] One should know, therefore, that one kind of term is universal, another singular. [1.1.1]

[10] A *singular* term is one that applies only to itself and is not common to many, i.e., one that is predicated of one thing alone (like an individual), as are 'Socrates', 'Plato', 'Cicero', 'this white', or 'this one who comes'. A *universal* is what is naturally suited to be predicated of several things, as are 'man', 'ass', and 'animal'.[1] And so a singular term is the same for a logician as a proper noun is for a grammarian. A universal term, for the most part, is the same as an appellative name, because every universal is the same as an appellative, although not vice versa in the sense in which we are now speaking of a universal, because no equivocal is a universal nor of this kind. And so a common name in logic corresponds to an appellative noun in grammar more than a universal name does, for the name 'dog' and the like are common names, but not universal ones.[2] Let what is called a suppositum in grammar be called here in this doctrine a subject, and what is there called an appositum is here called a predicate. And the basis for this will be made more clear later on (238).[3] [1.1.2–5]

[11] There are five universals, namely, genus, species, differentia, proprium, and accident. [1.1.6]

[12] *Genus* is what is predicated of more than one thing differing in species in respect of what they are (*in eo quod quid*), as 'animal' is predicated of more than one thing differing in species in respect of what it is,

1 Around the middle of the thirteenth century there was a variety of ways to define the term 'universal'. See, respectively, William of Sherwood's *Introductiones*, trans. Kretzmann, p. 51; Peter of Spain's *Tractatus* 2.1, trans. Kretzmann and Stump, *CTMPT*, pp. 80–81; and Lambert of Auxerre's *Logica*, p. 51.4–21.

2 Or, to put it another way, all common names are appellative nouns and are also universal names except those common names/appellative nouns like 'dog' (meaning a barking, four-footed animal, a celestial constellation, the "Dog star," or a certain sea creature) that are equivocal.

3 In classical grammar the subject of a sentence was called a *suppositum*, i.e., a term placed under a broader term (the predicate), which latter was thought of as being apposed (*appositum*) to the former.

that is, of more than one species, e.g., *man, ass*, and *cow* and the other species of animals, because a man is an animal, an ass is an animal, and a cow is an animal.[4] Genus is predicated of these in respect of what they are because, to the question raised about something, "What is it?" one should reply, "It is an animal," just as to "What is a man?" [the response is] "An animal," and so on. [1.1.7]

[13] *Species* is what is predicated of more than one thing differing in number in respect of what they are, as 'man' is predicated of more than one individual or singular, e.g., of Socrates and Plato, and so on of others, and 'ass' of Burnellus and Balduinus, and thus of other species and other individuals that are individuals of one species. I say "differing only in number," i.e., in respect of the number of the seven accidents [described] by Porphyry and Boethius, which are: country, family, form, figure, place, time, and proper denomination.[5] Or this way according to Boethius in his commentary *On Porphyry*: "in number," that is, in terms of the units by which they are counted, because the unit in terms of which Socrates is counted is different from that by which Plato is counted.[6] Or this way: "differing in number," that is, in respect of the number [of distributions] of a common form or species throughout different matter, because the matter of one individual is different from that of another whereas their form is the same in essence, granted it differs in being (*esse*), because the division of species into individuals is through material, not formal, parts, as is written in Book Three of the *Metaphysics*.[7] And in agreement with this is what is said in Book Seven of the same, namely, that the cause of difference is matter.[8] Thus individuals differ in virtue of the multiplication of a common form in different matter in such a way that diversity is causally attributed to matter, and occasionally to form, as is made clear elsewhere (25).[9] There is some-

4 The phrase "*in eo quod quid est*" is a Latin translation of Aristotle's phrase "ἐν τῷ τί ἐστι" in *Topics* 1.5.102a33–102b3, and is translated in various ways, all of which refer to an essence in some way: that which serves to distinguish *kinds* of things. I have translated the phrase by "in respect of what" because of the explanation that follows in Bacon's and Aristotle's text.

5 Jacqueline Hamesse, ed., *Les Auctoritates Aristotelis: Un florilège médiéval, étude historique et édition critique* (Porphyry), Philosophes Medievaux, vol. 17 (Paris: Béatrice-Nauwelaerts, 1974), p. 300, no. 13.

6 Boethius *In Isagogen Porphyrii Commenta* 2.6, ed. Samuel Brandt, 2nd ed., Corpus Scriptorum Ecclesiasticorum Latinorum, vol. 48 (Vienna and Leipzig: F. Tempsky and G. Freytag, 1906), p. 191.5–8.

7 See Aristotle *Metaphysics* 3.4.999b21–24.

8 Aristotle *Metaphysics* 5.6.1016b32.

9 To what is Bacon referring when he says that numerical difference is *occasionally* attributed to form? Probably to the claim in 25 that the names of the sun, moon, and Phoenix are universal terms because the forms of what they name *could* be

thing somewhat similar to this in the case of an image in a mirror that is multiplied when the material parts of the mirror are broken. And species is predicated of individuals in respect of what they are because, to the question raised about individuals in respect of what they are, one should reply with reference to their species. Thus, "What is Socrates?" "A man." "What is Burnellus?" "An ass," and so on. [1.1.8–12]

[14] *Differentia*[10] is what is predicated of more than one thing differing in species in respect of how they are qualified (*in eo quod quale*), as 'nonrational' is predicated of an ass or a cow, which differ in species, and 'mortal' of a man and other things. It is not predicated in respect of what it is, but in respect of how it is qualified because, to the question raised by how it is qualified in respect of some species, one should reply by reference to a differentia. Thus, how is *man* qualified? "As mortal and rational." How is *ass* qualified? "As nonrational and mortal." [1.1.13]

[15] One should know, moreover, that one kind of genus is a most general genus, one kind is a subalternate one; one kind of species is a lowest species, one kind a subalternate; and one kind of differentia is a differentia that divides a genus, one kind one that constitutes a species. A most general genus is one above which there is no overarching genus, and thus a genus that in no way is a species. A subalternate genus is one that is a genus and a species. And likewise a subalternate species is said to be a species in comparison to higher things; in comparison to lower things they are said to be genera. A lowest species is what is a species in such a way that it is in no way a genus, and beneath which there is no other lower species, but only individuals. And this is clear in every category. Let one be taken as an example, namely, the category Substance, in which *substance* is the most general genus. *Animate body, animal body*, and *rational animal* are subalternate genera and subalternate species; *man* is a lowest species.[11] *Corporeal* and *incorporeal* and the others that are subalternates are divisive and constitutive differentiae because *corporeal* divides *substance*, and it, added to *substance*, constitutes its species, namely, *body*; and *animate* divides

---

multiplied if they did not exhaust all the matter in their respective species, which he thinks each does. In his *Questiones altere supra libros prime philosophie Aristotelis* Bacon says that supercelestial bodies "are not things capable of being multiplied, neither on the part of matter nor on the part of form," because each comprises all the matter in its own species. (Ed. Robert Steele, *Ohi*, fasc. 11, p. 154.10–11, trans. Thomas S. Maloney, *Three Treatments of Universals by Roger Bacon*, Medieval & Renaissance Texts & Studies, vol. 66, p. 64.)

10 This Latin term is anglicized to underscore the fact that it has, as will be seen, more a technical meaning than 'difference' ordinarily conveys.

11 The translation takes "*corpus animal*" as a scribal error for '*corpus animale*'. (See *Sd* 1–2, p. 178, 19.3.) The term does not reappear in the ensuing discussion in this paragraph.

body and it, added to *body*, constitutes *animate body*; *sensible* divides *animate body*, and it, added to *animate body* constitutes *animal*; *rational* divides *animal* and constitutes *rational animal*; and *mortal* divides *rational animal* and thus constitutes *man*. Likewise, other differentiae divide those same genera, but constitute other species, as will be clear in [the discussion of] the categories and as is clear in this figure:[12]

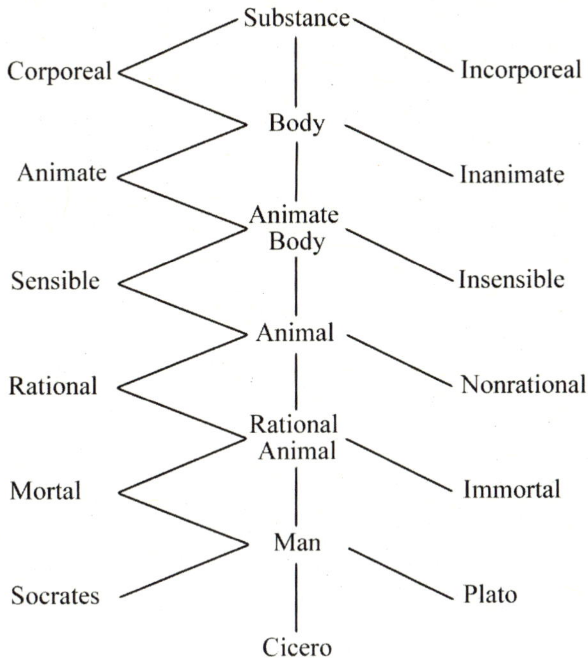

[1.1.14–20]

[16] A *proprium* is spoken of in four ways.[13] In one sense it is said to be what applies to a species and to it alone, but not to every individual of that species, as to be a physician, to be a grammarian, and the like are

12 The schema that follows is traditionally called the Tree of Porphyry because of its somewhat conical shape and the fact that it is suggested by a passage in Porphyry's *Isagoge*. In the center columns under *substance* are the various subalternate genera/species down to *man*, a lowest species. On the sides are differentiae, and those on the left, added to the genus immediately above, constitute the succeeding species, each also a genus for the next lower species. Note, however, that 'Socrates', 'Plato', and 'Cicero' are the names of *individuals* of the species *man* and not lowest differentiae. For comment on the species *immortal rational animal* see 64.

13 The Latin term is anglicized to alert to the fact that it does not convey exactly the same sense as 'property' does today.

propria of *man*. In a second sense a proprium is said to be what applies to every individual of some species but not [to that species] alone, as to be two-footed is a proprium of *man* and to be four-footed is a proprium of *horse*. In a third sense it is said to be what applies to a species and every individual, but not always, as to grow gray-headed applies to a man in old age. In a fourth sense it is said to be what applies to a species and every individual of that species, and always,[14] as to be able to laugh is a proprium of *man* and to be able to bray of *ass*, and to be able to moo of *cow*, and so on. And this proprium is a proprium in the strictest sense, for it is properly a proprium. One should know, however, that a proprium is spoken of in respect of an ability and not an actuality. Hence, *man* is not said to be able to laugh because he is always laughing, but because he is naturally suited to laugh. Likewise, *man* is not said to be two-footed because he has two feet, but because he is naturally suited to have such. It is, therefore, a proprium in the last sense that is converted absolutely with a species and is applicable to all its individuals and always, and is thus predicated in the sense of an aptitude in respect of a qualification.[15] So, how is *man* qualified? One answers correctly, "As able to laugh." How is *ass* qualified? "As able to bray," speaking of a convertible, accidental quality, not an essential one, as will be stated later.[16] [1.1.21–27]

[17] An *accident* is what is present and absent without the corruption of a subject, as is whiteness, blackness, knowledge, heat, cold, good, bad, wet, dry, sweet, bitter, and the like.[17] All these are present to a subject without the corruption of the subject because they are not part of the essence of a subject, since the essential parts of anything are matter and form, as the soul of Socrates is a form and his body matter, which alone constitute and make up Socrates. The case is similar with *man*, which is a species. Therefore, the genus *rational animal* is matter and *mortal* is form.

14 Bacon has inadvertently (here and later in this paragraph) omitted to add "and it alone" to the phrase "to some species" in this traditional definition. Cf. William, Peter, and Lambert. Respectively, *Introductiones*, trans. Kretzmann, p. 56; *Tractatus* 2.14, trans. Kretzmann and Stump, *CTMPT*, p. 85; and *Logica*, p. 61.8–9.

15 For example, whatever is true of a man is also true of something able to laugh, and vice versa.

16 See 35.

17 'Accident' is the Aristotelian term for what we might today call an attribute or a characteristic which serves for the description of something. (See Aristotle *Topics* 1.5.102b3–8.) The corruption of something is its total destruction. Thus to talk about accidents is to talk about attributes a thing might have at one time and not at another, and still be essentially (substantially) the same *kind* of thing. Following Aristotle the medievals speak of nine classes (genera) of accidents, and each of these, together with "Substance," will be the subject of the next section. See *Topics* 1.9.103b22–24 and also, below, 38.

All the other things, however, accrue to a man outside his essence and form, and so do not constitute a subject, and hence are present without the corruption of a subject. Those same things are absent without the corruption of a subject, like coldness; and any of the others can be absent from *man* or Socrates without *man* or Socrates undergoing corruption. [1.1.28]

[18] Nevertheless, one should know that the absence of an accident from a subject can be considered in two ways: either in respect of existence or in respect of understanding. The absence, moreover, is understood in both ways in the matter at hand. One sort of accident is separated from a subject in respect of existence, as is whiteness from Socrates as well as black or cold and hot, whereas another sort is absent only in respect of understanding, as is blackness from a crow and whiteness from a swan,[18] because, since an accident is not an essential part of a subject (it being neither matter nor form),[19] it is clear that an accident can be absent from a subject either in respect of existence or in respect of understanding without the subject's corruption, because only essential parts give being or nonbeing (corruption) to a subject, since through their presence they give being and through their absence they give nonbeing. [1.1.29–30]

[19] But one should note that for an accident to be absent in respect of understanding is nothing other than to understand a subject in terms of its essential principles and not in so far as it has accidents. And this way of thinking is true, but the other is not, that is, the understanding of a subject as not being under an accident. This [latter] is something absurd, because a bodily substance cannot be considered as not having quantity, nor a swan as not having whiteness, though they can be considered and thought of without attending to their having such.[20] [1.1.31–32]

[20] But then one should further know that substance has a two-fold being: the being of nature, i.e., natural being, and temporal being. If one speaks of the natural being of a subject, it can be said that an accident can be absent from a subject absolutely – in respect of existence and understanding – without the corruption of the subject. And according to this kind

18 Bacon says we can only *think* of swans as black because, as Kretzmann notes, medievals knew only of white swans and hence thought of their color as a contingent but unvarying characteristic. Black swans were later discovered in Australia. (*Introductiones*, trans. Kretzmann, p. 55, n. 14.)

19 In 17 Bacon used 'form' to refer to the soul as a co-principle of the essence of man, and the term is to be taken in the same sense here, i.e., as referring to a *substantial* form. In a broader yet customary use of the term, accidents are called *accidental* forms.

20 The occurrence here of 'cannot be considered' is a poor choice of words, given the last part of the sentence. To set up the contrast perhaps a more precise statement might be: "because a bodily substance cannot *fail to have* quantity nor a swan fail to have whiteness ... ."

of being, namely, natural being, substance is naturally prior to accident.[21] But if one speaks of temporal being, [the subject] can at least be understood without attending to its not being under an accident. And so an accident can be absent in respect of understanding, although not in the way it temporally exists, because perhaps an accident like quantity exists at the same time as a composed bodily substance. And the case is the same for any subject with its own proper characteristic (*cum sua propria passione*).[22] [1.1.33–34]

[21] These things having been explained, it is clear that there are two kinds of accidents: an accident separable from a subject because it does not always accompany its subject, but sometimes is in it, sometimes not, just as running, arguing, whiteness, blackness, knowledge, virtue, vice, and the like are accidents separable from a man. But there is also an inseparable accident that accompanies its subject, as blackness is an accident inseparable from a crow, an Ethiopian, and an Elanis, and whiteness from snow, a swan, and others.[23] And here let us speak of separation and lack of separation in connection with the act of existing, and not of the separation of an accident in connection with understanding, because in this [latter] sense every accident is separable from a subject. [1.1.35–36]

[22] But should one pose an objection in respect of death, corruption, generation, and combustion – for these cannot be present to a subject without its constitution nor be absent without its corruption,[24] [or, more accurately], for generation cannot be present without the constitution of a subject, nor the others without the corruption of a subject – one can reply

21 Substance is naturally prior in the sense that changes in accidents do not affect a substance essentially, though, were the substance to be destroyed, the accidents could not remain.

22 We can think (abstractly) of *man* without thereby thinking of any particular gender, size, shape, or color, or as existing at any particular time in history. But, says Bacon, no entity could exist that way, at least, not if it is a bodily substance (which must have quantity) or a substance having a proper accident, i.e., a proprium. (Since the context requires that 'perhaps' be construed with 'quantity' and not 'exists', the text can be accurately read when omitting 'perhaps'.)

23 De Libera informs me that Priscian identifies the Elanes as a people in Arabia, and that he chose the reading in MS. S. ("*Elani*") over that in MS. O. ([*ebeno*] [*ebano*]), which means ebony, on the principle that the more difficult reading is to be preferred. The example of ebony is found in the *Isagoge* itself. See Porphyry *Isagoge*, trans. Warren, p. 62.

24 In the translation, the words from the dash to the point of the insertion of the note number seem like something the author wrote and fully intended to erase. What is said incoherently and inaccurately here is restated clearly and accurately in what follows immediately. In making sense of the paragraph I suggest one simply omit the clause.

that some things are accidents that are a path to the being and nonbeing of a subject, like these, whereas others are they that follow upon the being of a subject and adhere to it, disposing it separably and inseparably.[25] Generation and corruption are in the prior group, and yet Porphyry does not speak of such; here he has the others in mind. Or, one could reply that the subject of generation and corruption is the material source of something capable of being generated and corrupted, because it always remains without its own corruption. And so generation and corruption can be absent without the corruption of their subject, and likewise with respect to death and combustion. [1.1.37–39]

[23] But according to the first solution, [i.e., when we speak of things in the natural order (20)], it is probably correct to say that species is not always predicated of more than one thing, as 'Phoenix' is not, for there is only one Phoenix and likewise only one sun, moon, earth, and the like.[26] Similarly, differentia is not always predicated of more than one thing, e.g., that differentia which constitutes the Phoenix, the sun, and the like. For all species are constituted by some differentia, and likewise for all others. For Boethius says in his commentary *On the Categories* that Porphyry defines 'differentia' and 'species' the way he does – and one is to understand them in this way – not because every differentia is always predicated of several species and individuals, but because "it is more frequently predicated of several things than of only one."[27] One should add that such informatory remarks (*notificatio*) are not substantial definitions or accidental descriptions that are still true, but certain common and accidental explanations (*explanatio*). Thus it is not necessary that they agree entirely with all [instances]. The case is similar in respect of [Porphyry's] description of, or observation about, accident, because the observation is general; and because of this it more frequently than not fits accidents, but not in all cases. [1.1.40–43]

[24] One should know that a qualification (*quale*) is spoken of in three ways, namely, as a substantial, i.e., essential, qualification, which pertains to the substance, i.e., the essence, of a thing, like a differentia, which is a substantial form.[28] An accidental qualification is something else, and it is

25 Reading at *Sd* 1–2, p. 182, 37.7, '*ipsum*' against '*eum*' in MSS. O. and S. and the text. I am indebted to Sten Ebbesen for calling my attention to this grammatical error in the MSS.

For the notion that generation and corruption have a kind of intermediary, ontological status between that of substance and accidence see Aristotle *Metaphysics* 10. 7.1057a18ff.

26 For further comment on such one-member classes see 25, 225, 239, and 240.

27 Boethius *In Categorias Aristotelis libri quattuor* 1, PL 64.177D.

28 This observation and what follows in 24 are very helpful clarifications not found in the treatment of predicables in the texts of William, Peter, and Lambert.

spoken of in two ways: one is convertible with a subject, and such is a proprium that is converted with the species of which it is predicated; the other is an accidental qualification that is common to many things and is not reserved to any one. Such is an accident, for an accident is predicated in respect of a qualification; but not all, as Boethius says in his second commentary *On Porphyry*.[29] He says that an accident in the category Quality, e.g., knowledge, virtue, whiteness, blackness, and the like, is predicated in respect of a qualification, and only such, for all the others of the eight categories are predicated in respect of how a thing presents itself, as, were one to ask, "How does Socrates present himself?" one will answer correctly that he is two cubits tall, is doing something, is being acted upon, exists today, is in England, is in Paris, is lying down, is sitting, has his shoes on, or is armed. Nevertheless, the older ones distinguish eleven modes of predicating something of a first substance, and this is correct: Does the thing exist? What is it? How many are there? How does it relate to others? What are its qualities? Where is it? When is it? How is it situated? What does it have? What does it do? What does it undergo? The first question pertains to an entity that is common to the ten categories. After it there are ten questions because of which the ten categories were invented.[30] [1.1.44–47]

[25] But one should know that a universal is not always predicated of several things that are actually more than one. For it is not for this reason that it is said to be a universal, but because it is naturally suited to be predicated of several things. And because of this these are universals: 'sun', 'moon', 'Phoenix', because, although they are not predicated of things actually more than one, yet they are naturally suited to be predicated of more than one thing, because the forms of the sun, the moon, and the Phoenix could be multiplied in several individuals, if they existed. But, because the form in each of these occupies all the matter naturally suited to it in one individual, there is no more than one, and because of this it is not predicated of more than one. Yet of its nature it could be predicated of more than one thing. Hence, when it is said that genus is predicated of

---

Medievals often use the term 'quality' equivocally and with no further indication of its precise meaning in the context. When they say that names signify a substance together with a quality, the quality in question is to be understood in the sense described here: a substantial form, a differentia.

29 Boethius simply points out that accidents are predicated in respect of a qualification. (Boethius *In Isagogen Porphyrii Commenta* 5.11, ed. Brandt, p. 317.3–17.) The qualification is explained immediately below.

30 Reading at *Sd* 1–2, p. 184, 47.6, '*post quam*' against '*Postquam*' in the text.

The order given here by Bacon, though slightly different from that given by Aristotle in the *Topics*, is the following: Existence, Substance, Quantity, Relation, Quality, Place, Time, Position, State, Activity, and Passivity. See *Topics* 1.9.103b23–24.

more than one thing, and other things likewise, predication there is based on an ability and not on an actuality. [1.1.48]

REMARKS PRELIMINARY TO A DISCUSSION OF THE CATEGORIES[31]

[26] Since the five universals have been discussed (which help in understanding the categories) one should now attempt to show the differences among the categories. But Aristotle prefixes certain preliminary clarifications to them which first need to be explained, since there are three kinds of predicables: a univocal, an equivocal, and a denominative.[32] [1.2.1–2]

[27] An equivocal cannot be in a category.[33] But univocals are all the things that are principally in a category.[34] Denominatives are reduced to the nature of a category, although they are not as properly recognized to be in a categorical genus as univocals are, because Aristotle says in Book Three of the *Topics* that a just thing and a good thing are not in a genus, and so on for every other denominative.[35] These should be understood principally to be things capable of being placed in order in a line, just as genera, species, and differentiae are reduced to one common genus. And also the nine categories of accidents are predicated denominatively of a substance, as will be clear later (30). [1.2.3–5]

31 Up to this point Bacon has introduced his students to five ways in which things are said of their subjects. Now he presents ten categories of things that can be said of something in one of those five ways. A discussion of categories is not found in all medieval textbooks on logic – William of Sherwood's *Introductiones in logicam* lacks one – probably because of a conviction that the notions of substance and accident are sufficiently clear from their discussion under the heading "Predicables." When, however, they are discussed, it is clear that they represent for the most part an attempt to present and clarify what Aristotle has to say about them in the *Categories* and *Topics*.

32 When medievals, following Aristotle's terminology in *Categories* 1.1a1–15, speak of univocals (equivocals, denominatives) they can mean either names or what is signified by names, or both. Hence, '*Animal est univocum*' can mean both that the term 'animal' is a univocal term and that the *animality* in a tiger and a human being is captured in the same notion of animality. The translation will discriminate when the context is clear. For Peter's and Lambert's discussion of univocals, equivocals, and denominatives see, respectively, *Tractatus* 3.1, trans. Kretzmann and Stump, *CTMPT*, p. 88, and *Logica*, pp. 65.1–66.25.

33 For the definition of 'equivocal' see 28.

34 For the notion of univocals see 29.

35 In the *Topics* Aristotle points out that, while justice (*iustitia*) is in a category under the genus *good*, the denominative, a just man (*iustus*), is not. (See 3.1.116a23–28.) In other words, while a man can be said to be just, he cannot be said to be justice, and to understand this is to recognize that the nine classes of accidents are predicated denominatively. For the definition of 'denominatives' see 30.

[28] Thus Aristotle says that equivocals are those things whose name alone is common and the concept of their substance different, just as 'animal' is equivocal for a true animal and a pictured animal, and 'dog' for what can bark, a sea creature, and a heavenly star.[36] But only the name 'animal' is common to these and the name 'dog' to the others, whereas the concept of their substance, that is, the substantial concept, which is here said to be a definition or description, is different.[37] A definition is an expression indicating what the being (*esse*) of a thing is. Such is composed of a genus and a differentia, as the definition of 'true animal' is "sensible, animate substance," whereas the definition or description of 'pictured animal' is "insensible, inanimate image." Let this be said by way of example. A description is a kind of informatory locution that arises from a genus and accidental characteristics (*quaedam notificatio ex accidentibus proprietatibus*), as a description of man is "naturally domestic animal" or from substantial differentiae outside a genus applied to composed things, as in "A man is a mortal, rational animal." And sometimes it arises outside a genus and outside a substantial differentia, consisting only of properties, as is the description of substance: "what is the subject of accidents."[38] [1.2.6–8]

[29] "Univocals are those things whose name is common and the concept of their substance is the same," as true *animal* is something univocally common to *man*, *lion*, and other species, and the concept pertaining to the name 'animal' is the same when predicated of *man* and *lion*, because it is *sensible animate substance*.[39] And *man* is something univocal in respect of its individuals, because it is predicated of all these according to one concept, which is *mortal rational animal*. [1.2.9]

[30] Denominatives are whatever have their appellation from something from which, in respect of their name, they differ only in case ending, e.g., 'grammarian', 'musician', 'white', and 'black', and every adjective is of

36 Aristotle *Categories* 1.1a1–12. Later, in the "*De signis*" of 1267, Bacon will distinguish between signification and imposition (the free act by which words are designated to stand for things) and contend that univocation and equivocation are differentiated, not on the basis of whether one or several things are signified by one name, but rather on whether the one name was imposed for only one thing or several. (See "*Ds*" 36.) According to Kretzmann the sea creature traditionally called a dog-fish was a kind of shark. (*Introductiones*, trans. Kretzmann, p. 102, n. 159.)

37 Aristotle says a definition is "a phrase signifying a thing's essence." (*Topics* 1.5.101b38–39, trans. W. A. Pickard-Cambridge, in *CWA*, vol. 1, p. 169.) See also *Topics* 7.3.153a15–16.

38 Given what is stated in this paragraph, it would seem that 'informatory locution' stands to 'definition' as genus to species: a definition is a kind of informatory locution. Presumably, then, 'description' is to be taken in the second sense given here.

39 The unacknowledged quotation is from Aristotle *Categories* 1.1a6–12.

this kind.[40] So, the substantival names 'whiteness', 'blackness', 'music', 'grammar', and the like are said to be abstract or principal names, and from these are derived those adjectival names that are called denominative or concrete names. Those are said to be denominative names that are spoken of or denominated from these that are principal, as 'white' from 'whiteness' and 'musical' from 'music'.[41] Those are said to be concrete names that signify a thing concretely and with an inclination to the subject or matter in which the accident exists, because 'something white' means the same as 'white thing', for 'white thing' denominates a subject or matter in which there is whiteness.[42] Again, they are called derivative names because they are taken and derived from principal ones according to the requirements of the Topic [from coordinates].[43] And besides this, other [names]

40 Aristotle *Categories* 1.1a13–15. The concrete, adjectival term 'white' is derived or denominated from the abstract, substantive term 'whiteness' as 'grammarian' from 'grammar' and 'musician' from 'music'. See also below, 31, for three conditions for "full denomination," and 32 for problems with certain adjectives. For a thorough discussion of denominatives and predications involving them see Desmond Paul Henry, *The* De grammatico *of St. Anselm: The Theory of Paronomy* (Notre Dame, IN: University of Notre Dame Press, 1964), and for a rebuttal of some of the claims of that work see John Malcolm, "A No Nonsense Approach to St. Anselm," *Franciscan Studies* 41 (1981): 336–345. For an excellent study of the relations among concrete and abstract substantive terms ('man', 'humanity') and concrete and abstract accidental terms ('white', 'whiteness') see Sten Ebbesen, "Concrete Accidental Terms: Late Thirteenth-Century Debates about Problems Relating to Such Terms as '*Album*'," in *Meaning and Inference in Medieval Philosophy – Studies in Memory of Jan Pinborg*, edited by Norman Kretzmann, Synthese Historical Library, vol. 32 (Dordrecht, Boston, and London: Kluwer, 1988), pp. 107–161.

41 The Latin text has the adjective '*musicus*' which can mean "musical" or "knowledgeable about music." Only the former serves to illustrate the point at issue.

42 In medieval grammatical theory a noun is said to signify a composition of a substance (matter, subject) with a quality (form). For example, 'man' signifies "something having humanity." The composition is also called the inclination of the quality toward the subject. In concrete nouns the inclination is signified as having terminated in the subject whereas in abstract nouns the inclination of the quality is signified but without signifying that the quality is formalized in the subject. Radulphus Brito mentions four theories about what concrete adjectival terms signify. See Ebbesen, "Concrete Accidental Terms," pp. 117–118. See also Joke Spruyt, trans., *Peter of Spain on Composition and Negation*, Artistarium Supplementa, vol. 5 (Nijmegen: Ingenium, 1989), pp. 119–123.

43 Here Bacon uses two verbs, '*sumere*' and '*derivare*', to indicate the way denominatives are formed, and then proceeds to speak of denominatives as *sumpta*. Since I take these two verbs to be synonymous here, the translation will render '*sumpta*' by 'derivatives'. For the Topic from coordinates see 364.

are said to be principal ones because [concrete names] are derived from them. They are also called abstract because they signify their significatum absolutely, without reference to a subject or matter, as is clear. [1.2.10–14]

[31] But one should know that there are three kinds of derivatives. One kind of derivative is what differs from that from which it is derived in ending and beginning, as 'studious' from 'virtue'. A derivative is spoken of in a second way when the principal name and the one derived agree in beginning and end, as 'maiden' (in the feminine gender and as an adjective) agrees with the substantival name 'maiden'.[44] In a third way the name derived and that from which it is derived agree in beginning and differ in ending, as 'white' from 'whiteness', 'to sit' from 'a sitting', 'to stand' from 'a standing', 'to run' from 'a running', and the like, because not only are names said to be denominatives but also verbs, as Aristotle says.[45] But in the first sense there is no denomination in the strict sense, but only in the broad sense. In the second sense it occurs in the strict sense, and in the third sense in the strictest sense, because Boethius says in his commentary *On the Categories* that three things are required for full denomination, namely, that there be present the participation of an existing thing in a subject, i.e., an accident with a subject (which is the same thing because only an accident is a thing existing in a subject), and the nature of something having this is what designates an accident.[46] A second condition is that it have a name derived from another, because many accidents do not have derivative names.[47] And [third], there is required an agreement in the beginning and an inflection at the end, that is, a difference. These three, moreover, combine for denomination in the most proper sense, but not for the others. [1.2.15–19]

44 Bacon's targeted word here is '*grammatica*' but in translation this would not serve as an acceptable example as it would have to be rendered in English, respectively, by 'grammatical' and 'grammar', themselves, however, examples of the next class of derivatives. Hence I have substituted 'maiden', which is both an adjective and a noun in the feminine gender. One could also note that, while '*grammatica*' as here used in the Latin text does not strictly fit the definition of 'denomination' in 30 – no difference in case ending – , it does square with the first two conditions given by Boethius and related in a "second sense" immediately below.

45 I have not found this reference.

46 Reading at *Sd* 1–2, p. 187, 19.6, '*<in> subiecto*' against '*subiecto*' in MSS. O. and S. and the text.

Boethius *In categorias Aristotelis libri quattuor* 1, PL 64.168A. This is a condition because what is being named denominatively is not a form alone but that form now concretized in some subject, and hence the form's latter condition sets up the need (and justification) for a new name: when something receives *whiteness* (*albedo*), it is called a white thing (*album*).

47 Accidents are accidental forms and, when considered independently of any inherence in some substance, *can* be given abstract names. When these forms are predicated of some object, however, they must be given concrete names.

[32] But what is to be said about these: 'rational', 'human'? Likewise, 'mountainous', 'forested', 'mantled', 'tuniced'? Also, 'A plant is healthy', 'Urine is healthy', and the like? Or, 'Oneness is one', or 'Quantity is quantified', and so on? One should reply that in the case of the species or differentiae of a substance there is no denomination, unless in a very broad sense and by stretching the name 'denomination' to the extreme.[48] The case is the same in respect of the other names, like 'mountainous' and 'forested', because 'mountain' and 'forest' name substances, from which there is no strict denomination, except when they happen to be places – a place is a thing existing in a subject. Then, in that sense, it could be said that denomination is present.[49] Likewise, 'mantled', 'tuniced', and the like can be said to be denominatives because they signify a thing existing in a subject, namely, mantleation and tunication, which are in the category Possession; and ['mantled' and 'tuniced'] are derived from ['mantleation' and 'tunication'] according to a logician, not from 'mantle' and 'tunic'. But when one says 'A plant is healthy', or 'Food is healthy', and the like, there is no denomination, because every denomination occurs with respect to form. Rather, health is included there effectively because the sense is: 'A plant is healthy', that is, it can cause health, and the case is similar for a medicinal potion. Likewise: 'Diet is healthy', that is, it preserves health, and 'Urine is healthy', that is, it is indicative of health. 'A healthy animal' – there 'healthy' is said in the strict sense of 'denomination', because it is formally predicated of an animal and it is in it as an accident is in its subject. It is there in urine as a sign, in diet as something that preserves, in food or a plant and in a medicinal potion as something that brings it about. With respect to oneness one should know that according to some 'one' is predicated only as a cause of it, as in 'Oneness is one', that is, it is effective of oneness; and 'Quantity is quantified', that is, it is effective of quantity, just as one says that a color is white because it makes something to be white. According to Boethius' previously mentioned exposition (31), denomination is not taken strictly, because '*unum*' (a one) does not signify an accident, a thing existing in oneness, nor '*quantum*' (something quantified) a thing existing in quantity, but rather in a substance, which is a thing having

48 Presumably 'rational', 'human', and the names of species are ruled out because they violate Boethius' first condition: they are not names of accidents.

49 Names of complete existing substances like 'mountain' and 'forest' are not abstract and do not name accidental forms. In that sense 'mountainous', meaning "like a mountain," and 'forested', meaning "covered with forest," cannot be said to be denominatives derived from them. But, says Bacon, they could be said to be derived from the abstract name of those accidents of place: 'mountainous' from 'mountainess'.

oneness or quantity.[50] But things in the category Quantity or one of the others receive a reflexive predication in the previously mentioned sense because of their simplicity. Because of this they reflect on themselves through a complete return, as is clear in *On Causes*, as understanding understands itself, and the intellect understands itself.[51] But a sense faculty does not sense itself and sight does not see itself, and likewise neither do natural nor gross things return upon themselves, as in 'Whiteness is white' and 'Blackness is black'. And so in things that are not natural there is a return of the same upon itself, of which sort are things of the mind, like goodness, evil, and likewise quantities. Here there is no strict denomination, as has been said, just as neither in the case of substantial differentiae, like *rational* and *mortal*, on the basis of which denomination signifies a thing existing in a subject, as one speaks here of denomination.[52] [1.2.20–27]

[33] It can be said that denomination occurs with respect to every sort of form, whether it be substantial or accidental; here, however, the focus is on accidental form. Every denomination arises for the knowledge of a subject; but knowledge by way of the senses (which is our kind of knowledge) principally arises by way of accidents; and so those things are said to be denominatives in the strict sense that are derived from accidental forms. [1.2.28]

50 Reading at *Sd* 1–2, p. 189, 27.3, '*quantum*' against '*quantitas*' in MSS. O. and S. and the text.

What we understand in these sorts of expressions is not due to denominational factors but to the fact that what is predicated is in the subject as a transitive cause of an effect (or as a sign) of some other entity; it is not there as an attribute of the subject.

51 *Liber de causis* 14 (proposition 15), no. 124, Adriaan Pattin ed., *Le Liber de causis* (Louvain: Editions du Tijdschrift voor Filosofie, [1966]), p. 79.50–51: "Every knower who knows his essence is one who is returning to his essence by a complete return."

52 Bacon's solution appeals to a distinction between denominative and reflexive predication, and to grasp its import one must catch the difference intended here between a thing existing in oneness and a thing having oneness (*res existens in unitate* and *res subiecta unitati*): the former, he says, is an accident, the latter a substance. With these stipulations he then makes two unsupported assertions: 'one' in 'oneness is one' and 'quantified' in 'Quantity is quantified' do not signify accidents. Presumably we are to draw on the conventional understanding of an accident as something that serves to characterize a subject in such a way that the former can come or go without the destruction of that subject. (See 17.) With this in mind 'one' is surely not the name of an accident because oneness would not be the *kind* of thing it is without what it names. And since denominative terms are names of accidents alone (see 17), 'one' cannot here be predicated denominatively. In the Latin text without the emendation from '*quantitas*' to '*quantum*' one could say that 'quantity' in the expression mentioned does not name an accident that is

[34] One should know, however, that not all concrete names are said to be denominatives, because a concrete substantial form distinguishes the matter in which it exists, just as an accidental form does. So the names 'man', 'animal', 'lion', 'goat', 'Socrates', 'Plato', and all the names of species, genera, and individuals in the category of Substance are said to be concrete names because they signify a substantial form as concrete and united to matter. But the names 'humanity', 'animality', 'assinity', 'Socrateity', 'Platoneity', and so on in all the cases where names are made up are not concrete, but abstract, because they signify substantial forms without an inclination to or union with matter. Thus Aristotle says that denonimative names are "whatever are different from a name" (as from a principal or abstract name) "only in case ending," that is, in their ending, the last part of those words, e.g., 'white' and 'whiteness'.[53] Or "only in case ending," i.e., they are different because of the descent or formation of the one from the other, for according to a logician 'white' is taken and derived from 'whiteness', although the contrary is true according to a grammarian. But derivation with respect to what is signified rather than derivation with respect to the signifying utterance is said to be the work of the logician,

being (denominatively) predicated for the simple reason that it names a "substance," the subject of the expression. (I have used quotation marks around 'substance' because the "substance" being talked about is not something in the category Substance, but an accident in the category Quantity.) But if 'one' and 'quantitative' are not predicated denominatively, they are, says Bacon, predicated reflexively. In "oneness is one" oneness is said to have the form *oneness*, which is to say that oneness is predicated of itself. What is signified by the predicate is a simple form and is not different from what is signified by the subject, and hence the expression is reflexive.

Evidently the proper analysis of these kinds of expressions was highly disputed in Bacon's time, for in the "*De signis*" of 1267 he returns to the issue when discussing various problems with equivocation. (See "*Ds*" 72–80, esp. 72–73.) There he makes it clear that subjects can have forms either as part of their essence or as an accident, and then contends that, for these reflexive expressions (there called double predications ["*Ds*" 80]), one must understand the predicates to name essential forms and not accidental ones. (See "*Ds*" 73.) Thus, he says, to say that oneness is oneness and to say oneness is one is to say the same thing absolutely and then concretely. (Ibid.) Extending this notion to all accidents he says, "Consequently, if oneness can be concretely (*in concretione*) predicated of itself because of the unity of itself with itself, so whiteness [can be predicated concretely] of itself, and such will be the case for all others." (See "*Ds*" 70.) And evidently the issue was still alive in 1292, for in his *Compendium of the Study of Theology* he writes: "But here there is a serious problem and vehement long-windedness [worthy] of an extended discussion which will be explained in the chapters that follow." (*Cst* 2.133.) Unfortunately, either he never wrote additional chapters or they are now lost.

53 Aristotle *Categories* 1.1a13–14.

because a grammarian takes into consideration the characteristic of an utterance and says that what has fewer syllables – and also sometimes fewer letters – is the source of that which has a greater number of syllables or letters. And since such is the case with almost all concrete names when measured against abstract ones, he says (both of verbs and nouns) that nouns are derived from verbs and substantival nouns from adjectives. I say this happens for the most part, but not always, e.g., where that characteristic is found in a verb or an adjective. And this can be confirmed because a beginning is very small in quantity yet very great in power and potential, as Aristotle says at the end of *Sophistical Refutations*.[54] A logician, however, does not consider the characteristic of an utterance in respect of this – or at least not principally – as does a grammarian, and so does not propose such a derivation. For he principally considers the condition of the thing signified and the nature of the thing signified by those words. And so, since something abstract is the cause of the concrete and its source, namely, something formal, he says that a concrete name descends from an abstract one as from its source. Again, a grammarian is a crude and gross philosopher, attentive to things of the senses. And so of more importance to him is a starting point that is composed and less simple, which is something concrete, and because it is concrete, he is naming a form with matter. [But when one names] something abstract, [one is naming] only a form, because it is more simple than something composed of a subject and that form. But a logician is a subtle philosopher and more intellectual, and so, since to his way of thinking form is prior to a composite (because a composite is not understood or known except through a form), the logician says the abstract is prior to the concrete.[55] Or, this way: "only in case ending," that is, only in the termination of a form in matter and in a subject, because, as is often said, a denominative name signifies a form united to matter and to a subject, whereas an abstract one does not. [1.2.29–35]

[35] Therefore, one should know that no genus is predicated equivocally of its inferiors – nor are differentiae and species – but univocally.[56] An individual, moreover, is predicated univocally of one thing alone. But a

54 Aristotle *Sophistical Refutations* 34.183b18–25.

55 The issue whether the name of a composite is principally the name of the whole thing or its substantial form is discussed briefly in the "*De signis*" and then at length in *Compendium of the Study of Theology*. (See, respectively, "*Ds*" 126 and *Cst* 69–82.) Those who held the second view are unnamed but called "quite foolish" in the "*De signis*," while Averroes (1126–1198) is named in the *Compendium* and thoroughly excoriated.

56 In "*De signis*" (42) and *Compendium of the Study of Theology* (137) Bacon describes the logician's claim that genus is predicated univocally as superficial, and points out that in natural philosophy it is said to be predicated equivocally (analogically). See respectively "*Ds*" 42 and *Cst* 137, and cf. above, 10 and 27.

name of an individual is predicated equivocally of several individuals, as the name 'Peter' of several Peters, because it is predicated with a different understanding and signification of this Peter and that one. The case is similar in connection with a proprium and an accident, and more than the other [predicables] these two agree in the same ways of predicating because a proprium, in truth, is a convertible and essential accident, without which the thing whose it is can neither be nor be understood.[57] But the accident about which Porphyry speaks is an accident that is not convertible with one species but is naturally common to several, without which a thing can be, as was said above (17). A common accident or a proprium, therefore, can be compared to those things that are under it in its genus, and then it is predicated of these univocally, because, just as there are genera, species, individuals, and differentiae in the category Substance, so in the categories of accidents. And then an accident will be either a genus like *color*, or a differentia like *piercing*, or a species like *white*, or an individual like *this whiteness*, all of which must be predicated in the previously mentioned way.[58] Or, it could be considered as it is predicated of a substance, or one accident of

57 When treating the predicable Proprium (16, 24) Bacon made it abundantly clear that a proprium is not an essential accident, but simply an accident that is so inseparable from the species of which it is predicated that it is convertible with the latter. This is the traditional notion of a proprium. (See, e.g., *Tractatus* 2.14, trans. Kretzmann and Stump, *CTMPT*, p. 85.) It would seem that Bacon either has misspoken himself here, or that he is taking the term 'essentially' in a broad sense, or that what he wants to say about a proprium is simply that it is intimately associated with the essence of something (species), that there are no individuals of that species that are not naturally suited (*apta nata*) to have it, and that it is unique to that species, all of which conform with what he has (correctly) said in his discussion of Proprium. For Porphyry's contrast between species and proprium see *Isagoge*, trans. Warren, pp. 60–61.

58 For this definition of 'white' see Aristotle *Topics* 3.5.119a31–33. The Greek reads "τοῦ λευκοῦ ἐστὶ λόγος χρῶμα διακριτικὸν ὄψεως," and Boethius translates this by "*albi est ratio color disgregativus visus.*" In English the Greek has been rendered by "'white' is 'a colour which penetrates the vision'" by E. S. Forster and by "a colour which disperses the vision" by W. A. Pickard-Cambridge. (Respectively, ed. Bekker, trans. Forster, Aristotle, *Posterior Analytics [and] Topica*, The Loeb Classical Library, 1960, p. 408.31–32, and trans. Pickard-Cambridge, *CWA*, vol. 1, p. 200.) Allan Bäck translates the phrase "*disgregativum visus*" by "standing out in sight." See his "The Structure of Scotus' Formal Distinction" in *Medieval and Renaissance Logic in Spain*, edited by Ignacio Angelelli and Paloma Pérez-Ilzarbe, Acts of the 12th European Symposium on Medieval Logic and Semantics, held at the University of Navarre, Pamploma, 26–30 May 1997, Philosophische Texte und Studien, vol. 54 (Hildesheim, Zurich, New York: Georg Olms, 2000), p. 415. It is not immediately clear to me how the original definition fits one color more than any other.

something of another category, and in this sense it is not absolutely predicated univocally, because it is required for univocal predication that something be predicated in accord with its name and in accord with its concept. But not all accidents are predicated of a substance in accord with their name, as will be known (36), but some are. None, however, is predicated in accord with its own concept. For example, whiteness can be predicated of a body in accord with a name denominatively derived from it, as in 'The body is white', but the concept of whiteness cannot be denominatively predicated of a body. For the concept of whiteness is "color piercing sight," and this cannot be predicated of a body.[59] [1.2.36–42]

[36] If someone objects that [the concept] can be predicated just as the name can be predicated, as in 'A body is something colored piercing sight', one should reply that Aristotle was speaking about the concept, the definition, in a way in which the nature of the definition remains intact. But a definition does not arise from a denominative or concrete genus, but only from an abstract one.[60] This, however, requires further discussion, because perhaps neither is 'something colored piercing sight' predicated of Socrates, for it is not applicable to a substance, since, as it seems, [the substance] would be [said to be] piercing sight. For since the differentia of whiteness is "piercing sight" and is predicated of whiteness under a denominative utterance, it does not seem that it would be predicated of its subject under the same utterance, just as a genus itself, like 'color' (which is predicated in abstraction from whiteness), is not predicated of a subject under the same form of its [name]. For one does not say that Socrates is a color, and so neither, likewise, 'Socrates is piercing sight'. And so it seems that because of this Aristotle says that the concept or definition of whiteness is not predicated of a subject, whose confirmation, however, should be inquired about elsewhere.[61] [1.2.43–44]

59 This follows from what has been said above about denominative predication (31). Thus while one can say that this body is white, one cannot correctly say that this body is whiteness, i.e., color piercing sight. While the accidental form *whiteness* is predicated of a body, it can be predicated only concretely and under a denominative name.

60 The definition of a term (in the Aristotelian sense of an essential definition) requires that the genus be named in the abstract and not denominatively, as 'whiteness' instead of 'something white'. Hence, while there is nothing wrong with the predication 'A body is something colored piercing sight' ('some body is something white'), what is predicated is not a definition of 'whiteness', and hence neither the definition of nor the name 'whiteness' is being predicated. These can be predicated of an individual (concrete) substance only when the name and concept (definition) have taken a denominative shape.

61 Can an individual have within it the form that is the differentia of a higher genus? Can a Caucasian Socrates be said to be piercing sight? Bacon says No because the

[37] Of those things that are said, that is, utterances, one kind is uncombined, like 'man', 'Socrates', 'runs', and any term; the other is combined, e.g., an expression like 'Socrates runs'.[62] [1.2.45]

[38] Of those things that are, some are said of a subject but are not in a subject, like all universals in the category Substance, such as genera and species and differentiae, e.g., *man* and *mortal rational animal*.[63] Some things are in a subject but are said of no subject, like particular accidents, such as this quantity, this quality, this whiteness, and this blackness.[64] Others are said of a subject and are in a subject, like universal accidents such as quantity, quality, whiteness, blackness, the different kinds of knowledge, and the like.[65] Others are neither said of a subject nor are they in a subject, like singular or particular things, e.g., some man and Socrates, which are in the category Substance.[66] To be said of a subject is nothing other than to be said of something below itself in its genus. To be in a subject is to be in a substance as an accident is in something. [1.2.46–51]

[39] But one should know that being-in is spoken of in eight ways.[67] The first way is as an integral part is in its whole, as a hand is in Socrates, and as a wall is in a house. The second way is the converse, as a house is

---

differentia of the genus color should not be able to be predicated of a subject and the species formed by that differentia and its genus under the same name and concept. If *whiteness* can be defined as *piercing sight*, then a (white) car should not be able to be said to be *piercing sight*. The reason for this is that a differentia in a category of Accident is predicated essentially of its genus and species, but only accidentally of an individual. Thus one can say that *whiteness* is something piercing sight, but not that a car is something piercing sight, and mean the same thing. As Aristotle says, "Color is in body and therefore also in an individual body." (*Categories* 5.2b1–2, trans. J. L. Akrill, in *CWA*, vol. 1, p. 5.)

62 Paragraphs 37–38 are paraphrases of Aristotle's *Categories* 2.

63 To this Aristotle adds: "(By 'in a subject' I mean what is in something, not as a part, and cannot exist separately from what it is in)." (*Categories* 2.1a23–24, trans. Akrill, in *CWA*, vol. 1, p. 3.) Hence, what is being said here is that universals in the category Substance are not individual substances themselves, though they are parts (forms) of individual substances.

64 Aristotle adds: "... and the individual white is in a subject, the body (for all colour is in a body), but is not said of any subject." (*Categories* 2.1a27–29, trans. Akrill, *CWA*, vol. 1, p. 3.) Thus one never says, "This dog is whiteness."

65 Aristotle adds: "For example, knowledge is in a subject, the soul, and is also said of a subject, knowledge-of-grammar." (*Categories* 2.1b1–2, trans. E. M. Edghill, in *CWA*, vol. 1, p. 3.)

66 These cannot be present in, or a constitutive (formal) part of, an individual substance because they are already existent as individual things themselves. Bacon is not speaking here of an object composed of two previously and separately existing things.

67 See Aristotle *Physics* 4.3.210a14–26.

in its wall. The third way is as a subjective part is in its universal whole, as an individual is in a species, like Socrates in *man*, and as a species is in a genus, like *man* in *animal*.[68] The fourth way is the converse, as a genus is in a species and a species is in an individual. The fifth way is as a form is in matter, and this occurs in two ways: either as a substantial form is in matter, like animality in an animal, fireness in a fire, and so on, or as an accidental form is in matter, that is, in its subject, like whiteness in a wall. And here 'to be in a subject' is taken in this way and only in this way. The sixth way is as sovereignty is in a sovereign and the origin of movements is in a thing that moves another. The seventh way is as something is in its goal, like virtue in happiness. The eighth way is as something is in a place. [1.2.52–60]

[40] Aristotle, moreover, adds two rules or maxims, the first of which makes clear what it is to be said of a subject by showing the mutual relationship between those things that are ordered in the same category, and it runs: "Whenever one thing is said of another as of a subject, it is also said of the subject."[69] For example, if *animal* is said of *man*, and if *body* or *substance* or something else is said of *animal*, all these latter things will be said of *man*. For if a man is an animal, and an animal is a substance, then a man is a substance. For all the higher things are predicated of the lower ones, and such is the case within the other categories. One should be careful, however, not to take something that would not be in the same category and say it of that category, for the rule does not hold for those. For example: 'A man is an animal, an animal is white, therefore a man is white'; or '*Man* is *animal*, *animal* is a genus, therefore *man* is a genus'. For 'genus' and 'white' are not in the same category, nor are they superior to 'animal', and so the part "of the subject" is not fulfilled. A subject here is called what is below in the same categorical line. [Aristotle], moreover, subjoins another rule which principally distinguishes different categories from each other in respect of species and differentiae and it is this: "The species and differentiae of different genera that are not subalternate to one another are different."[70] But by this rule not only are the different categories distinguished, but also the various genera that are dispersed throughout the same category. Those things, moreover, are here called "genera not posited in the way of a subalternate," of which one is not placed under the other as a

68 Note that the difference between the first way of being-in and this one lies in the fact that a whole can be predicated of a subjective part but not of an integral part: one can say that Socrates is a man but one cannot say a wall is a house.

69 Aristotle *Categories* 3.1b10–12.

70 This seems to be a restatement of what Aristotle says in *Categories* 3.1b16–19 where he points out that, while *two-footed* is a differentia of the genus *animal*, it does not serve to distinguish various species of the genus *knowledge*.

lower under a higher, as are all genera existing in the different categories, for example, *animal* and *knowledge*. These have different species and differentiae, for the differentiae of *animal* are *rational*, *mortal*, *two-footed*, *four-footed*, and the like, whereas the differentiae of *knowledge* are *linguistic*, *moral*, *rational*, *mathematical*, and the like. Having assumed these things, we must now proceed to the principal topic. [1.2.61–65]

CATEGORIES IN GENERAL

[41] One should know that every thing is either a substance or an accident. Substance is one category, but Accident is divided into nine, namely, Quantity, Quality, Relation, Action, Passion, Where, When, Situation or Position, and Possession. And since these nine along with Substance make ten, there are only ten categories.[71] [1.2.66–67]

[42] One should know, therefore, that a category is spoken of in different ways by different people. Because of this various significata must be assigned to the name 'category'. Sometimes it signifies a category. For example, Aristotle says in *On Interpretation* that "these composed things are posited so that every category may be one."[72] Sometimes it signifies a

71 As the text reads Bacon would be read to hold the view that the number ten is exhaustive. It should be noted, however, that the word 'only' is found only in MS. S. and not in MS. O. As one can see by comparing the texts of Bacon, Peter, and Lambert, there is only a partial sacredness about the order in which the nine categories of accidents are enumerated and discussed. When they simply enumerate them, Quantity, Quality, and Relation are always so ranked, and variation is permitted in the remaining six; and when they discuss each individually, Quantity remains first but Relation precedes Quality, with variation again tolerated among the remaining six. Hence, there seems to be a rationale behind the rankings, at least of the first three categories, and Lambert (alone) seems to offer the key, while attributing all to Aristotle, without, however, any references. Thus Lambert says that for the initial enumeration Quality precedes Relation because it is more easily observable and is better known, since it is in a subject whereas Relation is not, being a mere *respectus*. But when discussing categories, he continues, one proceeds according to the natural order both because Relation does not presuppose Quality and because, while both Quantity and Quality are causes of Relation, Quantity is a sufficient cause. Thus, to place Relation between them is to honor the fact that what is intermediary stands between extremes. Finally, Quantity is always placed first in both orders because its presence is more immediate than Quality's: as soon as there is a substance there is a quantity. For the enumerations see, respectively, Bacon, 41; Peter, *Tractatus* 3.5, trans. Kretzmann and Stump, *CTMPT*, p. 91; and Lambert, *Logica*, p. 50.14–15. For the rationale behind the two rankings see Lambert, *Logica*, pp. 77.26–78.24, reading at p. 78.21 '*immediatius*' against '*immediatus*' in the text.

72 *On Interpretation* 11.20b31. Aristotle goes on to indicate various ways in which two predicates in two different statements can be combined in one statement:

treatise, as when I say, "Aristotle wrote the *Categories*." Sometimes it signifies a word, i.e., a term, e.g., a predicable utterance in general, as it is used by Aristotle in *On Sophistical Refutations* when he says, "Since we have various classes of categories,"[73] and Boethius when he says, "Affirmations arise from categories," that is, propositions arise from utterances and words.[74] In none of these senses, however, is a category spoken of in the way we are speaking of a category here, namely, in the sense in which I say universals are contained in the categories, about which different people hold different views. [1.2.68–72]

[43] Some say a broadest genus is a category and so they posit that there are ten categories because there are ten broadest genera. So they place some things in a category because these are contained under the broadest genus which they judge to be similar, as in 'The sun is in Leo', because it is under Leo, for the sun does not enter the sign, but passes under the sign. [1.2.73]

[44] Others claim a category is a way of predicating, because there are ten ways of predicating. For example, one is the way of predicating in respect of what (*in quid*), another in respect of quantity (*in quantum*), another in respect of quality (*in quale*), and so on. These people, moreover, say that all species and all genera are in the category Substance, because they are predicated in respect of what. Hence, Substance is not the first category because this genus embraces single subsisting things contained in that category.[75] But because the things of this category are predicated in respect of *substance*, that is, in respect of what – 'quiddity' and 'substance' are taken here for one and the same thing – consequently it is clear that all ten broadest genera are in the category Substance, because they are predicated in respect of what, for there are ten rich men in one city, with no one dominating another, no one richer than another.[76] Such an opinion is given by Aristotle in Book One of

"A man is an animal with two feet." (11.20b31–21a7.) But he warns that one encounters absurd results if one attempts to do this with all predicates. For what is said here in 42 de Libera suggests one also see *Tractatus Anagnini* 1, ed. de Rijk, *LM*, vol. 2.2, p. 224.31–34, and *Ars meliduna*, MS. Oxford, Bodlean Library, Digby 174, fol. 223ra, mentioned by de Rijk, *LM*, vol. 2.1, p. 314.

73 Aristotle *Sophistical Refutations* 22.178a5–6.

74 The source for the quotation is not known to me.

75 Reading at *Sd* 1–2, p. 196, 74.6–7, '*praedicamento*' with MSS. O. and S. against '*praedicamenta*' in the text.

76 It would seem that the claim that all ten broadest genera are in the genus *substance* is what the other claims seek to establish, and this seems to seek to honor the notion that each accident is something, not nothing, by claiming that each is justifiably called a substance. Thus *man*, in this opinion, is a substance and so is *whiteness* and *hereness* and all the genera and species of the ten categories: they are all something said of something else. If everything predicated is a substance,

the *Topics* when he says, "After this we must distinguish the genera of the categories in which are the four mentioned differentiae. They are, moreover, ten in number: Quiddity, Quality, Quantity, etc."[77] Hence, they say that, just as the first declension is the first way of declining, so the first category is the first way of predicating, namely, in respect of what. For just as all names declinable in a similar fashion are of the same declension, so all universals predicable in the same way are in the same category. [1.2.74–75]

[45] But others argue that, just as we say in grammar there are eight parts of speech – that is, eight principal classes of words that are such that one cannot be the other nor be contained under the other, and under which are contained all the parts of speech – and likewise, just as we say in rhetoric that there are seven circumstances, that is, principal classes of attributes (e.g., Who? What? Where? With whose help? Why? How? When?) of which one is not the other, so in logic there are said to be ten categories, that is, ten classes of predicables, ways of being (*maneries*), which are such that one is not the other nor contained by the other, under which every predicable is contained and of which one is said to be the category Substance, another the category Quantity, etc.[78] [1.2.76]

[46] And they are said to be categories in respect of what and qualification by Aristotle in Book One of the *Topics*, not because there are ten ways of predicating, as the prior opinion asserted (44–45), but because they are named from the effects that are in them, according to which they are assigned to true substances.[79] Hence, these people gloss the words of Aristotle this way: "After this we must distinguish, etc.," that is, we must distinguish the differences in the ways of predicating in respect of primary substances, which are called individuals, as will be seen later (48). For that genus of predicables is said to be the category Substance to which belong all those predicables by whose assignment what it is is determined of a primary substance.[80] But that genus of predicables is said to be the cate-

---

then 'categories' is not a name for ten classes of things – there are no such – or ten kinds of predicates, but simply a name for ten ways of predicating these "substances." The fundamental flaw in this theory, if I have understood it correctly, is the failure to recognize an essential difference between what exists in its own right (a substance) and what exists only in dependence on another (an accident). Each is something, not nothing, and has title to be called a substance, but in different senses and under the name 'substance' taken equivocally. For Bacon's response see 46.

77 Aristotle *Topics* 1.9.103b20–24.

78 This opinion also does not envision an Aristotelian category as a predicate of a certain kind, but, like the former, as a way of predicating, and draws analogies from grammar and rhetoric.

79 Aristotle *Topics* 1.9.103b20–104a1.

80 Such predicables would be genus and species.

gory Quality to which belong all those things that determine with respect to a primary substance how it is qualified.[81] Likewise, that genus of predicables is said to be the category Quantity which is of such a kind that all predicables contained in it point out with respect to a primary substance how it is quantified, and so on. Or, [the point can be stated] another way: the genus of all things predicable in respect of what of primary substances, together with the primary [substances] themselves, is the category Substance; therefore, [the genus] of all things predicable in respect of single qualities in the singular things, together with those [single qualities], is the category Quality, and so on. [1.2.77–81]

[47] Still others say that a category is a collection of predicables, just as Substance and all its inferiors – both genera as well as species and individuals – are one category. Quality, however, with its inferiors, is another category, and so on. Let the vote on which of these opinions is first be left for discussion. Now that what a category is in general has been seen, let us run through each of them. [1.2.82–84]

SUBSTANCE

[48] The first category is the category Substance, whose division Aristotle proposes briefly in these words: "Of substances, one is primary, the other secondary."[82] A primary substance is what is properly, principally, and in the strictest sense said to be a substance, like a man, an ass, and a lion, which are singular things in the category Substance. But a secondary substance is a species or genus: a species, like *man* and *ass*; a genus, like *substance* and *animal*. [1.2.85–87]

[49] But to understand this claim a greater distinction should be added.[83] Thus it should be said that a substance is either matter or form or a composite. But matter and form are the principles of any substance and are not in a category as is a genus, species, or individual, but are reduced to principles in what has principles. *Composite*, i.e., *composed substance*, comprehends all the genera, all the species, and all the individuals in the category Substance.[84] [1.2.88–90]

81 Such would be differentia, property, and accident.

82 "A *substance* – that which is called a substance most strictly, primarily, and most of all – is that which is neither said of a subject nor in a subject, e.g., the individual man or the individual horse. The species in which the things primarily called substances are, are called *secondary substances*, as also are the genera of these species." (Aristotle *Categories* 5.2a12–19, trans. Akrill, in *CWA*, vol. 1, p. 4.)

83 Reading at *Sd* 1–2, p. 198, 88.1, '*divisionis major*' against '*dictionis maius*' in MSS. O. and S. and the text. I am indebted to Sten Ebbesen for the suggestion.

84 Only complete individual substances composed of matter and form are said to be in this category in the fullest sense. Hence, Bacon implies here that the principles or metaphysical components of an individual substance are called substances only

[50] One should consider, therefore, what a broadest genus is and proceed on from there. On Porphyry's authority, moreover, we have it that *substance* is a broadest genus whose subalternate species are *corporeal substance* and *incorporeal substance*. Under *incorporeal substance* are two subalternate species, namely, *intelligence* and *intellectual soul*.[85] [1.2.91–92]

[51] *Intelligence* is called *angel*, but this is not the name of a nature, but of an office (as philosophers say, and also others), because 'angel' means the same as 'messenger' does. Under *intelligence* are many species in accord with their hierarchies or orders. These are named both by philosophers and the Saints in this way: *angel*, *archangel*, *virtues*, *dominations*, *principalities*, *powers*, *thrones*, *seraphim*, and *cherubim*, according to what is said in Book One of Bernardus Sylvestris' *Philosophy*.[86] Different philosophers propose another distribution of intelligences, especially Algazel in Chapter Five of his *Metaphysics*, which is entitled *Flowers of Things Divine*, about which we are not to concern ourselves at this time.[87] [1.2.93]

[52] *Soul* has species under it, like *vegetative soul* and *sensitive soul*, which, according to some, are subalternate species containing many species of various plants and animals under them, and *intellectual soul*, which, according to Aristotle, does not exist except in man, but which, according to Plato and others, is in supercelestial bodies, like the heaven, stars, the moon, and planets.[88] And then one could say it would be a subalternate species, because a man and the stars are different in species. Individuals, moreover, i.e., primary substances, in these classes are each an intelligence. [1.2.94]

[53] But although the substantial forms of things and differentiae are in the category Substance, they are not species and genera; they are the principles of substances, namely, formal principles, and are reduced to the category Substance as principles to what has principles. Aristotle, moreover, suggests these principles when he says in the *Categories*: "Not only is it proper for a secondary substance to be predicated univocally, but also for differentiae."[89] Through this it is clear that a differentia is not a sec-

---

equivocally. See also 53. From here to the end of his discussion of Substance Bacon presents numerous examples not mentioned earlier when he described the Porphyrean Tree (15) and not found in the similar treatments of Substance by Peter and Lambert.

85 Porphyry *Isagoge*, trans. Warren, , pp. 35–36.

86 Bernardus Silvestris *De mundi universitate libri duo* [*Megacosmos et Microcosmos*], Book 1, lines 3–20, ed. Carl Sigmund Barach and Johann Wrobel, Bibliotheca Philosophorum Mediae Aetatis, vol. 1, p. 15.

87 See Algazel *Metaphysica* 1.1.5, *Algazel's Metaphysics*, ed. J. T. Muckle, (Toronto: St. Michaels College, 1933), p. 121.3–26.

88 See Aristotle *On the Heavens* 2.1.284a27–b5.

89 See Aristotle *Categories* 5.3a34 and 3a21–22.

ondary substance, because it is neither a species nor a genus. And it is clear that it is not a primary substance because it is not an individual. Likewise, neither is the First Cause in the category Substance, although *incorporeal substance* is said of It, because *substance* is predicated equivocally of It and created things, as is clear on the authority of Boethius in his book *On the Trinity* and of others, for It is above every category, both the cause and the source of all things.[90] [1.2.95]

[54] The other subalternate species of *substance* is *corporeal substance* or *body*, under which are subalternate species, namely, *simple body* and *composed body*. [1.2.96]

[55] Under *simple body* are the subalternate species *heavenly body* and *elemental body*. [1.2.96]

[56] Under *heavenly body* are lowest species, e.g., *ninth sphere*, *starry sphere*, *sphere of Saturn*, *sphere of Jupiter*, *sphere of Mars*, *sphere of the sun*, *sphere of Mercury*, *sphere of Venus*, and *sphere of the moon*.[91] Also there are lowest species in the genus *sphere*, like *moon*, *Venus*, *Mercury*, *sun*, *Mars*, and *Jupiter*, which are the seven planets,[92] and they differ in species because a planet does not differ from its sphere in essence, since it is the brightest part of a sphere, as Averroes says [in his commentary] on *Heaven and Earth*.[93] And other stars differ in species from planets. But whether they differ in species among themselves, as do the parts of an animal, is up to now still in doubt. And yet it seems better that they do not; but this is wont to be inquired about elsewhere. [1.2.97]

[57] Under *elemental body* are four species, namely, *earth*, *water*, *air*, and *fire*. [1.2.98]

[58] Under *composed body* are two subalternate species, namely, *animate body* and *inanimate body*.[94] [1.2.99]

90 Boethius *De Trinitate* 4, *Boethius: The Theological Tractates*, trans. H. F. Stewart and E. K. Rand, Loeb Classical Library, pp. 16.7–18.44. See also below, 250 and 251, for an analogous point made by Boethius.

91 In Bacon's time the physical universe was thought of as consisting of concentric spheres which rotated daily around the earth. The sun, moon, planets, and stars were thought to be the more luminous and more dense part of their respective spheres, as Bacon will immediately point out.

92 Bacon has left out reference to Saturn, though it is mentioned immediately above.

93 For the reference see Averroes *De coelo* 2, *comm.* 42, *Aristotelis opera cum Averrois commentariis*, vol. 5, fol. 125vG,L.

94 MS. S. adds the following at this point: "under *composed animate body* there are these kinds of species: *vapor*, which is a subtle body lifted from earth and water by the heat of the sun; and bodies created from vapor are impressions, like comets, which are bodies sublimated by the power of a star, having roundness through the transition of rays from that rotundity in the manner of comets and firebrands; and other impressions like ascending and descending assub with other

[59] Under *inanimate body* there are species.[95] One kind of inanimate body is material for all inanimate bodies, and goes by the common name 'vapor'. But vapor is properly spoken of in so far as it is lifted up from the earth and from water, whether this be in their own spheres or in a mixed one, smoke from the earth and from the air in a mixed one, a spirit from fire in a mixed one, since [vapor] is said to be spirit because of its spirituality. But these names are taken interchangeably for each other. A body is indeed lifted up from the earth and from water by the heat of the sun and of the other stars, as something fine from something gross, just as fine droplets are lifted up from water boiling in a pot toward the opening of the pot. Or, there is no such material, but it is generated from [vapor], and then there is a body either elevated by the power of a star, like a comet, which is generated within the confines of air and fire from vapor elevated by the power of the star by which it is drawn, just as iron by a magnet. [Or perhaps there is] another kind of inanimate body that is not elevated in this way by the power of the heavens, but principally retains an elemental power, and then it is either generated from ignited or nonignited vapor.[96] If it is generated from an ignited vapor, then it exists in five ways that do not differ in species.[97] One is a perpendicular fire, which appears in the air like the flame from burning wood, broad at the bottom and narrow at the top.[98] Another

---

openings; and there is a clear white body appearing in the air in the manner of an ascending and descending star. Among others there are, moreover, cold bodies generated from vapor, like clouds, mist, hail, snow, rain, hoarfrost, dew. But there are other species of *inanimate body*, like stones and metals, sulfur and other such, about which Aristotle speaks in the book *Meteorology*. Under *composed body* are two subalternate species, namely, *animate body* and *inanimate body*." (*Sd* 1–2, p. 201, n. 6.)

95 After a lengthy reflection on the possible sources for the discussion in this paragraph de Libera concludes that the notions are derived from Aristotle's *Meteorology* as translated by Gerard of Cremona. See *Sd* 1–2, p. 151.

96 In this reading, *Sd* 1.2.101 and the opening "or" in Sd 1.2.103 should be taken as introducing a hard disjunction: the matter common to all inanimate bodies is either vapor (*Sd* 1.2.101) or something generated from vapor (*Sd* 1.2.103). Then the second option is said to be either elevated by the power of a star (*Sd* 1.2.103) or to act from its own elevated power (*Sd* 1.2.104), in which latter case it is generated either from ignited or nonignited vapor (*Sd* 1.2.104). An alternate reading would take the *aut* ... *aut* construction in *Sd* 1.2.103 to signal a hard disjunction but would result in a rather confusing paragraph. In either reading the Latin syntax is less than perfect.

97 For comment on the five kinds of fire in 59 and their significance for a claim for Bacon's originality see *Sd* 1–2, pp. 149–150.

98 Reading at *Sd* 1–2, p. 202, 106.2, '*ascendentis*' against '*accendentis*' in MSS. O. and S. and the text. I am indebted to Sten Ebbesen (University of Copenhagen) for the revision.

is an elongated fire like a spear or a beam, having greater length than width. The third is a round fire like that of a candle. The fourth is called ascendant assub and it is a clear body, proportionally very long and wide.[99] And these four are generated in the highest part of the air. The fifth, however, is descendant assub, which is seen to fall in the evening and at night, as if it were a star falling from the heavens. But should [the inanimate body that principally retains an elemental power] not be the one that is generated from ignited vapor, then it is either generated from vapor alone, or from vapor together with the irradiation of a star. For if it is generated only from vapor, then it is generated either in air or in earth and water. If in air, either it is a cloud, or it is rain, or it is mist (which is the calm part of a cloud left rolling in the air after a rain), or it is dew, or frost, or snow, or hail. What is to be said of the things that are generated in water and earth will be clear later.[100] But should an inanimate body be generated with the irradiation of a star, then, either it is generated indifferently by the irradiation of any star, and then it is said to be a circle about the star, or only by the irradiation of the sun and moon, and then it is said to be a rainbow, or only by the irradiation of the sun, and then it is said to be a perpendicular, which is a clear body diversified by colors, like a rainbow, having a long flame like a beam or lance, appearing in the air to the side of the sun.[101] [1.2.100–114]

99 In the *Opus maius* Bacon will later say: "Flaming impressions in the air from ignited vapors like stars which are called in Arabic ascendant and descendent assub are bodies of small quantity, but which seem to have a long light because of their distance and the swiftness of their movement." *The 'Opus Maius' of Roger Bacon*, ed. John Henry Bridges, vol. 2 (Oxford, 1897; reprinted Frankfurt am Main: Minerva, 1964), pp. 102–103.

100 The reference is unclear.

101 Reading at *Sd* 1–2, p. 203, 114.3, '*perpendiculare*' against '*perpendicularis*' in MSS. O. and S. and the text, and at p. 203 n44.8, '*cuminum*' against '*cruinum*'. MS. O. adds here: "under an opposite body. There are two subalternate species of [*body*], namely, *animate body* and *inanimate body*. Under *inanimate body* there are species of this sort, namely, *fusible* or *malleable body*, which is something metal, and *nonfusible*. Under *metal* are species of this sort: *gold*, *silver*, *iron*, *alloy of silver and lead*, *bronze*, and the like. Under *nonfusible body* are subalternate species of this sort, namely, *corpus terribile* and *corpus non terribile*. Under *corpus terribile* are species of this sort: *salt*, *pepper*, *cumin*, *cinnamon*, *clove*, and the like." (*Sd* 1–2. p. 203 [44].) The above seems to be a belated additional division of the genus *body*. See 54. I have not been able to find a translation for '*corpus terribile*'.

The distinction between malleable and nonmalleable metal is derived from Aristotle; the further classification of metals, says de Libera, comes from Isidore of Seville's *Etymologiae*. (See, respectively, *Meteorology* 4.9.386b18–387a4, and *Etymologiarum sive originum libri xx* 16.17, ed. Lindsay [Oxford: Clarendon Press, 1911].) For the significance of such references see *Sd* 1–2, p. 148.

[60] Under *animate body* there are two subalternate species, namely, *sensitive animate body* and *nonsensitive animate body*. [1.2.115]

[61] *Nonsensitive animate body* is, e.g., *plant*, for it has a vegetative soul, which is a principle for nourishing, growing, and generating, yet is nonsensitive in the sense that it cannot sense, because it does not have a sensitive soul. Under *plant*, moreover, there are subalternate species, e.g., *tree* and *grass* and *vegetable* and *shrub*, which [latter two] are intermediary between *tree* and grasses; but *vegetable* more closely approximates *grass*, and *shrub* more closely approximates *tree*.[102] A shrub is a plant that has many branches from one root without a stem, like a bush, a bramble, a thorny shrub, and a reed; a vegetable is a plant that has many stems from one root and has many branches, e.g., *rue*, *lettuce*, *sage*, and the like. But a tree is what has one trunk and many branches, e.g., *apple*, *pear*, *olive*, and the like; and grass is what has no stem, but only leaves with a root. [1.2.116–118]

[62] *Sensitive animate body* is *animal*, under which there are subalternate species, like *rational animal* and *nonrational animal*. [1.2.119]

[63] Under *nonrational animal* there are different species, both lowest and subalternate, e.g., *ass*, *lion*, *snake*, *fish*. [1.2.120]

[64] Under *rational animal*, according to Porphyry, there are two species, namely, *mortal* and *immortal*, each of which is a lowest species, e.g., *mortal rational animal*, because this alone is *man*; the other is a subalternate species, like *immortal rational animal*, under which are many species, e.g., *sun*, *moon*, *heavens*, *Mercury*, and so on.[103] Nevertheless, according to Aristotle one should not make such a claim, because he does not consider heavenly bodies to be animals; and so only *rational animal* converts with *man* and does not have different species under it. Hence there is no immortal rational animal; each is mortal.[104] And so Porphyry, since he followed Aristotle, considers heavenly bodies to be animals by reciting the opinions or falsehoods of Plato and others, whose falsehood the truth of Aristotle damns. [1.2.121–123]

102 De Libera says that the description of ambragyon descends in direct line from Nicholas of Damas' *De plantis*, a work on which Bacon commented during his first Parisian period. (*Sd* 1–2, p. 148.) See also Bacon's *Questiones de plantis*, ed. Robert Steele, *Ohi*, vol. 11, pp. 173–252.

103 Porphyry *Isagoge*, trans. Warren, p. 44.

104 Aristotle *On the Heavens* 2.1.284a27–b5.

QUANTITY

[65] Quantity is divided into *continuous* and *discrete quantity*. [1.2.124]

[66] *Discrete quantity* is what has parts that do not come together at the same boundary, and this is divided into *number* and *expression*.[105] *Number* is, e.g., binary, trinary, etc.[106] A number is a discrete quantity because its parts are not continued to a boundary, as the parts of a binary number (which are two unities) are not joined together. An expression is a definite measure of any composed spoken utterance, for every composed spoken utterance is either a syllable, a word, or an expression. But an expression, which is a quantity, is not one of these, but is a quantity and measure of these. *Expression* is divided into species like *meter*, *foot*, *longness*, and *shortness*. For as one attends to *expression*, so under it there is *meter*, which is divided into *two-meter* and *three-meter*; as one attends to *word*, so under it is *foot*, which is divided into *dactyl*, *spondee*, *trochee*, etc.; and as one attends to *syllable*, so under it is *longness*, *shortness*. Or, *expression* is spoken of in another way as one attends to *syllable*: *two-letterness*, *three-letterness*; as one attends to *word*: *two-syllableness*, *three-syllableness*; as one attends to *expression*: *two-wordness*, *three-wordness*. Thus can the species of *expression* be taken in a certain sense because we have no proper names by which to signify those species.[107] An element is the measure, the quantity, of a simple utterance, which is a letter. And one should know that *quantity* is a broadest genus, and *discrete quantity* is a subalternate genus, under which

105 Were two parts to be joined by a common border, the result would be a continuous quantity, like a line or surface (67). Apropos of *number*, one must think of each number as a part. Thus, as Aristotle remarks, while five and five make ten, the parts are separate and have no common boundary. (*Categories* 6.4b27–28.) Similarly, with regard to a vocal expression, one must think of the individual sounds of the letters, syllables, and words as separate parts, but as having no boundaries at which they are joined. (Ibid., 31–36.) Aristotle adds that it is evident that *speech* (Bacon's *expression*) is a subalternate species of *discrete quantity* because it can be measured in long and short syllables. (Ibid., 31.) It follows from all this that a quantity is something (an accidental form, not a complete substance) having parts: if the parts border one another it is a continuous quantity, whereas if they do not, it is a discrete quantity.

106 A binary number is the number two. Bacon will discuss numbers at great length when presenting the category Relation. See 72–83.

107 As evidenced in this paragraph, Bacon often resorts to the names of differentiae ('shortness', 'two-letterness', 'two-syllableness') to name various subalternate species for which, he says, no names have been coined. But if the species of *meter* (*metrum*) are appropriately named by him 'two-meter', 'three-meter' (*dimetrum, trimetrum*), why would not those of, e.g., *syllable* (*syllaba*) be appropriately named 'two-syllable', 'three-syllable' (*bisyllaba, trisyllaba*)? At one point (73) he pauses to acknowledge the error in substituting abstract for concrete names, but then proceeds with the abuse.

are *number* and *expression* as subalternate genera. Under *number* are lowest species, namely, *binary*, *ternary*, and the other numbers. Under *expression* are the subalternate species already noted, e.g., *meter* and *foot*, and lowest species, like *longness*, *shortness*, *two-letterness*, etc. [1.2.125–132]

[67] *Continuous quantity* is a subalternate genus under which are many subalternate genera, e.g., *line*, which is the continuous quantity from whose participation length alone can be judged to be in a thing, for it consists in length without breadth and density, under which are lowest species, namely, *foot*, *pace*, *stadium*, *mile*, *league*. Under *continuous quantity* there is a subalternate species, like *surface*, which is the continuous quantity from whose participation breadth alone can be judged to be in a thing, for a surface has length and breadth without depth. And it has under itself subalternate species, namely, *triangle*, *quadrangle*, *pentagon*, *hexagon*, and so on. Each of these, moreover, is divided into its lowest species as *triangle* is divided into *scalene*, *isosceles*, and *quadratus*, and so on.[108] Under *continuous quantity* there is a third subalternate species that is called *body* and this is the continuous quantity from whose participation density alone can be judged to be in a thing, for a body has a threefold dimension, namely, length, breadth, and density or depth. And it has under it lowest species, namely, *cube*, *pyramid*, *solid with sides one cubit long*, and *stignum*.[109] Again, under *continuous*

108 Reading at *Sd* 1–2, p. 205, 134.7, '*quadratus*' for '*gradatus*' in MSS. O. and S. and the text.

A *triangulus quadratus* is a scalene triangle (no sides equal), and is usually contrasted with an equilateral and an isosceles one. (See Peter *Tractatus* 7.108.) Bacon's term '*gradatus*' is curious, but it appears again in 320.

109 Reading at *Sd* 1–2, p. 205, 135.6, '*cubum*' for an uncertain spelling of either '*cubicum*' or '*cubitum*' in MS. O. and against '*cubitum*' in the text.

This paragraph merits several comments. First, the reference to four species of body would seem to recall at least part of Plato's fourfold division of solids in the *Timaeus* (55c–56b) into *cube*, *pyramid*, *octahedron*, and *icosahedron*. But note: the text at 55c is beyond the part translated by Calcidius (17a–53b) and directly available to Bacon, and the second two solids in Bacon's division do not correspond to Plato's second two. I am indebted, however, to James Marchand for pointing out that Bacon refers to Plato's four solids in his *Opus maius*. (See the chapter on Mathematics, op. cit., vol. 1, pp. 159.18–160.5; trans. Robert Belle Burke, *The Opus Maius of Roger Bacon*, vol. 1 [Philadelphia: University of Pennsylvania; London: Humphrey Milford; Oxford: Oxford University, 1928] pp. 180–181.) What one finds there is that Bacon became aware of Plato's classification through Averroes' commentary on Aristotle's *On the Heavens* where Aristotle rejects the notion that the basic four elements can be assigned four (and only four) different figures. See 3.8.306b2–308b28.

Second, surely '*latricubitus*' is a mistake: a body measuring one cubit (the length of a forearm) on each side is simply an individual of the species *cube*, along with others measuring two, three, four, etc. cubits on each side.

quantity there is a fourth subalternate species, namely, *time*. Time is the measure of movement, and it has lowest species under it, namely, *hour*, *day*, *week*, *month*, *year*.[110] Under *continuous quantity* there is a fifth subalternate species, namely, *place*, which is a boundary, the ultimate immobile thing containing something, under which can be assigned species, namely, *modius*, *sextarium*, and other capacities, which, although they may name substances, signify capacities and places.[111] [1.2.133–137]

[68] And one should know that what has parts coming together at a common boundary is said to be a continuous quantity, like the parts of a line at a point, the parts of a surface at a line, the parts of a body at a surface, the parts of time in an instant (like the past and the future to the present), and the parts of a place at that capacity which corresponds to a surface joining the parts of a body, as Boethius says and other expositors.[112] One should know, moreover, that *body*, in as much as it is a threefold dimension, is a species of *continuous quantity*, but that, in as much as it is that to which that threefold dimension belongs, is in the genus Substance. And it is there in two ways: in one way it is a universal whole and is a subalternate species of Substance; in the other way it is an integral part of any singular, animate, corporeal substance, like Socrates and a tree. One should know, finally, that more and less of the same essence constitute different species in mathematics, although not so in material things, because five and six differ only because of the greater and lesser number of units, and so on for all numbers. And similarly for lines, bodies, and all quantities. The case is not the same for substances, because a man does not differ from a man in species because he is bigger or smaller.[113] [1.2.138–140]

Third, I have not found the term '*stignum*' in any dictionary or word list, and so it has been left in Latin.

Finally, while Peter treats *body* as a separate species of Quantity, Lambert seems to want to treat it together with *place* and then proposes a distinction between continuous quantity made up of parts (a) having a position relative to each of other and (b) not having such a position. (*Logica*, p. 73.19–40.)

110 This definition of *time* is found in Aristotle's *Physics* 4.11.220a25, trans. R. P. Hardie and R. K. Gay, in *CWA*, vol. 1., p. 373: "... time is 'number of movement in respect of the before and after'."

111 A *modius* was a Roman dry measure equivalent roughly to a quarter of a bushel; a *sextarium* was a measuring vessel holding about one pint.

112 Boethius *In Categorias Aristotelis libri quattuor* 2, PL 64.205C–206A, commenting on Aristotle *Categories* 6.4b20–5a14.

113 Peter and Lambert add three points at the end of their treatments of this predicament: (1) nothing is contrary to a quantity; (2) Quantity does not admit of a more or less in the sense that, e.g., one line is more a line than another; and (3) it is unique to Quantity that something can be said to be equal or unequal with respect to it, e.g., one line can be said to be equal or unequal to another with

RELATION

[69] The third category follows in which Relation or Position is the broadest genus, and under it are two subalternate species: first, *aequiparantia*, second *nonaequiparantia* or *inaequiparantia* (to coin a name).[114] [1.2.141]

[70] *Aequiparantia* occurs when a relative form has its extremes signified by the same name. Under it is a subalternate genus, namely, *opposition*, and this has under it four species, namely, *contradiction*, *contrariety*, what occurs on the basis of privation and possession, and *relation*. The first occurs in contradictory opposites, as in these: 'Socrates runs,' 'Socrates does not run'.[115] The second occurs in contrary opposites, as in these: something healthy and something sick, which are direct contraries, and

---

respect to their quantities. (Respectively, *Tractatus* 3.16, trans. Kretzmann and Stump, *CTMPT*, p. 14.16, and *Logica*, pp. 76.26–77.11.) Lambert alone calls attention to the fact that we often speak in an inexact way when we use such phrases as 'much white' (in reference to a large white surface), 'a long time', or 'much motion'. (*Logica*, pp. 173.40–174.8.) Ordinarily Bacon ends his discussion of a predicament with a reference to individuals of that category. (See 85, 91, 100, 102, 105, 109.) Surely, then, what is stated in 85 (with corrections) should have been stated here or has been misplaced in the manuscript transmission.

114 The closest Bacon comes to a definition of 'relation' is in 84. Aristotle clarifies the notion by speaking of relatives (things that are related). Thus, e.g., Aristotle opens his discussion of this predicament in this way: "We call *relatives* all such things as are said to be just what they are, *of* or *than* other things, or in some other way *in relation to* something else." (*Categories* 7.6a36–39; trans. Akrill, in *CWA*, vol. 1, p. 10.) The fact that what is said in 84 is found near the end of the discussion of this predicament is, from a pedagogical point of view, curious. In 69–72 Bacon discusses notions that are ultimately derived from *Categories* 7, but the bulk of his treatment (72–83) focuses on subalternate and lowest species of multiple, itself a subalternate species of *prior/superior position nonequiparous relation* (see 72 and its note). Again, Bacon's names of species will sometimes be seen to be names of the differentiae of those species. In 73 he acknowledges the problem. I have not been able to think of a good English translation of '*aequiparantia*'. Such would have to be extensive enough to contain under it all the species of relations mentioned by Bacon. Peter gives as an example of it the case where similar is said to be similar to similar and neighbor is said to be neighbor to neighbor – each of the terms of the relation is called by the same name with respect to the other – and Kretzmann and Stump translate his phrase '*secundum aequiparantiam*' by 'on the basis of a comparison'. (*Tractatus* 3.18, trans. Kretzmann and Stump, *CTMPT*, p. 95.) Bacon gives no additional subalternate species of *aequiparantia*, but see 70 for the names of its lowest species.

115 A contradictory relation is one where both the terms cannot be said of a subject at the same time truthfully or both falsely.

something good, something bad, which are indirect contraries.[116] The third species occurs in privative opposites, of which sort are blindness and sight.[117] The fourth species occurs in related opposites, of which are a father and his child, and a lord and a servant. And one should note that the name 'relation' is equivocally said of the broadest genus (Relation) and of the relation that is a species of opposition. Under *aequiparantia* are lowest species, e.g., *likeness*, *unlikeness*, *equality*, *inequality*, *identity*, *friendship*, and *society*. Such can be said figuratively and by way of examples.[118] [1.2.142–148]

[71] *Nonaequiparantia* occurs when the relative form has terms signified under different names, and it contains under it subalternate species, namely, *prior position* and *inferior position*, i.e., *superior position* and *subjection.*[119] [1.2.149]

[72] *Prior position* or *superior position* has under it various lowest species, e.g., *paternity*, *domination*, and the like, and various subalternate species, e.g., *multiple*, *superpartient*, *superparticular*, *multiple superpartient*, and *multiple superparticular.*[120] [1.2.150]

116 A contrary relation is one where both the terms cannot be said truthfully of the same subject at the same time, though they can both be said falsely of it.

117 A privation is a lack of some faculty or attribute that ought to be present. Thus blindness and sight are not *privative* opposites of a stone.

118 Friendship is a relation wherein the two terms are both named by the same: 'friend of'.

119 While, technically, one could argue that the pairs mentioned here indicate different kinds of relations, Bacon makes no use of such a distinction, and hence they may be taken as synonymous.

120 Here *multiple* is presented as a subalternate species of *prior/superior position*, and in 73 it is said to have the lowest species *double*, *triple*, etc. (In 78 it is given as a species of *inferior position/subjection*, bearing the prefix 'sub' to indicate the relation of a lower number to a higher.) In 75 it appears as a subalternate species of *number*, with *double* as one of its species. Then it appears as a genus of *superparticular* (76) and *supertripartient* (77), along with each of their several subalternate species (76 and 77, respectively) in a context where these are all species of *number*. While Boethius' treatise *De arithmetica* is clearly the ultimate source for the ensuing treatment of numbers in the category of Relation – he speaks of the categories mentioned here as the five parts of *greater inequality* – de Libera notes that Bacon may well have drawn on an anonymous Parisian author of the *Accessus philosophorum VII artium liberalium* of the 1230s as a kind of "working drawing" (*l'épure*) for his own analysis. (See, respectively, PL 63.1099D–1110A; *Sd* 3, p. 187, n. 63; and Anonymi Magistri Artium Parisienses *Accessus philosophorum VII artium liberalium*, in *Quatre introductions à la philosophie* au *XIIIe siècle, Textes critiques et étude historique,* ed. Claude Lafleur, Publications de l'Institut d'études médiévales 23 [Montréal: Université de Montréal; Paris: Librairie philosophique J. Vrin, 1988], pp. 192–194.) In pointing this out de Libera is calling yet further attention to the fact that Bacon used modern as well as older sources.

[73] *Multiple* is what contains something else added more than once.[121] Its lowest species are *doubleness*, *tripleness*, and so on. And, likewise, other species can be proposed, but it is more appropriate to give concrete names for abstract ones, since abstract names are not imposed [for the names of species]. [1.2.151–152]

[74] A *superparticular number* is a number related to another number and containing all of that plus some part of it, namely, any one part.[122] And under it are these kinds of parts: *sesquialter*, which contains the whole [of another number] plus its other part or half, as three stands to two; and *sesquitertius*, which contains something plus its third part, as four stands to three; and *sesquiquartus*, which contains something plus its fourth part, as five stands to four; and so on.[123] [1.2.153–154]

[75] A *superpartient number* is one that contains something, [another number,] plus some parts of it.[124] Its species are: *superbipartient*, which contains a number plus two-thirds of it, as five stands to three; or two-fifths of it, as seven stands to five; and so on for all uneven numbers taken

121 A multiple number is any whole number more than 1. A superpartient number involves a fraction where the numerator is 1, and a superparticular number involves a fraction with the numerator being a whole number more than 1. Thus a multiple superpartient number would involve a whole number above 1 plus a fraction with 1 as the numerator, and a multiple superparticular number would involve a whole number above 1 plus a fraction with the numerator a whole number more than 1.

122 A superparticular number, then, is the *larger* of two numbers compared. It contains another number (the smaller) plus *one* part of the *latter*. Later, Bacon will discuss numbers that are *smaller* than another when he presents subalternate species of *inferior position/subjection*. See 78–83, esp. 79. To derive a superparticular (or superpartient) number simply express the difference between the two numbers ($1\,{}^{1}/_{2}$, $1\,{}^{1}/_{3}$, etc.) as a fraction (${}^{3}/_{2}$, ${}^{4}/_{3}$, etc.), and then state this as a ratio with the larger number first (3:2, 4:3, etc.). All of these pertain to the same equivalence class.

123 Sesquialter: $1\,{}^{1}/_{2} = {}^{3}/_{2} \sim 3:2$. The sesquialter superparticular number is 3 because it contains 2 plus ${}^{1}/_{2}$ of 2; sesquitertius: $1\,{}^{1}/_{3} = {}^{4}/_{3} \sim 4:3$; sesquiquartus: $1\,{}^{1}/_{4} = {}^{5}/_{4} \sim 5:4$.

The translation here (and throughout the discussion of this category) employs the names of cardinal numbers ('two', 'three', 'four', etc.) where the text has the names of distributive numerals ('binary', 'ternary', 'quaternary', etc.). The change in no way affects the meaning of the text.

124 Superpartient numbers are derived in the same way as superparticular ones, except that one adds to the second number (the denominator) *more* than one of the latter's parts. Shortly it will be further stipulated that numbers containing twice a number (Bacon's "double numbers"), numbers reducible to superparticular numbers, and even numbers are excluded from this class.

in order.[125] But this is not so with respect to even numbers, because, should it contain two halves, or two-fourths, or two-sixths, or two-eighths, it will not be a superbipartient number, but a multiple number or a superparticular number. Should it contain two halves, it will be a multiple number, because it would be a double multiple, as four stands to two. Should it contain a number [plus] two-fourths of it, then there will be a sesquialter proportion, as six stands to four; should it contain a number plus two-sixths of it, then there will be a sesquitertius proportion, as eight stands to six; and should it contain a number plus two-eighths of it, then there will be a sesquiquartus proportion, as ten stands to eight. Another species of *superpartient number* is what is called *supertripartient.* It is such that it contains something and three-fourths of it, as seven stands to four; or three-fifths of it, as eight stands to five; or three-sevenths of it, as ten stands to seven; or three-eighths of it, as eleven stands to eight.[126] But not three-sixths, because then there will be a sesquialter proportion, as nine stands to six; nor three-ninths of it, because then there will be a sesquitertius proportion, as twelve stands to nine. Another species of *superpartient number* is said to be *superquadripartient number*, which contains something and four-fifths of it, as nine stands to five; or four-sixths of it, as ten stands to six; or four-sevenths of it, as eleven stands to seven; or four-ninths of it, as thirteen stands to nine.[127] But not four-eighths, because then there will be a sesquialter proportion; and one is to keep such things in mind from here on. Similarly, other species of *superpartient number* can be added without limit in accord with multiplicity. But it would take a long time to enumerate them and they are clear to one who diligently inquires. Thus they are to be omitted.[128] [1.2.155–162]

[76] There is a *multiple superparticular number* as often as a number, compared to another, contains it more than once plus one part of it, that

125 A multiple number is any whole number more than 1. Thus the other whole number plus ${}^{2}/_{2}$ would be a multiple number. The others would be superparticular numbers because they reduce to fractions with the numerator 1 (74).

126 $1\,{}^{3}/_{4} = {}^{7}/_{4} \sim 7{:}4$; $1\,{}^{3}/_{5} = {}^{8}/_{5} \sim 8{:}5$; $1\,{}^{3}/_{7} = {}^{10}/_{7} \sim 10{:}7$; $1\,{}^{3}/_{8} = {}^{11}/_{8} \sim 11{:}8$, where the supertripartient numbers are, respectively, 7, 8, 10, 11.

127 A superquadripartient number is one exceeding another by $1\,{}^{1}/_{4}$, and which is reducible neither to a superparticular number or a double number. Thus, e.g.: $1\,{}^{4}/_{5} = {}^{9}/_{5} \sim 9{:}5$, with 9 the number because it is $1\,{}^{4}/_{5}$ times greater than 5; $1\,{}^{4}/_{6} = {}^{10}/_{6} \sim 10{:}6$; $1\,{}^{4}/_{7} = {}^{11}/_{7} \sim 11{:}7$; $1\,{}^{4}/_{9} = {}^{13}/_{9} \sim 13{:}9$. Note, however, that the example he gives of $1\,{}^{4}/_{6}$ is reducible to $1\,{}^{2}/_{3}$, which is a superbipartient number. (See 1.2.156). See also 77.

128 To derive these additional species take a whole number and add to it fractions having their numerators 5, 6, 7, etc., but avoiding those reducible to a superparticular number or a double number, e.g., $1\,{}^{5}/_{6}$, $1\,{}^{6}/_{7}$, $1\,{}^{7}/_{8}$, etc. (See 75.) The phrase "in accord with *multiplicity*" reminds that these numbers are species of *multiple number*. See 73.

is, contains it either twice, or three times, or four times; or as many as have [it more than once] plus some part of it, either a half, or a third, or a fourth, or a fifth, etc.[129] And it has under it many species, of which the first is *double superparticular number.* And these species have many species under them, of which the first is *double sesquialter*, which has double the other number plus half of it, as five stands to two; or *double sesquitertius*, which contains [double] the other plus one-third of it, as seven stands to three; or *double sesquiquartus*, as nine stands to four, and so on.[130] The second principal species is *triple multiple superparticular number.* There are many species of this sort of which the first is *triple sesquialter*, as seven stands to two; *triple sesquitertius*, as ten stands to three; and *triple sesquiquartus*, as thirteen stands to four, etc.[131] The third principal species is *quadruple superparticular number.* The first species of this sort is *quadruple sesquialter*, as nine stands to two; *quadruple sesquitertius*, as thirteen stands to three; *quadruple sesquiquartus*, as seventeen stands to four; and thus can be multiplied the species of *multiple superparticular number.*[132] [1.2.163–169]

[77] There is a *multiple superpartient number* as often as one number compared to another number has in itself the whole of it more than once plus two or three parts of it, or it contains several parts.[133] The first subalternate species of this is *double superpartient number*. And this has many species of which the first is *double superbipartient*, which contains twice some number plus two-thirds of it, as eight stands to three; or it contains it twice plus two-fifths of it, as twelve stands to five; and so on, in accord with which a superpartient number is multiplied.[134] Another species is *double supertripartient*, which contains twice some number plus three fourths of it, as eleven stands to four; or plus three-fifths, or three-sevenths, on the basis of which a supertripartient number is extended.[135] Yet another species is *double superquadripartient number*, which contains twice some

129 E.g.: $2^{1}/_{2}$, $3^{1}/_{2}$, $4^{1}/_{2}$, etc., and $2^{1}/_{2}$, $2^{1}/_{3}$, etc., and $3^{1}/_{2}$, $3^{1}/_{3}$, etc.

130 Double sesquialter: $2^{1}/_{2} = {}^{5}/_{2} \sim 5{:}2$, where 5 is the double sesquialter superparticular number because it is $2^{1}/_{2}$ times greater than 2. Similarly, double sesquitertius: $2^{1}/_{3} = {}^{7}/_{3} \sim 7{:}3$; double sesquiquartus: $2^{1}/_{4} = {}^{9}/_{4} \sim 9{:}4$.

131 Reading at *Sd* 1–2, p. 209, 167.4, '*quaternarium*' for '*quinarium*' in MSS. O. and S. and the text.

132 Reading at *Sd* 1–2, p. 209, 169.2, '<*ut novenarius se habet ad binarium; quadruplex sesquitertius,*>' as an addition immediately prior to '*ut tertiusdecimus*'.

133 A multiple superpartient number is one that is more than one and parts greater than another number, but avoiding numbers reducible to a superparticular number or a double number (see 75), e.g., $2^{2}/_{3}$.

134 $2^{2}/_{3} = {}^{8}/_{3} \sim 8{:}3$; $2^{2}/_{5} = {}^{12}/_{5} \sim 12{:}5$.

135 Reading at *Sd* 1–2, p. 210, 173.1–2, '*continet aliquem numerum bis et*' with MSS. O. and S. and against '*continet et*' in the text.

number plus four-fifths of it, as fourteen stands to five; or plus four-sixths, or four-sevenths, and so on, in accord with which a superquadripartient number proceeds.[136] The second subalternate species of *multiple superpartient number* is *triple superpartient*, and these are multiplied as before. Its first species is *triple superbipartient number*, which contains something three times plus two-thirds of it, as eleven stands to three; or plus two-fifths of it; or two-sevenths, in accord with the progression of a superbipartient number. Its second species is *triple supertripartient number*, which contains three times some number plus three-fourths of it, as fifteen stands to four; or plus three-fifths of it; or three-sevenths, in accord with the multiplication of a supertripartient number. Its third species is *triple superquadripartient number*, which contains three times some number plus four-fifths of it, as nineteen stands to five; or four-sixths of it; or four-sevenths; in accord with the division of a superquadripartient number, and so on. The third subalternate species of *multiple superpartient number* is *quadruple superpartient number* and this is multiplied as was the preceding. Its first species is *quadruple superbipartient*, which contains four times some number plus two-thirds of it, as fourteen stands to three; or two-fifths of it, etc., on the basis of which occurs the progression of a superbipartient number. Its second species is *quadruple supertripartient*, which contains four times something plus three fourths of it, as nineteen stands to four; or which contains four times something plus three-fifths of it; and so on, in accord with which a supertripartient number is multiplied. Its third species is *quadruple superquadripartient*, which contains four times some number plus four-fifths of it, as twenty-four stands to five; or [four]-sixths, or [four]-sevenths, etc., in accord with the multiplication of a superquadripartient number.[137] [1.2.170–182]

[78] *Inferior position* and *subjection* contain various lowest species, e.g., *sonship*, *servitude*, and the like, and subalternate species, like *submultiplicity*. And this is divided into lowest species, namely, into *subdouble*, *subtriple*, and so on.[138] [1.2.183]

136 $2^4/_5 = {}^{14}/_5 \sim 14{:}5$; $2^4/_6 = {}^{16}/_6 \sim 16{:}6$; $2^4/_7 = {}^{18}/_7 \sim 18{:}7$. Note, however, that $2^4/_6$ is a bad example because it is reducible to $2^2/_3$, a double superbipartient number.

137 Reading at *Sd* 1–2, p. 211, 182.3, '*sextas*' and '*septimas*' against '*sex*' and '*septem*' in MSS. O. and S. and the text.

138 The prefix 'sub' in 'submultiplicity' indicates a multiple diminution or decrease in a number, whereas 'subdouble' and 'subtriple' mean a decrease by a half and a third, respectively. Cf. 72 where 'double multiple' would mean an increase brought about by doubling a number. Boethius is not totally consistent in his terminology, though his intent is clear. Thus at one point in *De arithmetica libri duo* he speaks of submultiple numbers, subsuperparticular ones, and subsuperpartient ones, and at the same time multiple (not submultiple) subsuperparticular and subsuperpartient numbers, while at another point calling these submultiple superparticular and superpartient ones. Respectively, PL 63. 1100A and 1107D.

[79] A *subdouble number* is one that is twice contained in another; a *subtriple number* is one that is contained three times in another, and so on for all the species of *submultiplicity*. Any species of it corresponds to one species of *multiplicity* as does an opposite relative to its opposite.[139] A *subsesquialter number* is one that is contained in another plus its own other part, as two stands to three; a *subsesquitertius number* is one that is contained in another plus its own third part, as three stands to four, and so on, for *sesquialter* and *subsesquialter* are proportionately relative species.[140] Likewise, *sesquitertius* and *subsesquitertius*, and *sesquiquartus* and *subsesquiquartus*, and so on. [1.2.184–185]

[80] Another subalternate species of *subjection* is *subsuperparticular* [*number*], and a subsuperparticular number is one contained in another plus one of its own parts, whose species are *subsesquialter*, *subsesquitertius*, *subsesquiquartus*, and so on indefinitely.[141] [1.2.186]

139 The number 2 is a subdouble number because it is twice contained in 4; 3 is a subtriple number because it is thrice contained in 9. Thus, e.g., 4 is both a double number and a subdouble number: it is twice more than 2 and twice less than 8. This is the case with all even numbers 4 and above.

140 Reading at *Sd* 1–2, p. 211, 185.1, '*subsesquialter numerus*' with MSS. O. and S. against '*numerus sesquialter*' in the text, and at 1.2.185.2 '*subsesquitertius*' with MS. S. against '*subsesquialter*' in MS. O. and the text.

This reconstruction of the text is proposed for the following reasons: (1) the unemended text gives a definition of *sesquialter number* that is in clear opposition to that given in 74 for a sesquialter one and which has been coherently used up to now. (2) The prefix '*sub*' was introduced in 78 as a sign that Bacon is now discussing *multiple* as a species of *inferior position/subjection;* hence the number under discussion will be *lower* than the one to which it is related: a superparticular number is higher (74), a subsuperparticular number is lower (79). (3) A subsesquialter number involves $^1/_2$, not $^1/_3$, as the unemended text claims. (4) With the proposed emendations the ratios indicated turn out to be correct – no others are subsequently given with which to check them – but only on the condition that '*eius*' be understood to be reflexive. (The text would have been clearer had Bacon used '*sua*' in place of '*eius*'.) If the subsesquialter subsuperparticular (lower) number were one contained in another number plus half of the latter – the more grammatically correct use of '*eius*' – the second number would have to present a fraction and would not preserve the stated ratio. And (5), this last point serves to explain what is meant by the claim that "*sesquialter* and *subsesquialter* are proportionately relative species": 3:2 and 2:3.

Finally, it can be noted that the numbers presented assume one has in mind subsuperparticular numbers, because the diminution in both species is by only *one* part ($^1/_2$, $^1/_3$). See 80.

141 To derive a (subsuperparticular) subsesquialter number simply reduce the difference between the two numbers to a fraction, and state the ratios. The lower number will be the subsuperparticular number. Thus, e.g., subsesquialter: $1^1/_2$ = $^3/_2$ ~ 2:3, where 2 is the subsesquialter subsuperparticular number because

[81] Another subalternate species of *subjection* is *subsuperpartient number*. It is the number contained in another plus its own two parts, or three, or four, or however many in another. Its species are *subsuperbipartient, subsupertripartient, subsuperquadripartient*, and so on. A *subsuperbipartient number* is one that is contained in another plus its own two-thirds or two-fifths parts, etc.; a *subsupertripartient number* is one that is contained in another plus its own three-fourths or three-fifths parts, etc., and so on, always comparing one species of *subsuperbipartient* number to one species of *superpartient number*.[142] [1.2.187–188]

[82] Another species of *subjection* is *submultiple subsuperparticular number*, whose subalternate species is *subdouble subsuperparticular*. Its species are: *subdouble subsesquialter, subdouble subsesquitertius, subdouble subsesquiquartus*, and so on.[143] Another subalternate species is *subtriple subsuperparticular*. The third species is *subquadruple subsuperparticular*, and so on indefinitely, whose lowest species are multiplied as stated in the first species, namely, on the basis of the division of superparticular number. [1.2.189–191]

[83] Another subalternate species of *subjection* is *submultiple subsuperpartient number*, one species of which is the subalternate *subdouble subsuperpartient*. Its species are *subdouble subsuperbipartient, subdouble subsupertripartient, subdouble subsuperquadripartient*, and so on, always proceeding in accord with the division of a superpartient number.[144] Other species of *submultiple subsuperpartient number* are *subtriple subsuperpartient, subquadruple subsuperpartient, subquintuple subsuperpartient*, and so on. The species of these must be taken as has been described with respect to *double subsuperpartient number*. [1.2.192–194]

---

it is contained in 3 plus $^{1}/_{2}$ of itself, i.e., it is $1^{1}/_{2}$ times smaller than 3; subsesquitertius: $1^{1}/_{3} = {}^{4}/_{3} \sim 3{:}4$; subsesquiquartus: $1^{1}/_{4} = {}^{5}/_{4} \sim 4{:}5$.

142 Reading at *Sd* 1–2, p. 212, 188.3, '*et eius tres quartae, vel quintae*' against '2, 3, 4, 5, *vel quintae*' in MS. O. and '*duae quartae, vel quintae*' in MS. S. and '.2. *et eius duae* .4. *vel quintae*' in the text. (A subsupertripartient number is at issue.) E.g.: subsuperbipartient: $1^{2}/_{3} = {}^{5}/_{3} \sim 3{:}5$, $1^{2}/_{5} = {}^{7}/_{5} \sim 5{:}7$, where the first subsuperbipartient number is 3 because it is contained in 5 plus $^{2}/_{3}$ of itself, i.e., it is $1^{2}/_{3}$ less than 5; subsupertripartient: $1^{3}/_{4} = {}^{7}/_{4} \sim 4{:}7$, $1^{3}/_{5} = {}^{8}/_{5} \sim 5{:}8$.

143 E.g., subdouble subsesquialter: $2^{1}/_{2} = {}^{5}/_{2} \sim 2{:}5$, where the number is 2 because it is twice and $^{1}/_{2}$ itself contained in 5, i.e., it is $2^{1}/_{2}$ times less than 5; subdouble subsesquitertius: $2^{1}/_{3} = {}^{7}/_{3} \sim 3{:}7$; subdouble subsesquiquartus: $2^{1}/_{4} = {}^{9}/_{4} \sim 4{:}9$.

144 A subdouble subsuperpartient number is one which is contained twice and some parts of itself in another. Thus: subdouble subsuperbipartient: $2^{2}/_{3} = {}^{8}/_{3} \sim 3{:}8$, with 3 the number because it is two times and two parts of itself contained in 8, i.e., it is $2^{2}/_{3}$ times less than 8; subdouble subsupertripartient: $2^{3}/_{4} = {}^{11}/_{4} \sim 4{:}11$; subdouble subsuperquadripartient: $2^{4}/_{5} = {}^{14}/_{5} \sim 5{:}14$.

[84] One should note that the names 'relative', 'related', and 'relation' differ. A relation (*relatio*) is the possession itself, like *paternity*, *doubleness*, etc. A relative (*relativum*) is something taken concretely from such, e.g., a *father*, *double*. A thing related (*relatum*) is that whose possession is designated by a relative or a relation, like Socrates, to whom *paternity* or *that he be a father* accrues.[145] [1.2.195–198]

[85] Individuals of this category, e.g., *this expression*, *this number*, *this line*, *this surface*, *this body*, *this time*, *this place* are in the category Quantity.[146] [Individuals] in the category Relation are of this kind: *this likeness*, *this unlikeness*, *this equality*, *this paternity*, *this sonship*, and so on. [1.2.199–200]

QUALITY

[86] With respect to the fourth category it should be known that Quality is a broadest genus of which there are four subalternate species. [1.2.201]

[87] The first is *habit* and *disposition*, for these are two names of this species. They differ in that 'disposition' names something incomplete in this species and 'habit' something complete, as do 'boy' and 'man'. This is what Boethius intends in his commentary *On the Categories*.[147] A *disposition* is an easily altered quality, like *heat* and *cold* in the body of an animal and the like, that quickly passes away. But a *habit* is altered only with difficulty, like *knowledge*, *virtue*, and *vice*, which are subalternate species. Such as these do not easily take their leave of that in which they are. Under *knowledge* there are subalternate species, namely, *mechanical knowledge* and *liberal knowledge*. Under *mechanical knowledge* are such as these: *wool processing*, *agriculture*, *weaponry*, *acting*, *hunting*, *sailing*, *medicine*. Under *liberal knowledge* are species of this sort: *rational*, *divine*, and *mathematical*. Under *rational knowledge* are *grammar*, *logic*, *rhetoric*; under *divine knowledge* are *moral* and *metaphysics*; and under *mathematical knowledge* are *the art of measurement*, *music*, *geometry*, and *astronomy*.

145 The things related are also called the terms (*extrema*) of a relation. See 70.

146 Reading at *Sd* 1–2, p. 213, 199.1, '*istius praedicamenti*' against '*istum praedicamentum*' in MSS. O. and S. and the text.

Without the emendation this paragraph makes the false claim that individuals of the ten categories are all in the predicament Quantity. With the emendation the text is either a belated statement about individuals in the predicament Quantity or one that has become misplaced in the transmission of the MSS. It is best read when placed between 68 and 69.

147 Boethius *In Categorias Aristotelis libri quattuor* 3, PL 64.242A, commenting on Aristotle *Categoriae* 8.8b28–9a4.

Under *virtue* are species of this sort: *fortitude*, *chastity*, *liberality*, *nobility*, *magnanimity*, *desire for honor*, *gentility* or *humility*, *friendship*, *truth*, *liveliness* (the virtue of choosing the mean with respect to amusements), *modesty*, *righteous indignation* (which detests evil in another).[148] Under *vice* are species of this sort: *fear*, *temerity*, *incontinence*, *insensitivity*, *prodigality*, and *avarice*, and so on for the other extremes of other virtues. Every disposition can become a habit over a period of time. Things of this species accrue to a subject from without and by effort. [1.2.202–210]

[88] The second species is *natural power* or *lack of power*, and it is signified by these two names, as before (87). But one name can be imposed, e.g., 'capability', just as 'effort' was before (87). *Natural power* is a quality contingent on the natural disposition of the members of something to do something easily, or to not be easily affected by something harmful, as the ability to run is a quality of this sort for running, and the ability to box for boxing. Thus runners and boxers are so-called, not because they fight or run, but because they can do this well by their very nature and not by art or industry or practice, i.e., not by contrivance. Likewise, health-makingness, to coin a name, is the natural power by means of which one who makes himself healthy does not easily suffer anything from bad food or drink or from other things that induce sickness. And so he is said to be one who makes himself healthy, not because he becomes healthy, but because he is able to be unaffected by others because of his naturally well-endowed and strong constitution. Nor would this be owing to medicines, potions, and the like, for these would not affect him. And likewise hardness is the natural power of something hard in virtue of which it does not easily undergo sectioning. *Natural lack of power* is a quality contingent on the natural disposition of parts in virtue of which someone cannot easily do something or be affected by nothing harmful.[149] That natural lack of power in virtue of which someone cannot easily do something is a quality opposed to the ability to run and likewise to the ability to box. It is then (to coin a name) inability to run and inability to box. That natural lack of power in virtue of which someone is unable to be affected by nothing harmful, that is, in virtue of which he is easily affected [by something harmful] – because two negatives make an affirmative – is, e.g., ill-makingness, if I may coin a name, for in virtue of this, one who makes himself ill easily suffers something. For one who makes himself ill cannot resist the accidents that accrue to his body from without, not because he is ill, but

148 The reference to the mean is to Aristotle's notion that virtue stands between the extremes of excess and defect, for which see his *Nicomachean Ethics*, e.g., 2.2.1104a11–25.

149 I.e., it is the natural lack of ability to do something easily or the natural ability to be easily harmed.

because he has a weak constitution. And likewise softness is the natural lack of power in virtue of which something soft easily undergoes sectioning. *Ability to box* and *ability to run*, *health-makingness*, and *hardness* are, moreover, lowest species of *natural power*; the others are lowest species of *natural lack of power*. [1.2.211–217]

[89] The third species is *passion* and *passive quality*, which, as do *disposition* and *habit*, differ as does the complete from the incomplete. A *passion* is a momentary quality accruing to a subject, not by effort, but by chance or nature: by chance, like a blush that comes from shame or a pallor from fear; from nature, as in the case where someone acquired a quality in the womb of his mother (like redness or some such) and it endured for a moment. A passion exists when someone by his natural constitution acquires a quality that is not long-lasting. But a *passive quality* is an enduring and long-lasting quality accruing to a subject, not by effort, but by chance or nature. There is the example just mentioned with respect to a passion: any quality (which a passion is) becomes a passive quality if it lasts for a long time. *Passion*, moreover, and *passive quality* contain lowest species under them, of which sort are: *sweetness*, *bitterness*, *austerity*, *heat*, *coldness*, *whiteness*, *blackness*, and the like. [1.2.218–222]

[90] The fourth genus or subalternate species of Quality is *form* or *figure*, *straightness*, and *curveness*. It can be said there is no name imposed for this species by Aristotle, but let it be called *composition of a thing*. This is divided into its species, namely, into the composition that is observed in connection with a body, this is called a *form*; and into the composition that is observed in connection with a surface, this is called a *figure*; and into the composition that is observed in connection with a line, this is called *straightness* or *curveness*. [1.2.223]

[91] There are individuals of this sort in this category: *this knowledge*, *this virtue*, *this vice*, *this ability to run*, *this ability to box*, *this whiteness*, *this blackness*, *this form*, *this figure*, *this straightness*, *this curveness*, and others of this sort. [1.2.224]

ACTION

[92] The fifth category follows and Action is the broadest genus in it.[150] Its subalternate species are these two primary ones, namely, *corporeal action* and *spiritual action*. [1.2.225–226]

[93] *Corporeal action* contains species of this sort, namely, *cutting*, *burning*, *drinking*, *eating*, *reading*, *arguing*, and the like, which are low-

150 Bacon's treatment of this category is a good example of how much further medievals went in discussing some of the categories than Aristotle did. See Aristotle *Categories* 9.11b1–7.

est species. Perhaps it contains many subalternate species, of which sort are *fabricating*, *carpentering*, and the like, should one wish to create names.[151] [1.2.227]

[94] *Animal* or *spiritual action* contains species under it of this sort: *understanding*, *thinking*, *knowing*, *using the senses*, all of which are subalternate genera. [1.2.228]

[95] But one should know that according to some nothing is properly in the genus Action unless it is signified by a verb [signifying something] happening to a rational thing. Such, moreover, is one that causes another to undergo something. This is perhaps true, if one were to consider those things that most properly are in the genus Action. And, since an action in the most proper sense causes another to undergo something, only a verb that produces an effect of itself, absolutely, and in every [grammatical] person [on that other person] will signify a thing that is in the category Action.[152] And this is a verb [signifying something] happening to a rational thing, and so it most properly signifies a thing in the category Action. Less properly, however, do those that signify a thing happening only to a nonrational thing signify something in the category Action, because these do not, of themselves, cause other things to undergo something in every person, but only in the third, as Priscian proposes.[153] For nonrational things do not, of themselves, speak, which is proper to the first person, nor does one address them, which is proper to the second person. Broadly and least properly do those verbs that are not transitive but neutral, e.g., 'I run' and the like, signify a thing in the category Action.[154] [1.2.229]

151 These actions are named by abstract nouns (*sectio*, *ustio*, *bibitio*, etc.) instead of concrete verbs like 'to cut', ' to burn', 'to drink', 'to eat', etc., because of a point Bacon wants to make in 97.

152 Reading at *Sd* 1–2, p. 217, 229.4, '*verbum ex se*' with MS. O. against '*verbum cum altero ex se*' in MS. S. and the text.

153 Reading at *Sd* 1–2, p. 217, 229.9, '*haec*' against '*hoc*' in MSS. O. and S. and the text.

For the reference to Priscian see *Institutiones grammaticae* 8.10, ed. Martin Hertz, in *GL*, ed. Keil, vol. 2, p. 375.13–21.

154 I am indebted to Sten Ebbesen for the following plausible interpretation of the rather obscure theory in this paragraph, though neither of us is aware of who the "some" are to whom it is attributed. In the strict sense, only those acts (*res*) are to be classified in the category of Action which cause a person (*res rationalis*) to undergo some effect (*passio*) and which acts can be expressed in all three persons in both the active and the passive voice. Only in this strict sense do actions bring about effects whereby Action and Passion can be seen as fully contrasting categories. Thus, e.g., the verb 'love' fits this description because one can say 'I love', 'you love', 'he/she loves', and the case is similar when the object of the action signified by this verb is a person: 'I am loved', 'you are loved', 'he/she is loved'. If, however, one considers a different kind of act, e.g., typing, one can offer parallels

PASSION[155]

[96] The sixth category is the category Passion. In this the broadest genus is *passion*, one subalternate species of which is *corporeal passion*, and likewise, *spiritual passion*: e.g., *a cutting*, *a burning*, *a reading*, and the like.[156] [1.2.230]

[97] It is no wonder that the utterances signifying action and passion are the same, since these are used equivocally, because a cutting can be an action or a passion, and so on. Because of this, to make the difference between these categories clear – especially the species in the concrete – let us designate these in such a way that *acting* is the broadest genus in the category Action, and *reading*, *arguing*, and the like are its species. Let *undergoing*, however, be the broadest genus here, and *to be read*, *to be argued*, *to be cut*, and *to be burned* be species of *corporeal passion*. And similarly let the species of *spiritual passion* be of this sort: *to be understood*, *to be thought*, *to be judged*, and the like. [1.2.231–232]

POSITION

[98] The seventh category follows and its broadest genus is Situation or Position. A situation is something accruing to a subject by which the arrangement or disposition of the parts of the subject is manifested in a place. [1.2.233–234]

[99] It contains these first subalternate species: one kind of *position* is proper to animate things, under which are its lowest species, e.g., *sitting*,

---

in the active voice but not in the passive, except in the third person: 'It is typed', but not 'I am typed', 'you are typed'. Hence, in this theory the latter sort of verbs are not to be considered actions in "the most proper sense" because they do not cause a person to undergo (*pati*) something and hence do not allow themselves to be evocative of passion in the highest sense, that which a person would undergo.

At the end of his discussion of this category and the next Bacon omits reference to their individuals. Peter and Lambert add at the end of their discussions of Action: (1) every action infers a passion; (2) action (and passion) admit of contraries (cooling/heating, enjoy/sadden); and (3) action and passion admit of more and less. Respectively, *Tractatus* 3.27, trans. Kretzmann and Stump, *CTMPT*, p. 98, and *Logica*, pp. 90.39–91.4.

155 A word about the name of this category. English seems to have no one descriptive word to name the class of all things that happen to a person or thing, though we can easily speak of them as things that happen to us or other things, things we undergo, etc. In Latin these are properly called (via Boethius) *passiones*, and for lack of a good substitute most translations (as here) simply name the category Passion, and then call attention to the fact that one is not talking here about emotions like love and anger, which are qualities, for which see 89.

156 Note that in 97 Bacon supplies the more readily recognizable verbal names of both actions and passions.

standing, *reclining*, and the like; another to inanimate things, which has lowest species under it, of which are *the rough*, *the smooth*, *the thin*, *the thick*. [1.2.235]

[100] Individuals, i.e., singulars, in this category are this sitting, this reclining, this rough, and so on. [1.2.236]

WHEN

[101] The eighth category follows and its broadest genus is When, the species of which are *to be in [present] time*, *to have been in time*, *to be in future time*. *To be in [present] time* has species under it: *to be at an hour*, *to be on a day*, *to be in a week*, *to be in a month*, *to be in a year*, *to be in a five year period*, *to be in a century*, *to have been at an hour*, *to have been on a day*, etc., *to be at a future hour*, *to be on a future day*, etc. [1.2.237–238]

[102] Individuals are: to have been on this day, to have been at this hour, in this year. [1.2.239]

[103] And this accident occurs when there is something existing in a subject by which one tells at what time it exists. [1.2.240]

WHERE

[104] The ninth category follows and its broadest genus is Where. [1.2.241]

[105] It is divided into four subalternate species, namely, *to a place*, *in a place*, *through a place*, and *from a place*. *To a place* contains species under it, e.g., *to a region*, *to a city*, *to a church*, *to a house*, and the like. They have individuals under them, e.g., to Europe, to Italy, Paris, home, to England, to France, Rome, London, and so on for all the singular places and for the others. *Through a place* contains lower things under it, like these species: *through a region*, *through a city*, *through a house*, *through a church*. These are their individuals: through Europe, through Italy, through England, Rome, Vernon, and the like. *From a place*, likewise, contains lower species under it, e.g., *from a region*, *from a city*, *from a house*, *from the field of battle*, *from the country*, *from a church*, and the like. These, moreover, are their individuals: from Europe, from Italy, from Vernon, from this house, from this church, and the like.[157] *In a place* contains species under it and individuals, just as *to a place*, *from a place*, and *through a place*. [1.2.242–246]

157 The preposition '*de*' could also be translated by 'of' in this context as in 'William of Ockham'. Vernon, here and in 105, is a French town in the Eure Department, sixteen miles east-north-east of Évreaux, on the left bank of the Seine. The significance of this town for Bacon is unknown.

POSSESSION[158]

[106] The last category follows whose broadest genus is Possession. [1.2.247]

[107] To have is to possess something extrinsically accruing [to a subject], not something innate to the possessor, and this is to possess. For 'possession' serves here just as well as 'having'. And should the same thing be described by the same, this is not inappropriate, because a poverty of words has caused this. Or better, let it be said that Possession is the broadest genus in this category. And it is described by Aristotle in this way: "Possession is a form that something has in as much as it has something decorating the body having it or surrounding the parts of the body, something movable with its motion."[159] In accord with this [one finds the following] in the first book of Algazel's *Metaphysics*: "It is clear that under this are contained the things signifying something possessed that decorates and adorns a body."[160] [1.2.248–249]

[108] Under this broadest genus are these subalternate species: *having a covering on*, which pertains to the whole body, and another species, which pertains to the parts of bodies, for no name has been imposed [for this species], but it is called [by the letter] 'a'. Under *having a covering on* are these sorts of species: *having weapons on* and *having clothing on*, i.e., *clothed*. Under *having weapons on* are these sorts: *having chain mail on*, *having a helmet on*, and the like. Under *clothed* are these sorts: *having a tunic on*, *having a mantle on*, *having a pallium on*, and the like. Under 'a' are *having an amulet on*, *having a necklace on*, *having earrings on*, and the

158 This category is called State by Aristotle and, while he does no more than name it and give an example in the *Categories* and *Topics*, he concludes the *Categories* with a comment on the various senses of 'to have', the third of which refers to apparel and ornaments, and this later becomes the basis for a medieval discussion of this category. See, respectively, *Categories* 4.1b25–26, *Topics* 9.103b23, and *Categories* 15.15b21–24. Lambert also presents the six kinds of "possession" where the third is the one that constitutes this category, but he does this at the end of his next chapter, "*Post Predicamenta*" (After the Categories). (*Logica*, p. 101.8–27.) Prior to this, and at the end of his discussion on the categories, he addresses his tenth called *Habitus* and provides a definition from *Six Principles*: "Possession pertains to bodies and things that adorn a body," adding that 'things that adorn a body' refers to the parts of the body. *Logica*, pp. 94.23–95.14. Bacon goes to the *Metaphysics* for a definition of the name of this category, and adds additional explication from Algazel. See 107.

159 Aristotle *Metaphysics* 5.20.1022b4–8.

160 Algazel *Metaphysica* 1.1.4, ed. Muckle, p. 20.18–27.

like, to coin some names. For names have not been imposed for these species, and thus they are more conveniently designated by the letters 'a', 'b', 'c', 'd'. [1.2.250]

[109] Individuals, singulars, of this category are: this having weapons on, this having a helmet on, this having a tunic on. [1.2.251]

Part Two

Statements

SOUNDS

[110] Since terms about which the first part of Logic concerns itself have already been discussed, we must next speak of statements, which the second part of Logic treats, namely, *On Interpretation*. The first things to be looked at when considering a statement are its parts, and such are a noun and a verb, as Aristotle proposes.[1] We must speak, therefore, of these. But because every noun is an utterance and every utterance is a sound, we must begin with sound as from the more worthy part. [2.1–3]

[111] Sound is described in this way: a sound is the ear's own sensible thing.[2] "The ear's sensible thing" is stated because sound is not audibly recognized by another sensory part of the body, as is clear when one senses. "Own" is stated, that is, [sound is] a proprium of, and something perceptible by itself by, the ear, not in consequence [of something else] like a bell or a man, since these are perceived not by themselves but by their sound. The ear as an instrument of sensing and something fashioned for hearing senses nothing but sound, although as flesh or something having nerves it senses heat and cold and the like. And so the ear is not of itself an instrument of touch. [2.4–6]

[112] One kind of sound is vocal, the other nonvocal. [2.7]

[113] *Nonvocal sound* is, e.g., the sound of a bell, the collision of rocks, the crash of trees, the clamor of feet. [2.8]

1 Here medievals present a problem for a translator because throughout their discussions of statements (and beyond) they use the word '*nomen*', which can be rendered by 'noun' and by 'name'. Apropos of this and as a general rule, grammar can be said to treat of nouns, logic of names, and with this as a guide, '*nomen*' will be translated by 'noun' from here through 132 where Bacon is presenting the grammatical components of expressions, and by 'name' from 133 on, except, of course, where the context clearly indicates the contrary. For the reference to Aristotle see *On Interpretation* 5, 17a10–11, and 10, 19b10. For the notions of an expression (*oratio*), a statement (*enuntiatio*), and a proposition (*propositio*) and their differences see, respectively, 135 and 136.

2 As a matter of historical interest Lambert holds that, should a sound occur and no one perceive it, the sound still exists because it is still able to be heard (*audibilis est*). *Logica*, p. 6.13–14 and .32–34.

[114] *Vocal sound* is the same as an utterance, but 'utterance' is taken in two ways: commonly and properly. In one sense 'utterance' indicates whatever is perceived by an ear, because one speaks of the "call" of the trumpet and the "voice" of thunder, and in this sense 'call', 'voice', and 'sound' are synonymous names.[3] It is described in this way: an utterance is the sensible thing that is proper to hearing. But if it is taken properly, it is still taken more and less properly, for, should it be taken specially and more properly, it is only the voice of animals that do not modulate their sound, like a cow and suchlike, as Aristotle says in Book Four of *On Animals*.[4] ('*Vox*' is derived from '*calo*', '*calas*', which is the same as '*resono*', '*resonas*', as P[eter] Helias says. From this verb, likewise, '*boo*', '*boas*' is derived, or vice versa.)[5] But if it is taken less properly, then it is taken broadly for every kind of voice of an animal, namely, for a clamor and for the hiss of snakes. Similarly, the voice of a cow as well as the locutions of animals who do modulate their sound in the fashion of men [would be utterances in the broad sense], as Aristotle distinguishes in Book Four of *On Animals*.[6] [2.9–13]

[115] In another sense an utterance is said to be a sound produced by the mouth of an animal and is described in this way: an utterance is the percussion of air exhaled by the soul in those parts that are in the vocal passage, that is, in the throat. Or, in this way: an utterance is a sound produced by the mouth of an animal and formed by these natural instruments: lung, throat, teeth, tongue, palate, and lips. But Boethius offers a different definition of 'utterance' in his commentary on *On Interpretation*: an utterance is a sound produced by the mouth of an animal, formed by the plectrum of the tongue, that is, by a plectrum which is the

3 'Utterance', 'call', and 'voice' are all translations of '*vox*'; hence, they are all synonyms of 'sound' in this sense of the term.

4 Cf. Aristotle *History of Animals* 4.9.536a33–b3, where he distinguishes between the voice and sounds of animals, and points out that animals without lungs, tongues, or lips have no voice or language. But see n. 6.

5 The Greek verb is actually spelled "βοάω, βοᾷς" (I shout, you shout) and the reference should be to Priscian *Institutiones grammaticae* 1.2, *GL*, vol. 2, p. 6.4–5: "*Vox autem dicta est vel a vocando ut dux a ducendo, vel,* ἀπὸ τοῦ βοῶ *ut quibusdam placet.*"

6 Aristotle *History of Animals* 4.9.536b1–20. In this text Aristotle states clearly that language is unique to humans, but then goes on to say: "[B]ut articulate sound, that one might reasonably designate 'language', differs both in various animals, and also in the same species according to diversity of locality ... ." (Ibid., trans. D'Arcy Wentworth Thompson, in *CWA*, vol. 1, p. 848.) This, respectively, strict and broad notion of language could be the foundation for Bacon's distinction above; and Book Four, Chapter Nine, could also serve as the basis for later comments by Bacon on the communication of animals within a species. See 117.

tongue.[7] It is said to be a plectrum because, just as in the case of musical instruments the strings are altered by a plectrum to create harmony, so we have a tongue to make utterances, a kind of plectrum. Because the tongue is the principle instrument in the formation of an utterance, so Boethius creates a definition with reference to the tongue more than to anything else. A cough, exhalation, and inhalation, however, are not utterances in the last sense, although they are in the first sense. [2.14–18]

[116] Some utterances are ones that signify, others ones that do not signify. [2.19]

[117] A *nonsignifying utterance* is one by which nothing is represented, e.g, 'buba', etc. [2.20]

[118] A *signifying utterance* is one by which every animal communicates something to all or some of its species. Every animal can do this because nature did not give each a voice in vain. We can see this clearly, because the hen clucks differently to her chicks when she calls them to eat and when she teaches them to beware of a hawk.[8] Brute animals, moreover, communicate with each individual of their own species, as an ass with every ass, a lion with every lion. A man does not communicate with every man, but with some, because a Frenchman communicates only with a Frenchman, a Greek with a Greek, a Latin with a Latin, and so on. Also,

7 "An utterance is the percussion of air by the tongue which is produced by an animal through certain parts of the throat which are called passages." Boethius *In librum Aristotelis Peri hermeneias* 1, 2nd ed., ed. Karl Meiser, in *Anicii Manlii Severini Boetii Commentarii in librum Aristotelis ΠΕΡΙ ΕΡΜΕΝΕΙΑΣ* (Leipzig: Teubner, 1880), p. 4.18–20.

8 Earlier (n. 6) it was pointed out that Aristotle's *History of Animals* could well have served as the basis for these claims about animal communication, and here Bacon notes that such are open to empirical verification. Note, however, that the only other time he alludes to "chicken talk" – he omits it in the "*De signis*" of 1267 – is in his last work, *Compendium of the Study of Theology* (1292), and there the text that spurs his reflection, he says, is in Augustine's *On Christian Doctrine*. (See *Cst* 2.36 and 25.) But it seems to me that there are good reasons for contending that Bacon's division of signs (natural and at pleasure) and his detailed comments on communication among animals have more of a Aristotelian cast about them than an Augustinian one, however much in later years he strove to cast an Augustinian patina upon them. For a discussion of this issue see Thomas S. Maloney, "Is the *De doctrina christiana* the Source for Bacon's Semiotics?", pp. 126–142. For the view tracing Bacon's division to Augustine see Jan Pinborg, "Roger Bacon on Signs: A Newly Recovered Part of the *Opus maius*," *Miscellanea Mediaevalia* 13, no. 1 (1981): 403–412, and more recently Irène Rosier, "Variations médiévales sur l'opposition entre signification 'ad placitum' et signification naturelle," in *Aristotle's Peri hermeneias in the Latin Middle Ages*, edited by H. A. G. Braakhuis and C. H. Kneepkens, Artistarium Supplementa, vol. 10 (Goningen-Haren: Ingenium, 2003), pp. 165–205.

no animal communicates something to any individual of another species, unless improperly; at least it communicates nothing by its own utterance except to those that are of its own species. Nevertheless, should an animal be able through hard work and practice to use the utterance of another species, as a magpie uses the utterance of a man, it can, in a certain sense, improperly and unnaturally, signify something to a species other than its own, e.g., man. Although a man could by chance understand something by a magpie's utterance, that utterance, strictly speaking, is not one that signifies, since it does not arise from the magpie with an intent to signify. Although a man could understand something by such an utterance, the magpie, strictly speaking, signifies nothing by it. Likewise, a cock's crow, strictly speaking, signifies nothing to us as a signifying utterance, but a cock's crow signifies the time of day to us, just as red in the morning sky signifies rain to us. [2.21–23]

[119] Some signifying utterances are ones that signify at one's pleasure, others naturally.[9] [2.24]

[120] An utterance signifying *naturally* is one that is directed by nature to signify, like the groans of the sick and each utterance or sound of wild animals. [2.25]

[121] An utterance signifying *at one's pleasure* is one that signifies something by human institution, as do each Greek and Latin dialect. Of these, one is a word, another an expression. Some words are nouns, others are verbs. [2.26–28]

NOUNS

[122] A *noun* is an utterance that signifies at one's pleasure, apart from time, finite and direct, no part of which taken by itself signifies anything.[10] "An utterance that signifies" is included to distinguish it from a nonsignifying utterance. "At one's pleasure" is placed there to distinguish it from a naturally signifying utterance. "Apart from time" to distinguish it from a verb, which signifies together with time. (A noun, however, can indeed signify time, as do 'day' and 'year', but it does not consignify time or signify together with time, that is, time does not accrue to what it prin-

9 For the rationale behind the translation of '*ad placitum*' by (some variant of) "at one's own pleasure" instead of by "conventionally" or by "arbitrarily" see Engels, "La doctrine du signe chez saint Augustine," pp. 366–373, and his "Origine, sens et survie du terme boècien '*secundum placitum*'," 87–114. In the former he writes: "A curious fact: whereas the definition of a sign formulated by Augustine passed down through the Middle Ages, the collective aspect of the linguistic sign, although pointed out by him, has been almost eclipsed by the Boethian '*ad placitum*'" (p. 373).

10 For a comment on the translations of '*nomen*' as noun, see above, n. 1. See also Aristotle *On Interpretation* 2.

cipally signifies.) "No part of which" is included to distinguish it from an expression, whose parts taken by themselves do signify. The parts of no noun signify anything by themselves or as its parts, because neither do the parts of a noun composed of two whole nouns, like 'almshouse':[11] in as much as 'alms' is part of this one word, it has the force of a syllable and not the force of a word, and a syllable as a syllable signifies nothing by itself. "Finite" is included to distinguish it from an infinite noun because an infinite noun is not a noun.[12] [2.29–30]

[123] An *infinite noun* comes about by the addition of a negation. By the phrase "by the addition of" I mean by composition, not by apposition, e.g., 'nonman', 'nonlion'.[13] Boethius says that those things that can be signified by an infinite noun are an infinite number of things, and in this sense an infinite noun is called a noun.[14] For a nonman can be a horse, a stone, a house, Antichrist, Caesar and, generally speaking, any entity or nonentity, because in whatever the privation of humanity can be found, that can be said to be a nonman.[15] Hence, past Caesar is a nonman and the future Antichrist is a nonman. So it asserts nothing, because it indicates neither an entity nor a nonentity, since it is common to both, just as 'animal' does not

11 I have substituted 'almshouse' for '*respublica*' in the text with no alteration in the point being made. The translation of '*respublica*' by 'republic' would not illustrate his point.

12 At this point the explication of the terms in the definition of 'noun' is interrupted by a digression on the notion of an infinite term (123–125). In 126 Bacon will complete it with the explication of the term 'direct' (*recta*). Additional comment on infinite terms is found in 128.

13 Were the negative sign apposed instead of added to a term the result would be a negative term or denial, like 'not man'. (In some English translations infinite terms appear with a hyphen, like 'not-man'.) Thus one must distinguish among a finite term ('man'), an infinite term ('nonman'/'not-man'), a privative term ('unjust'), and a negative term ('not man').

14 "When I say 'nonman', I signify something – that which is not a man but this infinite thing." (Boethius *In librum Aristotelis ΠΕΡΙ ΕΡΜΕΝΕΙΑΣ* 1.2., 2nd ed., ed. Meiser, p. 62.3–5.) Lambert holds a different view: the reason why infinite terms are *not* nouns (names) is because such are not able "to put an end to a question (*finire questionem*) to which one is responding." *Logica*, p. 10.24–27.

15 In the strict sense 'privation' designates a lack of something that ought to be present, e.g., sight and justice in man. (See Aristotle *Topics* 6.6.143b34–35.) Thus Bacon is correct in saying that an infinite term can name things lacking humanity that ought to have it, for all things named by a privative term are also correctly named by infinite terms. E.g., all unjust people are also nonjust (as well as not just). But the converse does not hold, and hence the clause here introduced by 'because' does not supply a reason for the immediately preceding (accurate) claim.

indicate an ass or a lion, since it is common to them.[16] It is not inappropriate for something presenting itself in the form of a privation or negation to be common to an entity and a nonentity, although nothing presenting itself in the form of a possession or position could be common in this way.[17] [2.31–33]

[124] [To make a term infinite] differs from the negation of a term, because by means of negations nothing can be understood in virtue of the locution, as when I say 'no man'. But by means of an infinite term both an entity and a nonentity can be understood, as when one says 'nonman', just as by 'animal' an ass, a lion, and a goat can be understood. I say this with respect to most cases, but not to all, because to make 'entity' and 'one' and 'something' infinite indicates nothing; nor can anything be understood by them if I say 'nonentity', 'nonsomething'. But this is not because of the force of the denial, but because of what the things signified by the term have in common, because it is common to all things that are, and so its privation is found only in a nonentity. In spite of this the nature and way of negating and making a term infinite are not the same. [2.34–36]

[125] These things are to be understood of substantival nouns and not of adjectives, because an infinite adjective, like 'nonwhite', designates the privation of a quality and indicates an indefinite substance. Hence, it should be known that for a term to be able to be infinite through the reception of a negation, it is necessary that it signify a predicable thing, that it signify a finite quality, and that it be composed of two whole terms. Because of the first condition signs and syncategorematical words in general cannot be made infinite.[18] Because of the second, indefinite nouns like 'who', 'of such a kind', etc., and pronouns cannot be made infinite because "a pronoun signifies a mere substance," which without a quality is confused and indefinite.[19] Because of the third the signs '*nemo*', '*nullus*',

16 To say in this context that an infinite term "posits nothing" seems to mean that it posits something, but that what it posits is indefinite in the sense that it can be anything other than what is signified by the finite form of the term. (See 124.) In 153 he will say explicitly that an infinite term presents something to be understood. By contrast in 124 he will correctly note that the infinite term 'nonentity', 'no one', [i.e., 'not-one',] and 'nonsomething' do indeed posit nothing, because (124) of the comprehensivity of the significata of their corresponding finite terms.

17 Habits and positions are accidents and as such can only exist as attributes of existing substances. (See 87 and 98.) Thus, e.g., a given quality or posture does not signify or connote a nonentity having it. See also 125.

18 For the notion of syncategorematical terms see 129. Thus, e.g., one does not correctly formulate such terms as 'nonevery', 'nonsome', or 'nonno'.

19 See Priscian *Institutiones grammaticae* 12.15, *GL*, vol. 2, pp. 585.32–586.2: "Pronouns signify only a substance, not a quality, in connection with the utterance of a word."

'*neuter*', etc., cannot be made infinite. '*Nemo*', moreover, is composed of two corrupt terms, whereas the others are composed of a corrupt term and a whole one.[20] Connectives, moreover, and prepositions and some adverbs and interjections cannot be made infinite because they do not signify something predicable or finite. But some – those that signify something predicable – can be made infinite, e.g., 'well', 'poorly', and the like. The participles of a verb will be understood later (133). [2.37–41]

[126] "Direct" is included to distinguish the case of a noun, because, as Boethius says in *On Categorical Syllogisms*, every noun joined to a verb indicates something true or something false, as, should you say 'It is daytime', this is either true or false.[21] But, should you join an [oblique] case, you effect something neither true nor false. For should I say 'It is to a day', nothing is indicated that would be true or false. Boethius says, "What is called a noun with merit is only the nominative case," saying, "That word which those who impose names for things first spoke, that alone is called a noun with merit. For who first imposed the name 'circus' for a circus seems to have spoken in this way: 'Let this be called "circus"'; and so this first case, which is called the nominative, is a noun."[22] [2.42]

[127] According to a grammarian there are thirty-three different kinds of nouns in all, of which four are apportioned to proper nouns, namely, *agnomen*, *cognomen*, *first name*, and the *name itself* of a thing. Four are common to proper and appellative nouns, namely, *corporeal* ones, *incorporeal* ones, *synonyms*, and *homonyms*, i.e., equivocal nouns. Six are apportioned to derivatives, namely, a *patronymic*, a *possessive*, etc. But there are nineteen common to original nouns and derivatives, namely, an *adjective*, *something said with reference to something*, etc. But these do not pertain to our present purpose. [2.43–46]

[128] For a logician 'noun' is spoken of in many ways. For there is a *finite noun*, e.g., 'man', 'stone', and an *infinite* one, such as 'nonman', 'nonstone'. There is a noun in the *nominative* case, e.g., 'Cato', and one in

20 The terms have been left in Latin because I can think of no English equivalents that fit what is said of them.

21 Boethius *De syllogismo categorico libri duo* 1, PL 64.795D: "For every noun, when it is joined with a verb, indicates something either true or false." The nominative, vocative, and sometimes the accusative cases are said to be direct (*rectus*), whereas the genitive, dative, and ablative oblique (*obliquus*).

22 Boethius *De syllogismo categorico* 1, PL 64.796A: "That alone with merit will be called a noun which they who were imposing names for things first uttered as a word. For who first imposed the name 'circus' for a circus seems to have spoken this way: 'Let this be called "circus"'. And so this first case is called the nominative because it is a name." See Priscian *Institutiones grammaticae* 5.72, *GL*, vol. 2, p. 185.11–12: "That is direct which is called nominative, for through it naming occurs, as in 'Let this one be named "Homer," that one "Virgil"'."

an *oblique* case, such as 'Cato's', and 'Caesar' [can be expressed] obliquely. There is a *universal noun* that is said of many things with one signification, e.g., 'man', 'animal'; and there is a *singular noun* that is said of only one thing with one signification, such as 'Socrates'. There is a *noun of first intention*, e.g., 'a man', 'an animal', and whatever signifies something that is in nature outside one's imagination; and there is a *noun of second intention* that does not signify a thing itself, but a concept that an intellect places over a thing, e.g., 'genus', 'species', and the like. Nouns of first intention are nouns signifying predicable things. Nouns of second intention are not of this sort, because 'proposition', 'syllogism', 'genus', 'species', etc., are not in a category.[23] [2.47–54]

[129] Also according to a logician there are nouns such as a *categorematical noun* and a *syncategorematical noun*. A categorematical noun is any noun that signifies a predicable thing and similarly any noun of second intention. Syncategorematical nouns are those that signify modes and dispositions of those others, e.g., signs such as 'all', 'every', 'no', 'neither', etc. 'Syncategorematical' is taken from '*syn*', which means with, and '*categorema*', which means signifying, as it were, consignifying, that is, signifying in connection with another and not by itself. This is to be understood finitely, because 'all', 'every', 'no', and so on for the other syncategorematical words signify nothing finitely. But they signify something indefinitely because they signify a substance together with a general and indefinite quality. I say this of the syncategorematical words that are nouns. [2.55–56]

[130] There is, moreover, a *noun of possession* and a *noun of privation*: nouns of possession, e.g., 'sight', 'hearing', 'just'; nouns of privation: 'blind', 'unjust', and the like. And, some nouns are *equivocal*, some *univocal*, and some *denominative*, about which we have already spoken (34). [2.57–58]

VERBS

[131] A *verb* is an utterance that signifies at one's pleasure together with time, finite, direct, no part of which taken by itself signifies something. All the parts of this definition are clear from what has already been said (122), except 'finite' and 'direct'. [2.59–60]

[132] An infinite verb is not a verb because every verb with a noun can constitute a perfect statement, but an infinite verb cannot do this, as will be clear later (153).[24] But a verb is called infinite because it indicates nothing definite, for what nonwhitens can redden, become black, and be

23 These are not in a category in the same sense as extramental objects are not, but all of these as concepts (simple or compound) are qualities of the mind and hence predicated of a mind.

24 A perfect statement is one that expresses a complete thought. (See 138.)

pale, run, and do nothing and an unlimited number of other things, because of which such a verb is called infinite.[25] Boethius says, therefore, that "an infinite verb does not remain infinite in an expression."[26] This is shown in this way: when a verb is placed in an expression, it actually faces a suppositum, i.e., a subject, to which it is united and with which it is composed, and thus there occurs an actual union of an action with a substance or to a substance. Because of this a verb is essentially related to the other as to a subject when it is placed in an expression, and it cannot be freed from the relation to the subject. So, should a negation enter (which introduces a division of one thing from another), it divides absolutely the action signified by the verb from the substance signified by the noun. Such a negation, moreover, constitutes a negative expression, as will be known later (153); therefore, that negation will purely negate and not make the verb infinite. Because of this I say that a verb in an expression cannot be made infinite, but only negated. [2.60A–63]

[133] One should know in addition that only a verb in the third person can be made infinite outside an expression, and not a verb of the first or second person, because of the previously stated reason (132), for the latter provide the understanding of a perfect expression because a definite nominative is understood in them, as Priscian says, and so they have an actual subject.[27] Also, certain verbs in the third person signifying certain actions (*exceptae actiones*) cannot be made infinite for the same reason, examples of which are 'strikes' and 'thunders', because a nominative is

25 Apropos of the translation of infinite terms, '*non currit*' and '*non laborat*', which William uses as examples of infinite verbs, should have been translated by Kretzmann by 'nonruns' and 'nonworks' (or 'not-runs' and 'not-works') instead of by 'does not run' and 'does not work', respectively. See *Introductiones in logicam*, ed. and trans. (German) Hartmut Brands and Christoph Kann. Philosophische Bibliothek, vol. 469 (Hamburg: Felix Meiner Verlag, 1995), p. 8.8, and cf. trans. Kretzmann, p. 24.

26 "Infinite verbs which have been joined [to subjects] in a proposition produce not an affirmation but a negation, and so he [Aristotle] remains silent about these, because these [considerations] which derive more from an infinite verb pertain to one quality of a proposition, i.e., the negative one. For there always occurs a negation from an infinite verb." Boethius *In librum Aristotelis ΠΕΡΙ ΕΡΜΕΝΕΙΑΣ* 4.10, 2nd ed., ed. Meiser, p. 258.16–21.

27 While de Libera suggests Priscian *Institutiones grammaticae* 8.3, Priscian simply says there that 'he' is understood in verbs like '*rogat*'. (See *GL*, vol. 2, p. 370.22–23.) But on p. 448.15–17, Priscian says that first and second person verbs are finite because a definite subject is understood in them, whereas third person verbs often need an (expressed) pronoun to make them definite. The reasoning seems to be that in first and second persons one knows clearly who the subject is, but there is something indefinite about the third person: he? she? it?

understood in them, namely, Jupiter. It must be said that the verb 'is' can be made infinite, as was said of the noun 'entity' (123). When a verb is made infinite, nothing is indicated, just as neither in a negation, because an infinite verb is common to an entity and a nonentity, as Aristotle says.[28] Yet, something can be understood when some verbs are made infinite, as was said of nouns (123).[29] With respect to a participle it should be known that it can be made infinite, just as an adjective: it asserts something because an indefinite substance is indicated and an action is privated. Verbs in the infinitive mood can be made infinite, just as verbal nouns, because they signify the same thing. For although such a verb is infinite as to significance or mood, yet it is finite as to what is signified, and so it can be made infinite.[30] An impersonal verb can be made infinite because it in no way provides an understanding of something in the subject position. [2.64–70]

[134] "Direct" is said to distinguish the cases of a verb. The case of a verb is past and future. Direct is present. But one should know that a perfect expression or statement can arise from the case of a verb together with a noun, because the direct is understood in the case of a verb, as in 'will be' [there is understood] 'is in the future', and in 'was' [there is understood] 'is in the past'; and so just as the expression 'Socrates is' is perfect, so these: 'Socrates was' or 'Socrates will be'. But a perfect expression [need] not arise in this way from the case of a noun together with a verb, because the nominative case is not understood as the case of [every] noun, for 'lord' is not understood when I say 'of a lord' or 'to a lord'. [2.71–72]

EXPRESSIONS

[135] A logician posits the parts of an expression in this way, namely, a name and a verb, whereas a grammarian posits eight.[31] A logician, however, includes a pronoun under 'names' because of the agreement of what is signified and the pronoun's function, which is to submit a subject

28 While I do not find what is claimed by Bacon expressly stated by Aristotle, it is reasonably inferred by what is said in his discussion of the use of negative, privative, and infinite terms in propositions. See Aristotle *On Interpretation* 3.16b13–25 and 10.19b5–20b10, and *Prior Analytics* 1.46.51b5–52b34.

29 If Bacon is speaking only of those verbs in the third person outside an expression that can be made infinite, then his position is coherent. But if this is a reference to some verbs other than the verbal forms mentioned next, then he needs to become more explicit to ensure such consistency.

30 The term 'significance' (*significantia*) has been supplied by de Libera for '*signatum*' in MS. O. and '*significatum*' in MS. S.

31 For sources of this two-fold division see Aristotle and Priscian. Aristotle says, "I mean, for example, a man is just; here I say that the 'is' is a third component – whether name or verb – in the affirmation." Priscian says that dialecticians divide expressions (*oratio*) into *nomen* and *verbum*, but notes that Stoics propose a five-

to a verb.[32] An adverb is included under 'names' because Boethius says this in *On Categorical Syllogisms* in these words: "An adverb is a name whose finite signification is apart from time and it makes no difference that it is not declined through cases, for it is not a proprium of a name to be declined, for there are some names that cannot be declined which are called *monoptota* by grammarians."[33] A participle is included under 'verbs' because the same Boethius says: "That which is called a participle is put in the place of a verb, since it indicates time."[34] And also it is sometimes taken for a noun because it shares in the nature of a name. But connectives and prepositions are not included in the parts [of an expression] strictly speaking and with respect to signification, but rather with respect to function. Boethius says that these are "additions to an expression," for just as the cinches and bridles of a four-horse team are not their parts but in some sense bindings and additions, so connectives and prepositions are not parts of a statement but certain things that bind [the parts together].[35] An interjection is included under 'adverbs', as Priscian maintains.[36] [2.73–78]

[136] But, since a logician considers expressions and their parts because of the nature of a syllogism, which latter needs only parts that can

---

fold division and unnamed others speak of nine, ten, and eleven parts of speech. See respectively, *On Interpretation* 10.19b19–20, trans. Akrill, in *CWA*, vol. 1, p. 31, and *Institutiones grammaticae* 2.17, *GL*, vol. 2, pp. 54.23–55.3. Bacon seems to be in the camp of those who disagree with Aristotle when he takes the copula 'is' as a third part of speech. William stands with Bacon. See William, *Introductiones*, trans. Kretzmann, p. 27. Bacon mentions the copula again in 140 but only to distinguish an implicit and explicit copula.

32 Bacon seems to have in mind here the case where a pronoun is the subject of a verb. Hence, whatever it signifies functions as the subject of a verb – this is the agreement he speaks of – and because names do this whereas verbs generally do not, pronouns are classified as names and not as verbs.

33 Boethius *De syllogismo categorico libri duo* 1, PL 64.796D–797A. Cf. also Boethius *In Aristotelis librum* ΠΕΡΙ ΕΡΜΕΝΕΙΑΣ 1.1, 2nd ed., ed. Meiser, p. 15.5–7. According to Priscian monoptota names are nouns that have the same ending in all the grammatical cases, e.g., the names of numbers from four to one hundred, '*mille*', and letters of the alphabet. Those with two endings are diptota, etc. *Institutiones* 5.13, *GL*, vol. 2, pp. 184.6–8 and 188.4–9.

34 Boethius *De syllogismo categorico libri duo* 1, PL 64.796D.

35 Ibid.: "The only two parts to be thought of are the name and the verb, for the others are not parts but additions to an expression. For just as the bridle and cinch are not parts of a four horse team but are in a certain sense bindings, and as has been said, additions are also not parts, so connectives and prepositions and other suchlike are not parts of an expression but things that bind [the parts] together."

36 Cf. Priscian *Institutiones grammaticae* 15.40, *GL*, vol. 3, p. 90.6–9.

be a middle term, a major extremity, or a minor extremity (about which we must speak later [290]), he posits only those parts of an expression that can be converted into these. Only a name and a verb can appropriately be of this sort (as will be clear [135, 290]), since a syllogism arises from universal and particular propositions and no universal or particular expression can be made from a pronoun in the position of a subject. So pronouns cannot be the terms, the complete parts, of a syllogism, just as neither can adverbs nor interjections nor prepositions and connectives, because none of these can be a major or minor or middle term, or receive a universal or particular sign upon itself. A participle, however, passes for a verb because it signifies together with time and because it is more naturally suited to be said of another than to function as a subject with respect to another. Because of this a logician posits only two parts of an expression, namely, that about which the other is said, namely, a name, and that which is said of the other, namely, a verb. [2.79–81]

[137] An expression is an utterance that signifies at one's pleasure, each part of which taken by itself signifies something. Boethius says, "Whose parts are at one's pleasure is at one's pleasure; the parts of an expression are a name and a verb; but these are at one's pleasure; therefore, an expression is at one's pleasure."[37] Principally and *per se* a name and a verb are at one's pleasure; consequently, so is an expression. It should also be known that a part of an expression is two-fold, namely, a principal one, like a word, which always signifies when taken by itself; the other, however, is secondary, like syllables and letters, and these do not signify when taken separately. The parts "apart from time" and "along with time" are not included in the definition of 'expression' because some "expressions" signify apart from time, e.g., those that are made up of names only, whereas others along with time, as do those in which a verb is placed.[38] [2.82–85]

[138] Some expressions are perfect, others imperfect. An *imperfect expression* is one that generates an incomplete thought in the mind of the listener, e.g., 'white man'; a *perfect expression* is one that generates a complete thought, etc., as does 'A man is an animal'. Some perfect expressions are indicative, e.g., 'A man runs'; some are imperative, as is 'Build a fire'; and some are optative, e.g., 'Would that I were a good cleric'.[39] Some

37 Boethius *De syllogismo categorico libri duo* 1, PL 64.797A.

38 An expression made up only of names and no verbs could only be an expression in an equivocal sense, given that the parts of an expression have been said to be a name and a verb. Hence, the quotation marks around 'expression' (*oratio*) in the translation.

39 Reading at *Sd* 1–2, p. 231, 88.2, '*essem*' with MSS. O. and S. and against '*esse*' in the text. This supports the notion that Bacon did not become a Franciscan until after this work was written, though, if Stewart Easton is correct, he would have

indicative expressions are interrogatory, e.g., 'Do you think the soul is immortal?' Others make a statement, as does 'The soul is immortal'. An entreating expression is reduced to an optative one according to Boethius, as is 'Would that God would act'; a vocative one is reduced to an imperative one, e.g., 'God, be with me'.[40] Yet it is commonly said that an entreating expression is contained under 'imperatives', e.g., 'God, have mercy on me'. Boethius does not speak of an expression with a connective in it because it does not constitute an expression *per se* but only together with another verb to which it is subjoined.[41] In this sense it ought to be denominated more from the other verb, just as 'Should you come to me, I shall give you nothing' is an indicative one. So, an expression with a connective in it when taken *per se* is contained under 'imperfect expressions'. An expression that makes a statement is the same in substance as a proposition, for each is an expression signifying something true or false. But none of the other expressions signifies something true or false.[42] [2.86–93]

[139] Some propositions are simple, others composed, i.e., some are categorical, others hypothetical.[43] A *categorical proposition* is one whose

---

entered the Order very soon after its composition. Easton suggests about 1252 in England for his entry into the Order of Friars Minor. See Easton, p. 139. The classification of types of expressions seems to be rather unsettled at this time. In 136 Bacon distinguishes various species of expressions but, along with William's *Introduction*, fails to mention those in the subjunctive mood as a class in themselves. In contrast Peter distinguishes among indicative, imperative, optative, and subjunctive expressions and gives as an example of a subjunctive expression, 'Should you come to me, I will give you a horse', the same example (with an insignificant change) Bacon will shortly present as an indicative expression with the (subordinate) clause in the subjunctive and consider an imperfect expression. *Tractatus* 1.16.

40 Lambert agrees apropos of entreating expressions, but not with the claim about vocative ones. (*Logica*, p. 12.3–4.) Boethius says: "There are five species of *expression* in the narrowest sense. Interrogative, e.g., 'Do you think the soul is immortal?' Imperative, e.g., 'Take the book'. Optative or entreating, e.g., 'Would that God would act'. Vocative, e.g., 'God, be present'. One that makes a statement, e.g., 'Socrates walks'." *De syllogismo categorico libri duo* 1, PL 64.797C.

41 Boethius *De syllogismo categorico libri duo* 1, PL 64.797C–D.

42 Lambert points out that 'expression' is a generic term with numerous species. Consequently, he continues, an expression taken by itself is called a statement (*enuntiatio*); when sought by an opponent, a question (*questio*); when given to an opponent in a debate, a *dictio*; when an opponent takes it in the manner given by the respondent, an assumption (*sumptum*); when placed in an order (with others) to infer a conclusion, a proposition (*propositio*); and when it is concluded from premises or a premise, a conclusion (*conclusio*). *Logica*, p. 12.15–23.

43 For Bacon's treatment of simple and composed propositions see 175.

force consists in a predication, that is, one that has a subject and a predicate for its parts. A *hypothetical proposition* is one whose force consists in there being something that follows or one that has categorical propositions for its parts, e.g., 'If it is day, there is daylight'. Let us speak first of categorical propositions. [2.94–97]

CATEGORICAL PROPOSITIONS

[140] A *categorical proposition* is the same as one that predicates, from '*categorizo, -as*', which is 'I predicate', 'you predicate'.[44] Its parts are a subject and a predicate, as was already said (136), and a copula. A *subject* is that about which the other is said; a *predicate* is what is said about the other; and a *copula* is what joins a predicate to a subject.[45] For example, in 'A man is an animal', 'man' is the subject, 'animal' the predicate, and 'is' the copula. But sometimes the copula is explicit, as in 'A man is an animal', sometimes implicit, as in 'This man runs'. [2.98–100]

[141] Some categorical propositions are affirmative, others negative. That is *affirmative* in which the copula or principal verb is affirmed, as in 'A man is an animal'. That is *negative* in which the copula or principal verb is negated. I say this if there are two [verbs], as in 'A man is not an animal that runs' and 'A man who runs does not argue'. Likewise, 'A man is an animal that does not run' is affirmative, whereas 'A man is not an animal that runs' is negative. The name 'that' is always linked with the nonprincipal verb, by whose negation or affirmation the expression is never denominated negative or affirmative. [2.101–104]

[142] Some categorical propositions are universal, others particular, others indefinite, others singular.[46] [2.105]

[143] That is a *universal proposition* in which a common, universal term determined by a universal sign functions as the subject. What sort of term is common and universal has already been stated (128). Universal signs are, for example, 'all', 'every', 'any one at all', 'each one of', 'whoever', 'each and every', 'wherever', 'always', 'any sort of', 'however

44 While William and Lambert also present 'καθηγορίζω, –ζας' as the Greek source of 'categorical' the correct verb (as Kretzmann points out) is 'κατηγορέω'. Respectively, *Introductiones*, trans. Kretzmann, p. 27, and n. 26, and *Logica*, pp. 12.40–13.2.

45 On some occasions the subject is stated as what is subordinated (*subici*) to the predicate. In these cases it will be translated by 'what serves as the subject'.

46 Bacon (and other medievals) often use '*infinita*' when '*indefinita*' would be more informative. (See 152 and cf. 145.) Note that when MS. S. reads '*infinita*' MS. O will often present '*indefinita*', as for example here. (*Sd* 1–2, pp. 232, n. 68 and 233, n. 89.) For the definitions of the four kinds of propositions see, respectively, 143, 144, 145, and 146.

much', 'unlimited', 'whole', 'both', 'each of two', 'none', 'neither', 'never', 'in no part', 'nothing', and the like. Therefore, these kinds of propositions are universal: 'Every man is just', 'No man is just', 'Both of these run', etc. And by an actual pointing-to made by a pronoun, the name of the species is understood that is common to the things pointed to by the pronoun 'of these', e.g., 'man' or 'ass'. 'A man always runs' is equivalent to 'A man runs at every time': 'time' is a subject, and 'every' is a universal sign. Likewise, 'God is everywhere' is the same as 'God is in every place'. But one should know that there are two sorts of subjects, namely, a subject of attribution and a subject of locution.[47] A *subject of attribution* is a noun in the nominative case to which a verb conforms; a *subject of locution*, however, is one in an oblique case determined by a sign. Sometimes, therefore, a proposition is said to be universal in virtue of having a subject of locution determined by a universal sign, and sometimes in virtue of having a subject of attribution determined in this way. But 'the whole of' causes a proposition to be universal when it is added, not to a common and universal term, but to a discrete and singular one, as in 'The whole of Socrates is white'. The explanation for this is that it is equivalent to 'Any part of Socrates is white' or 'With respect to any of his parts Socrates is white'. Both of these are universal: the first in virtue of having a subject in the nominative case determined by a universal sign, the second in virtue of having a subject in an oblique case. [2.106–115]

[144] A *particular proposition* is one in which a common term determined by a particular sign serves as the subject. Particular signs are of this sort: 'some,' 'any', 'a certain', 'the other', 'the remaining', 'sometimes', 'somewhere', 'some sort of', 'a certain amount of', and the like. So, these propositions are particular: 'Some man runs', 'Any man runs', etc. [2.116–118]

[145] An *indefinite proposition* is one in which a common term determined by no sign functions as the subject, neither by a pronoun nor by anything contracting the common term to a singular one, e.g., 'A man runs', or 'The son of Sophronicus runs' (if Socrates is his only son), and the like. The proposition 'This man runs' is not indefinite. [2.119–120]

[146] A *singular proposition* is one in which a discrete term or pronoun along with a common term or something contracting a term serves as the subject, e.g., 'Socrates runs', 'This man argues'.[48] [2.121]

47 With regard to the two kinds of subjects: a subject of attribution is the subject of a sentence or clause, that which has something attributed to (predicated of) it by the predicate. A subject of locution, however, is simply the object in a prepositional phrase or the subject of an infinitive in the accusative case. See 187 and 229.

48 An example of "something contracting a term" would be 'the *second* house *on the left*'.

[147] One should know, moreover, that to the question raised about what kind one would answer "categorical or hypothetical"; to the question raised about quality "affirmative or negative"; and to the question raised about quantity "universal or particular or indefinite or singular."[49] [2.122]

[148] Some propositions do not share a term, e.g., 'A man runs' and 'An ass drinks'; others share only one, as do 'A man argues' and 'A man reads'; and some both terms. But [this latter happens] in two ways: either in *reverse order*, e.g., 'A man is an animal' and 'An animal is a man', or in the *same order*, as in 'Every man is an animal' and 'Some man is an animal'. [2.123]

[149] Some of these are *contraries*, namely, the universal affirmative and the universal negative, e.g., 'Every man runs' and 'No man runs'; some are *subcontraries*, as are the particular affirmative and the particular negative, e.g., 'Some man runs' and 'Some man does not run'; some are *subalterns*, as are the universal affirmative and the particular affirmative, and the universal negative and particular negative; and some are *contradictories*, namely, the universal affirmative and the particular negative, and the universal negative and the particular affirmative.[50] Examples of these are

49 Apropos of the notions of quantity and quality Kretzmann notes that these are not Aristotelian but originated in the logic of the twelfth century, and he cites Peter Abelard, *Super perihermenias*, in *Abaelardiana inedita*, ed. Lorenzo Minio-Paluello, in *Twelfth Century Logic: Texts and Studies*, vol. 1 (Rome: Edizioni di Storia e Letteratura, 1958), p. 23. (*Introductiones*, trans. Kretzmann, p. 29, n. 29.)

Peter's treatment is much like Bacon's, though it offers in addition the following mnemonic (*Tractatus* 1.12):

quae ca vel ypo	What kind ca[tegorical] or hypo[thetical]
qualis ne vel aff	Quality ne[gative] or aff[irmative]
un quanta par in sin	Un[iversal] quantity par[ticular] in[definite] sin[gular]

50 Bacon (as well as William, Peter, and Lambert) call the affirmative universal and singular (A–I), and negative universal and singular propositions (E–O) subalterns (*subalternae*). Where there is need to distinguish them the universal is called the subalternant (*subalternans*) and the particular the subalternate (*subalternata*). (Respectively, *Introductiones*, trans. Kretzmann, p. 30; *Tractatus* 1.12; and *Logica*, p. 19.32.) For a brief comment by Kretzmann on these terms see *Introductiones*, trans. Kretzmann, p. 30, n. 34. Kretzmann notes that William does not describe the relations here as oppositions though the term had been standard since Boethius' translation of *On Interpretation* of Aristotle. (Ibid., p. 29, n. 33.) I would add that neither Bacon nor Peter nor Lambert call these relations oppositions at this point in their treatises, though of course they all do when they present the four species of opposition. Although the examples used by William and Bacon make it clear, it is interesting from a pedagogical point of view that only Peter and Lambert explicitly state in this context that the rules of opposition

clear in the following figure:[51]

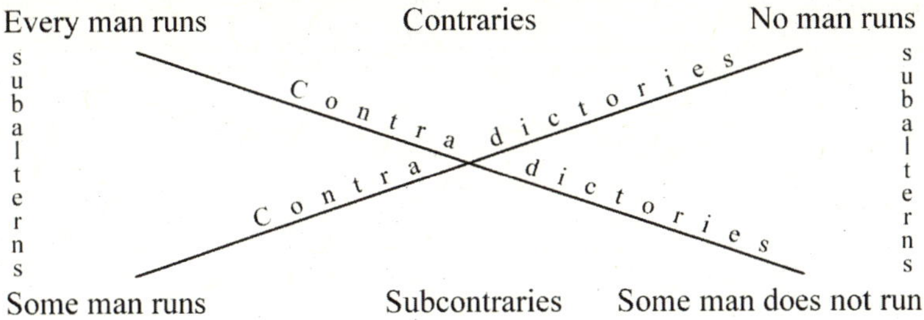

[2.124]

[150] Besides these things one should know that the matter of a categorical proposition is three-fold, namely, necessary, separate, and contingent.[52] A proposition pertaining to *necessary* matter is one in which the predicate always agrees with the subject, an existing subject, in such a way that the predicate could not fail to inhere in it, as in 'A man is an animal',

hold only for propositions having the same terms and those terms in the same order. (Respectively, *Tractatus* 1.12, and *Logica*, p. 18.20–22; cf. *Introductiones*, trans. Kretzmann, pp. 29–30.) And only Bacon among the four does not even define the names of the four relations in the immediate context. But see 151.

51 Kretzmann notes that the square of opposition "has some remote ancestors in the tables to be found in [*On Interpretation*], Chapter 10, but it occurred in this traditional form as early as the second century A.D. in the logic manual of Apuleius of Madaura" (*Introductiones*, trans. Kretzmann, p. 32, n. 39). Interestingly, Alessio's edition of Lambert's *Logica* presents no diagram of the square of oppositions. MS. O. also presents an additional series of squares of opposition, for which see *Sd* 1–2, p. 234, n. 5:

Every man is just	No man is just
A certain man is just	A certain man is not just
Both of these run	Neither of these runs
One of these runs	Another of these does not run
God always is	God never is
God sometimes is	God sometimes is not
God is everywhere	God is nowhere
God is somewhere	God is not somewhere

52 Cf. William, Peter, and Lambert. The matter Bacon calls "necessary" they call "natural." Lambert adds that natural, contingent, and remote matter is also called, respectively, necessary, accidental, and impossible. Kretzmann notes that the doctrine of the matter of statements dates to at least the *Dialectica* of Garland the Computist in the eleventh century. (*Introductiones*, trans. Kretzmann, p. 33–34 and n. 41; *Tractatus* 1.13; and *Logica*, pp. 19.4–20.27.)

'A man is able to laugh'.[53] A proposition pertaining to *separate* (impossible) matter occurs when the predicate can never be in the subject, as in 'A man is an ass'. A proposition pertaining to *contingent* matter occurs when the predicate can be and not be in the subject, as in 'A man is white', 'A man runs'. [2.125–128]

[151] There is, therefore, a law of contraries such that, if one contrary is true, the other is always false in every sort of matter. And it is not converted because both can be false in contingent matter, e.g., 'Every man runs', 'No man runs'.[54] The law and nature of subcontraries is such that,

53 Peter states explicitly what is shown by way of the examples: "Natural matter is that in which the predicate pertains to the essence of a subject or is its proprium" (*de esse subiecti vel proprium eius*). A little later he makes it clear that inseparable accidents (for which notion see Bacon 21) are to be treated as natural matter. (*Tractatus* 1.13 and 14.)

54 For 149 cf. William, Peter, and Lambert, respectively, *Introductiones*, trans. Kretzmann, pp. 30–33; *Tractatus* 1.12 and 14; and *Logica*, p. 19.20–36. These propositions must have the same terms and the latter must be in the same order, as the examples serve to illustrate. What is important to catch here is that the oppositions in the original square of opposition obtain only when the propositions are about *contingent* matter. Lambert's presentation seems to be the most thorough of the four, but none calls attention to all the implications of oppositions that arise when propositions pertaining to *natural* matter and those involving the predication of inseparable accidents are involved. Among the four writers no explicit attention is called to the fact that, if one man is an animal, then all are, and if one is not, none is, and that therefore there are no subaltern, contrary, or subcontrary relations as defined for use in the square of opposition. Thus in necessary matter the following relations hold: A–E, I–O, A–O, and I–E are contradictory, and A–I and E–O are such that if one of the pairs is true the other must be true also, and if one is false the other must be false. Putting all this together we get the following change in the square of opposition for propositions pertaining to *natural* (necessary) matter or predicating inseparable accidents:

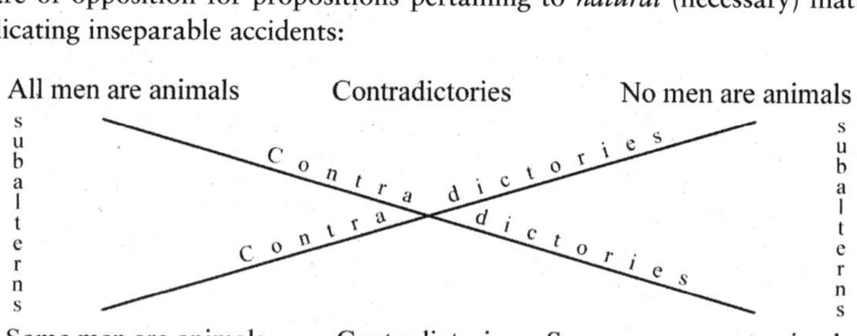

Some curious things accompany these insights in the four texts: (1) William uses propositions pertaining to natural matter as examples when presenting the notions of contraries and subcontraries (no examples are given when defining subalterns and contradictories), but uses contingent propositions in his diagram of the square

if one is false, the other will always be true and in every sort of matter. It is not converted because both can be true in contingent matter, e.g., 'Some man runs', 'Some man does not run'. The law of subalterns is such that, if a universal is true, its particular will always be true and in every sort of matter, and it is not converted. And if a particular is false, its universal is always false and in every sort of matter, and it is not converted. The law of contradictories is such that, if one is true, the other will be false, and vice versa, always and in every sort of matter. One should know that not only the already mentioned propositions that were said to be contraries are contrary, but also a universal affirmative and a singular negative, e.g., 'Every man is just' and 'Socrates is not just', because they can be at the same time false but not true; and also a universal negative and a singular affirmative,[55] which is clear in this figure:

---

of opposition. (2) Peter follows the opposite course: when presenting the four oppositions he uses contingent propositions as examples, but switches to necessary ones in his diagram. (3) Lambert presents no diagram, but provides examples of propositions reflecting contingent matter to illustrate subcontraries and contradictories, but examples involving natural matter when illustrating contraries and subalterns. And (4) only Bacon uses contingent propositions as examples in his diagram and his discussion of the oppositions. Respectively, *Introductiones*, trans. Kretzmann, pp. 32–33; *Tractatus* 1.12–14; *Logica*, p. 18.28–40; and Bacon 149.

55 William calls attention to this difference, i.e., when a singular proposition is related to a universal one and the subjects are, respectively, a discrete term (or its equivalent) and a universal term. Kretzmann says that he is unaware of any logician prior to William pointing this out, granting that Aristotle had recognized it in *On Interpretation* (7.17b28, 18a2). The fact that Peter fails to mention this, he thinks, makes it possible that "it is not a regular feature of treatments of traditional logic," and one can add here that Lambert also fails to make this point. Nevertheless, Bacon does include it (using different examples), so two of the four major treatises (preserved) from this period do include it. (*Introductiones*, trans. Kretzmann, p. 31, and n. 38.) One should note also, however, that Peter and Lambert omit a further point made by William, this time about two singular propositions with the same terms in the same order, but one an affirmation and the other a negation, namely, that such are not subcontraries but contradictories: 'Socrates runs', 'Socrates does not run'. (Ibid.) But worse, while Bacon fails to make the point in his text, the relation between two such singular propositions is incorrectly labeled "subcontrary" in the diagram that follows immediately in the text in MS. O. (fol. 56v), though no diagram is provided in MS. S. Kretzmann (ibid.) sums up: "The result of his [William's] discussion of singular statements is that they are like particulars (with respect to the forms of opposition) only in that a universal and a corresponding singular of the same quality will be subalterns." For a hexagon of oppositions that includes singular propositions see the diagram in *Introductiones*, trans. Kretzmann, p. 33.

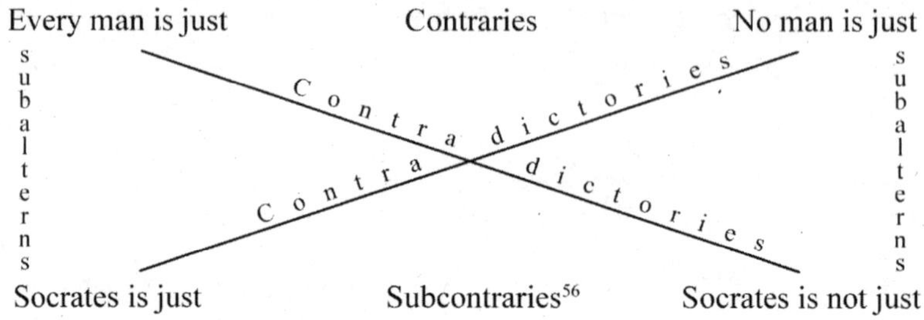

[2.129–133]

[152] One should know about the equipollence of these propositions that a negation placed before any sign is equipollent to its contradictory sign; placed after to its contrary sign; and placed before and after to its subaltern sign.[57] Examples make this clear: a negation placed before a common term is equipollent to a universal sign; a negation placed after a particular to a negative sign; placed before and after a universal to an affirmative sign. It should be noted that a particular and an indefinite proposition are converted.[58] But it should be known that a double negation related to the same thing in the same way, absolutely, and in no way to different things always causes one affirmation, namely, what remains were the negations to be removed, just as 'A man does not not-run' is the same as 'A man

56 This relation is mislabled in MS. O; the two propositions are contradictory, not subcontrary. (See fol. 56va.) In MS. S. a space is provided for the figure, but is not filled in. See fol. 78vb.

57 Alexander Broadie introduces the notion of equipollence this way: "Given that of two propositions one is contradictory, contrary, subaltern, or subcontrary to the other, then the question can be raised: By what (if any) placing of negation signs in the first proposition is it transformed into a proposition equivalent to the second? The rules of equipollence provide an answer to this question." (Alexander Broadie, *Introduction to Medieval Logic*, 2nd ed. [Oxford: Clarendon Press, 1993], p. 153.) Thus William passes on the following verse as an aid to memory for the rules of equipollence (*Introductiones*, trans. Kretzmann, p. 38):

(1) Pre-[negation produces] the contradictory
(2) Post-[negation produces] the contrary
(3) Pre- and Post-[negation produce] the subaltern

Thus, e.g., where the italicized negatives are the additions: (1) '*Not* every man runs' is equipollent to 'Some man does not run'; (2) 'No man does *not* run' to 'Every man runs'; and (3) '*Not* some man does *not* run' to 'Every man runs'.

58 This would seem to be true except where an indefinite proposition predicates a definition or proprium, the "necessary matter" mentioned in 150. Thus 'A man is an animal' is an indefinite proposition, but it is universal, not particular. Kretzmann notes that Aristotle subtly dismisses indefinite statements for syllogistic purposes. See *Introductiones*, trans. Kretzmann, p.30, and n. 36, and *Prior Analytics* 1.7.29a27.

runs'. When, however, I say 'It is not the case that a man does not run', the negations do not refer absolutely to the same thing, but in a certain sense to different things.[59] They do not refer in the same way also because one falls upon the subject of the first negation, negating it with respect to the verb, whereas the other falls only on the verb and in no way on the subject. So, they do not bring about the affirmation 'A man runs' but another, namely, 'Every man runs'. One should know about singular propositions that it makes no difference whether one places a negation before or after a singular term, as when I say 'It is not the case that Socrates runs', this is the same as 'Socrates does not run'. And so in whatever way the negation is doubled, they always bring about one affirmation.[60] [2.134–137]

[153] But one should know that some terms are negated, as in 'It is not the case that a man runs', [i.e.,] when the negation 'not' does not combine with a term. This is the case likewise in 'A man is not just' – 'just' is negated there.[61] Some terms are infinite, namely, when the negation combines with the term, as has already been said (123), as in 'Nonman is nonjust'. Some terms are privative, as in 'A man is unjust'. In each of these there is the force of negation, but in the first there is pure negation, negation that negates; in the second there is the negation that makes a term infinite; and in the third there is the negation that makes a term privative, which is called privation. These differ from one another since a negation that negates, pure negation, always causes a negative proposition, posits nothing, and presents nothing to understand, but is always directed to the composition of an action with a finite substance, i.e., the verbal composition. It also both negates and indifferently separates the one from the other, whatever it might be.[62] The negation that makes a term infinite, however, is added to the term by composition, and it does not indifferently cause a proposition to be negative because it is not directed to the composition of the action with the substance, which composition is verbal – the composition, I say, that concerns a finite substance and an actual suppositum, as has already been said (123–124, 132). But it can be directed to the composition of a verbal action with a substance

59 Reading at *Sd* 1–2, p. 236, 136.5, '*non homo*' for '*non-homo*' in the text. See the claim two sentences below where it is said that the proposition in question yields 'Every man runs'. I am indebted to James Cain (Oklahoma State University) for calling my attention to the need for the emendation.

60 One could place the two "nots" before 'Socrates', or before 'run', or separate them as in the example, and all three would result in affirmative propositions.

61 In the second example the point is illustrated in the Latin but not in the English translation. To make the point in English one would have to write: 'A man not is just', so that 'not' negates 'just' even though separated from it by 'is'.

62 The composition spoken of here is that of the subject with the predicate of an expression. Hence, this kind of negation separates the predicate from the subject, denying that the predicate is truthfully said of the subject.

designated by a participle and to the composition of an action with a verbal substance that concerns an indefinite substance and not an actual suppositum, as is clear in the case of a verb in the third person. But it indicates nothing, as was just said.[63] An infinite term, however, presents something to understand and it negates, i.e., privates, something indifferently of any subject, whether that subject be susceptible of something negated and made privative or not, just as one appropriately says 'A stone is nonjust', 'A man is nonjust'.[64] In the case of nouns, however, it requires the composition of a quality together with a substance, like 'nonman'.[65] The privation of a quality pertains to such a composition in most cases. For example, should I say 'an unjust one', 'an inept one', and the like, they do not cause a negative proposition and they indicate something as a subject susceptible of a privated thing, and so do not cause a privation except in a susceptible subject. For example, one appropriately says 'A man is unjust', but inappropriately 'An ass', and so on for the other names of privation, just as one appropriately says 'A man is blind', but inappropriately and falsely says 'A rock is blind'. So, it is clear that this follows: 'If he is unjust, he is nonjust, and in consequence is not just', and that it is not converted. [2.138–146]

HYPOTHETICAL PROPOSITIONS[66]

[154] Categorical propositions have been discussed and so now we must speak of hypothetical ones. An hypothesis is the same as a supposition or condition made in connection with some conclusion. An hypothet-

63 Reading at *Sd* 1–2, p. 237, 143.7, '*substantia verbali*' against '*substantiam verbalem*' in MSS. O. and S. and the text. Participles and gerunds made infinite are exceptions to the rule that this kind of negation does not separate a verb from its subject. In 'nonman' no verbal actions are involved, but because of the grammatical relation of participles, gerunds, and gerundives to verbs, this cannot be said of, e.g., 'nonknown' and 'nonknowing'. For verbs in the third person see 133.

64 'Nonman' causes one to think of all things (existing or not) other than man. Since most classes have a complementary one – for examples of those that do not, see 122 – Bacon says that '*non*', when joined to a class name, deprives, i.e., removes that class from consideration indifferently, i.e., no matter what the class. Since all but the most general classes are "negated" in this sense, it is somewhat rhetorical to add "whether they be susceptible ... or not." This latter is probably stated to present a contrast with privations (70) which are only of things that in some sense ought to have a certain quality and do not.

65 Understood by contrast with what is said in 70 about privative terms, this is said to point out that an infinite negation attacks the whole notion (substance plus quality) named by the name to which it is attached, whereas the privative negation denies only a certain characteristic in the thing named, not the subject itself.

66 In the terminology of the period (and since at least Galen; see William and Mary Kneale, *The Development of Logic* [Oxford: Clarendon Press, 1962], p. 182) any proposition made up of two categorical propositions is called a hypothetical propo-

ical proposition is one in which something is indicated to follow from another either in word and in understanding, i.e., principally and *per se*, or only in understanding and as a consequence. A conditional proposition functions in the first way, a disjunctive one in the second way. [2.147–149]

[155] A *conditional proposition* is one in which two propositions are joined by means of the conditional term 'if' or the term 'when', as in 'If Socrates runs, Socrates is moved'. A disjunctive proposition is one in which two propositions are joined by means of a disjunctive connective, as in 'Socrates is healthy or ill'.[67] A conditional proposition comes about by means of 'when', as Boethius says in his book *On Hypothetical Syllogisms*, for he says that 'if' and 'when' signify the same thing and have the same force with respect to a consequence.[68] For through these, two propositions are connected, joined, to one another in such a way that one actually follows from the other. A *disjunctive proposition*, however, comes about by a disjunction between contradictory and directly contrary things. [2.150–153]

[156] Those propositions are contradictory that cannot be true or be false at the same time, as has already been stated (151). There are two kinds of contraries: either *complex* ones, about which we have spoken (151), or *incomplex* ones. And these are of two kinds: either *indirect*, as among those that have a middle, among which are black and white, and

---

sition, and the three most prominent species are conjunctions, disjunctions, and conditionals. Interestingly, and in contrast to Peter, William, and Lambert, Bacon makes only a passing reference to conjunctions in this section (158), deferring consideration to his next topic (165), and the reason is provided in 170: he does not consider them to be hypotheticals.

67 In treatises on Logic in this period 'or', 'and', and 'if' are called *coniunctiones* or *coniunctivae*, although 'and' is more specifically called a *copulatio* or *copulativa*. This results in the sometimes confusing phrase 'disjunctive conjunction' if these notions are translated literally. To avoid this, I shall employ 'connection' and 'connective' to translate the former pair when they refer to 'or' and 'if' specifically or all three generically, and 'conjunction' and 'conjunctive' to translate the second pair. If the disjunctive proposition defined here is a species of hypothetical proposition, then the example, more appropriately stated, should read: 'Socrates is healthy or Socrates is ill'. As it stands it is a categorical proposition with a disjunctive predicate, about which he will speak later. See 159.

68 Boethius *De syllogismo hypothetico libri duo* 1, PL 64.834. The conjunctive 'when' is a translation of the Latin '*cum*', which could also and perhaps more illustratively be translated by 'since'. However, Boethius' example is '*cum homo est, animal est*' which, because of the use of the indicative mood, is properly translated 'When it is a man, it is an animal' and not 'Since it is a man, it is an animal', which latter would have required the subjunctive mood. One could also note that Lambert classifies temporal clauses as hypothetical ones. See *Logica*, pp. 16–17.

good and evil, since between white and black there are dark and pallid, etc., and between good and evil there is man, who is neither good nor evil, as is said in Book Ten of the *Metaphysics*.[69] In connection with this the Commentator says, for example, that a man who is a hermit, who is not part of a city, is neither good nor evil, but someone in between.[70] *Direct contraries* are those between which there is no middle, among which are something healthy and something ill. A disjunctive connective truly disjoins direct contraries or contradictories since it makes a proposition hypothetical, as in 'Socrates either is healthy or is ill'. [2.154–157]

[157] But there is doubt about the sense in which a disjunctive proposition is a conditional one since it does not have in itself the mark of a condition, but rather the mark of a disjunction. One should reply that every disjunctive proposition can be resolved into what is actually a conditional one, because Boethius says this at the end of *On Hypothetical Syllogisms*.[71] He thinks a disjunctive connective is one that does not allow the things that it disjoins to be at the same time. So when one part of a disjunction is asserted, the removal of the other follows, and vice versa. For example, 'Socrates is healthy or ill' [is resolved into] 'If he is not healthy, he is ill'. So a disjunctive connective conceptually as well as in terms of its force is a conditional connective. [2.158–159]

[158] But one should note that a disjunctive connective is sometimes taken disjunctively, sometimes subdisjunctively. When it is taken disjunctively it signifies one part to be and the other not to be, because it disjoins from each other what cannot be at the same time, as is the case with contradictories or direct contraries, for a disjunctive proposition is true in these cases, but in others false. [A disjunctive connective is taken] subdisjunctively in two senses, for sometimes it signifies that the two parts are at the same time, and then it is taken conjunctively, as in the example given by Terence in *Eunuchus*: "Or the king was always thanking me profusely" for "And the king."[72] Sometimes, however, it signifies that both are, but

69 Aristotle *Metaphysics* 10.4.1055b23.

70 Averroes *In Aristotelis Metaphysicam* 10.4, trans. Nova, commentary 16, *Aristotelis opera cum Averrois commentariis*, vol. 8: fol. 263vI. See also ibid., 5: commentary 27, fol. 135rB.

71 Boethius *De syllogismo hypothetico libri duo* 1, PL 64.875A, *ad sensum*.

72 Terence *Eunuchus* 399: "For instance the king was always profuse in his thanks for anything I had done ..." (*vel rex semper max[i]mas mihi agebat quidquid feceram*). *Terence*, vol. 1, Loeb Classical Library, p. 274, quoted by Priscian, *Institutiones grammaticae* 16.7 (and 17.11), *GL*, vol. 3, p. 98.3–8 (and pp. 114.23–115.4). I am indebted to Sten Ebbesen for calling my attention to the fact that the addition in MS. S. should read "*quod ponit Priscianus*" and not "*quod ponit prius*." The mistranscription leads de Libera to speculate on the work to which it refers. See *Sd* 1–2, p. 240, n. 92 and pp. 159–160.

not at the same time, as in 'Socrates lectures or argues all day', for it signifies lecturing at one time and arguing at another. [2.160–162]

[159] One should know, however, that a disjunctive sometimes disjoins terms, sometimes expressions: expressions, e.g., 'Socrates is healthy or Socrates is ill'; terms, as in 'Every animal is rational or irrational' – 'rational or irrational' converts with 'animal'. For the sake of an example let 'cleric' or 'layman' be said to be convertible with 'man'; in *Syncategorematicals* this will be made clearer.[73] When a disjunctive disjoins expressions, then the proposition is hypothetical, and when it disjoins terms, then it is categorical with a disjoined subject or a disjoined predicate.[74] The same applies to a conditional connective, because it either joins complex things like expressions – e.g., 'If it is a man, it is an animal' – and then the proposition is hypothetical, or it joins something complex to something incomplex. This can take place either within the subject – and then there is a categorical proposition with a conditional subject, e.g., '"The false is, if Antichrist is" is true' – or within the predicate, like 'Something false is "The true is, if Antichrist is"', for here there is joined the whole 'if Antichrist is' to 'is true'.[75] The following, however, is hypothetical: 'If Antichrist is, the false is true'.[76] [2.163–166B]

[160] It should be known that there are two parts to hypothetical propositions, namely, an *antecedent* and a *consequent*. In conditional propositions the antecedent proposition is that before which the sign of condition is immediately placed; the other is the consequent. In disjunctive propositions what is placed first in discourse is called the precedent or the antecedent; what, however, is placed second, the consequent, as Boethius says.[77] [2.167–169]

73 Whether the work referred to here is the same as the *Syncategoremata* found in MS. O. and an Erfurt manuscript is disputed. Kretzmann thinks Roger Bacon is the author; Braakhuis and de Libera opt on probable grounds for the Dominican Robert Bacon. See *Sd* 1–2, pp. 154–160.

74 Reading at *Sd* 1–2, p. 240, 165.2, n. 4, '*tunc est*' with MS. O. against '*nunc*' in MS. S. and the text.

75 The two examples, respectively, are: '*Falsum si Antichristus est est verum*' and '*Falsum est verum si Antichristus est*'. These examples of a categorical statement with a conditional subject and a conditional predicate are not the clearest he could have provided. Clearly, a third verb has to be supplied, presumably the copula 'is' (*est*). The first example has to be read in a way similar to '"The ground is wet, if it has rained," is true' and the second in a way similar to 'The false is "if Socrates is a man, he is immortal"'. The author of the *Ars emmerana* warns that those "less skilled" (*minus periti*) will take such to be hypotheticals when in fact they are categoricals. *LM*, vol. 2, pt. 2, p. 159.18–23.

76 Number 166 in de Libera's edition is repeated. To distinguish the two I have added 'a' and 'b', respectively.

77 Boethius *De syllogismo hypothetico libri duo* 1, PL 64.835D–836A.

[161] One should know, moreover, that a conditional proposition is true whose antecedent cannot be true without the consequent being true, e.g., 'If it is a man, it is an animal'; a conditional proposition is false whose antecedent can be true without the consequent being true, as in 'If it is an animal, it is a man'. Every conditional proposition that is true is necessary; every one that is false is impossible. A disjunctive proposition is true when one part of it is true, as in 'Socrates is healthy or Socrates is ill'; false when both parts of it are false, e.g., 'Socrates is an ass or Socrates is a lion'. [2.170–172]

[162] One should know that 'the whole' signifies in one sense the same as 'what is complete with respect to its parts'; in another sense the same as 'any part'. Here, however, it is taken as signifying the same as 'what is complete or whole with respect to its parts'. A hypothetical proposition is said to be affirmative when the whole proposition, i.e., the connection, is affirmed, even if both parts or one of them is negated, as in 'If Socrates is not moved, he does not run' and 'Socrates is not healthy or is not ill'. It is negative when the whole proposition, i.e., the connection, is negated, as in 'It is not the case that, if Socrates runs, Socrates is moved'. The reason for this is that, just as in the case of categorical propositions, an expression is said to be affirmative or negative because of the affirmation or negation of the connection that joins two things, namely, an antecedent and a consequent.[78] [2.173–176]

[163] If one objects that it is necessary that a negation be directed to a verb, one should reply that the action of one thing following from another in a conditional proposition is carried out by means of the connection itself, and it is to this that the negation is directed.[79] Or, [one should reply that] through the action carried out one understands a similar signifying action that can be apposed and to which the negation is directed, as in 'It is not the case that, if Socrates is an animal, Socrates is a man', that is, 'If Socrates is an animal, Socrates is a man' does not follow.[80]

78 I.e., subjects and predicates in the case of categorical propositions and antecedents and consequents in that of hypotheticals.

79 An affirmative categorical proposition is made negative by negating the verb (predicate). But one cannot deny a conditional (or disjunctive) by negating just any or all of its verbs; one must deny the relation between the two parts.

80 Reading at *Sd* 1–2, p. 242, 178.1, '<*et*> *cui*' against '*cui*' in MSS. O. and S. and the text.

Syncategorematical words like 'not' and the connectives 'if', 'or', and 'and' do not signify extramental things and their concepts as do nouns and verbs but actions as carried out, mental acts. Bacon is making the point here that, e.g., 'not' can be directed to an action as carried out and not just to an action as signified by a verb, and that the sort of signification appropriate to the two kinds of actions while not identical are (sufficiently) similar to permit the negation of the action carried out by

One is to understand a disjunctive proposition in a similar manner.[81] [2.177–179]

[164] One should know about quantity, however, that no hypothetical proposition is said to be quantified – it is neither universal nor particular, etc. – because every sort of quantity is caused by a subject, and there is no subject in it. But a proposition with a conditional predicate or subject is quantified in the same way as was indicated with respect to categorical propositions (142–143). Every proposition with a disjoined subject, moreover, is indefinite, unless a sign is added, because every disjunctive whole is predicated of two singulars. A proposition with a disjoined predicate acquires a quantity in the same way as do other categorical propositions.[82] [2.180–183]

SINGLE AND MULTIPLE PROPOSITIONS

[165] Some propositions are single or single in virtue of a connective, others are multiple.[83] A proposition is *single* to which one response can appropriately be given. A proposition is *multiple*, however, to which more than one response is to be given. We have already spoken of propositions that are single.[84] [2.184–187]

[166] One should know that, just as in the case of things where a thing is single in virtue of a simple form (e.g., an element, namely, earth and

---

the connective. For other uses of the distinction between signified acts as conceived and as carried out see 174 and 198. And for a very helpful study of the two kinds of acts here described see Gabriel Nuchelmans, "The Distinction *Actus Exercitus/ Actus Significatus* in Medieval Semantics," in *Meaning and Inference in Medieval Philosophy – Studies in Memory of Jan Pinborg*, pp. 57–90. See also D. Schlüter, "*Actus exercitus/actus signatus*," in *Historisches Wörterbuch der Philosophie*, vol 1 (Basel and Stuttgart: Schwabe, 1971).

81 E.g., 'It is not the case that either Socrates runs or Socrates argues'.

82 E.g., 'Some man is either healthy or ill'.

83 Reading at *Sd* 1–2, p. 242, 184.1, '*alia una sive coniunctione una, alia plures*' against '*alia una. alia plures sive coniunctione una*' in S. and the text, and '*alia una, alia coniunctione una sive plures*' in O. For the emendation see *Aristoteles Latinus*, vol. 1, pts. 1–2: *Categoriae vel Praedicamenta, translatio Boethii*, ed. Lorenzo Minio-Paluello (Bruges; Paris: Desclée de Brouwer, 1961), pp. 8.20–9.2.

Earlier (139) we saw, and later (175) we will see, where Bacon, following Aristotle in *On Interpretation* 5, divides propositions syntactically into simple and composed ones; here the criterion for division is semantical. Bacon is one of the few 12th and 13th century logicians to present a discussion of both divisions and to give such a thorough and innovative analysis of single and multiple propositions. See Thomas S. Maloney, "Roger Bacon on the Division of Statements into Single/ Multiple and Simple/Composed," *The Review of Metaphysics* 56 (2002): 321–356.

84 The reference is probably to those single/categorical propositions that have one subject and one predicate of the type 'Plato runs' that were announced in 139 and discussed in 140–142.

water, etc.) whereas another is single in virtue of a composed form (e.g., an animal, a tree, a stone, etc.), so is it the case with propositions: one sort is single in virtue of a simple form, another sort is single in virtue of a composed form. A proposition is single in the first way when one thing is predicated of one thing. But this happens in two ways: either in virtue of word and thing [signified], i.e., understanding, and in this way 'A man runs' is single, or only in terms of understanding and thing [signified].[85] And then in one of two ways: either in virtue of a connective, or without one. In the second way, as in 'A mortal rational animal runs'.[86] In the first way when a proposition has a conditional or disjunctive or conjunctive subject or predicate, because this can occur in three ways: either by means of a conditional connective, as in '"It is an animal if it is a man" [is true]'; or in virtue of a disjunction, as in 'Every animal is rational or nonrational', which has a disjunctive predicate; or in virtue of a conjunction in which the conjunction couples two things from which there arises one subject or one predicate, as in 'Socrates and Plato haul the boat in', according to which the action of hauling-in is denoted to apply to them together, namely, conjointly and not separately, as in 'A body and a soul are an animal', 'Two and three are five', and the like.[87] If, however, a proposition is single in virtue of one composed form, then it is conditional or disjunctive.[88] [2.188–195]

[167] But if there is a multiple proposition, its multiplicity is actual either in virtue of word and understanding, or in virtue of understanding

85 It is clear from what is said here and in 167 that 'thing [signified]' (*res*) and 'understanding' (*intellectus*) mean the same thing: they name what is signified by a term or a proposition. See 183.

86 Although each of the terms in the subject has its own signification, they all combine to signify essentially one thing, a man. This is to be contrasted with such phrases as 'white man knowledgeable about music' (*homo albus musicus*) that expresses no such essential unity (167). For a possible explanation why Bacon does not discuss the effect of a pause in speech (or the insertion of 'and') between 'mortal' and 'rational' in the example see 168 and its note.

87 In 166 three things need comment. First, an emendation is needed in the example of the conditional because of the description of the condition in 166. Second, from Boethius on, the paradigmatic example of a proposition single in virtue of a connective has been a statement with a conditional statement-connective (as presented in the MSS) and not three statements with compound subjects or predicates. So, with or without the emendation Bacon is breaking with tradition here. Third, the use of the conjunctive connective is especially unusual here. For additional explanation see 169.

88 Given the third type of single statement just announced and exemplified, what is said here is false. The converse, however, is true: any statement that is conditional or disjunctive is single in virtue of a composed form.

alone. If the first way, this occurs either in virtue of a connective – not just any, but a conjunctive one – as in 'Socrates runs and Plato runs', or without a connective, as in Priscian's example: 'Here was her armor here her chariot', in such a way, however, that in the latter case one would understand a pause in speech in place of a connective.[89] But if the multiplicity of a proposition is only because of understanding, i.e., thing [signified], this will occur in two ways: either with a connective or without one. If in virtue of a connective, this will be in virtue of a conjunctive connective, namely, when two things are joined in the subject, from which arises no predicate in the singular, as in 'Socrates and Plato run', and vice versa, e.g., 'Two fives are six and four'. If, however, without a connective, then there is either a multiplicity of terms such as several accidents with their subject – e.g., 'A white man knowledgeable about music runs' is a proposition that is multiple – or there is not, but instead only one utterance, whether it is an expression or it is a word. And so, an ambiguous expression is one that is multiple, just as that in which there is an equivocal term or one having different accents, and so on, as in 'A dog runs', 'God did nothing unwillingly', and the like.[90] [2.196–200]

[168] Yet one could object that a collection of propositions without a connective does not result in a proposition that is multiple but multiple propositions. So, someone might argue that a pause in speech does not suffice to result in a proposition that is multiple, for a proposition that is multiple could not be spoken of in the singular unless it had some sort of unity. But there is none, at least none indicated by the words; there is simply diversity and multiplicity. Thus it seems that that part [of the common opinion] ought not to be asserted, neither with respect to propositions nor likewise with respect to terms.[91] [2.201–202]

89 The second example is deliberately written without punctuation and without any device to indicate speech uttered with a pause. In 168 Bacon will comment on the way this proposition differs from a mere collection of propositions. For the quotation see Donatus *De arte grammatica libri* 3.4.5, ed. Keil, *GL*, vol. 4, p. 397.24, as derived from Virgil *Aeneis* 1.16–17, *Virgil: Eclogues. Georgics. Aeneid I–IV*, ed. and trans. H. Rushton Fairclough, vol. 1, Loeb Classical Library, p. 242.

90 'Dog' can mean the animal that barks, a heavenly constellation, or a sea creature. For further analysis of the fallacy in each of the three examples in this paragraph see Part Three, respectively, 528, 440, 564. As far as I am aware Bacon alone mentions the fallacy of Accent in the context of a discussion of single and multiple propositions.

91 In 168 Bacon seems to be telling us by way of an objection to which he provides no reply that he opposes the common opinion that pauses in speech render a statement multiple. His reason seems to be that, so long as the unity essential to constituting a locution a (multiple) statement is not destroyed, the result does not represent

[169] Next, one should know with respect to the connective 'and' that sometimes it joins two things in a third or under a third: in a third, as in 'Socrates and Plato run', and then it is taken as properly conjunctive; under a third, when two things are joined prior to receiving a third. This can happen in two ways: either because the third thing regards both equally principally, and then it is said to be taken in a uniting sense, as in 'My body and my soul are an animal', 'Two and three are five', and 'Evening and morning are one day'; or one principally and the other secondarily, and then it is said to be taken properly in an associative sense, as in 'I would prefer to be set free and be with Christ'[92] and 'This one eats bread and wine' (when he does not eat the wine or something made of these, but bread accompanied by wine). When 'and' is taken associatively, it has the same force as 'with'. But note that the word 'with' can be taken strictly, and in this sense it is taken associatively and so a verb in the singular appears with it, as in 'Socrates runs with Plato'; and in the other sense it is taken broadly, namely, conjunctively, and in this sense it requires a verb in the plural, as in 'Socrates [together] with Plato run'. [2.203–207]

[170] Next, one should know whether a conjunction constitutes a categorical or hypothetical proposition. It should be known that when it conjoins terms, it constitutes a categorical proposition with a conjoined subject or predicate or both, as in 'Socrates and Plato run', 'Five are two and three', and 'Socrates and Plato know grammar and music'. But when it conjoins propositions, then it causes neither a categorical nor a hypothetical proposition, in accord with what has already been said (140 and 154), the contrary of which, however, is commonly held. For it is argued that there are many species of hypothetical propositions, namely, conditional, conjunctive, disjunctive, causal (e.g., 'Because Socrates lectures, Plato brings to completion'), and expletive (*expletive*) (as in 'Socrates runs, however Plato argues').[93] And to these there are added some that are not single in virtue of a connective but in virtue of a relation, e.g., 'Socrates is where Plato is', which is called local, and 'Socrates hauls [the boat] in when Plato runs', which is called temporal, and still others of this sort for the same reason: 'Socrates is such as Plato is', 'Socrates is as big as Plato is',

(even with pauses) a mere collection of statements that reflects only "diversity and multiplicity." While this would explain why no comment on the effect of pauses was provided in 166, it does not provide much help in deciding just how much unity must be present for a locution to be a multiple statement and not a mere collection of statements.

92 This is a close rendering of St. Paul, Philippians 1:23.

93 Donatus gives the following examples of expletive connectives: '*autem*', '*tamen*', '*porro*', '*quidem*', '*equidem*', and '*quoque*'. *Institutiones artium*, *GL*, vol. 4, p. 143.34–36.

and 'Socrates runs as often as Plato argues'.[94] But the force of a conditional proposition is not understood to be actually in a conjunctive one. Thus a conjunctive proposition is not a conditional one, and so neither is it a hypothetical one, since a hypothetical proposition is the same as a conditional one because 'hypothesis' means condition. But a disjunctive proposition, as was previously stated (157), has the actual force of a conditional one since it can be resolved absolutely into a conditional proposition. So a disjunctive proposition is also a hypothetical conditional one, taking the name 'conditional' generally and by extension.[95] Boethius, in his book *On Hypothetical Syllogisms* where he teaches of what sort are hypothetical propositions and the syllogisms constructed from them, proposes only the conditional in the strict sense and the disjunctive to be hypothetical.[96] This makes sense because only a proposition that is single enters a syllogism and a conjunctive proposition is not a proposition that is single, but a proposition that is multiple. So the latter does not qualify to enter either a hypothetical or a categorical syllogism. Therefore, a conjunctive proposition will be neither a hypothetical nor a categorical proposition. But all propositions other than a conditional and a disjunctive one are reduced to a conjunctive one, as is clear to one who investigates the matter.[97] [2.208–216]

[171] One asks about the quantity of a conjunctive proposition. One should reply that, when [a conjunctive connective] joins propositions, [the result] has no quantity because it does not have a subject and predicate as its parts, but only propositions. When, however, a proposition has a con-

94 While this sentence could be read to mean that the causal and expletive hypothetical propositions mentioned in the previous sentence are not single in virtue of a relation, the similarity between their morphology and that of the types mentioned here would suggest that they are all to be considered single in virtue of a relation and not single in virtue of a connective. The mention of this sort of single proposition has the effect of introducing a third species of single propositions not mentioned in other treatises: propositions can be single without a connective, single in virtue of a connective, and single in virtue of a relation.

95 Reading at *Sd* 1–2, p. 245, 214.3, '*disiunctiva est*' against '*conditionalis est*' in MSS. O. and S. and the text. Cf. 155.

96 Cf. Boethius *De syllogismo hypothetico libri duo* 1, PL 64, 833B.

97 There is a controversy on this point. William (but not Peter or Lambert) explicitly says that only conditional propositions are hypothetical in the strict sense. (*Introductiones*, trans. Kretzmann, p. 34, 2.18.) Bacon seems to have arrived at that position by this point. He has said that all but conditional and disjunctive propositions are said to be reduced to conjunctive ones; conjunctive ones are said not to be conditional ones; (on interpretation of the referent of 'it') conjunctive propositions are not hypothetical ones; and disjunctive ones are said to be reduced to conditional ones. This leaves only conditional propositions to be hypothetical ones, and this is confirmed when 'hypothetical' and 'conditional' are said to mean the same thing.

junctive predicate, [the conjunctive connective] does not cause the quantity to be different, and one must treat of it in the light of the preceding. [2.217–219]

[172] But when [the inquiry] is about a conjunctive subject, there could be a doubt about its quantity. It would seem to be singular as in the case where 'Socrates and Plato run' is said, because something singular functions as the subject. Yet, one could also argue it might be universal because, were Socrates not running and Plato running, 'Socrates and Plato run' is false, and likewise 'Socrates and Plato do not run', and these cannot be true at the same time; therefore, they are contraries. But in the case of all contraries either one or both are universal. But what would make one of these universal would serve for the other; therefore, both are universal; therefore, the propositions are universal. One should reply that the proposition is universal although singular terms are taken in the subject, because each of those terms is not the subject but the whole made up of them, which can be understood as having universally and according to its understanding the concept of a quantitative whole whose singulars are 'Socrates runs' and 'Plato runs'.[98] But one should know that a universal proposition can be spoken of with respect to word and understanding or with respect only to understanding itself in which the universality is understood to be actual. For with respect to understanding it is the same as, e.g., 'Each of these two runs' (indicating Socrates and Plato), for one is explained by the other. So, granted with respect to word a singular is placed in the subject, yet, by resolution to what is understood, there is something universal there, just as in 'Each of these two runs' the name of the species of those who are indicated by the pronoun is understood. Or, one should reply that in virtue of the conjunction a universal is designated in which the things joined are united, not by way of a concept, but by way of an affect. [2.220–224]

[173] It is clear, therefore, that, when [a subject] is taken conjunctively, it produces a universal proposition; and the case is similar when it is taken in a uniting sense (169), because, just as 'Every man runs' is properly universal, and 'All the Apostles are twelve' is improperly universal, so 'Socrates and Plato run' is properly universal because the subject terms introduce division and distribution.[99] 'Socrates and Plato haul the boat in' is improperly universal because it designates a collection. The first is equivalent to 'Each of these two runs', the second, however, to 'Both haul the boat in together'. 'Each of two' marks out two by way of division and partition; 'both' by way of collection. When a sign distributes a subject for parts taken separately, then the proposition is properly universal. When,

98 See 173 for this notion of universal.

99 Reading at *Sd* 1–2, pp. 246–247, 225.2–226.1, '*similiter, quia*' against '*similiter. Quia*' in the text. See 349 for further analysis of this last example.

however, it distributes for parts taken collectively, then it is improperly universal. Even if a proposition is multiple, it can still have quantity, because there the multiplicity is not entirely according to word and understanding, but according to understanding alone. [2.225–229]

[174] One should know regarding negation and affirmation that [a conjunctive proposition] is not said to be affirmative or negative from an affirmation or negation of one or both of its parts, but when the whole conjunctive proposition and the conjunction itself is denied, as in 'It is not the case that Socrates and Plato run' and 'It is not the case that Socrates runs and Plato argues'. For, since it is a proposition, in some sense it has a unity and one affirmation or agreement, yet not from the signified action given in the expression, but from the action carried out through its conjunctive function, which is the action of being together at the same time, or from a similar signified action designated by the action carried out which is understood through the force of the conjunction yet not needing to be expressed because the same action is carried out.[100] It can be competently said that in conjunctive expressions as well as in disjunctive and conditional ones a negation is directed to an action as carried out. Although the action as carried out is not a part of the expression, and only the parts of an expression are ordered and referred to one another, nevertheless, because that action is carried out through an actual part of the expression – e.g., through a disjunction, conjunction, or condition – it is to that extent included in the words.[101] But should it be signified through part of an expression, a part of an expression like a negation can well be referred to

100 The theory presented here (as in 163) speaks of two kinds of actions that signify in similar but not identical ways: as conceived and as carried out. That much is clear. But then it goes on to speak of a signifying action designated by the action carried out. In what sense can a (speech) act as carried out (and not the mark of such) signify the act that is at the basis of the unity of a conjunctive expression? The act as carried out exemplified by the connective 'and' is what unifies a conjunctive expression.

101 Here Bacon takes a shot at trying to explain in what sense 'not' and what it exemplifies is and is not part of the (conjunctive, disjunctive, conditional) expression it negates. The thought seems to be this. Consider the expression 'It is not the case that Socrates runs and Plato runs'. 'It is not the case that' is not a (properly formed) expression and hence 'not' in it is not part of an expression. But for 'not' to exercise its negative function it needs to be within an expression, says Bacon. Since 'not' in 'It is not the case that' negates the conjunction in a proper conjunctive expression like 'Socrates runs and Plato runs', there is a sense in which its act of negation "is carried out through an actual part of an expression," i.e., it operates on the conjunction *within* the conjunctive expression and it does this precisely by affirming or denying what is indicated by the sign of conjunction, (disjunction, condition) in such expressions. See 163.

such an action, and a conjunction can be negated by one negation through the relation of the negation to that action. And the sense of the proposition 'It is not the case that Socrates runs and Plato runs' is that 'Socrates runs' and 'Plato runs' are not true at the same time. In as much as a proposition is multiple it has some unity, and so it has one affirmation and one negation. If, however, we look at the actual multiplicity of the proposition, it will be said that it does not have one negative, but more than one, nor is there one affirmative, but more than one, and so they are negative from the negation of both parts. [2.230–235]

SIMPLE AND COMPOSED PROPOSITIONS

[175] Again, some propositions are simple, others composed.[102] A *simple proposition* is one in which there is no composition through a mark of condition or disjunction or conjunction or of any other sort of connection or relation.[103] A *composed proposition*, however, is one that has such a composition. So, a proposition that is single with respect to understanding and word is simple.[104] And a proposition that is multiple in understanding arises when there is a multitude of terms as in an ambiguous expression, e.g., 'A dog runs'.[105] All others, however, are either composed because of a connective or relation or because of the ambiguity of a word. But the composition that arises from the apposition of a connective or relation is said to be composition in the strict sense. [2.236–242]

MODAL PROPOSITIONS[106]

[176] Some of the already mentioned propositions are modal, others are assertoric. That is *assertoric* at whose extremity or extremities lies being or nonbeing absolutely, as in 'A man is' and 'A man is an animal'. [2.243–244]

[177] A *modal proposition* is one next to whose extremity or extremities lies a to-be or a not-to-be disposed by a disposition potentially indi-

102 See 139 and 165. While Bacon's treatment of these types of propositions is very brief, it is unusual for any discussion to be provided.

103 This would seem to refer not only to statement connectives but also to "term-connectives" as in 'Socrates and Plato run'. For propositions containing relations see 170.

104 E.g., 'A man runs'.

105 See n. 90. Paragraph 175 reminds us to keep clear the differences between single/multiple statements and simple/composed ones. The reason the former are inserted in a discussion of simple/composed propositions is possibly to remind that, while some single propositions are also simple, not all multiple propositions are also composed.

106 For the influence of Aristotle's modal logic on the development of modal theories in the Middle Ages see Simo Knuuttila, "Modal Logic," in *CHLMP*, pp. 342–357.

cated by an assertoric proposition.[107] For example, if I say 'God is', I understand its dictum, namely, that God is. Besides this I understand that it is true and that there is falsity in its opposite. Therefore, the dispositions *true* and *false* were potentially indicated by the proposition 'God is', and in consequence also those that are contained under them. Under *true* are *contingent* and *necessary;* under *false* are *possible* and *impossible.* Consequently, a mode of this sort is designated by its assertoric proposition. [Some] potency is more remote than *true* or *false*, namely, bad and good, useful and useless, white and black, and the like. These are never understood by an assertoric proposition, and so they do not make a proposition modal. [245–249]

[178] But it should be known that some sort of determination falls on either of the extremes of the composition in a proposition.[108] This happens either absolutely (as is clear from categorical determinations like 'white' and 'black' that dispose a subject and predicate with reference to what the subject or predicate is), or there are other determinations that determine a subject and predicate as subject and predicate, that is, in comparison and not absolutely, e.g., a subject in comparison to a predicate, or vice versa (such are syncategorematical words like 'all', 'every', 'no', and the like). Neither of these determinations makes a proposition modal. [2.250–251]

[179] A determination that falls directly upon the composition, however, is different, and this can happen in two ways: either it adds something to the composition or it does not. If it does not, and only privates or posits and confirms, such a determination is not a mode – such are adverbs of negating and affirming. But if it adds something, either it adds it from

107 "Disposed by a disposition" is a reference to the function of the modal operator. See 179. 'Socrates is running' is an assertoric proposition; and 'It is possible that Socrates is running' (or 'That Socrates is running is possible') and the less explicit form 'Socrates possibly runs' (or 'Possibly Socrates runs') are modal propositions. The extremities of the assertoric formulation are 'Socrates' (subject) and 'running' (predicate); 'is' (in the terminology used in this context) names the being which lies next to (between) the extremities, i.e., affirms the predicate of the subject; and 'It is possible' and 'possibly' express the mode that disposes the assertoric expression 'Socrates is running'. Assertoric propositions potentially designate modes in the sense that to say 'X is Y' is to imply 'It is true that X is Y' and that it is false to say the opposite.

108 In an assertoric proposition the extremes are the subject and predicate, but in a modal proposition they are (in the more explicit form) the subordinate clause (dictum) and the main clause which expresses the mode. While '*alterum extremum*' could be read in the Latin text to refer to the *second* of these extremes, this is certainly not the case here since the dictum can be either the subject or the predicate in a modal proposition, and Bacon acknowledges this in 190. Hence, the phrase is translated by 'either of the extremes' here and in similar contexts.

our part or from the thing's part. If the first way, it will still also not be a mode, as in the case of the nouns and adverbs 'doubtful', 'doubtfully', 'probable', 'probably', and the like.[109] But if from the thing's part, it adds either a quality or quantity. If it adds a quantity, it is said that '*only*' and '*alone*' are modes, which, however, does not seem to be entirely true, if we assume what has already been said (178), namely, that a determination falling directly on either of the extremes, whether absolutely or in comparison, does not make a proposition modal. But if it adds a quality to the composition, then indubitably it makes a proposition modal.[110] This happens in two ways: either it adds truth unqualifiedly or falsity unqualifiedly, in which case it adds *true*, *false*, *truly*, *falsely*, or a restricted truth or falsity. If it adds a restricted truth, either it is an infallible truth, and this is necessity, or a fallible truth, and this is contingency. And so there are four other modes, namely, *necessary*, *contingent*, *necessarily*, *contingently*. If the falsity is restricted, then either it is fallible, and then there is possibility; or infallible, and then there is impossibility. And so there will be four additional modes, namely, *possible*, *impossible*, *possibly*, and *impossibly*. Thus, there are twelve modes in all: six nominal and six adverbial. The adverbials make propositions modal if they are added to those propositions, nominals, if they are added to the dicta of the propositions. [2.252–263]

[180] The dictum of a proposition, moreover, can be expressed in many ways: either by changing a nominative into an accusative and a verb of the finitive mood into a verb of the infinitive mood, e.g., '(that) Socrates runs' is the dictum of the proposition 'Socrates runs'; or by prefixing to the whole proposition the connective 'that', e.g., 'that Socrates runs'; or the word 'whether', e.g., 'whether Socrates runs'.[111] [2.264]

[181] These, then, are modal propositions: 'It is true that Socrates runs', 'It is false that Socrates is an ass', 'That God is is necessary', 'That an animal is white is contingent', 'That Antichrist is not is possible', and 'That a man is an ass is impossible'. Likewise with respect to the adverbials: 'Socrates truly (or falsely, necessarily or contingently, possibly or impossibly) runs'. The phrase *of necessity* makes a proposition modal. *True* and *false* make a proposition modal, both because they fall directly on the composition and not on either of the extremes, and because the propositions in which they are asserted have to be affirmed and negated just as other

109 'Probably' in 'He is probably from the South' does not make the expression modal, or in 'It is probably true that he is from the South', though the latter is modal because of 'true'.

110 I.e., if it stands in the predicate of the *main* clause and is not in the dictum.

111 The infinitive referred to here (and subsequently) appears in Latin but not in the English translation. An example of the change at issue is the following: '*Sor currit*' to '*Sortem currere*', or in English: 'Socrates runs' to '*that Socrates runs*'.

propositions in which the words *necessary* and *contingent*, etc., are asserted, as will be clear later (196).[112] [2.265–268]

[182] Propositions made modal by these follow directly from their own assertoric [formulations], and vice versa: 'If it is true that Socrates runs, Socrates runs', 'If it is false that Socrates runs, Socrates does not run', and vice versa. This, however, does not prevent them from making propositions modal since the latter (181) have a way of making a statement modal whereas the former (177) do not. For it does not follow that just because two things follow from each other they are of the same nature, just as the ability to laugh and a man follow from each other but the ability to laugh is an accident and a man is a substance. But although *false* and *impossible* may signify privation, nevertheless they do not signify by way of privation and negation as does the word 'not', and so they add something by way of an assertion and can make a proposition modal, although the word 'not' cannot. [2.269–271]

[183] But one should know that some adverbs determine a verb thanks to the composition alone, as do adverbs of affirming and negating, because they denominate the composition (for only a proposition is said to be affirmative and negative). Since, however, the thing [signified] by the verb is incomplex and designated by a word, it is not said to be affirmative or negative, for affirmation and negation pertain only to something complex, namely, an expression. The other sort of adverb determines a verb thanks only to the thing [signified] by the verb, such as 'well', 'badly', and almost all others that do not denominate the composition but only the thing [signified] by the verb, as in 'Socrates runs well', 'Socrates' running is good', 'Socrates runs fast', 'Socrates' running is fast'. One cannot denominate a composition by them because it cannot be said that a composition is good or a composition is fast. The second sort of adverbs, but not the first, makes a proposition modal. The second sort of adverbs can determine the composition and the thing [signified] by a verb, such as 'truly' and 'falsely', for I can say that 'Socrates truly argues' and that 'His disputation is true', and so they determine the thing [signified] by the verb. 'The composition "Socrates argues" is true' can also be uttered, and in this sense it indicates a composition, and so on. They make a proposition modal only because they are determinative of a composition. Why I can speak this way, however, will be clear later.[113] [2.272–277]

112 Bacon's acceptance of *true* and *false* as modal operators is controversial. William argues that they "do not distinguish a modal proposition from an assertoric statement" because 'Socrates runs' and 'It is true that Socrates runs' say the same thing. Lambert agrees, but then returns to discuss them when he treats the conversion of modal propositions. See respectively, *Introductiones*, trans. Kretzmann, pp. 40–41, and *Logica*, pp. 29.39–30.3 and 34.16–38.25.

113 The reference is too general to locate, but see 190.

[184] One can inquire about the quality and quantity and other differences of propositions. These are clear, if we see what the subject and the predicate are in these cases. [2.278–279]

[185] Aristotle says that being and nonbeing are subjects in these, whereas modes are appositions, i.e., predicates.[114] According to Boethius he understands by 'being' an affirmed dictum and by 'nonbeing' a negated dictum.[115] Then, it seems, the whole dictum is the subject in a modal proposition and the mode will be the predicate.[116] Yet the contrary of this seems to be the case because, if the dictum of a proposition and the mode are the extremes of a modal proposition, then the composition introduced by the infinitive verb will be the composition of the modal proposition. But this cannot be since that composition is not made modal. But the composition is explained by the dictum, i.e., by the infinitive, which is clear when 'That Socrates runs is true', is explained by 'The composition "Socrates runs" is true': it denominates the true composition of the verb 'runs', and not of the verb 'is', because then the sense would be [that of] 'The composition "That Socrates runs is true" is true', which is false. Therefore, the composition of an infinitive will constitute the composition of a modal proposition, and thus the extremes will be the subject and the predicate. Therefore, an accusative will be the subject and an infinitive will be the predicate, or an accusative of a participle will be the predicate. 'To be', however, will be the composition. [2.280–284]

[186] Again, when I utter 'A man is an animal', this proposition is not denominated [modal] from 'animal', or [when I say] 'A man is white', this proposition is not denominated from 'white', because a whole proposition is never denominated from its predicate or its subject. For no essential part of a proposition (which would be the subject or predicate) suffices to give

114 Aristotle *On Interpretation* 12.21b30–31.

115 "And so also in these which are spoken modally being is the subject as a sort of thing, but the mode is predicated of the being. For, when we say 'That it rain today is possible', the being has functioned as the subject and we have predicated possibility." Boethius *In librum Aristotelis ΠΕΡΙ ΕΡΜΕΝΕΙΑΣ* 5.12, 1st ed., ed. Meiser, p. 175.6–12.

116 In a modal proposition such as 'That Socrates runs is contingent' there are two verbs: 'runs' and 'is'. Boethius says that Aristotle says that 'runs' is the predicate of the claim (*dictum*) and 'is contingent' the mode (or modal predicate of the whole statement). From what was seen in 179 it is clear that Bacon allows the dictum to stand in either the subject or predicate position of the whole statement; so does William, judged by examples. But there is a controversy here. Peter expressly requires it to be in the subject position and Lambert requires a construction of the type 'For Socrates it is contingent to run'. For the debate (involving Aristotle) on the point see, respectively, *Introductiones*, trans. Kretzmann, pp. 43–46; *Tractatus* 1.22; and *Logica*, pp. 30.34–31.18. For Bacon's resolution see 190.

a name to the proposition, i.e., the composition. Therefore, neither will *true* and *false*, etc., denominate the proposition, because they are predicates. And there are many opinions on this. [2.285–286]

[187] Some say that there are two sorts of subjects: a *subject of locution* and a *subject of attribution*.[117] The dictum is a subject of attribution and the mode is the predicate corresponding to it. The accusative case is the subject of locution and the participle of an infinitive is the predicate. 'To be' is the copula; the mode is the determination of the composition and something that modifies it. Others say otherwise, namely, that a modal expression can be looked at as a proposition or as a statement. If it is looked at as a proposition, then an accusative is the subject and an infinitive verb the predicate. If, however, it is looked at as a statement, then the whole dictum is the subject, and the mode the predicate. For it is said that every statement has its subject in the nominative case because it arises from a name and a verb, as Aristotle proposes in *On Interpretation*.[118] [2.287–293]

[188] This is true, at least when speaking about statements in the strict sense, and such are principally assertoric expressions. A proposition, however, can indifferently receive a subject in the nominative case and one in an oblique case, because 'proposition' indicates a sort of positing for another. For it is a proposition in as much as it is asserted within a syllogism to prove a conclusion; but a syllogism equally arises from oblique cases as well as nominative ones. A proposition, therefore, with a subject in an oblique case and a statement differ with respect to subject and predicate, as has been said (187). But a proposition with a subject in the nominative case does not differ from a statement except accidentally, namely, because it is a statement in as much as it is taken outside a syllogism to make known externally what internally was within a soul. The same expression, however, is said to be a proposition when it is arranged within a syllogism to prove a conclusion. It is, therefore, the same to say that an expression can be looked at as a proposition and as a statement and as something with a subject in an oblique case and in the nominative case. Also, it is the same thing to look at [it as] an expression having a subject of attribution, as a proposition with a subject in the nominative case, and as a statement. It is the same thing to look at it as [an expression] having a subject of locution and as a proposition with a subject in an oblique case. A statement, taken strictly, is not one with a subject in an oblique case. [2.294–301]

[189] From these things it is clear what the subject in a modal expression is when it is a proposition with a subject in an oblique case,

117 For the distinction see 143.

118 Aristotle *On Interpretation* 5.17a10–11, and 10.19b10.

because the accusative case is the subject and the infinitive or participle understood in it is the predicate. And so it is truly modal since the composition of such extremes is made modal when one speaks in this way: 'That Socrates runs is possible', 'The proposition or composition "Socrates runs" is possible'. [2.302–303]

[190] To that, therefore, which is objected with respect to Aristotle and Boethius (185) one should reply that there are two classes of extremes, namely, natural and positive. Natural ones are the accusative case and the infinitive because the one reflects the other as what serves as a predicate and what serves as a subject. But positive extremes are the mode and the dictum because the dictum is the subject and the mode is the predicate, according to the position and arrangement of the utterance. This is clear in an example. The proposition '"Animal" is predicated of man' is true, and yet 'animal' is the subject. So, what is a natural predicate becomes a positive subject. Just as the proposition '"Animal" is predicated of man' redirects our intellect to the proposition 'A man is an animal', so every modal redirects our intellect to its assertoric, just as everything that is positive is redirected to what is natural, as is clear in other examples. Thus the words of Aristotle and his expositor are to be redirected to positive extremes, not to natural ones. The accusative, therefore, and infinitive are the extremes of a modal proposition, from which extremes it is said to be a proposition and also modal, because it will be said to be a proposition and modal from these same extremes. [2.304–310]

[191] It should be added that the dictum in a certain sense has the characteristic of a proposition. For if a proper attribute can in all instances be predicated of a proper subject as 'able to laugh' of a man, 'even' and 'odd' of a number, 'curved' or 'straight' of a line – for a man is able to laugh, a number is even or odd, a line is straight or curved, and so on – then it should be the case that the attribute *true* or *false* is predicated of a proposition, since it is its proper attribute. But nothing complete in the genus *proposition* and taken under the concept of *proposition* receives them as predicated, because there is no dictum in 'Socrates runs is true'.[119] Therefore, it is necessary that something incomplete in this genus have the name 'proposition', as has been said (188). A dictum, therefore, will be a proposition and a modal proposition when a mode is added to it. So, the extremes of a dictum will be the extremes of a modal proposition, and its composition will be determined by the mode, and not by any other thing. For this is less absurd than for a proper attribute not to be predicated of its proper subject. Thus it is clear how the extremes of a modal expression are to be posited, considering it with respect to a

119 '"Socrates runs" is true' is not a modal proposition; 'That Socrates runs is true' is such.

subject of locution and on the basis of its being a proposition with a subject in an oblique case. [2.311–316]

[192] But to those who consider it with respect to a subject of attribution, and on the basis of its being a statement or proposition with a subject in the nominative case, one ought to reply either that no statement is modal and its composition is not denominated from a mode, or that the determination is intrinsic to it, that is, that no form is added to its essence, as we see in many examples such as 'Unity is one', 'Goodness is good': the predicate adds nothing beyond the essence of the subject. This is the case here because something modal adds nothing to the statement or essence, or, [to put it] differently, because something modal is predicated there effectively and not formally, just as the sun is said to be hot effectively because it causes heat but not formally, because heat does not inform the sun nor dispose it. Thus something modal is predicated effectively of a modal statement because it makes its subject modal, and the thing signified by the word 'modal' does not inform a statement nor does it dispose it. A proposition, and not so strictly and authoritatively a statement, will truly be said to be modal when its composition is denominated by a mode, as is clear, unless someone argues that there could be a statement with a subject in an oblique case, as does occur with respect to propositions.[120] [2.317–318]

[193] If it is objected that the parts of a statement are a name and a verb, one should reply that this is true only of a statement in the strictest sense of 'statement'; of such, none is modal. [2.319]

[194] If someone, however, wishes, one can expound Aristotle in another way (cf. 185, 190) by saying that a subject with respect to a predicate can be called what is subordinated to the predicate and an apposite can be said to be the predicate that is apposed to a subject. In this sense Aristotle did not propose that being and nonbeing are subjects; modes, however, are predicates. In another sense a subject and predicate are said to be a subject with respect to the composition because they are subordinated to it, and the composition is said to be an apposition because it is apposed to them, as 'man' and 'animal' are subordinated to the whole composition, i.e., proposition, that results from them, or to the verb 'is' that is added to them when I utter 'A man is an animal'. And in a way similar to what was said about those assertoric propositions it is said that in modals the whole dictum functions as a subject for the mode, because, just as their extremes are subordinated to the composition, so here the whole composition comprised of subject and predicate, namely of accusative and infinitive, functions as a subject for the mode, whereas the determining and denominating mode functions as a predicate for it.[121] [2.320–321]

120 See 187–188.

121 Reading at *Sd* 1–2, p. 257, 321.8, '*hic*' with MSS. O. and S. against '*hoc*' in the text.

[195] With respect to quantity it is clear that, if we take a look at a modal expression having a subject of attribution and in as much as it is a statement or proposition with a subject in the nominative case, then every one of such is singular because a singular dictum functions as the subject. If we take a look at one having a subject of locution and in as much as it is a proposition with a subject in the nominative case, it receives its quantity from its assertoric. [2.322–323]

[196] With respect to quality, however, one should know that a modal expression should be said to be affirmative and negative from the affirmation and negation of the mode and composition of the substantival verb adjoined to it, as these two are negative: 'It is not possible that Socrates runs' and 'It is not contingent that Socrates runs'. 'It is possible that Socrates runs' or 'It is contingent that Socrates runs', however, is affirmative. But if a negation is added to the infinitive in such a way that it does not fall on the mode, it will still be affirmative, as in 'It is possible that Socrates does not run'. [2.324–325]

[197] How categorical propositions are assertoric and modal is clear. One should know about hypothetical propositions that a conditional one is said to be modal when the mode includes the condition and lies next to it, as in 'Necessarily, if there is a man, there is an animal'. But if it is included within the condition and precedes in the generation of the utterance, then it is not modal, as in 'If Socrates runs, he necessarily is moved'. The case is entirely the same as that for negation, for just as [a proposition] is said to be negative in virtue of the apposition of a negation to the whole conditional and when it includes the condition, so it is with a mode. The case is similar with respect to a disjunction, for if a disjunction includes a mode, it is not modal, as in 'Socrates runs or contingently argues'. But if a mode includes a disjunction and falls on the whole disjunctive, then [the proposition] is modal, as in 'Necessarily Socrates is healthy or Socrates is ill'. The case is similar with respect to a conjunctive proposition, for if a mode lies next to the whole and includes the conjunction, the proposition is modal, as in 'Necessarily God is and a man is an animal'. But if it is included within a conjunction, it is assertoric, as in 'God necessarily is and a man is an animal'.[122] [2.326–343]

[198] One should note that, just as it has already been said about negation in conjunctives, disjunctives, and conditionals (163, 174) that the negation is directed to the action carried out or to the signified action known through the action carried out, so it is here with respect to an adverbial mode because it does not fall on a verb placed in an expression (either conditional, disjunctive, or conjunctive), but on the action carried out by the effect of the condition, disjunction, or conjunction. And although the

122 The enumeration of paragraphs in the Latin text jumps from 331 to 342.

action carried out cannot be a part of an expression (because every action that is a part of an expression is signified), nevertheless, another part of the expression can well be referred to such an action since it is actually carried out by a part of the expression, just as here by the condition, disjunction, or conjunction. [2.344]

[199] With respect, however, to a host of these propositions in terms of opposition and consequence, they are to be clarified in the following way. [2.345]

[200] To whatever affirmed or denied dictum *necessary* is attributed, from its opposite *contingent* and *possible* are removed, and to the same *impossible* is attributed, as in 'It is necessary to be', 'It is not contingent not to be', 'It is not possible not to be', and 'It is impossible not to be'. Also: 'It is necessary not to be', 'It is not contingent to be', 'It is not possible to be', and 'It is impossible to be'. [2.346–347]

[201] Another rule is: From whatever affirmed or denied dictum *necessary* is removed, to its opposite *contingent* and likewise *possible* is assigned, and from that *impossible* is removed, as in 'It is not necessary that a man is', 'It is contingent that a man is not', 'It is possible that a man is not', 'It is not impossible that a man is not'. Also: 'It is not necessary that a man is not', 'It is contingent that a man is', 'It is possible that a man is', and 'It is not impossible that a man is'. [2.348–349]

[202] Some of these propositions are contraries, some contradictories, some subalterns, and some subcontraries. All propositions that are in the first series [below] are *contrary* to those that are in the second series. All that are in the third are *subcontrary* to those that are in the fourth. But the first and third are *contradictory*, as well as the second and fourth. The first and fourth are *subalterns*, as well as the second and third, as is clear in this figure:[123]

123 De Libera notes that the ensuing figure is supplied by him and is omitted in MSS. O. and S. (*Sd* 1–2, p. 259, n. 85.) Apropos of the diagram note the following.
(1) Traditionally, authors employ a square to diagram the relations of the four groups of modal propositions in the following manner:

IV III
I II.

But in contrast with placements on the traditional diagram of the square of oppositions among assertoric propositions, IV and III are subcontraries and I and II are contraries, all other relations remaining the same in the two diagrams. (See *Ut dicit*, *LM*, vol. 2, pt. 2, p. 394; *Cum sit nostra*, ibid., p. 431; *Dialectica Monacensis*, ibid., p. 483; William *Introductiones*, trans. Kretzmann, p. 48; and Lambert, *Logica*, pp. 32.39–33.15.)
(2) Peter presents two diagrams, the second of which labels the oppositions among the four groups. (*Tractatus* 1.24 and 25.) But Peter breaks with tradition (a) by naming the contrary groups I and II and the subcontrary groups III and IV, and (b)

I	II
It is necessary to be	It is necessary not to be
It is not contingent not to be	It is not contingent to be
It is not possible not to be	It is not possible to be
It is impossible not to be	It is impossible to be
IV	III
It is not necessary not to be	It is not necessary to be
It is contingent to be	It is contingent not to be
It is possible to be	It is possible not to be
It is not impossible to be	It is not impossible not to be

[2.350–354]

[203] One should know that all propositions that are in the same series are converted, and precede and follow from each other. One should also know that propositions with *true* and *false* in them are not included with these in a consequence because they do not follow from them nor are they absolutely in opposition, since *true* and *false* are [logically] superior to the other four. [2.355–356]

[204] And one should note that *true* and *false* have two senses. For there is an *incomplex* truth or falsity, as when we speak of a true denarius and a false denarius, and so truth is the reality of a thing, falsity its lack of existence or lack of reality. In a different way they speak of *complex* truth and falsity, namely, that in virtue of which a proposition is said to be true or false, and this truth is "the mutual agreement between states of affairs and how they are understood," whereas falsity is "the mutual dissonance between states of affairs and how they are understood," and they are referred in both ways to a composition. But one should note that there are two kinds of compositions: one is of a quality with a substance, and this is had by a name because "a name signifies a substance together with a quality"; the other is of an action together with a substance.[124] There are

by doing what William hinted could be done (*Introductiones*, trans. Kretzmann, p. 49), namely, placing the contraries on the top line and subcontraries on the bottom line, bringing the diagram of the relation of modal propositions in line with that of the relation of assertoric ones in the traditional square:

I II
IV III.

(3) When de Libera creates a diagram for Bacon he follows Peter's unorthodox arrangement of the groups in the *Tractatus*. And (4) de Libera also presents Bacon as breaking with all the above authors, including Peter, in presenting a novel sequence of modes within each group. Traditionally the sequence is from *possible* to *contingent* to *impossible* to *necessary*.

124 Priscian *Institutiones grammaticae* 2.18, *GL*, vol. 2, p. 55.6: "It is a proprium of a name to signify a substance together with a quality."

two kinds of the latter: one involves separated extremes, as in the case of a verb; the other is without separated extremes, as in the case of a participle. I say "involves separated extremes" because one understands in a verb a substance that precedes it, as in personal verbs, or that follows it, as in the case of impersonal ones, in such a way that it is not signified by the verb. So there the action stands at a distance from the substance, for the latter is not united to what is signified by the verb. "Without separated extremes" obtains in the case of a participle because the action is united to the substance in what is signified by the participle, for the latter signifies both a substance and an action because it signifies an action united to a substance; so there is no separation there. A complex truth, moreover, corresponds to the composition of an action with a substance. This involves a separation of the extremes, as in the case of a verb, namely, when it is actually arranged in an utterance to constitute a proposition. But an incomplex truth pertains to a composition of a quality with a substance or to a composition of an action with a substance without a separation of the extremes.[125] [2.357–365]

[205] *Necessary* sometimes means the necessity of a thing (about which nothing at present), and sometimes the necessity of what is statable, and this occurs in two ways because one sense of *necessary* is *per se*, and another *per accidens*. *Per se necessary* is what cannot, could not, and will not be able to be false, as in 'That God is'. That is *per accidens* necessary which cannot nor will not be able to be, but was able to be, as in 'That you were' and every true dictum about the past. Also, one sort of necessity is absolute, another is relative. Absolute necessity is what needs nothing in addition for its necessity, as in 'Every whole is greater than its part'. Relative necessity is what requires something in addition, as in 'That you are sitting while you sit is necessary'. As often as *necessary* is spoken, so often is *impossible* said, since of whatever *necessary* is said in one of its significations *impossible* is said of its opposite. For example, 'That God is not' is *per se* impossible because it cannot be, it will not be, nor could it not have

125 What Bacon seems to be saying in 204 is this, and I am indebted to Paul Spade for digging it out: While any expression is a unit, the subject and predicate are not (necessarily?) joined directly. This is masked in expressions like 'Socrates runs', but, if such are stated in their more explicit form, such as 'Socrates is running', one can readily see the point: a copula separates the substance from the verbal action, the extremes in question. The substance in the example clearly precedes the verbal action. But what is meant by the reference to subjects that follow the verb in the case of impersonal verbs? Possibly Bacon has something in mind like 'It is said that Socrates runs'. Technically, 'it' is the subject, but in another sense the clause "that Socrates runs" fills the bill, since it is the referent of 'it'. Such separation of substance from verbal action, however, is not the case with participial phrases, as can be seen in 'the running Socrates' where there is no such separation.

been true. 'That you were not' is *per accidens* impossible because it cannot nor will not be able to be true, but it could have been true. 'Not every whole is greater than its part' is absolutely impossible as well as 'That a man is an ass' because it needs nothing in addition for its falsity. 'That you are not sitting while you sit' is relatively impossible because it needs something in addition for its falsity. [2.366–372]

[206] *Possible* is spoken of in as many ways as potency. Some potency is spoken of in an extended sense, some truly and properly. *Potency in an extended sense* is the same as permission, as in 'He can eat meat on Thursday and not on Friday'.[126] *Potency taken strictly* is either rational or nonrational. That potency is *rational* which is in those things having reason, as in the intelligences and man. Hence, either it is *active* as an agent intellect is, e.g., in the intelligences (which is clear elsewhere), or it is *passive* and receptive as a possible intellect is, e.g., in man.[127] *Nonrational potency* is also of two sorts: one belongs to matter, like the potency of clothes to be torn or not torn, but before that to wear out; the other is the potency of an efficient cause, like the potency of fire to warm. *Rational potency* (at least the passive sort) is receptive of opposite sorts of things. The potency of matter is receptive of opposite sorts of things. The potency of an efficient cause is not, but is directed to one goal.[128] *Active potency* is a principle of transformation into another, that is, something by which someone can act. *Passive potency* is a principle of transformation by another, that is, by which something is able to be acted upon by another. Of almost all of these some are with act, others are before act. [Some potencies are] *with act*, e.g., an intellect can understand when it understands, and matter can be cut

126 Reading at *Sd* 1–2, p. 261, 375.2, '*et non in die*' with MSS. O. and S. against '*in die*' in the text.

127 For the notion of intelligences see 51–53 and 64. The notions of active and possible intellects pertain (in part) to the medieval dispute over the causal activity which enables humans to form abstract concepts. For Bacon's position in the controversy see Theodore Crowley, *Roger Bacon: The Problem of the Soul in His Philosophical Commentaries*, pp. 182–188, and Dorothea Sharp, *Franciscan Philosophy at Oxford in the Thirteenth Century* (New York: Russell & Russell, 1964), pp. 160–165.

128 In MS. S. we find the following addition at this point: "*Per se* it does not have the ability to influence things opposed to it, but it does accidentally, because what is hot makes something cold accidentally, as is clear in the case of hot water that is to be frozen, because hot water is frozen more quickly than cold. So heat contributes to freezing, but accidentally, because the very thing that is cold excites the intentions to make it warm. Something similar happens in the case of the generation of hail. And what is cold warms accidentally, just as in winter digestion and the strength of natural heat are greatly fortified because of the cold surrounding the body." *Sd* 1–2, p. 262, n. 22.

when it is cut, and fire warm when it warms; [other potencies are] *before act*, e.g., an intellect is able to understand something before it actually understands, just as a boy geometry, and so on. Then, too, some potency is *proximate*, as a soldier can perform military service; another is *remote*, as a boy can perform military service. Also, some potency is *accidental*, as that which needs only an accidental mover to result in act, namely, by removing what restricts act. For example, a stone is in potency to descend when it is actually up; and a grammarian, knowing grammar but not actually thinking of it or while asleep, has grammar potentially; and an eye while sleeping sees potentially. Another potency is *essential*, which requires an essential mover to bring about something in act, namely, by generating and transfiguring. For example, a boy is in potency to knowing grammar, and earth is in potency to becoming water, and seed is in potency to becoming an animal. But so that all meanings of *possible* may be clearer, *contingent* should be distinguished. [2.373–389]

[207] *Contingent* in one sense comprehends every proposition that does not have *impossible* in it, whether it has *necessary* in it or not. In another sense it is opposed to *necessary* in the sense in which we say 'Some true things are necessary, others contingent'. This [latter] sort of *contingent* can be [taken] in three senses: for either it is equally open to being and nonbeing, and then it is called *indeterminately contingent* or *indefinitely* or *equally*, as in 'That you sit'; or it occurs for the most part, and it is then called *contingent-for-the-most-part*, i.e., *naturally contingent*, as in 'That a man becomes gray-headed in old age'; or it occurs occasionally and then is called *contingent-in-a-few-cases*, as in 'That diggers find a treasure'. [2.390–392]

[208] *Possible*, however, is commonly spoken of in one way when it includes every proposition that does not have *impossible* in it, as is clear in *Prior Analytics* and in *On Interpretation*, and so is converted with *contingent* in the first sense (207).[129] The names are synonymous except in the rarest sense. For all grant that 'That God is' is possible, but not that 'That God is' is contingent, because, although it could be true, yet it is greatly closer to *necessary* than *contingent* is, because *contingent* is what can be otherwise. But this [last clause] is to be understood of the second sense of *contingent* (207), if it is true. In another sense *possible* is opposed to *impossible* in so far as we say 'Some false things are possible, others impossible'. In this way *possible* is related to falsity as *contingent* in the second way is to truth. *Possible*, however, is so-called because of the truth it does not yet have and can have; *contingent* because of the truth it has and can lose. *Possible* and *contingent* taken in this way have the same supposition, though it receives them as predicates at different times, as 'That you are a bishop'

129 Aristotle *Prior Analytics* 1.13.32b10, and *On Interpretation* 13.22a32–38.

is possible before you are a bishop; once you are a bishop, it is contingent, and so on. But *possible* interpreted in this sense is spoken of in as many ways as *contingent* is taken in the second sense, i.e., *indeterminately*, *for the most part*, *occasionally*. [2.393–397]

[209] But the relation of these to, and their consequence for, their assertoric propositions is of this sort. Every proposition with *true* in it precedes its assertoric one and follows from its assertoric one, as in 'It is true that Socrates runs; therefore Socrates runs', and vice versa. Every proposition with *false* in it is equipollent to its opposite assertoric one, as in 'That you sit is false; therefore you do not sit', and vice versa. Every proposition with *necessary* in it precedes its assertoric one, and not vice versa, as in 'That God is is necessary; therefore God is'.[130] Every proposition with *impossible* in it precedes its contradictory assertoric one, and not vice versa, as in 'That you sit is impossible; therefore you do not sit'. Every proposition with *contingent* in it in its first signification (207) follows from its assertoric one, and is not converted. Likewise a proposition with *possible* in it in its first signification (208), for these follow: 'If Socrates runs, that Socrates runs is possible' and 'that Socrates runs is contingent', and these are not converted. [2.398–404]

[210] And I say this truthfully, although with respect to the way we speak some say that it always follows except in the rarest sense, as in 'God is; therefore that God is is contingent', because what is proposed seems to be falsified. If reason and truth set aside the force of custom, these propositions do not precede their assertoric ones, as is clear to one who reflects on the matter. But likewise [propositions with *contingent* or *possible*] in their second signification in them (207, 208) do not follow from their assertoric ones, for 'God is; therefore that God is is contingent (or possible)' does not follow.[131] But every proposition with this sense of *contingent* in it precedes its assertoric one, as in 'If that Socrates runs is contingent, Socrates runs', and not vice versa, because it follows in this way: 'If it is contingent, it is true' and every proposition with *true* in it precedes its assertoric one, and hence, so does every proposition with this sense of *contingent* in it. So, this follows: 'If that God is is contingent, God is'. But the first is false, and from something false follows something true, although not vice versa. Every proposition with *possible* in it taken in the second sense (208) precedes its opposite assertoric one, as in 'That Socrates runs is possible; therefore Socrates does not run'. In the mentioned consequences pertaining to modals, however, *contingent* and *possible* were taken not in

130 Reading at *Sd* 1–2, p. 264, 401.2, '*Deus est*' with MSS. O. and S. against '*Deum est*' in the text.

131 Reading at *Sd* 1–2, p. 264, 407.1, '*sequuntur*' against '*sequitur*' in MS. S. (omitted in MS. O.) and the text.

their second signification but in their first (207, 208), because in this sense they were converted. [2.405–411]

THE PROPERTIES OF TERMS[132]

[211] Granted that parts are prior to their whole, yet many properties of parts are not known without a knowledge of the whole, because in the whole the parts acquire new conditions and properties that they did not

132 Up to this point Bacon, as he will immediately point out, has discussed the relation of words to sounds and signs, has distinguished the parts of speech and components of a proposition, and has discussed various kinds of propositions. Such is the contribution of the "old logic," most of which was drawn from Aristotle via Boethius. Now he inserts in his textbook the contribution of the "new logic," a focus on terms in propositions and the many ways in which we use them to stand for various things. In great part, then, what is presented in this section is Bacon's view of the medieval contribution to a theory of reference as distinguished from meaning, though modern commentators will be quick to point out that the medieval notions of signification and supposition do not correspond exactly to those of meaning and reference (respectively) in the current sense. Nevertheless, the clear focus and heart of this new medieval treatise on the property of terms is an attempt to understand and spell out how terms in propositions stand in various ways for things. For excellent overviews of the notions of signification, supposition, appellation, ampliation, and restriction discussed in this section and their historical development from earlier grammatical theories see de Rijk, "The Origins of the Theory of the Property of Terms," *CHLMP*, pp. 161–173; Paul Spade, "The Semantics of Terms," *CHLMP*, pp. 188–96; Desmond Paul Henry, "Suppositio and Significatio in English Logic" in ed. H. A. G. Braakhuis et al., *English Logic and Semantics: From the End of the Twelfth Century to the Time of Ockham and Burleigh*, Acts of the Fourth European Symposium on Medieval Logic and Semantics, Leiden-Nijmegen, 23–27 April 1979, Artistarium Supplementa, vol. 1 (Nijmegen: Ingenium, 1981), pp. 361–387; and Kneale, pp. 246–265.

Paul Spade has also written a very penetrating study of the development of supposition theory in which he attempts to explain why its dual facets of being a theory of reference and a theory of descent and ascent from common terms became separated in the early fourteenth-century, the former dropping out. He hypothesizes that by that time the linking of the theory of reference to quantification had such problems that that aspect of supposition theory was rejected and this left the theory of modes of supposition with no question to answer: it was no longer a theory of truth conditions or analysis. This leads him to say, "No wonder it has proved so hard for scholars to agree about what it was trying to accomplish. By the early fourteenth century, it was no longer trying to accomplish anything at all!" ("The Logic of the Categorical: The Medieval Theory of Descent and Ascent," in *Meaning and Inference in Medieval Philosophy*, pp. 187–222, quotation on p. 212. Section IX of Spade's work, "Suggestions Regarding the Nature of the Theory," is especially valuable for pre-fourteenth-century theories of supposition, for which see ibid., pp. 208–213.) In his formal presentation of supposition Bacon will be seen to use the

previously have.[133] Since treatment has already been given to the parts of speech – considered in and of themselves as well as in propositions, with respect to all the properties of functioning as subject and predicate, and with respect to a proposition itself in all its differences (112–210) – now there are to be addressed certain aspects of the properties of the parts that go by the names of 'supposition', 'appellation', and 'copulation'. [2.412–413]

Supposition

[212] 'Supposition' is used in many ways.[134] In one way supposition is said to be a property of a common term compared to the individuals that are its supposita, according to which we say that a common name like

---

term 'descent' only rarely (219–220, and 430) and 'ascent' never, though the latter is implied once (217) by way of example.

Alan Perreiah proposes a theory of supposition that denies that it is a theory of quantification and takes it as a system of conceptual notation, "a convenient shorthand for noting that a categorematic term was subject to certain logical rules in a given context." ("Supposition Theory: A New Approach," *The New Scholasticism* 60 [1986]: 213–231.) For the more specialized issue of Bacon's role in creating the divergences in semantic theories that became so pronounced in the fourteenth century at Oxford and Paris see Alain de Libera, "The Oxford and Paris Traditions in Logic," *CHLMP*, pp. 174–187.

133 Note that Bacon, by stating that he intends to focus on the function of terms *within* propositions and not on their signification outside of their use in such reveals that he is in the camp of those who no longer consider signification a property of terms in the technical sense but rather a precondition of their ability to stand for extralinguistic (and linguistic) entities. (See 212.) Later we will see him say that a term has a certain kind of supposition *because* it is the *name* of the suppositum in question. See 222.

134 The double notion of supposition that follows is given in MS. S. whereas MS. O. inserts two additional definitions prior to those: "[1] [I]n one way supposition is said to be a request for or an acceptance of some [proposition] without proof when [that proposition] needs to be or could be proven; [2] in another way supposition is said to be the substantive designation of a thing, just as we say that substantive names supposit their thing, i.e., substantively designate; [3] in a third way it is said to be a property of a common term compared to the individuals that are its supposita, according to which we say that a common name, like 'man', signifies a quality together with a substance, i.e., humanity, and supposits individuals, namely, Socrates, and Plato, and others; and [4] in a fourth way supposition is said to be a property of a subject term or of a subject in as much as it supposits for another (*alii supponit*) and functions as the subject in an expression," reading at *Sd* 1–2, p. 265, n. 84.3–4, with MS. O. '*substantive designant*' against '*substantiva designant*' in the text.

Textbooks differ on which definitions of 'supposition' are relevant to a study of logic. William provides only one definition and says, "Supposition, however, is an

'man' signifies a quality together with a substance, i.e., humanity, and supposits individuals, namely, Socrates and Plato and others. In a second way supposition is said to be a property of a subject term (a suppositum) in as much as it supposits for another and functions as the subject in an expression.[135] My present focus is on the latter usage. From this it is clear that supposition is not a property except of a term actually ordered within an expression, and not outside it. Signification, however, is a condition of an utterance and a term in and of itself and not in comparison to another under which it is placed. So it signifies both outside an expression and

---

ordering of the understanding of something under something else" and Kretzmann promptly points out that this definition plays "no important part in the remainder of the chapter" on supposition. (*Introductiones*, trans. Kretzmann, p. 105 and n. 3.) Peter also passes on only one definition: "Supposition is the acceptance of a substantive term for something." (*Tractatus* 6.3, and trans. Mullally, p. 3.) Lambert on the other hand provides the four definitions found in Bacon's MS. O., with Bacon's first and second reversed as well as the third and fourth. In addition he offers a comment on each of the four. Supposition in Bacon's first sense (in MS. O.), he says, pertains to propositions and not to terms, since in disputations one assumes propositions, not just terms. Clearly Bacon's way of formulating the definition is broad enough to allow terms as well as propositions to be supposed, i.e., assumed. It may also be the case, however, that Bacon's indefiniteness in speaking of supposition in this sense as "*petitio alicuius*" was careless and he should have written "*petitio alicuius propositionis.*" Supposition in Bacon's second sense as the substantive designation, i.e., indication (*signatio*) of something, Lambert says, is a kind of signification of a term naming a species (*significatio specialis termini*), not a property of it, though the line of reasoning he employs to justify this is somewhat obscure. Supposition in Bacon's third sense (first sense in 212) is what logicians talk about when they write tracts on the supposition of terms, whereas supposition in Bacon's fourth sense (second sense in 212) is of interest principally to grammarians when they speak of the difference between subjects and verbs in sentences: subjects supposit and predicates appose. *Logica*, pp. 206.21–207.8, trans. Kretzmann and Stump, *CTMPT*, p. 106–107, reading at *Logica*, p. 206.32 '*pro se*' against '*per se*' in the text. See ibid., p. 207.16 for confirmation. For the development of supposition theory see Sten Ebbesen, "Early Supposition Theory (12th and 13th Century)," *Histoire, épistémologie, langage* 3 (1981): 35–48.

135 Reading at *Sd* 1–2, p. 265, 416.2, '*suppositi*' against an uncertain reading in MS. S. and '*suppositio*' in MS. O. and '*suppositio est*' in the text.

In traditional terminology subjects of sentences were thought of as being placed under, subordinated to, their predicates, which latter, being general terms and broader classes (for the most part), were thought of as standing above their subjects, thus giving rise to the metaphor of *descending* to particulars from general terms. Hence, this notion of supposition is of interest primarily to grammarians. See Bacon's fourth definition in MS. O. and Lambert's third. See also, respectively, the preceding note and *Logica*, p. 206.26–31.

within an expression, although it supposits only within.[136] One sort of supposition is simple, another personal.[137] [2.414–420]

[213] *Simple* supposition occurs when a term does not stand for another person or an inferior thing, but rather for an utterance, as in '"Man" is an utterance'; or for what is signified, as in 'Man is the noblest

136 A word acquires the ability to be a sign of something when a person by an act of his/her free will, called imposition, attaches some meaning to the term or designates it as the name of something. Bacon's paradigm case of imposition probably already is, but certainly by 1267 will become, the naming of infants at Baptism and pets, for which see "*Ds*" 155 and 158 and *Cst* 2.97, 99, and 125. For Aristotle's theory see Norman Kretzmann, "Aristotle on Spoken Sound Significant by Convention," in *Ancient Logic and Its Modern Interpretations*, ed. John Corcoran (Dordrecht: Reidel, 1974), pp. 3–21. For studies of Bacon's theory see Karin Margareta Fredborg, "Roger Bacon on '*impositio vocis ad significandum*'," in *English Logic and Semantics*, pp. 167–192, and Thomas S. Maloney, "Roger Bacon on the *Significatum* of Words," in *Archéologie du* signe, ed. Lucie Brind'Amour and Eugène Vance, Recueils d'études médiévales/Papers in Mediaeval Studies, vol. 3 (Toronto: Pontifical Institute of Mediaeval Studies, 1983), pp. 187–211. In spite of what Bacon says in the next sentence, it is clear that his focus is on the first of the two definitions, granted he does discuss grammatical issues in 238. For the rationale for translating "*de isto modo*" by 'on the latter usage' see *Sd* 1–2, p. 252, para. 274, where we find "*Ista autem adverbia, nec priora* ... ."

137 Of all the divisions of supposition the greatest divergence among authors occurs in the initial division, and in great part this is because of a lack of agreement on how to think about the way terms stand for themselves and concepts as opposed to extramental entities, and whether to separate from the outset discrete terms, like proper names, from common appellative nouns. Thus William's initial division is one between the capacity of a term to supposit (*secundum habitum*) and an actual occurance within an utterance (*secundum actum*), a distinction reflected in the divisions by Peter and Lambert called, respectively, natural and accidental supposition. William then divides between terms that stand for utterances (what he calls material supposition) and those that stand for what a term signifies, i.e., a form (what he calls formal supposition). (*Introductiones*, trans. Kretzmann, p. 107.) He then proceeds to a subdivision of his formal supposition and separates the supposition of discrete terms like 'John' or 'this man' from common ones like 'man', thus giving rise to what he calls discrete formal supposition and common formal supposition. *Introductiones*, trans. Kretzmann, pp. 108.

Peter, on the other hand, thinks that one should at the outset separate the reference of discrete and common terms and therefore presents an initial subdivision between what he calls (respectively) discrete and common supposition, and then proceeds in a subdivision of common supposition to separate what he calls natural and accidental supposition. The former draws on a notion that by mere imposition a common term of itself *can* stand for anything (existing or not) for which it can be a sign, i.e., for anything that can participate in the universal form or nature signified by the term. Thus it seems that natural supposition for Peter is the ability of a

of creatures'; or for a signifying utterance, as in '"Man" is a name'; or for a property of an utterance, as in '"*Homo*" is a two-syllable word' and '"*Homo*" is a trochaic foot'; or with respect to the properties of what is signified, as in 'Man is a universal' and 'Man is a species'; and there are many others of this sort.[138] Augustine clearly shows at the end of his *Dialectics* that a name can thus be interpreted differently and in many other ways, and comment will later be made on this.[139] [2.421–422]

[214] *Personal* supposition occurs when a term supposits for its individuals and inferiors, as in 'A man runs' and 'A man disputes'. One sort of personal supposition is discrete, the other common. [2.423–424]

---

word to stand for something by itself whether in or outside discourse. (See L. M. de Rijk, "The Origins of the Theory of the Property of Terms," *CHLMP*, pp. 168–169.) By contrast, accidental supposition for Peter is that which a common term has when it is accidentally determined by (i.e., when it has) a qualifier as 'man' in 'A man exists' or 'A man runs' (read, 'A man is running') or 'white man'. (See *Tractatus* 6.5, and trans. Mullally, pp. 5–7.) Clearly, Bacon has no need of this distinction because for him all supposition would be accidental. (See 212.) For the distinction see L. M. de Rijk, "The Development of *suppositio naturalis* in Medieval Logic," *Vivarium* 9 (1971): 71–107.

Lambert's initial division is Peter's second, i.e., one between the supposition terms have by themselves (natural supposition) and that which they have only within discourse in virtue of being adjoined by some other term (accidental supposition). This latter is then subdivided along the lines indicated by Peter, including a last subdivision between mobily and immobily confused supposition. *Logica*, pp. 208.28–211.26, trans. Kretzmann and Stump, *CTMPT*, pp. 109–113. See also, however, ibid., p. 207.9–29, trans., p. 107.

138 Thus we see that Bacon's simple supposition includes what William calls material supposition and also the first part of the latter's third division, simple (common) supposition, namely, the supposition of terms for what they signify, i.e., a species or nature, as 'man' in 'Man is a species'. (*Introductiones*, trans. Kretzmann, p. 107.) It also includes what Peter subsumes under what he calls simple (accidental common) supposition when he describes common terms that stand for their species (whether in subject or predicate position). (*Tractatus* 6.6, and trans. Mullally, pp. 7–9.) Finally, it reflects what Lambert calls simple accidental supposition. In this context Lambert also speaks of simple supposition in a broad sense where a common term "is not related to the supposita determinately and yet has a relation to them indeterminately." He gives two examples: 'I know there is a man in England' and 'Pepper is sold here and in Rome' where 'man' and 'pepper' are the terms at issue. (*Logica*, p. 209.1–22, trans. Kretzmann and Stump, *CTMPT*, p. 110.) For Bacon's analysis of the latter proposition see 266 and 267–268.

139 Augustine *De dialectica*. ed. Jan Pinborg, trans. B. Darrell Jackson, *Augustine: De dialectica*, Synthese Historical Library, vol. 16 (Dordrecht and Boston: D. Reidel, 1975), pp. 112–114. See also "*Ds*" 88.

[215] *Discrete* supposition occurs when a discrete term or a demonstrative pronoun functions as a subject, as in 'Socrates sits' or 'This man runs'.[140] This occurs in another way when a universal becomes the name of its individual either by an uncertain imposition, or by transposition, or by conjunction with a word, as happens in the case of the name 'relation', which is the name of a genus and species, as is clear in Book Two of Aristotle's *Physics*; and in this way a transfer occurs from one name to its singulars.[141] [2.425–426]

[216] *Common* supposition occurs when a common term stands for its inferiors.[142] This is of two sorts, the one determinate, the other confused.[143] [2.427–428]

140 See 231 where Bacon will take up the case where a proper name supposits for many individuals of the same name, e.g., for many people called Socrates.

141 Reading at *Sd* 1–2, p. 266, 426.2, '*per adiunctionem in dictione* –' against '*per adiunctionem*', in the text.

Aristotle *Physics* 2.2.194b8 and 3.1.200b28–32. Bacon is speaking here of equivocation as happens when a name, originally imposed for one thing, is transposed for another, or when a term like 'man' that is common becomes restricted or ampliated (broadened) by a qualifier as in, respectively, 'this man' and 'dead man'. This emphasizes the fact (212) that how a term is used in a proposition determines its supposition. Thus we see here a subtle hint of what will be stated clearly later in this work and the "*De signis*" of 1267, that all modes of supposition along with restriction and ampliation are at root the result of new impositions that then equivocate with the original ones. (See 264 and "*Ds*" 48–52.) The phrase 'by uncertain imposition' (*impositione incerta*) seems to be an early Baconian way of speaking about the act by which these equivocations come about: because universals are so bound up with their individuals, he says, to say 'man' and yet refer to Socrates is to equivocate without realizing it. Later Bacon will clearly distinguish between tacit (*apud mentem*) and vocally expressed imposition see "*Ds*" 50 and 154–161, and *Cst* 2.125.

142 In addition to the definitions of the names of the three modes of common supposition that follow see 430 for further comment.

143 Apropos of the ensuing three-fold distinction of common supposition Paul Spade points out that such is based on (1) the syntactical consideration of the position of the term in a sentence, and (2) the ability to descend to and ascend from singulars covered by the common term in question. With respect to (1), rules will be mentioned here and there by Bacon that indicate the kind of common supposition that is operative, and this is shown to depend on whether the term falls under the scope of a negation or of a particular or universal quantifier. With regard to (2), Spade says that the theory of ascent and descent depends on an account of inferential relations between a sentence and its singulars with respect to a term occurrence, and, since these were generally regarded as necessary, formal validity or invalidity of such inferences did not depend on contingent matter that happened to be realized, i.e., 'Socrates is a Greek; therefore every man is a Greek' was taken as formally invalid even were Socrates the only man who ever lived. Paul Spade, "The Logic of the Categorical," pp. 190–192.

[217] It is *determinate* when the proposition in which the common term is placed requires one singular for its truth, as in 'A man runs' (if Socrates runs), and this suffices for its truth.[144] [2.429]

[218] It is *confused* when the term stands for all its singulars and requires the truth of each of its singulars. This is of two sorts, the one confused and distributive, the other merely confused. [2.430–431]

[219] *Confused and distributive* (*mobile*) supposition occurs when an affirmative sign is joined to a common term directly and with identity in case and number, or, when a universal negative sign or the negation that negates precedes a common term either indirectly or directly. For example, in 'Every man runs' or 'The ass of no man runs' both 'man' and 'ass' stand confusedly and distributively.[145] Confused and distributive supposition occurs, therefore, when a common term supposits for all its inferiors and there can be a descent to any one of them, as in 'Every man runs; therefore this man runs, and that one, etc.'. [2.432–433]

[220] *Merely confused* supposition occurs when a common term supposits for all its inferiors, and there can be no descent to [just] any one of them. For example, in 'Any man's ass runs', 'ass' stands merely confusedly because one may not make a descent from it.[146] For it is commonly said that, when a term follows indirectly a universal affirmative sign, it supposits merely confusedly.[147] One should know, however, that a negation

144 Interestingly, while Bacon is clearly exemplifying determinate supposition in terms of ascent here, I find no other place where ascent is implied as a way of understanding this kind of supposition, and it is never mentioned explicitly. Descent is expressly mentioned in 219–220 and 264.

145 Supposition is called mobile when one can infer from the suppositing term to any of its inferiors, and immobile if one cannot. Thus 'Every man runs' is true only if every person is running, and 'No man runs' is true only if no individual person is running: the subject term in universal affirmative and negative propositions is distributed. If 'no man's ass is running', then no individual ass is running, assuming, of course, that every ass belongs to someone. For the notion of "a negation that negates" see 153.

146 We are told to read the subject term as having merely confused supposition, i.e., in such a way that one cannot descend from it to just any of its particulars. It would seem, then, that the example would have to be understood in some way analogous to what is said in 'Every human has some ass (or other) and each ass runs'. For the example in the text see 236–237, 425, and 432.

147 To follow indirectly means that there is at least one word between the noun in question and the sign. Thus the predicate term in a universal affirmative proposition would follow the universal sign indirectly and the subject term would follow it directly. The rule mentioned here by Bacon is the subject of some controversy. In a lengthy discussion Peter points out that it does not hold in cases where something essential is predicated of something, as in 'Every man is an animal'. The predicate

does not by itself confuse merely confusedly, but only confusedly and distributively.[148] So neither a negative universal sign nor a negation confuses merely confusedly. But a universal affirmative sign can indeed do this.[149] [2.434–437]

[221] There are those, however, who have doubts about what has been said (210). A term has discrete supposition when it supposits for something discrete and singular, but, when it stands for its own utterance or for what it signifies, it stands for a discrete and singular thing; therefore it will have discrete supposition then. But every discrete supposition is personal; therefore simple supposition will be personal. And this seems to be the case since 'person' is taken here for an individual and a singular thing. Therefore, personal supposition occurs in all such cases. [2.438–442]

[222] One can reply that personal supposition can be taken broadly or narrowly. If it is taken *broadly* and commonly it includes every supposition of a term on the basis of which a term supposits for any individual or singular thing, whether [the individual] is a singular of it or whether it is a singular of another [term], such as the latter's significatum or its own utterance, because it is the name of all of these and can supposit for each one. And in this sense personal supposition includes simple supposition under it. But if [personal supposition] is taken *narrowly*, it then includes only the supposition of a term on the basis of which a term supposits for its individuals or singulars. These are said to be "persons" with respect to its significatum and its utterance, which ["persons"] participate in [the sig-

---

has, he says, simple supposition. (*Tractatus* 6.6 and 9–12, and trans. Mullally, pp. 7 and 9–19.) (See 253 where Bacon will be seen to give a similar analysis of 'A man is an animal'.) Lambert, however, acknowledges no such exception, saying that 'animal' there has weak, immobile confused supposition (Bacon's merely confused supposition). (*Logica*, p. 211.6–11, trans. Kretzmann and Stump, *CTMPT*, p. 112.)

148 In 'No man runs' one is not blocked from validly disjoining the predicate from every person.

149 MS. S. adds at the end of this paragraph: "One should know, however, that a considerable difficulty is associated with merely confused supposition, which we are not resolving now because of an opinion that requires a distinction, which, however, [will be treated] in its proper place." (*Sd* 1–2, p. 267, n. 11.) It is perhaps helpful to keep in mind the following application to universal, particular, indefinite, and singular propositions of that part of supposition theory that pertains to subject and predicate terms with common supposition. The number in parenthesis indicates the kind of *common* supposition the preceding term has: (1) Determinate; (2) Confused and Distributive; (3) Merely Confused.

Every man (2) is an animal (3)	Every man (2) is not an animal (2)
Some man (1) is an animal (1)	Some man (1) is not an animal (2)
A man (1) is an animal (1)	A man (1) is not an animal (2)
Socrates is an animal (1)	Socrates is not an animal (2)

nificatum and the utterance].[150] In this [narrow] sense it does not supposit for what it signifies or for its own utterance, and so is distinguished from simple supposition, which occurs for the utterance itself and its signification. It is clear, therefore, that not every supposition of a term will be personal [in the narrow sense]. And so the supposition that occurs for what a term signifies or its own utterance will not be discrete in so far as discrete [supposition] is called personal [in the narrow sense], because discretion is taken in this [narrow] way with respect to what [a term] supposits, i.e., [its] individuals. There is, nevertheless, [this other] discretion because [supposition] occurs for something discrete, and in that sense, therefore, every supposition will be discrete and not personal [in the narrow sense].[151] [2.443–448]

[223] This can be stated another way since 'person' is taken here for an individual and something singular and an individual [can be taken] in two ways, strictly and broadly. *Strictly* speaking an individual is what is in no way common, as are individuals of the lowest species. *Broadly* and, so to speak, in a certain respect an individual is what is common absolutely speaking, but is individual with respect to something, as is the case with every universal. For example, 'man' is common absolutely because it signifies a form common to many, yet it is singular with respect to 'species', just as the thing signified by 'animal' is common to the latter's species, though singular with respect to 'genus'. Likewise, the thing signified by 'rational' is common to all men, and yet singular with respect to 'differentia'. And such is the case with 'proprium' and 'accident'. When, therefore, a common term supposits for what it signifies, it supposits absolutely for what is common, and broadly and in a certain respect for a singular. When, however, it supposits for its own supposita, it supposits absolutely for what is singular and individual. When, therefore, 'person' is taken here for an individual and a singular, it is clear that 'person' has two senses, and 'personal supposition' does likewise. For example, when supposition occurs absolutely and strictly for a person, this is called personal supposition in the narrow sense, but when supposition occurs broadly and in a certain respect for a person, this is called personal in the broad sense and, so to speak, such [supposition is] "personal" [only] in a certain respect. [Supposition] occurs in the second way when a common term stands for its own significatum, in which case it will not be called absolutely or strictly personal but simple, receiving denomination from the simple form for which

150 The final clause is ambiguous on several counts. Presumably one could say that individuals participate in the significata of their names (and, stretching it a bit, in the terms themselves), but it makes no sense to speak of the significatum of a term participating in the individual of that term. Thus the insertions as provided.

151 This paragraph needs considerable interpretation, as the brackets suggest.

it supposits, just as personal from the person for which it supposits. Or, it is said to be simple because it stands for what it signifies in the absolute sense, not as it picks out the things for which it supposits. [2.449–454]

[224] It is clear, therefore, that, when a common term supposits for what it signifies, as in 'Man is a species' and 'Man is the noblest of creatures', it has simple supposition. Likewise, it can indeed be taken and stand for what it signifies when it is interpreted for what it signifies, as in 'Man is an animal'; but in a different way for what it supposits. Nevertheless, if a singular term supposits for what it signifies, the supposition is not simple, because the significatum is in no way something common, but is absolutely individual, because the significatum is the same thing as the suppositum that corresponds to such a term. This [suppositum], however, is absolutely singular, and therefore the significatum is absolutely singular. And so the supposition will be absolutely personal. [2.455–456]

[225] Should anyone argue that, when one says 'Man is a species', here ['man'] stands for the concept of what is signified, and [does this] in its function as a proper and singular name with respect to the species, but [that] this is not the case with 'Man is an animal' and 'Man is the noblest of creatures', because there ['man'] does not stand for anything with respect to which it is proper, one should reply that this does not prevent it from suppositing in the same way and for the same thing. This is because,[152] if I say 'Socrates is an individual' or 'Socrates is an animal', the term supposits in both cases for the same thing and in the same way, since the thing signified by 'Socrates' is individual and it is an animal. This is what happens when looked at from this point of view. Hence, the thing signified by the name 'man' is a species and it is an animal, and so it always stands for the thing itself and not for a pure concept, but for the thing under a concept, which thing is individual with respect to the species, though common when looked at from a different point of view, namely, by comparison to its own individuals. But with respect to animal or to something higher it is neither an individual nor something common. But because it is common to its inferiors and is an individual of a species, it is subordinated to animal and the other higher things, just as 'Socrates' (which is individual in every way) is subordinated to animal.[153] [2.457]

152 MS. S. inserts here: "... perhaps it does not stand for a concept alone nor for a pure property, but rather for a property and a concept. And this is what I wanted to say earlier when I said that a term stands for a property of what is signified ... ." *Sd* 1–2, p. 270, n. 56.

153 The objection seems to be this: (1) 'Man' in 'Man is a species' stands for the concept of man, i.e., rational animality, and not for the nature itself; and (2) it also stands as a proper name for a single species; but (3) in 'Man is an animal' and 'Man is the noblest of creatures' it is not taken as the proper name of a species because the

[226] But what is to be said about these: '"Man" is an utterance', '"Man" is a name', and the like? Here one cannot distinguish a two-fold sort of individual, in the narrow and broad sense, because 'man' is absolutely a singular utterance and a singular name and is in no sense something common; and so it seems that it would always supposit for something discrete. Therefore, there will always be discrete and personal supposition. This must be conceded from this [broad] point of view, although the opposite might be able to be sustained in accord with the preceding [narrow point of view] (222, 223).[154] [2.458–461]

[227] If one asks about [expressions] like these: 'The Seine flows' and 'England is a good land', [or] what sort of supposition the term has in 'The Phoenix is', 'The sun is', and the like, one should reply that, since 'Seine' is the proper name of a river, it will have discrete supposition. But, if it is said that it agrees with many things because the water flowing at Paris is the Seine and the water flowing elsewhere is the Seine, therefore it is a common name, then some argue that such names are common and have individuals on the basis of different sites and different places.[155] According to them, terms of this sort will have determinate personal supposition, not discrete. But this is not true, because the name 'Seine' is imposed for all the water flowing from one end to the other, and it is not the name of some part by imposition.[156] And so the water flowing at Paris in one sense can be said truly to be the Seine, but not in another sense. If we speak of that signate part that flows there, it is not the Seine, but a part of the Seine, and so on. If, however, we say that the water flowing at Paris and elsewhere is the Seine, this is true. 'Seine' is not, therefore, common to many by appellation, but to one, just as one does not apply 'Socrates' to a foot or a hand. Nor does one take the parts of the Seine without the Seine, just as the hand of

---

predicates in these expressions are broader than their subjects: 'man' is not the proper name of a genus. Bacon's response is simply to note that in each of these cases, while the suppositum of the predicate may change, that of 'man' remains the same: it is a species, an animal, and the noblest of all creatures, and it is not a concept but an individual that comes under that concept. Note, however, that in the response he concedes that from another point of view 'man' is a common term and stands for individual people. When Bacon (in the last sentence) speaks of man as "an individual *of* a species," I suspect he means "an individual species," i.e., the name 'man' can be a common name of individual people and a proper name of one species of animals. See 223 for a similar problem in interpretation.

154 See 213, where 'man' in that context is said to have simple supposition, and 238, where a predicate term standing for an utterance is said to have discrete supposition with no allusion to a possibility of simple supposition.

155 For 'Phoenix' see 23 and 241–242.

156 In later years Bacon will return to this issue and present an analysis based on equivocal imposition. See "*Ds*" 41 and 47–52, and *Cst* 2.136.

Socrates without Socrates, so long as the hand is joined to him. Just as Socrates is not predicated of his parts, so neither is the Seine predicated of its parts.[157] [2.462–465]

[228] With respect to the other [claims] (227) one should reply, as is the case with other common terms, that these terms are universal, not because they are actually predicated of more than one existing thing, but because they are naturally suited to be predicated of more than one thing. They can stand for what is signified and so have simple supposition. But, if for an utterance, then they have discrete supposition;[158] if for an individual, determinate. [2.466]

[229] In connection with this one should know that there are two sorts of pointing-to (*demonstratio*).[159] One is *personal*, as when numerically the same thing is pointed to, as in 'this man', 'that man'. The other is a *simple pointing-to*, as when, in pointing to an individual, the concept of the species intervenes either nominatively or obliquely, as when one says: 'This plant grows in my garden', i.e., 'A plant of this species grows, etc.'.[160] Here there occurs a pointing-to with respect to the intellect, because species is an intelligible thing. If one asks what the quantity is, it can be said in one sense that it is indefinite, but in another sense singular, just as when one says '*Asinus Sortis currit*' (An/the ass of Socrates runs). If it is considered to have a subject of attribution (which is in the nominative case), then it is indefinite; but if it is considered to have a subject of locution (which is in an oblique case), then it is singular.[161] There is, however, doubt about this, but because it will be treated elsewhere in its proper place (425, 432), I offer no solution in this Part. [2.467–471]

[230] One should know, however, that something relative sometimes creates a simple relation, sometimes a personal one. Something relative is that which calls to mind something previously mentioned. For example, in 'A man runs and he debates', 'he' is a relative because it represents something already mentioned, namely, 'a man'. So, one sort is a relative of *identity*, e.g., 'that one', 'he', 'the same one', and 'who'; another sort is one of *diversity*, such as 'another', 'the other (of two)', and 'the one remaining'. One should know, therefore, that a relative sometimes refers to its ante-

157 The translation takes '*sibi*' to be improper grammar for '*ei*'. (*Sd* 1–2, p. 271, 465.6.)

158 MS. S. inserts here: "but differently, then, in accord with the two positions treated" (*diversimode tunc, secundum positiones duas tactas*). (*Sd* 1–2, p. 271, n. 91.) See 222 and/or 223–226.

159 With this paragraph begins Bacon's treatment of relative pronouns which he pursues through 230 (with a brief further comment in 237), though MSS. O. and S. show no major break.

160 For the notions of "directly and obliquely" (*recte et oblique*) see 126.

161 For the distinction between a subject of attribution and subject of locution see 143 and its note.

cedent on behalf of the same singular thing for which its antecedent stood, and then it has personal reference, as in 'The woman who damned has saved'. If this constitutes a *personal relation*, then 'who' is interpreted for Eve and refers 'woman' to Eve, because the antecedent already stood for her, and in this sense the expression is false. A *simple relation* occurs when a relative refers to its antecedent on behalf of the same species in this sense: 'Womankind who damned has saved', that is, 'A woman has damned and a woman has saved'.[162] Similarly, with respect to a relation of diversity, as here: '"H" is written among other letters'.[163] If the stated relative of diversity ['other'] refers for things numerically different, then [the above expression] is false, because then one indicates that 'h' differs from the others only numerically and not specifically, and then it would follow that 'h' would be a letter [among letters of the same species]. But should it refer for things different in genus and species, and not just numerically [different, the expression] is true in this sense: '"H" is written among letters that are other [kinds of things] than "h"' is. In the first sense the relation is personal, and in the second it is simple, as is commonly said. Similarly, one ought to be able to distinguish this: 'Socrates sits among other asses', and the like.[164] [2.472–481]

[231] Having treated difficulties pertaining to the difference between simple and personal supposition, now we must take a look at the various sorts of personal supposition.[165] [There are four claims]: (1) Since 'Socrates' and any name of an individual is common to many by appellation, its supposition will, therefore, be common to many. Since the supposition of such a term is discrete, discrete will be common.[166] (2) Since what

162 See 386, at the end.

163 In the discussion of the supposition of this letter of the alphabet the fact that capital ('H') and lower case ('h') are used is of no significance for the problem. The issue is this: does the expression in question assume that every letter is an 'h' and hence mean that 'h' is merely one of a kind (personal supposition), or is 'h' taken as different in species from other letters of the alphabet (simple supposition)? Or, to put it another way, are all letters of the alphabet substantially different or different merely *per accidens*?

164 If the supposition of 'other' is personal, then the expression assumes that Socrates is of the same species as the asses and implies he is one among many asses, and the expression is false; if, however, 'other' has simple supposition, then the expression makes no such assumption and means that Socrates, an individual of one species of animals, sits among individuals of a different species, in which latter case the supposition of 'other' is simple, and the expression is true.

165 Paragraph 231 resumes the treatment of supposition. For the definitions of these types see 214, 215, 216, 217, 218, 219, and 220.

166 Discrete supposition picks out only one individual whereas common supposition designates more than one. Here Bacon raises the question of the proper classification of the supposition of a proper name which is had by more than one person. For his response see 232.

is determinate and what is discrete are the same, or share more, or have more in common than what is determinate and what is common (since the latter are, as it were, opposites), determinate supposition will more be discrete than it will be common. (3) Since a common term without a sign is more likely to bring about indefinite supposition or an indefinite proposition than a determinate one (since what is indefinite and what is indeterminate are the same), its supposition will be indeterminate. But indeterminate and confused supposition are the same; therefore it will not have determinate supposition.[167] (4) Since there is personal supposition that is said to be determinate because it stands for a determinate person and therefore for a determinate individual – such is nothing but a singular significatum and a unique thing –, it will stand for a unique, singular significatum. But to stand for a unique, singular significatum is to supposit discretely; therefore determinate supposition will be discrete.[168] [2.482–496a]

[232] One should reply to these claims that an individual name is something proper. Under one concept or signification it is not common to many, but applies to one thing alone. So, when mention is made of its supposition, it is interpreted as signifying one thing and not more than one, and, since that is discrete and singular, it will have discrete supposition.[169] When, however, it is said that it applies to more than one by appellation, this is to be understood equivocally and under different significations. Thus it does not follow that it is common, because to apply to more than one, as a common name does, is to apply to more than one univocally and under one signification.[170] [What is to be said] about equivocal supposition will become clear later (424–432). [2.496b–498]

[233] To the second [one should reply] that two conditions are required for determinate supposition, namely, that the suppositing term be common and that it stand for some individuals under a disjunction of one thing in reference to another in such a way that for its truth it requires verification in only one singular. Its determination, therefore, consists in this

167 The objection turns on the proper understanding of 'determinate' in 'determinate supposition', as will be seen in 233 and 235.

168 The paragraph enumeration in the Latin text skips from 485 to 496 and 498 is repeated. To remedy the latter I have added 'a' and 'b' to 498.

169 'John' is a name common to many men, but when it is used in an expression and has personal supposition, it will stand, says Bacon, for only one of these persons. Hence it will not have common, but discrete supposition.

170 Common supposition requires a (common) term that is predicated univocally of many, as 'man' of every person. When one proper name is used for many persons in a way that seems universal with regard to that group, such names are not universal for the simple reason that, implies Bacon, the intent of the namers was in no way thereby to join the entities signified into one univocal concept, which would make the name a univocal term.

that one singular alone suffices for it, although it have more than one. But it does not stand for that determinate thing or for that significatum, but rather for this one or that one; hence it stands for a vague individual (*pro personali vago*).[171] Determinate supposition, therefore, involves something common both on the part of what is supposited and on the part of the thing [signified] for which the supposition occurs, namely, because it can stand for this or that significatum, and in this sense it is said to be common. Determinate supposition, however, does not have discretion in the sense in which supposition is said to be discrete, because in the latter case discretion is taken both with respect to the supposition and with respect to that for which the supposition occurs, both of which are absolutely determinate and discrete. [2.499–501]

[234] Because of this the response to the last objection is clear: it is said to be determinate because it supposits for individuals taken disjunctively in such a way that the discretion of one singular suffices for its truth, and not because it supposits precisely and discretely or absolutely for one significatum and one discrete thing. [2.502]

[235] To the remaining [third] objection [one should reply] that a term can well cause a proposition to be indefinite and indeterminate even though it supposits determinately, because this indetermination equivocates here and there. For the indetermination or indefiniteness of a proposition is so-called because the subject can indifferently receive any quantity of determination on itself, either a particular sign, or a universal one, or a demonstrative pronoun. But a term is said to supposit determinately not for this reason but for the previously mentioned one (233–234). Therefore, it is not necessary for a term in an indefinite proposition to stand indeterminately.[172] [2.503]

[236] There are doubts about confused supposition. It has been said that a term that has been directly adjoined is confused confusedly and distributively (219), so, if one says 'Any sort of man runs', 'man' confuses confusedly and distributively. Therefore 'Any sort of man runs, therefore Virgil' follows, which is false, given that there be four men and any one of the three has one quality and runs, and the one [remaining] has every quality and does not run. [2.504–505]

[237] One should reply that 'man' is not directly adjoined according to the understanding of the expression, because 'any sort of' conveys by its

171 Reading at *Sd* 1–2, p. 274, 499.6, '*Non tamen stat pro illo determinato vel*' with MSS. O. and S. against '*Non tamen stat*' in the text.

172 Basically, Bacon's response here is to point out that what makes a term indefinite is its lack of quantification whereas what makes a term to have determinate supposition is not through quantification, but by use in an expression such that the latter can become true by verification of at least one of the term's inferiors.

concept a distribution and the matter of a distribution, i.e., a subject, for what has been said is the same as 'A man of any quality runs'. [The term 'any sort of'] does not distribute the term 'man' for its appellatives, but distributes its qualities.[173] So, one should understand that, if a term is added directly to a sign with identity in case and number, in such a way that it is a subject and the matter of distribution, it is confused confusedly and distributively. Then all the cavils that can be raised are excluded. For if one says 'Both of these run', it is clear from what has been said that 'of these' should not be confused, since it is not the matter and subject of distribution, nor is it added with identity in case and number to the sign. Rather what is understood there is the subject, namely, a name common to those that are denominated by the demonstrative pronoun. With respect to the supposition of a relative pronoun one should know that (as is commonly said), if it refers to the antecedent with the latter's distribution, then it stands confusedly and distributively.[174] If it refers without distribution, then it stands determinately. [2.506–510]

[238] From what has already been said (212) it seems that supposition is only of a subject, since only a subject presents what functions as the subject of a verb.[175] This is to be conceded, strictly speaking. For just as

173 Paragraphs 236–237 must be understood in the following way: 'any sort of' (*qualislibet*) should (219) distribute 'man' so that one thinks of each and every person. But, says Bacon, 'sort' bespeaks qualities of persons, not the individuals themselves, i.e., not the appellatives of 'man'. So, to say 'Any sort of man runs' is to mean a man of any qualilty runs. With this understanding 'man' is not distributed for all people (since it only has determinate supposition) but for the qualities people possess. The inference from 'A man of any quality runs' to 'Virgil runs' is readily seen then to be invalid because of the change in supposition (and supposita) in the subjects of the two propositions: in the antecedent the subject supposits determinately whereas in the consequent discretely. Paul Spade (in a personal communication) suggests that what is unstated in the example and must be assumed is that the three other than Virgil each have (in addition to running) only one other quality and that quality is different for each of the three.

174 For the earlier treatment of relative pronouns see 230. Since the kind of supposition a pronoun has is totally determined by the supposition of the term to which it refers, the translation understands '*sui*' to be poor grammar for '*eius*'.

175 There is controversy over this claim. William acknowledges this claim (*Introductiones*, trans. Kretzmann, pp. 122–123) but throughout gives examples of the supposition of substantive terms in the predicate position (e.g., ibid., p. 108), and Peter gives no evidence he has any problems with predicate supposition. (See, e.g., *Tractatus* 6.6, and trans. Mullally, p. 7.) Lambert, also, does not address the issue directly, but treats of predicate supposition when discussing the status of predicates in universal affirmative and negative propositions. (*Logica*, p. 210.26–30, trans. Kretzmann and Stump, *CTMPT*, p. 112.) L. M. de Rijk has emphasized the fact that supposition theory has clear roots in grammatical theory where subjects sup-

supposition is a property of what is supposited and what is a subject, so apposition is a property of what is predicated and of what is apposed. But because one is to speak with the majority yet think with the minority, let us accede to the customary terminology and extend the name 'supposition' to a property of a predicate.[176] For a predicate is taken either with a sign or without a sign. If with a universal sign, it stands confusedly and distributively. If without a sign, it is either a discrete term, and then it has discrete supposition whether it stands for an utterance or for a signification or for a suppositum,[177] because each of them is discrete and singular absolutely, or, it is a common term, and then it stands either for a signified form, and then it has simple supposition, or for a suppositum, and then it has determinate supposition, or for the utterance itself, and then it has discrete [personal supposition in the broad sense of 'personal supposition'], as has already been said (222 and 226).[178] But, it is commonly argued that, when

---

posit and predicates appose, and what we see here with Bacon is simply an example of one who is not happy with this new departure from grammatical custom. See de Rijk, "The Origins of the Theory of the Property of Terms," *CHLMP*, pp. 161–173, passim.

176 MS. S. adds at the end: "so that 'supposition' be taken with the majority. Then, a standing for, or for a word to stand for, some significatum are the same, and thus both the subject and the predicate supposit. If one [speaks] properly, [however], then only the subject has [supposition]. Consequently, the predicate 'supposits', i.e., stands for or is taken for something which is said about a subject." (*Sd* 1–2, p. 275, n. 68.) Apropos of this issue Paul Spade notes that his study of the theory of supposition in Walter Burley, John Buridan, and William of Ockham (all early fourteenth-century) reveals that, while all three profess that supposition properly speaking is only of subject and predicate terms, in practice all common terms in a sentence are treated as having supposition. ("The Logic of the Categorical," p. 195.) This practice seems also to be adopted by Bacon without explicit acknowledgment when in 237 talk about the distribution of 'quality' surfaced in analyzing 'A man of any quality runs'. But then this raises a question as to whether or not it makes a difference whether one descends (ascends) first from the subject term or first from the predicate term. Alexander Broadie shows that it does and presents the following rule: descend first from determinate supposition, then from confused and distributive, and finally from merely confused supposition. (Broadie, *Introduction to Medieval Logic*, pp. 41–42.)

177 To distinguish between a suppositum on the one hand and an utterance or signification (species, form) on the other is to restrict the meaning of 'suppositum' used throughout this treatment of supposition. In 212–213 species and utterances as sounds are said to be simple supposita.

178 Earlier (226) Bacon was willing to grant that 'man' in '"Man" is an utterance' has discrete supposition (in the broad sense of 'personal supposition'), though he added that the opposite might also be able to be held, i.e., that it has simple supposition, as stated in his original claim in 213.

a universal sign is placed in the subject position, the term in the predicate position stands merely confusedly, as in 'Every man is an animal'.[179] When two signs are placed in an expression, one in the subject position, the other in the predicate position, it is said that the first immobilizes the second, as in 'Every man is every man'.[180] This, however, I think is false, but let the resolution of these things be left for disputation.[181] Now that supposition has been treated we must discuss appellation. [2.511–520]

Appellation[182]

[239] It is said that appellation is the signification of a predicable term apart from time.[183] This is false because appellation is spoken of with ref-

179 The predicate term supposits confusedly and immobily because, though the supposita of 'animal' are any animals, the expression cannot be true of just any animal: one cannot infer from the expression in question 'This man is this animal'. But Alexander Broadie claims that one can descend from the predicate term in a universal affirmative categorical proposition to a disjunctive predicate and ascend from one of the singulars. See Broadie, *Introduction to Medieval Logic*, pp. 39–40.

180 Presumably the argument would be the same as the one just given in the preceding note: if 'man' in both positions is taken distributively and mobily, then one could validly infer 'Socrates is Plato'.

181 Although the text is ambiguous since the referent of 'this' is unclear, I suspect Bacon accepts the former claim as true and wishes to challenge only the latter one. Peter considers the expression to be a sophism and false, and says its "proof" is guilty of the fallacy of Consequent due to an insufficient enumeration of particulars: it fails to recognize that, were the proposition true, one could validly infer these: 'Plato is every man' and 'Every man is Plato', which are both false. (*Tractatus* 12.13, and trans. Mullally, p. 79.)

182 Appellation differs from supposition in that only terms naming things currently existing, i.e., at the time of utterance, have appellation as a property, and the term must be truly predicated. For later treatments of appellation by Bacon see "*Ds*" 134–164 and *Cst* 2.85–128. Throughout the discussion of appellation Bacon will use the terms '*praesentia*', '*praesentes*', '*praeteriti*', and '*futuri*' (or their declined forms) to name what it is that terms appellate. The first clearly indicates present *things*; the third and fourth clearly indicate, respectively, past and future (male) *persons*; and the second is ambiguous: it could be short for '*praesentes res*' (present things) or for '*presentes homines*' (present persons), more probably the latter. The translation will provide 'persons' when the third or fourth terms are used and 'things' when the first is used. The second will be rendered by either as the context suggests. Although Bacon's use of Latin requires this attention by a translator, the use of 'things' or the more narrow 'persons' signals no nuance in the theory of appellation itself. Hence, 'things' can be substituted for 'persons' with no danger of misunderstanding the theory.

183 While Bacon will consider most arguments against his position to be foolish, he says in 1292 that he considers the one based on this definition to be "reasonable," though no such qualification is made in the "*De signis*" of 1267. See "*Ds*" 139 and

erence to the appellata to which it relates. Since, therefore, a subject term and a predicate term are equally related to appellata, a subject will have appellation as well as a predicate does. Since every appellation involves significations, every appellation will be personal. [184] Moreover, just as personal supposition is divided, so appellation can be divided, because some is discrete and the other is common, etc. The same examples serve [for terms] in the subject position as well as in the predicate position. [2.521–525]

[240] Yet there are two opinions on appellations because some argue that a term by itself appellates present, past, and future appellata and is common to entities and nonentities.[185] Others contend that a term is the name only of present things, and that there is nothing common to an entity and a nonentity (i.e., something past, present, and future), in accord with what Aristotle says in Book One of the *Metaphysics*.[186] Because the first opinion is common, let us investigate it first. [2.526–528]

Cst 2.105. William defines appellation as "the present correct application (*praesens convenientia*) of a term – i.e., the property with respect to which what the term signifies can be [truly] said of something through the use of the verb 'is'." Peter defines it as "the acceptance of a common term for an existing thing," but then a little later speaks of the appellata of singular terms. Lambert presents four meanings of the term and accepts the fourth for his discussion here: "... appellation is the acceptance of a term for a suppositum or for supposita actually existing," and then later specifies that only common terms can appellate. For Lambert, appellation is a species of supposition, i.e., supposition for existing things. Respectively, *Introductiones*, trans. Kretzmann, p. 106; *Tractatus* 10.1 and 2, and trans. Mullally, p. 45 (note that Mullally's Latin text and translation omit the word 'common'); and *Logica*, ed. de Libera, "*Le traité*," pp. 251.4–252.11 and p. 255.18, trans. Kretzmann and Stump, *CTMPT*, pp. 113–114 and 115. For the notion of a noun see 122.

184 William and Lambert agree that all appellation is personal. Peter, however, speaks of simple appellation, that which 'man' has in 'Man is a species'. (*Tractatus* 10.3.) Bacon will later say that, while antonomastic supposition and appellation are always personal, metonymic can be simple *per accidens*, though the expression in question is also then said to be false. (See 266–268.) He will also say in his "*De signis*": "A word (*dictio*) does not supposit for something in speech unless it signify it and unless it be imposed for it," which is to say that supposition presupposes imposition and signification. See "*Ds*" 50.

185 For a discussion of Bacon's role in this controversy see de Libera, *Sd* 1–2, pp. 163–165. The definitions of 'appellation' given by William, Peter, and Lambert indicate that they are not to be thought of in the camp described by Bacon in this paragraph. (See n. 183.) For later treatments by Bacon see "*Ds*" 134–135 and *Cst* 2.88.

186 Aristotle *Metaphysics* 1.9.992b12–15, trans. Nova, in *Aristotelis opera cum Averrois commentariis*, vol. 8: Averroes *In Aristotelis Metaphysicam*, fol. 25vG; and Averroes, ibid., 1: commentary 46, fol. 25vK–L. Bacon defends the second opinion

[241] A term not restricted to nonpresent persons, functioning as the subject of a present-tense verb having no ampliating force and in an affirmative proposition, supposits only for present persons, as in 'A man is' and 'Caesar is'.[187] I say "not restricted to nonpresent persons" because were it restricted, it would not supposit for only those present, as in 'A man who has been is' or '[A man] who will be is'. A term not restricted to present or future persons, functioning as the subject of a past-tense verb, can supposit indifferently for past and present persons, as in 'A man was'. If, however, 'A man who is (or who will be) was' is proffered, it would be restricted to present or future persons. A term not restricted to present or past things, functioning as the subject of a future-tense verb, stands for present and future things, as in 'A man will be'. A term not restricted to present, past, or future things, functioning as the subject of a verb having an ampliating force, stands for those things that are as well as for those that are not. For example, if one ampliates to future things, it stands for present and future things; if to things in the past, it stands for present and past things. An example of the first is 'That a man is is contingent' and 'A man can be'; an example of the second is 'A man usually is'. They say in this opinion (240) that a term, functioning as the subject of a future-tense verb having an ampliating force, stands for present persons and for nonexistent persons

---

here, and will continue to support it in the "*De signis*" of his *Opus maius* around 1267 (136–144) and finally at the end of his life (1292) in his *Compendium of the Study of Theology* (2.85–111). In the latter he names one of his principal opponents on this issue from the 1250s, Richard of Cornwall. (*Cst* 2.86.) Here in 240 Bacon appeals to Book One of the *Metaphysics* whereas later ("*Ds*" 135 and *Cst* 2.88) reference is to Book Two. Alain de Libera claims that Bacon's reference is to 992b12–15 and explains the discrepancy with respect to chapter as rooted in the division of Book One into two books in a subsequent translation of the *Metaphysics*. For this see *Sd* 1–2. p. 165. In 241 Bacon will declare his position (with a modesty uncharacteristic of his later life) to be (only) "sufficiently probable."

187 An ampliating force is the broadening effect one term has on another and is the opposite of a restriction. Thus 'every' when joined to 'man' ampliates the latter, whereas 'white' joined to the same restricts it. Here the emphasis is on the ampliating force of verbs as a result of their tenses. 'Existed' in 'Caesar existed' broadens the temporal frame of the subject to include the past, whereas 'will exist' in 'My child will exist' broadens to the future. (Bacon will add in this paragraph that he is speaking of an unrestricted common term having sufficient appellata.) For comment on the sources of the claims in this paragraph see de Libera, "*Le traité*," p. 242. For Bacon's treatment of ampliation and restriction in the "*De signis*" see "*Ds*" 89–99; they are simply mentioned in *Compendium of the Study of Theology*. (See *Cst* 2.85.) For additional brief remarks on the significance of the use of the notions of ampliation and restriction see de Libera, "The Oxford and Paris Traditions in Logic," *CHLMP*, pp. 174–187.

because the present is understood in such verbs, and so they can restrict a term to present persons. Terms, moreover, in virtue of their own proper nature, namely, by reason of their condition of being past and future or by reason of ampliation, can stand for nonexistent persons.Then again they argue that the first rule is to be understood with respect to a term having enough appellata, and not with respect to others, of which 'Phoenix', 'sun', and 'world' are [examples].[188] For if I say 'Every Phoenix is', 'Every sun is', or 'Every world is', [each subject term] stands for present, past, and future things. [2.529–538]

[242] But, since either a sufficiency or an insufficiency of appellata in no way affects the supposition of a term, one should reply that, whether the term has enough or not, it supposits for a present person when it is adjoined to a present-tense verb, but it is not restricted to nonpresent persons. Hence, these are incongruous: 'Every Phoenix is', 'Every sun is', and the like, because the sign requires three supposita, yet each term has only one. Nor is it improper for a sign to be joined to a subject term that is naturally common, that is, for it to be conformed to [a term] in gender, case, and number.[189] But because of the special nature of such an adjunct – which is the nature of an individual bearing a relation to more than two single things because the sign 'every' requires three appellata, and in such a substantive there is only one – [the "expressions"] are neither true, nor false, nor propositions, nor do they have contradictories. [2.539–541]

[243] A term in the predicate position stands according to the requirement of the verb. For example, if the verb is in the present tense, the term stands for present things, as in 'Socrates is a man'; if it is in the future tense, it stands for future things, as in 'Socrates will be a man'; if in the past tense, it stands for past things, as in 'Socrates was a man'. If the verb is one that ampliates, [the term in the predicate position] stands for that to which [the verb] ampliates: if it ampliates to past things, it stands for past things; if to future things, it stands for future things. [2.542–543]

188 In 242 Bacon will note that for a common term ampliated by 'every' to have sufficient appellata it must stand for a minimum of three things. For the reason for "three" see William and Peter; Lambert rejects this requirement. The quantitative sign 'both' would be used for a distribution for two. Respectively, *Introductiones*, trans. Kretzmann, pp. 124–126; *Tractatus* 12.7, and trans. Mullally, pp. 67–69; and *Logica*, ed. de Libera, "*Le traité*," p. 260.6–7, trans. Kretzmann and Stump, *CTMPT*, p. 118.

189 Reading at *Sd* 1–2, p. 278, 541.1, '*adiunctum*' against '*adiuncti*' in MSS. O. and S. and text. 'Man', as such, is a common term and can stand for a male or a female (gender), can be used as a grammatical subject, object, etc. (case), and can indicate one or many persons (number). Signs affixed to such terms play a role, especially in Latin, in indicating the gender, case, and number, of the terms they modify, especially where the common term turns out to be ambiguous on the point.

[244] When, however, Aristotle says in Book One of the *Metaphysics* that nothing is common – nor is there a disposition common – to what was and to what will be and to what already has the force of being, i.e., to something present, it seems that a common term will not be common to present, past, and future appellata.[190] If it is common in some sense, it will be common in the sense that 'man' is common to a dead man and a living man, for what is past is dead and so a dead man will be a man only in a certain respect and not absolutely.[191] For the same reason a future man will be [a man only] in a certain respect. Wherefore, what is common there will be of that sort according to which something is common to one thing absolutely and to another in a certain respect, just as white [is said] of [the color] white absolutely and of the white in a foot [only in a certain respect]. Because of this [a common term] will be common to an entity and a nonentity so long as it presents itself in the form of a privation.[192] For it is of course true that something presenting itself in the form of a privation can be common to an entity and a nonentity, e.g., 'nonman'. Therefore, 'man', since it is the opposite of that and something presenting itself in a positive way, will be a name only of entities. [2.544–548]

[245] Also, an entity is understood along with every name, as is clear, whether it signifies a substance or an accident, because each of these is an entity. 'Man', therefore, will be the same as 'man-the-entity'; therefore, since 'man-the-entity' is not common to an entity and a nonentity, neither likewise will 'man' be. [2.549–550]

[246] If one objects that there the noun 'entity' is understood, not the participle 'being', and [that] the noun 'entity' can be common to an entity and a nonentity [...].[193] On the other hand the noun 'entity' is the proper

190 Aristotle *Metaphysics* 1.9.992b12–15, trans. Nova, *Aristotelis opera cum Averrois commentariis*, vol. 8: Averroes *In Aristotelis Metaphysicam*, fol. 25vG. See 238, "*Ds*" 135, and *Cst* 2.88.

191 The appeal to the distinction "in a certain respect and absolutely" in this context will also be seen in "*Ds*" 140, and *Cst* 2.98 and 110.

192 Later Bacon will speak of privative, infinite, and negative terms and give examples, respectively, of 'unjust', 'nonjust (not-just)', and 'not just'. (See below, 261.) In the next paragraph 'nonman' seems to be taken as a privative term in a broad sense, i.e., in the sense that any term with the prefix 'non' can be said to deprive the class named by the term to which it is attached of its ordinary meaning. Apropos of this Aristotle presents four kinds of privation and then continues: "There are just as many kinds of privations as there are of words with negative prefixes ..." (*Metaphysics* 5.22.1022b23–33, trans. W. D. Ross, in *CWA*, vol. 2, p. 1615). What is common to all the definitions is that one is speaking of something that in some sense ought to be present and is not, as indicated in the terms 'unjust' and 'blind'. For a later treatment see *Cst* 2.106.

193 For a similar discussion see *Cst* 2.102.

subject of the being of what is signified by the verb 'is', from which it takes its origin, and not the participle 'being', since a participle specifying composition or being itself is always co-understood with a verb. Therefore, since being is neither the operation nor the action of anything but an entity in act, it must be the case that the noun 'entity' signifies only something actual. [2.551–552]

[247] This same thing is seen in the nature of ampliation, since every term supposits the ampliation of the supposition of that term. But, should the term be common to something present, past, and future, its supposition can in no way be ampliated; therefore, it will not thus be common.[194] Therefore, it will only be a name of present things, which should be conceded. [2.553–555]

[248] One should reply, therefore, that a term is only a name of present or existing things – what I call a noun by signification.[195] Hence, it should be noted that, just as in grammar there is a word that is a noun by signification and an adverb by construction or some other part [of speech], and likewise [just as] one word is a participle by signification and another part [of speech] (like a noun) by construction, so with respect to the other parts of speech, just as here one word is a noun by signification and a noun by construction. But in so far as a word is taken as a noun by signification it is a name only of present and existing things. But in so far as it is a noun by construction and a noun by constitution it can be a name of nonexisting things and supposit for nonexisting things, namely, when it is construed with something that has the nature of nonexistence, namely, of the past or future, because a term in and of itself only distinguishes present things and by its nature supposits for them. It will, however, be able to stand for past and future things in virtue of the nature of a past-tense or future-tense verb, or one having their nature, like verbs that ampliate.[196] [2.556–559]

194 The argument in 247 seems to be this: if common terms by themselves were common to entities and nonentities, they would already be ampliated and hence could not be further ampliated in virtue of a change in supposition as a result of an adjoined term or a past- or future-tense verb.

195 A noun by signification is simply a noun, but a noun by construction (see immediately below in this paragraph) is a noun used as some other part of speech: e.g., 'being' in 'John is a being' and 'John, being here, was happy'. What was a noun by signification in the first expression has become a participle by construction in the second. The distinction assumes a theory of original imposition whereby terms are given significations and presumably their grammatical classifications. By the writing of the "*De signis*" and *Compendium of the Study of Theology* this terminology seems to have been abandoned by Bacon.

196 Reading at *Sd* 1–2, p. 280, 559.6, '*poterit*' against '*poterunt*' in MSS. O. and S. and the text.

[249] From these things it is clear that a present-tense verb does not affect the supposition of a term in the subject position, since it cannot make a term stand for anything except present things, and a term has it by its very nature that it so stand. But because it does not have it by itself that it stand for past and future things, a past-tense or future-tense verb having the force of ampliation will be able to make it stand for things other than present ones. [2.560–561]

[250] From these things it is clear that a predicate in no way contracts a subject or restricts it, but only ampliates its supposition whether by reason of its own signification, as in 'usually is', 'can', 'is contingent', and the like, or by reason of its consignification, namely, of time, as in the case of a past-tense or future-tense verb. Ampliation is in such predicates determinately, as heat is in fire; therefore, its opposite, which is restriction, cannot be in it. A predicate, moreover, cannot contract its subject either to [its own] supposita or to [its own] mode of supposition, because the placement of what contracts to what is contracted is direct, and they collapse into one with respect to supposition and thing [signified].[197] But this is not the case with respect to a predicate and subject absolutely. [2.562–565]

197 Bacon wants to distinguish the case where, e.g., the adjective 'tall' when directly joined to the noun 'person' (as in 'tall person') does indeed contract (restrict) the reference of 'person' to only tall ones from the case where the qualifying term is separated from the noun by, e.g., the copula, as in 'Some person is tall'. In the latter, 'person' (independently of 'some') stands for all persons, not just tall ones. In so far as the sentence is true it is not, says Bacon, because the predicate contracted the reference of the subject in some way. Where the qualifying term adjoins the noun directly, contraction of the noun occurs and this affects the supposita of the noun, or as Bacon puts it, "[the adjective and noun] collapse into one with respect to supposition and thing [signified]." Bacon's analysis here likens restriction (not ampliation!) to a physical force, which cannot operate at a distance, and de Libera calls attention to the fact that such a notion is mentioned in Nicholas of Paris' *Syncategoremata*: a subject term cannot be restricted by the tense of the predicate "because restriction is an action and every action involves contact, as Aristotle says in *On Generation*. Therefore things that do not touch each other cannot act on one another and be acted upon. But the predicate does not touch the subject nor adhere to it directly because an intermediate composition always intervenes. Therefore what is in the predicate does not act on the subject." (See H. A. G. Braakhuis, *De 13de Eeuwse Tractaten over Syncategorematische Termen*, vol. 2 (Meppel: Krips Repro, 1979), p. 31.1–8; Aristotle *On Generation and Corruption* 1.6.322b5; and de Libera, "*Le traité*," p. 245, n. 56). De Libera (p. 246) also says that Bacon is the only person to hold this contact theory of restriction.

[251] Yet against this there is that which is commonly said: 'Subjects are of such sorts as their predicates allow'.[198] If "of such sorts" is explicated to mean contraction, then this is absolutely a lie; but we are not to concern ourselves with how it is to be explicated. If one claims, however, that Boethius spoke those words, one should reply that that is false. [2.566–568]

[252] Boethius says in his book *On the Trinity* that "predicates are of such sorts as their subjects allow."[199] As told by Valerianus, Metellus asserts this: "It is logical: predicates are of such sorts as their subjects allow."[200] Nevertheless, there is no contraction of a predicate by the subject, as is clear; therefore, no such contraction should be inferred.[201] But because many understand that proposition falsely, Boethius' understanding must be looked at. He says that, if one says 'God is just', the justice that is an accident is not predicated but rather that which is more a substance, though not the sort of substance that is contained in the category Substance, but that which is above every category. But should I say, 'A man is just', the justice predicated is a quality and an accident, and the same for all such.[202] Therefore, in this sense one may argue that the ambiguity and equivocation of a predicate is determined by its subject.[203] So, if one says 'A sea creature is a dog', the equivocation in the term 'dog' would be determined in such a way that it would stand for a sea creature only.

198 Contrast this with the opening quotation in 252. William employs this adage even though he acknowledges that Boethius says the opposite. Peter rejects this claim and contends that predicates restrict their subjects only with respect to the latter's consignification, not their principal signification. Thus in 'A Citizen is white' (*Civis est albus*) the subject is restricted to males but not to white things. Respectively, *Introductiones*, trans. Kretzmann, p. 113, and *Tractatus* 11.7.

199 Boethius *De trinitate*, trans. Stewart and Rand, p. 16.4–5: "These [categories] therefore are of such sorts as their subjects will allow." See also *Introductio ad sillogismos categoricos* where Boethius maintains that in 'Socrates is wise' the predicate term supposits an individual, since the subject is singular. (PL 64.768, as noted by Kretzmann, *Introductiones*, p. 113, n. 36.) How subjects do the "allowing" mentioned here Bacon does not say here, but see below where he says not by contraction (252) and not by a resolution (*determinatio*) by the subject (253), but by having their verbs agree with them (253).

200 In point of fact the exact opposite is said: "For it is logical, subjects are of such sorts as their predicates will allow" (*Logicum est enim, talia erunt subiecta. qualia permiserint praedicata*). Pseudo-Hieronymus *Epistulae* 36, n. 21, PL 30. 259A.

201 While Bacon wants to align himself with Boethius' claim that subjects dictate the supposition of their predicates, here he wants it understood that he is not saying such effects are properly called contractions.

202 For a later treatment see "*Ds*" 99.

203 This is not to be taken as Bacon's explanation of Boethius' statement (252) that subjects do the allowing; see 253.

This is false, for it can stand (truly or falsely) for any of its significata. It would then follow that there would be no distinction or ambiguity [in that term], which is against Aristotle. [2.569–575]

[253] One should reply that an equivocation in the predicate term is not resolved on behalf of the subject that receives only the one significatum.[204] But for a proposition to be true it is necessary that [the predicate] be taken for that significatum which is truly applicable, and so claims Boethius.[205] In order for 'God is just' to be spoken truthfully, the predicate 'just' cannot join an accident, but a substance. Consequently, [the rule] that "predicates are of such sorts as their subjects allow" should be understood to mean that for a proposition to be true the predicate should stand for that thing and significatum which would apply to and be in the subject.[206] But because our understanding is imbued with fantasy and deception, so we equally conceive within our understanding what is false as well as true, and we express these through an utterance. Hence, an utterance, just like an expression, can sometimes equally signify what is false as well as what is

204 I take the meaning of this to be that, when a predicate term is equivocal, it is *not* the subject that determines which of the predicate's significata is to be understood. (In 252 Bacon rejects a contraction *per subiectum* and a resolution *per subiectum*; here a resolution *propter subiectum*. Left unstated is just what does determine the supposition.) So, up to this point Bacon has told us that (some) predicates can ampliate the supposita of their subjects (249); that predicates never restrict their subjects (250); that, if the common adage "Subjects are of such sorts as their predicates may have allowed" is taken to imply restriction by the predicate, it is a lie (251); that Boethius says subjects do the allowing (252), but that one is not to infer that he meant that subjects restrict predicates, because they do not (252); and that, while Boethius may seem to imply in what he has to say about the equivocal predication of justice said of God and man (252) that subjects resolve any such ambiguity in their predicates (252), they do not (253). Bacon's resolution of the issue is given in what follows.

205 Here is the key element in Bacon's resolution of the issue of how subjects "affect" their predicates: predicates must *agree* with their subjects.

206 Here we have Bacon's solution to the problem, and it seems to be this: when we are confronted with an equivocal predicate, what dictates which of its significata it will stand for is not some kind of syntactical function exercised by the subject over the predicate, but rather what can be truthfully said of the subject in that particular utterance. It is *we* who select among the various meanings of the equivocal predicates and apply the one that enables the sentence to be true. This seems to hint at what will be stated much more clearly and directly later, in the "*De signis*." There Bacon's response draws on the notion of (equivocal) reimposition and says that in 'God is just' (and the like) the subject presents an occasion for transferring the name 'just', which by first imposition names human justice, to divine justice, with the result that the subject and predicate are then in agreement. See "*Ds*" 99.

true.[207] So [an utterance] does not necessarily have to express the truth, but can equally signify what is false. Therefore, 'God is just' in one sense is true, [i.e.], when it joins a substance, but in another sense false, [i.e.], when it joins an accident, and the same applies to all others. But when there is no equivocation in a predicate the term stands for its significatum, whether it is a genus or species. For example, in 'A man is an animal', 'animal' is predicated for a general significatum that belongs to all its species and individuals, and it is not predicated there for a rational animal. And when I say 'An ass is an animal', 'animal' is not predicated there for an irrational animal, but for a general significatum. [2.576–580]

[254] If one argues that predicates are of such sorts such as their subjects allow, [and that], therefore, when I say 'A man is an animal', the predicate 'animal' stands for a rational animal (a man), and so on, one should reply that, if the predicate 'animal' is taken in its generality and for its significatum without reference to any differentia, it is of such a sort as its subject allows, because the essence of a genus is truthfully predicated of any of its species, as is clear on the authority of Porphyry, Boethius, and Aristotle.[208] For genus is predicated of more than one thing differing in species, etc., and species are predicated of individuals. So it is not necessary that a genus predicated of some species stand for that species or for itself taken to include the differentia of that species. A subject allows both, if one inquires. [2.581]

[255] Granted these things, there is a doubt about something said earlier (122), [namely], that a name signifies apart from time. Therefore, since such terms as 'man' and 'Socrates' are names, they do not specify for themselves any particular time nor appellata more present than past or future.[209] [2.582–583]

207 When discussing the verification of utterances (*voces*) and expressions (*orationes*) earlier in this work (138) Bacon nowhere indicates that truth and falsity can be predicated of utterances but only of expressions that make a statement (*oratio enuntiativa*). Elsewhere he is given to this lack of precision when he speaks of "false wine" and means imaginary wine. See *Cst* 2.127.

208 Porphyry *Isagoge*, trans. Warrren, pp. 29–30 and 34–35. But see, e.g., "*Ds*" 42 and *Cst* 2.137, where Bacon will treat generic terms as equivocals. It is potentially confusing to find "it is of such sort as its subject may have allowed" in this sentence. Bacon has just made the point that subjects do *not* do any allowing (determining, contracting) with respect to their predicates (252), and his explanation of their relation was stated in 253 to be that one takes predicates (be they generic terms or equivocals) to stand for that which truthfully applies to and is in the subject. Perhaps he has included it in the sense that, well, if one must use (Boethius') adage, then understand that it only means that every subject permits its predicate to be what it is, and in the case of generic predicate terms, that they signify only generally. Such would not imply that subjects determine or contract their predicates. See n. 206.

209 For a later treatment see "*Ds*" 139 and *Cst* 2.97 and 107.

[256] The solution to this is that a name does not have time as its significatum, nor does it specify for itself present appellata as things that are consignified, as the objection assumes; but by reason of their signification they do assume such for themselves.[210] A name is imposed for a present thing and for something appellated in the present. For it is necessary that something present and an actual entity be that for which a name is imposed. But this is two-fold: either an entity actual and present in the natural order, e.g., a man or an ass, or something intentional, like a chimera and suchlike imaginary things within the intellect and knowledge.[211] For just as 'man' specifies men for itself by its signification, so these are present and existing men. [2.584–586]

[257] But consider: if a term were common only to present things, and this by itself and in virtue of its nature, then if nothing changes it, it would supposit for them. Therefore, were I to say, 'A man does not run', the term would stand only for existing things, because the negation follows the term and affects nothing in the term. So, if what has been said is true, it is the same as 'A man-the-entity does not run', which is contrary to many who say that a [subject] term in a negative proposition stands for an entity and

210 Bacon's theory of imposition implies this: the first time something is named, it is always and exclusively something present to the namer, for, as has been noted, his paradigm case is or will become one of naming infants at Baptism and pets (and "all things"). (See "*Ds*" 155 and *Cst* 2.97, 99, and 125.) Thus while the *name* itself neither causes one to think of a particular time nor connotes a temporal frame of reference, what is named is clearly in present time. Or, to put it another way, for Bacon names by original imposition signify temporal things, but they do not do this temporally.

211 The first part of the previous two sentences ("For it is necessary ... ") reads: "*Oportet enim, quod sit praesens et ens actu, cui nomen imponatur. Sed hoc dupliciter*: ..." (*Sd* 1–2, p. 283, 586.) The referent of 'this' (*hoc*) is unclear. Is the meaning (judged by the context) (1) merely that there are two kinds of things (extramental and mental) that can be named, or (2) that there are two kinds of *present, actual* things that can be named, implying that intentional entities have an ontological status sufficiently close to the present, actual one of extramental entities that they can be named, granted they are not natural things? A further question: do the examples of a chimera and imaginary things (3) limit the notion of "[something] intentional (*secundum animam*)," or does Bacon mean by this phrase (4) also to include concepts of extramental entities and genera and species? I suspect that though (2) and (3) are the more literal reading, Bacon intended (1) and (4). After all, the whole debate is whether common terms by themselves appellate entities and nonentities (240), and in the "*De signis*" and *Compendium of the Study of Theology* the naming of utterances, concepts of extramental things, chimeras, nothing, the void, infinites, and impossibles is always described as a case of equivocal, second imposition because they are all examples of nonentities. (See, e.g., "*Ds*" 155 and 162, and *Cst* 2.62, 91, 105, and 119.)

a nonentity.[212] They confirm this by what Aristotle says in the *Prior Analytics*, namely, that a negative particular is verified through the sense of a universal negative and through the sense of a particular.[213] For example, 'Some man does not run' can be true either because no man runs or because some man runs and some man does not. Thus similarly 'Some man is not' can be true either because no man is or because some man is and some man is not. So, a negative particular will be able to be verified for a nonentity. By the same reasoning [this is true] of an infinite negative, because they are converted.[214] Therefore, [they argue,] a term taken without ampliation will be common to an entity and a nonentity. [2.587–588]

[258] Also, Aristotle says in *On Interpretation* that a proposition about a denied predicate follows from a proposition about a privated or infinite predicate, as in 'A man is nonjust; therefore he is not just', and this is not converted because a negation asserts nothing; therefore, it will be able to be verified of a nonentity.[215] [2.589]

[259] Then too, Aristotle proposes in the same book that indefinite propositions can be true at the same time, as in 'A man is handsome', 'A man is not handsome'. He gives another example: 'This something is', 'This something is not', for he proves the negative in this way: 'What comes to be is not; something comes to be; therefore something is not'.[216] So, Aris-

212 Apropos of 'man-the-entity' Peter considers such cases as instances of what he calls nominal restriction and proposes an appropriate rule to govern them. (*Tractatus* 11.) See also Lambert, *Logica*, p. 228.3–25, reading at line 21 '*non*' for '*enim*' in the text.

213 The claim is actually made by Algazel in his *Logica* 3, ed. C.H. Lohr, *Traditio* 21 (1965): 255.107–115. See also Aristotle *Prior Analytics* 1.46.51b36–52a17. For later treatments see "*Ds*" 141 and *Cst* 2.107, where the reference is to Aristotle's *On Interpretation.*

214 The objection presented in this paragraph is the following: if names by first imposition appellate only existing entities, then they could not appear as subjects in negative propositions. But 'Some man does not run' makes sense when the subject is taken for existing people (entities) or for dead ones (nonentities). Hence the subject term in a negative proposition can name entities and nonentities. The same is verifiable through an infinite negative proposition: 'Some nonman does not run' makes sense whether the subject is taken for an *existing* rock or a *nonexistent* horse. For Bacon's response see 260. Cf. an alternate solution by Peter in n. 222.

215 Aristotle *On Interpretation* 10.19b23–32. For a later treatment see "*Ds*" 141 and *Cst* 2.106. Again the objector's principle point is that the subject in a negative proposition can name either an existing or nonexisting thing, contrary to the general (and Bacon's) theory of appellation. Here the objector shows this by what can be inferred from a proposition with a privative or infinite predicate. For Bacon's response to this objection see 261.

216 Aristotle *On Interpretation* 7.17b30–34. For a later treatment see *Cst* 2.107; the example is not mentioned in the "*De signis.*"

totle interprets 'Something is not' as true; therefore the subject necessarily stands for a nonentity. Hence, a term in a negative proposition will stand for an entity and a nonentity, which is entirely contrary to what has been argued (256).[217] [2.590]

[260] To these one should reply that a [subject] term in a negative proposition – I mean in an indefinite and particular one – stands for an entity, just as it does in an affirmative one, because a negation changes nothing in the term since it follows and does not precede.[218] There is doubt, however, about the case of a universal negative. And yet I think that in that case the term likewise stands for something present, because a negation negates the same thing that an affirmation affirms, and only it. So, either the negation will be one of two affirmations, which is against Aristotle, or there will be a negation for which there would be no preceding affirmation, as is clear if one thinks about it; but that is impossible.[219] To the first argument (257) one should reply that the verification of a particular through the sense of a universal is [available] for all predicates other than 'to be', and not in the case of the predicate 'to be'.[220] Or, one should

217 Here the objector reaches the same conclusion as in the preceding paragraphs, but arrives at it by drawing on the relation between subcontrary propositions. For the inferred negative proposition to be true, the objector says, one has to take its subject for a nonentity. Therefore, subject terms in negative propositions can name nonentities.

218 Here Bacon draws on the notion that one of the conditions for two particular propositions to be subcontraries is that the subject terms must remain the same. Hence if 'man' in 'Some man is handsome' names an existing man, then so must that term in 'Some man is not handsome'. What is denied in the latter, he implies, is that the (existing) man in question is handsome, not that he exists. For a later treatment see *Cst* 2.108.

219 Reading at *Sd* 1–2, p. 284, 593.4, '*aut*' against '*et etiam*' in MSS. O. and S. and the text.

Aristotle *On Interpretation* 7.18a1. In 'Every man runs' and 'Every man does not run' it is running that is affirmed in the first and denied in the second. If this were not true, then, explains Bacon, either there simply is no denial ("either the negation will be one of two affirmations") or the negative proposition will not have a contrary ("there will be a negation for which there would be no preceding affirmation"). Recall, contrary propositions must have the same subjects. De Libera notes that the theory embraced here is also held by Lambert. ("*Le traité*," p. 277, n. b, and *Logica* p. 222.11–17 and 30–33.) Note, however, that in de Libera's quotation of (Steele's edition) of Bacon's *Summulae dialectics* – line 8 of note b – the text should read: "*pro ente*" instead of "*pro non ente*."

220 This is easily seen by contrasting the existential condition of what 'man' stands for in 'Some man runs / Every man does not run' with 'Some man has existence / Every man does not have existence'. For later treatments see "*Ds*" 141 and *Cst* 2.107.

reply that Aristotle proposes that a particular may be verified through the sense of a universal, if the universal can be true in that sense. This is to be understood in this way: Given that every man be seated, 'No man runs' is true, so the particular coming under the latter is true.[221] But were it able to be truthfully posited that every man-the-entity is not, 'No man is' would be true, and its particular 'Some man is not' would be true. But the universal sense is not true, and so one must not conclude from it that the particular 'Some man is not' is true, nor that the subject stands for a nonentity.[222] [2.591–596]

[261] To the other argument (258) one should reply that Aristotle understands there only that the making infinite and privative of a predicate does not follow from the negation of a predicate. Infinitization does not follow for any other reason than because a proposition with an infinite predicate is affirmative, and so the being [of the predicate] is affirmed of the subject. In a negative, however, i.e., in a proposition with a denied predicate, the being [of the predicate] is denied of the subject,

221 Here Bacon appeals to Aristotle's notion of subalternation whereby particular propositions having the *same* terms as their universal propositions can be validly inferred from their universal ones: if no man is running, then 'Some man is not running' must be true. Here both the subject terms name entities.

222 Presumably Bacon intends this as a response to the last part of 257. The point is not that it is contrary to fact to say that no one exists, but that it is contradictory to say an *existing* man does not exist. Since according to Bacon the term 'man' by original imposition names only existing men, the use of that term with that supposition in 'Some man does not exist' and 'No man exists' (257) results in contradictions in each. For a later treatment see *Cst* 2.108. But not all medievals agree with Bacon here. In the process of investigating whether subject terms in negative and affirmative propositions are restricted by predicates in the same way, Peter discusses the notion that every negative proposition in which being is denied would have to be false without the qualification Bacon expresses here in 260, 263, and 264. Peter, for example, makes a distinction between existence and being present: entities and nonentities can be present, but only the former can exist. For example, assertibles (*enuntiabilia*), while false in the present, he says, are still present, yet they do not exist since no false assertible exists. Thus he says: "Consequently, 'to be' does not restrict to existing things but to present things. Hence, likewise, 'not to be' does not restrict to nonexisting things but to present things, since the time factor, which is the cause of the restriction, is the same for both." (*Tractatus* 11.16.) Also, he continues, general terms have two kinds of form: one (like humanity) applies only to existing things, the other (like assertibility) also to nonexisting things. Thus, he concludes: "Consequently, the meaning of the proposition 'A Rose is not' is not that a rose, which exists, does not exist, but rather this is the meaning: a rose, taken [Mullally's text adds: otherwise than] in the present, does not exist." (*Tractatus* 11.5–17, and trans. Mullally, pp. 57–61.)

and from the negation of something there does not follow the affirmation of the same.[223] Privation, moreover, does not follow, both because of the foregoing reason, and because it denies form to any subject. But privation only deprives a true form of a subject capable of having that form, and so 'It is not just, therefore it is unjust' does not follow.[224] It is clear, therefore, that a privative or infinite predicate does not follow from a denied predicate, because a denied predicate is common to an entity and a nonentity, but the others only to an entity.[225] I say this of an infinite predicate not in and of itself, since it could be common to an entity and a nonentity, but because of the affirmed being of which it is predicated.[226] 'Not to be just' can be said of a living and a dead thing, for, if we assume that he is unjust, I can say 'Socrates is not just' and I can say that dead Socrates is not just, but I cannot truthfully say that dead Socrates is unjust or nonjust. Indeed, 'Socrates is nonjust' and 'A man is unjust' are predicated only of an entity. And well do I say "of an entity," because 'Socrates' and 'Socrates-the-entity' are converted, and so is 'A man is unjust', and so on.[227] [2.597–600]

[262] But then someone might object that Aristotle gives examples of this type of consequence: 'A man is not just, [therefore] a man is nonjust, or a man is unjust'; hence, such an inference will not follow in [proposi-

223 The brackets "[of the predicate]" are twice inserted as otherwise Bacon would here be conceding that in negative propositions like 'A man is not just' the subject term would univocally name a nonentity, which would contradict his claims about such terms in 260. Thus, for example, from 'He is not just' (negation) one cannot infer 'He is unjust' (privation) or 'He is nonjust' (infinitization) because the denial in the first proposition would be true if one were talking about a dead man or a living one. But the two succeeding propositions are affirmations and in Bacon's view the subject terms in both were imposed for existing things. Hence the latter two propositions do not follow *necessarily* from the first one.

224 It is true to say of a rock that it is not just, but it does not follow from this that it would be true to say that a rock is unjust, since privations like a lack of justice assume that the characteristic in question in some sense ought to be there. (See 153.) For later treatments see "*Ds*" 141 and *Cst* 2.106.

225 This is the key argument for Bacon: a negative proposition like 'He is not just' does not tell one whether the subject is living or dead and could be true in either case. But propositions that are infinite ('He is nonjust') and privative ('He is unjust') are affirmations and hence assume the existence of the subject.

226 'Nonman' is the name of the class of all things that are not men; therefore it is the name of nonentities as well as entities other than men. But when it apposes (is predicated of) a subject in a proposition deduced from a negative proposition (whose subject names an entity), it names only an entity.

227 The claim that 'Socrates' and 'Socrates-the-entity' are converted assumes a living Socrates. See *Cst* 2.106, where Bacon says '"Socrates' is an ambiguous expression for an entity and a nonentity … ."

tions with] these terms.[228] So it is necessary, [they argue,] that the [subject] term in a negative proposition stand for a nonentity, because were it to do so for an entity, [an inference] would validly proceed from such a negative proposition to affirmative ones.[229] [2.601–602]

[263] I say to this that Aristotle does not clearly say that that is a consequence, nor up to that point does he directly give examples, but the masters assume that consequence from his text. Let it be granted that he affirmed that word for word. One should reply along with the author himself who says: "We do not give examples because they are true, but that he who learns might comprehend [by illustration]."[230] So one ought not fuss over his examples, for they are more for confirmation (*ad evidentiam*) than for truth.[231] Or, if the tenacity of the cavillator is not too intimidating, one should reply that in such examples the consequence holds only because of the [appellation of the subject] term and not absolutely, given that a term is only the name of present things. For, should a term that is common to an entity and a nonentity be taken, e.g., 'nonman', or one that would be a name of only a nonentity, e.g., 'dead Caesar' or 'the future Antichrist', such a consequence would not follow, just as 'A nonman is not just, therefore a nonman is nonjust' does not follow, nor 'Dead Caesar is not just, therefore dead Caesar is nonjust'.[232] Because, therefore, whatever

228 Reading at *Sd* 1–2, p. 285, 601.2, '*iustus*' <*ergo*>, against MSS. O. and S. and the text. The reference to Aristotle is possibly an extrapolation from *On Interpretation* 10.19b23–32. For a later treatment see "*Ds*" 141 and *Cst* 2.106, in which latter Bacon says he aired the solution of this objection some forty years previous, which would be around 1252. Most take this as a reference to the *Summulae dialectices*, but for a possible challenge to the claim see the Introduction, pp. xiii–xv and xviii.

229 If the consequences are not necessary, then the only reason can be because 'man' in 'A man is not just' can be the name of a dead man or a living one, and the ambiguity blocks an inference that is taken as necessary.

230 "We use the process of setting out terms like perception by sense, in the interest of the student – not as though it were impossible to demonstrate without them, as it is to demonstrate without the premises of the deduction." Aristotle *Prior Analytics* 1.41.50a1–2, trans. A. J. Jenkinson, in *CWA*, vol. 1, p. 80.

231 "... *non est curandum ... de exemplis suis.*" (*Sd* 1–2, p. 286.2, 604.) I suspect the use of the reflexive '*suus*' is poor grammar for '*eius*' (and the translation assumes this), but it is possible the sentence should read "One ought not always pay attention to one's own examples," which is more a directive to us about our use of examples than a comment about Aristotle's use of them. There are no later treatments in the "*De signis*" or *Compendium of the Study of Theology*.

232 To say that the consequence holds "because of the [appellation of the subject] term and not of the term absolutely" is to grant that any word originally imposed for an entity can be reimposed for a nonentity and used in 'A man is not just'. The subject term would then stand for a dead man, and the consequences in question do not validly follow. See 264, where reimposition and equivocation are expressly treated.

follows absolutely follows necessarily and always and not in virtue of a term, one should reply that in consequences like 'A man is not just, therefore a man is nonjust', etc., the consequence does not hold absolutely, since the term stands only for an entity. [2.603–606]

[264] To the other objection (259) [one should reply] that [Aristotle] does not interpret the indefinite propositions 'Something is' and 'Something is not' to be true, but these: 'Something comes to be' and 'Something does not come to be'.[233] So he means that propositions like the following can be true at the same time: 'A man becomes white', 'A man does not become white', and 'Air becomes fire', 'Air does not become fire'. The [subject] term in the negative propositions stands for an entity, as is clear. Or, one should reply that he did not take 'Something is', 'Something is not' to be subcontrary propositions, but 'It becomes something', 'It does not become something', with the result that the term 'something' in the predicate position would become its contrary.[234] Because of the brevity of his text – he is always concise in speech – we must supply subjects for those propositions however we wish, this way or that – 'An animal becomes something', 'An animal does not become something', 'An animal becomes a man', 'An animal does not become a man' – in such a way that something higher stands for something lower, namely, 'something' for a man or for something else, just as he does in many places, as is clear when one ambles about in his *Logic*.[235] So he meant nothing improper since 'An animal becomes a man' and 'An animal does not become a man' are true when the [subject] term stands only for an entity. Or, he is thinking of the propositions 'Something comes to be' and 'Something does not come to be', and these can be true at the same time for entities, as was just said. But it is not necessary to analyze the term 'something' for one of its inferiors. Hence, 'Something comes to be' and 'Something does not come to be' will be true, because an embryo, when it becomes something, becomes a man, and an

233 For a later treatment see *Cst* 2.108.

234 Recall, Bacon cannot accept as noncontradictory 'Something does not exist' because 'something' names an entity by original imposition. For a later treatment see *Cst* 2.108.

235 To say "something higher stands for something lower" is to say that in affirmative propositions employing the verb 'become' (implying natural generation) the subject must be broader than the predicate, i.e., that the subject must be higher on the Porphyrean tree. This is so, Bacon would argue, because generation proceeds from the more universal to the particular. (See Aristotle *On the Generation of Animals* 2.3.736a36–b4.) In his *Communia naturalium*, Bacon goes to great lengths to spell out this process when he treats of the relation of universals to individuals. See *Liber primus communium naturalium fratris Rogeri*, *Ohi*, vol. 2, pp. 97.14–98.2, of which the relevant part can be found in Thomas S. Maloney, trans., *Three Treatments of Universals by Roger Bacon*, pp. 91–92.

ass does not become a man.[236] Thus there are grounds, it seems, to sustain as sufficiently probable that a term that was imposed only for entities is common only to entities.[237] It will not be common to nonentities unless a new imposition occurs.[238] Then such a term will be one that equivocates for entities and nonentities, and the fallacy of equivocation will be incurred wherever it is asserted. [2.607–612]

[265] But one is wont to illustrate what has been said by these sorts of examples: 'Caesar is praised', when Caesar does not exist; 'Easter is a beautiful season', when it is not Easter; and 'Every woman is afraid when giving birth', 'Every man is afraid at sea', and the like, although no woman is giving birth and no man is on the sea.[239] Some argue that compositions of this sort are beyond time, since the words there stand habitually and not actually, and the previously mentioned rules are to be understood not to apply to them.[240] Others, however, contend that there are two sorts of

236 Earlier in this paragraph 'something' in 'Something comes to be' was said to need to be taken for its individuals, and one should add, individuals of the lowest species, i.e., complete individuals. Here Bacon says this is not always necessary, and gives an embryo as an example of an appropriate appellatum of 'something'. The theory he is drawing on, mentioned in the previous note, contends that human generation is a developmental process that involves various stages that reflect a descent on the Porphyrean tree, a natural process from the less determinate to the more determinate, wherein an embryo stands somewhere intermediary in the process. Given the theory, it seems that he would have to be committed to the claim that, before one is an individual of the human species, one was an *individual* of all the preceding genera. Hence, the intent here is to note that 'something' in 'Something comes to be' can name such generic individuals.

237 Reading at *Sd* 1–2, p. 287, 610.2, '*enti<bus>*' against '*enti*' in MSS. O. and S. and the text. As already noted, the caution, indeed humility, with which Bacon characterizes his theory of appellation here is in stark contrast with the boldness displayed at the end of his life in 1292 in *Compendium of the Study of Theology* (2.85–86 and 104). While he does not say the theory is only "sufficiently probable" in his "*De signis*" of 1267 (134–142) – he says it is "clear" and that others are infatuated with the contrary ("*Ds*" 135) – none of the animus and invective of his last treatment is found in the *Summulae dialectices* or "*De signis*."

238 And Bacon would say that this happened, e.g., when the first person uttered the name 'Caesar' after the latter's death: the name was thereby reimposed for a nonentity, a dead man. For a later treatment see, e.g., "*Ds*" 135 and 143–161, and *Cst* 2.91, 96, 105–106, and 118–128, passim.

239 See "*Ds*" 160, 135 and 153, and *Cst* 2.85, 100, and 111.

240 While Bacon does not pose this objection in the "*De signis*" it is clearly stated in *Compendium of the Study of Theology* (2.101) and given more detailed refutation than here. While William proposes the notion of habitual being and habitual supposition, H. A. G. Braakhuis correctly argues that William's views come under only partial condemnation by Bacon. See H. A. G. Braakhuis, "The Views of William of Sherwood on Some Semantical Topics and Their Relation to Those of Roger Bacon," *Vivarium* 15 (1977): 111–142.

present [time], namely confused and determinate.[241] The confused present of present time has no use because it represents no definite time, but is confused for any time, as is clear in the previously mentioned examples; the determinate present is what pertains to a definite time and a now. I think, however, that the verb 'is', taken strictly and absolutely, and taken with no determination, always copulates actual and determinate being. So these expressions are acknowledged only because of their use. Hence, these are more to be rebutted as a common and ordinary way of speaking than as expressing the truth. And so a term stands only for a present thing in these examples, as in others. Therefore, they are all false, if, abrogating use and custom, we attend to truth. [2.613–619]

[266] Besides the previously mentioned division of suppositions and appellations there is another division of supposition and appellation, namely this: some suppositions and appellations are gemina, others antonomastic, still others metonymical, and so on for the other figures of speech and construction. *Gemina*, as in 'Pepper is sold here and in Rome'.[242] *Antonomastic*, when a term stands for the individual to whom the name best applies either absolutely or as a predicate. When, for example, we say 'Philosopher', this word is understood of Aristotle by the Moderns because at the present he is reputed to be the best philosopher, although he was taken as a minor philosopher by earlier ones. Hence, Tully [apotheosizes] in *On the Nature of the Gods*, "Plato, the god of the philosophers," and so does Augustine, "Plato, the most illustrious of all philosophers."[243] With respect to a predicate term 'The Apostle PREACHED' is understood of Paul, who excelled in preaching.[244] There is *metonymical* [supposition and appellation] when [a term] indicating a container stands for the contents, as ['cup'] in 'Drink a cup', and so on.[245] There is no doubt

241 For later treatments see *Cst* 2.97–99, 101 and 103, especially the last two.

242 This is called *gemina* (twin) because a compound predicate is involved and the expression is analyzable into a compound sentence with 'pepper' the subject in each component. See 268.

243 "For let us hear Plato, that divine philosopher, for so almost he is to be deemed." (Cicero *De natura deorum* 2.12.32, ed. and trans. H. Rackham, Loeb Classical Library, p. 153.) "Of the pupils of Socrates, Plato was so remarkable for his brilliance that he has deservedly outshone all the rest." Augustine *The City of God* 8.4, trans. Gerald G. Walsh, Demetrius B. Zema, Grace Monahan, and Donald J. Honan, *Saint Augustine: The City of God: An Abridged Version* (Garden City, NY: Image Books, 1958), p. 148.

244 This is a curious example of antonomasia in a predicate term, for clearly 'The Apostle' is a case of antonomasia in the subject term. Given the explanation in the text, perhaps one is to bring out the antonomasia in the predicate in oral delivery by tonal emphasis and in written text by using caps, as supplied in the translation. The sense is that preaching was done supereminently by the Apostle Paul.

245 Other examples of metonymic terms: 'barker' and 'majesty'.

about antonomastic and metonymical [supposition and appellation] because antonomastic is always personal and determinate, likewise metonymical when taken strictly and *per se*; *per accidens*, however, it can be simple, as will be clear.[246] [2.620–624]

[267] With respect to gemina there is doubt whether it has simple supposition or personal. Not personal, [one might argue], because, when a term is asserted once, it only stands for one individual by disjunction, as is the case with every determinate supposition. But one and the same suppositum is not here and in Rome, and so the proposition will be false and therefore does not have personal supposition.[247] Nor [does it seem to have] simple [supposition, one argues], because selling is an accident and an exercise of an individual, because it is not applicable to a species.[248] [2.625]

[268] One should reply that, if the propositions are joined, then there must come to be an individual with respect to 'pepper' stated twice, and then it will have a double personal, determinate supposition in the sense of 'Pepper is sold here and pepper is sold in Rome'. Then one should not ask about the supposition of 'pepper' stated once, but twice.[249] If, however, the

246 An antonomastic term having simple appellation and supposition would have to name and stand for any utterance or essence (see 213) that fulfills the notion of utterance or essence in a way that excels all others. For a metonymic term to have simple appellation and supposition it would have to be a word that names and stands for an utterance or essence where the word is so closely associated with the utterance or essence that it can be taken for the latter. An acronym like 'NATO' would be an example of an equivocal metonymic term having both simple and personal appellation and supposition; were that organization to be disbanded, of course, it would no longer have appellation. Personally, it is the name of an international organization; simply, it is the name of the utterance 'North Atlantic Treaty Organization'. One could argue, however, it was originally imposed to name the utterance as a convenient way of naming the organization, and hence it names the organization *per accidens*.

247 The supposition of 'pepper', it is said, cannot be personal: not discrete, because the pepper in question cannot be one signate individual; not determinate, because the truth of the expression cannot be verified by disjunction; and not confused, because the expression is not true of all pepper. For the response see 268.

248 The reason given for rejecting simple supposition seems to be this: only individuals sell, and selling is an accident, not something characteristic of a species. If selling is an accident and an exercise of an individual and not of a species, then to-be-sold is an accident of and something endured by an individual and not of/by a species. With a move to the passive voice in the addition of the second insight the objector could then be understood to be pointing out that (1) a species cannot be bought and sold, and (2) even if it could, one would have two species different *per accidens*, as a suppositum for 'pepper': species-sold-here and species-sold-at-Rome. For Bacon's response see 268.

249 'Pepper' in each of the two instances would have determinate personal supposition under an implied reading of 'some pepper'.

terms are joined and there results a proposition with a compound predicate, then there can be simple or personal supposition: if personal, it is false; if simple, then it is true.[250] To the other objection (267, second part) one should reply, as Porphyry indicates, that accidents inhere principally and *per se* in individuals, secondarily in species and genera, and in that way they can be said of the [species and genera] in the same way as they inhere, and so the objection does not succeed.[251] [2.626–627]

Copulation[252]

[269] One should pass quickly through copulation since there is no difficulty with it. All adjectival names and all verbs and adverbs signifying some predicable concept copulate, that is, signify adjacently.[253] For copulation is the joining or adjacent [grammatical] inclination of a concept signified by the relation of one word to another.[254] Thus it does not pertain to substantival names, nor to parts of speech other than those previously

250 If 'Pepper is sold here and in Rome' is to be true, says Bacon, 'pepper' must be taken to have simple supposition. He seems to accept that it cannot have personal supposition because of the two different locations. What he says in this paragraph is intended to justify the claim that 'pepper' in this formulation can be taken as the name of a species and hence can have simple supposition. See 229.

251 Porphyry *Isagoge*, trans. Warren, p. 54: "Accidents exist principally in individuals, but genera and spec*ies* [sic] are naturally prior to individual substances."

252 Here we arrive at the third property of terms in expressions, copulation, the first two being supposition and appellation. Where the first two treated of substances, here we consider characteristics (accidents), and in consequence our attention will be directed to how adjectives, adverbs, and verbs stand for characteristics. A term copulates when it characterizes something.

253 To "signify adjacently" is to signify by being placed next to a word either directly, as 'beautiful' in 'The beautiful sky is blue' or by being indirectly linked by the verb 'is', as 'beautiful' in 'The sky is beautiful'. Verbs like 'runs' should be understood to read as 'is running' where the participle characterizes.

254 There is variation in how to characterize copulation. William defines it as "an ordering of the understanding of something over something else" (*ordinatio alicuius intellectus supra*); Peter terms it "the acceptance of an adjacent (Mullally: adjectival) term for something" (*termini adiectivi acceptio pro aliquo*); and Lambert speaks of it as "the acceptance of a term representing a dependent thing, in accord with which it can be interpreted for its own [signified] thing, or for a suppositum or supposita contained under its [signified] thing." Lambert also says that there is a sense in which copulation (as well as supposition) is also the signification of a term, not just its property. (*Introductiones*, trans. Kretzmann, p. 105; *Tractatus* 6.3, and trans. Mullally, p. 5; and *Logica*, pp. 207.30–32 and 208.13–17, trans. Kretzmann and Stump, *CTMPT*, pp. 107–108.)

mentioned. With respect to copulation, however, it should be known that copulation is either simple or personal.[255] [2.628–632]

[270] An adjectival or participial term can copulate simply or personally, as is manifestly clear, in accord with all the designated differentiae of supposition: [*simply*], as ['pierces'] in 'White pierces'; *discretely*, as ['this'] in 'This man runs'; *determinately*, as ['running'] in 'A running man argues'; *confusedly and distributively*, as ['white'] in 'Every white thing is colored'; and *merely confusedly*, as ['loving'] in 'Every thing having a good son is loving him'.[256] But a verb copulates simply and perhaps personally, just as was said of a predicate, but not merely confusedly nor confusedly and distributively. Adverbs sometimes copulate personally, as is clear in the case of temporal and personal adverbs like 'now' and 'indefinitely'. But adverbs of the following sort copulate [simply]: [ones that are] temporal, local, impersonal, and those of quality and quantity.[257] [633–635]

255 Since Bacon allows a division of copulation along the lines of supposition, presumably one can determine the type of copulation of adjacent terms simply by identifying the type of supposition of the terms they characterize. But this is not the case with William, for he says that one cannot divide copulation along the lines of what he calls material/formal, common/discrete, and simple/personal supposition. Indeed, according to him a copulating word used to stand for itself (his material supposition, Bacon's simple) is said to supposit, not copulate. He does, however, accept the applicability of the divisions determinate/confused and merely confused/distributively confused, and also acknowledges there can be immobile distributively confused copulation. (*Introductiones*, trans. Kretzmann, pp. 120–122.) If the differences between Bacon and William indicated here and spelled out in 270 are typical of the period, it is somewhat surprising that more attention is not given to copulation by all the texts on logic.

256 Reading at *Sd* 1–2, p. 289, 633.1, '*participialis*' against '*particularis*' in MSS. O. and S. and the text.
Since Bacon is addressing the modes of copulation of adjectives and participles some of the predicates here need to be transformed into ones with an expressed copula, i.e., from statements like 'He runs' to 'He is running'. 'White is piercing' is presumably an example of simple copulation because it expresses (part of) the definition of white, a species of color. See 35.

257 The textual status of this paragraph is so uncertain at crucial points that attempts to elucidate Bacon's theory of adverbial copulation must be highly conjectural. Note the following in this paragraph: (1) in MS. S. the ink is badly smeared, or at least so my microfilm would suggest; (2) '*incertim*' is a conjecture by the editor for '*ineatim*' in *both* MSS O. and S.; (3) the word 'simply' (*simpliciter*) naming the second type of adverbial copulation is also editorial conjecture for an omission in *both* MSS. O. and S.; and (4) temporal adverbs are listed in both groups. As the text now stands Bacon could be read to say, e.g., that 'greatly' in 'Mary loves him greatly' would copulate (only?) simply, i.e., that it characterizes the word 'loves' or the nature or species of the act of loving and not Mary's act of loving.

Part Three

Argumentation

ARGUMENTATION

[271] Since statements and their parts have been comprehensively treated with respect to all their differences, now we must speak of argumentation, in which the consideration of logic reaches its culmination. Therefore, we must see what argumentation is and how many species of it there are. [3.1–2]

[272] Argumentation is the rendering explicit of an argument by way of an expression. An argument is a reason that produces belief with respect to a matter that is in doubt. The power of inferring and proving a conclusion considered as a mental process is said to be an argument, as if from '*arguere mentem*' (to prove what one is thinking). But its expression by means of words is said to be argumentation. [3.3–6]

[273] There are four species of argumentation: Syllogism (275–257, 289–299), Enthymeme (300), Induction (301), and Example (302). One must first speak of Syllogism, but even prior to this it is necessary to know its parts. [3.7–9]

SYLLOGISM

[274] The parts of a syllogism are terms and propositions. Although, ordinarily speaking, any word might be called a term and any statement a proposition, taken strictly they differ in a certain respect. Whether something be a name or a verb it is said to be a *term* when it is within a syllogism, but a word outside such. A *proposition*, moreover, is arranged within the order of a syllogism, whereas a statement stands outside. Nevertheless, let us commonly take one for the other, as often in the preceding. A term is that into which a proposition is analyzed; a proposition is an affirmative or negative expression. [3.9–13]

[275] A *syllogism* is an expression (*oratio*) in which, certain things having been propounded, something else necessarily results from the things that were propounded.[1] 'Expression' is interpreted here for a group of sentences having one end, namely, to produce belief or something else. Tullius

1 See Aristotle *Prior Analytics* 1.1.24b18–20.

takes it this way in his *Rhetorica* because rhetoric is said to be an expression, i.e., a group of sentences tending to one end, namely, persuasion.[2] 'Expression', therefore, is here the same as 'argumentation', as it were, from '*oris ratio*' (a reason given by the mouth) and is not taken as in *On Interpretation* or as was previously the case.[3] [Aristotle] understands by the phrase "certain things" that two propositions must be asserted in a syllogism, for a multiple proposition approaches being a syllogism.[4] In saying "propounded" he calls attention to the way propositions are arranged in mood and figure; "something else necessarily results," namely, a conclusion; "from the things that were propounded," namely, by propositions that were already set forth. [3.14–18]

[276] Some syllogisms are perfect, others imperfect. A *perfect syllogism* is one that needs nothing for the evidence of its necessity except the things given. An *imperfect syllogism* is one that still needs one or more things. [3.19]

[277] Every syllogism, moreover, depends on a *said of all* or a *said of none*. A *said of all* occurs when there is nothing to take under the subject of which the predicate is not predicated, as in 'Every man is an animal'. A *said of none* occurs when there is nothing to take under the subject to which the predicate would be applicable, as in 'No man is an ass'.[5] After this one should know that there are three sorts of conversion of syllogistic propositions, and they need to be treated for the sake of clarity with respect to imperfect syllogisms. [3.20–21]

2 In Pseudo-Cicero *Ad C. Herennium de ratione dicendi* 1.2.2, ed. and trans. Harry Kaplan, Loeb Classical Library, 1954, p. 5, one finds: "The task of the public speaker (*oratoris officium*) is to discuss capably those matters which law and custom have fixed for the uses of citizenship, and to secure as far as possible the agreement of his hearers."

3 Aristotle *On Interpretation* 4.16b–26.

4 Since a multiple proposition is one in which more than one thing is said it offers at least the possibility of providing sufficient data to yield a conclusion implicit in that data. Clearly, however, not all multiple propositions do this – equivocal ones, for example, do not. For a discussion of multiple propositions see 165.

5 See 309 and 310. The reference here is to the A and E propositions and apropos of the point made here Kretzmann says: "The *dici de omni*, or *dictum de omni* (*et nullo*), was the most widely accepted formula for the essence of syllogistic reasoning. It is sometimes stated as 'what is predicated of any whole is predicated of any part of that whole,' which is traced to *Prior Analytics* 1.1.24b26–31: 'That one term should be included in another as in a whole is the same as for the other to be predicated of all of the first. And we say that one term is predicated of all of another, whenever no instance of the subject can be found of which the other term cannot be asserted; "to be predicated of none" must be understood in the same way.'" In *Introductiones*, trans. Kretzmann, p. 61, n. 22. Kretzmann is using the translation by A. J. Jenkinson, for which see *CWA*, vol. 1, p. 40.

[278] One sort of conversion proceeds with respect to terms, the other by means of opposite qualities. By means of *opposite qualities* a universal affirmative is converted to its contrary or subcontrary, as in 'It is contingent that every man runs; therefore it is contingent that no man runs; therefore it is contingent that some man does not run'.[6] *Conversion with respect to terms* is the change of a subject into a predicate, and vice versa.[7] Of this sort one is simple, one by limitation, and one by contraposition. But this last is provided by Boethius, not Aristotle.[8] [3.22–26]

[279] *Simple conversion* occurs when a predicate arises from a subject (and vice versa), the quality and quantity remaining the same. So a universal negative and a particular affirmative are converted in this way: the universal negative: 'No man is a stone; therefore no stone is a man'; the particular affirmative: 'Some man is an animal; therefore some animal is a man'. There is *conversion by limitation* when a predicate arises from a subject (and vice versa), the quality remaining the same but the quantity changing. So a universal negative and universal affirmative are converted in this way: 'Every man is an animal; therefore some animal is a man'; 'No man is an ass; therefore some ass is not a man'. Simple conversion, however, is said by Aristotle to be "a conversion with respect to terms and a whole," whereas conversion by limitation "a conversion with respect to a part."[9] *Conversion by contraposition* occurs when an infinite predicate arises from a definite subject and an infinite subject arises from a definite predicate, the quality and quantity remaining the same. So a universal affirmative and a particular negative are converted in this way: 'Every man is an animal; therefore every nonanimal is a nonman', and 'Some man is not an ass; therefore some nonass is not a nonman'. And there is a certain verse about these conversions:

Simpliciter feci convertitur, eva per acci,
Acto per contra. Sic fit conversio tota.[10]

'E' signifies a universal negative, 'I' a particular affirmative, 'A' a universal affirmative, and 'O' a particular negative. [3.27–30]

[280] But many examples are argued to stand against the stated conversions, e.g., 'No old man will be a boy', 'No virgin was a defiled woman',

6 The use of modal propositions as examples is a needless distraction for modes play no role in what Bacon wants to get across at this point.

7 The additional notion that the quantity and quality remain the same is not added here because under this heading also comes conversion by limitation. See 278.

8 Boethius *De syllogismo categorico libri duo* 1, PL 64.807A.

9 Aristotle *Prior Analytics* 1.2.25a5–9.

10 It seems impossisble to translate and preserve the function of the mnemonic. For two other versions of it see *Ut dicit* and *Cum sit nostra*, respectively, *LM*, vol. 2, pt. 2, pp. 385.34–386.4 and 427.2–3.

'No house is something in stone', 'No oven is something drawn from bread'. If these are converted, the conversions will be false, as is contended. Consequently, they call suchlike "impediments to conversion," seeking solace for their ignorance; but it is clear that there is no impediment. Let us suppose that in a proposition to be converted the participle of the verb is the predicate associated with it. This follows because a verb cannot be predicated since it cannot function as a subject, for every predicate in propositions that are to be converted can be changed into a subject, and vice versa. The first example, then, can be converted in this way: 'No old man will be a boy; therefore no future boy is an old man'; the second thus: 'No woman defiled in the past is a virgin'; the third in this way: 'No entity in stone is a house'; and the fourth thus: 'No thing drawn from an oven is bread; therefore no thing drawn from bread is an oven'. [3.31–32]

[281] But then there is doubt about propositions in the past tense of the active voice and in the present passive since they have no participles and so are not converted, because then the verb will necessarily be predicated and it cannot be changed into a subject, as in 'No man has loved', 'No book is read', and 'No questioner becomes a sophist'. One should reply that participles of such verbs are lacking in the Latin language, as Priscian says.[11] Since they do not signify by means of simple words, their participles are to be taken by circumlocution, as he teaches there, namely, by apposing the indefinite name of a substance to the same verb, just as the participle of the verb 'he loved' is this whole: 'one who loved'; and of the verb 'he is loved': 'one who is loved'; of such a verb as 'he becomes': 'one who becomes'. In propositions such as these that are to be converted the whole thing is the predicate. For if it is asked what the predicate is in such, one should reply that the whole thing is, namely, in as much as the propositions are ones that are to be converted. And [the whole thing] should be changed into a subject in this way: 'No man has loved; therefore no one who has loved is a man'; 'No book is read; therefore no one who is read is a book'; and 'No questioner becomes a sophist; therefore no one who becomes a sophist is a questioner'. For such should be analyzed in the manner of 'No man is one who has loved', and so on. Yet it could be said in another way that a participle in the present tense of the active voice is confused to signify a participle of the past and present, and a past participle in the passive voice is confused to signify a participle in the present and past. Hence these can be converted in this way: 'No man has loved; therefore no one loving was a man'; 'No book is read; therefore no thing read is a book'; 'No questioner becomes a sophist; therefore no one become a sophist is a ques-

11 Priscian *Institutiones grammaticae* 11.25, *GL*, vol. 2, pp. 564.25–565.3: "... in which because a past [tense] is lacking, in place of a participle we use a verb and an indefinite name, like 'who loved'."

tioner' (read in such a way that 'become' is in the present tense). But that way is very troublesome and not as applicable as the other. So, the first way is to be chosen. [3.33–36]

[282] There is still doubt also about: 'No citizen is a woman' and suchlike. It does not seem it may be converted otherwise than in this way: 'No woman entity is a citizen'. 'Every man is every man' does not seem to be converted because the whole phrase 'every man' is the predicate and it cannot become the subject because a sign cannot be part of a subject; so, it is not converted. There is doubt about exclusive and exceptive propositions, as, were I to say 'Only every man runs', this cannot be converted except in this way: 'Therefore only some running thing is a man', which is false. And so on. 'Every man except Socrates runs' should be converted this way: 'Therefore some running thing except Socrates is a man'. But this cannot be [acceptable] because an exception does not arise from a particular sign, but from a universal one. [3.37–40]

[283] To the *first* objection one should reply that in virtue of the locution the proposition 'No citizen, etc.' is the same as 'No masculine citizen or man is a woman', and in this sense it is legitimately converted in this way: 'Therefore no woman is a male citizen or a man'. To the *second* objection one should reply that 'Every man, etc.' should be converted thus: 'Therefore some entity every man is every man', and the sign can legitimately be part of the determination of the subject, though not part of the principle subject. To the *third* objection one should reply that the proposition 'Only every man runs' must be converted into its basic proposition in the manner of 'Therefore some running thing is a man' because the subject and predicate pertain to the basic proposition.[12] For an exclusive proposition is single absolutely and specifies for itself the extremes only of the basic proposition, because an exclusion adds nothing except some sort of precision with respect to a subject and predicate. So, if it is converted, it must be converted just as its basic proposition is, since simple conversion is accompanied by an exchange of extremes, namely, of one with the other. For conversion is so defined: "Conversion is the change of a subject into a predicate, and vice versa." So, since the subject and predicate of an exclusive proposition are from its basic proposition, conversions of an exclusive will only come about by changing the predicate of the basic proposition into its subject (and vice versa), the quantity being changed or not changed as the type of conversion requires. One should reply similarly with respect to an exclusive particular, as in 'Only some man runs; therefore some running thing is a man'. One should know about exceptive propositions that an affirmative is converted to the particular of the basic proposition, as in 'Every man except Socrates runs; therefore some running thing is a man', and a negative to a universal

12 The basic proposition of 'Only every man runs' is 'Every man runs'.

exceptive, thus: 'No man except Socrates runs; therefore no running thing except Socrates is a man'. [3.41–45]

[284] But then there is doubt about indefinite and singular propositions as to whether they are converted, and, if they are converted, how? One should reply that Aristotle did not touch on indefinite and singular propositions, the explanation for which Algazel seems to provide by saying that "a singular affirmative and singular negative and an indefinite affirmative and indefinite negative are ones that we do not use much in the sciences. For one does not treat of a singular, like Peter, in demonstrative sciences. Indefinite propositions," [he continues], "are taken in the sense of a particular, and without doubt because they signify something as a part does. Any universality in them," [he says], "is dubious because they relate to something indeterminately and so they are not definite but indefinite, and thus are excluded from demonstrative [sciences]. Accordingly, there remain four definite propositions, namely, the universal affirmative, the particular affirmative, the particular negative, and the universal [negative]."[13] These are the words of Algazel. From these things it seems that indefinite and singular propositions do not fall under science and art: indefinite ones because of their lack of definiteness, singulars because of their singularity. For this reason neither does their conversion properly fall under art. But if they have the ability to be converted, it will be reduced to that of the nature of a particular proposition because a singular is a particular, though signate. Likewise, an indefinite is converted with a particular with respect to the thing [signified]. So, they are converted simply when extending the name of conversion to them. But Aristotle says that a particular negative is not converted, and Algazel also.[14] This is to be understood of conversion in the strict sense. When extending the name of conversion to it, it is converted by contraposition, as Boethius testifies.[15] [3.46–50]

[285] With respect to the conversion of modal propositions one should know that propositions with *necessary* in them are converted in the same way as assertoric propositions because a universal affirmative with *necessary* in it is converted by limitation, as in 'Every man necessarily is an animal; therefore some animal necessarily is a man', and a particular affirmative is converted simply, as in 'Some man necessarily is a substance; therefore some substance necessarily is a man'. But a universal negative is converted simply and by limitation, as in 'No man necessarily is an ass; therefore no ass necessarily is a man' or 'Some ass necessarily is not a man'. According to Aristotle, however, a particular negative is not converted, just

13 Algazel *Logica* 3, ed. Lohr, 255.107–15. The quotation is accurate with a few inconsequential exceptions.

14 Aristotle *Prior Analytics* 1.3.25a35. See also Algazel *Logica* 3, ed. Lohr, 258.201.

15 Boethius *De syllogismo categorico libri duo* 1, PL 64.807A. See also 278.

as neither in the case of assertoric propositions, unless one speaks of conversion by contraposition, as in 'Necessarily some man is not an ass; therefore some nonass necessarily is not a nonman'.[16] All propositions with *necessary* in them, moreover, are converted in this way, except those of the sort whose predicate is in the subject neither in the first nor second way of speaking *per se* (311–312). The first way of speaking *per se* occurs when a predicate falls within the definition of a subject, as in 'A man is an animal'. The second way of speaking *per se* occurs when a subject falls within the definition provided by the predicate, as in 'A man is capable of laughing'. In other cases the consequence does not hold, as in 'Every thing with a knowledge of grammar or music necessarily is a man; therefore some man necessarily is knowledgeable about grammar or music'. The reason for this is that conversion is blocked by the different ways of predicating the adjectival names 'knowledgeable about grammar' and 'knowledgeable about music' and making them subjects, because, when they are predicated, they stand for a signified form, but when they serve as subjects, they stand for what they supposit.[17] And so one is true, the other is false. Or, since Aristotle says that these propositions with *necessary* in them are converted in the same way as those that are assertoric, this is to be understood of those with *necessary per se*, and not *per accidens* in them, of which sort are [the latter].[18] Or it can be said that, if a subject and a predicate are converted in the same way in which they stand, then [the proposition] can legitimately be converted, for the subject stands for what it supposits, and [the proposition] is true *per accidens* and not *per se*, in the sense that the following are true: 'Every thing knowledgeable about grammar necessarily is a man', i.e., 'Every thing that is subjected to being knowledgeable about grammar', i.e., 'Every thing that has grammar in it necessarily is a man'. Hence they are converted in this way: 'Therefore some man necessarily is that thing that has grammar in it'. What is to be converted and what has been converted are true. [3.51–60]

[286] Likewise one should know about propositions with *contingent* in them that, since there are three senses of *contingent*, namely, *necessary*, *possible*, and *nonnecessary*,[19] propositions with *contingent* taken for *necessary* and *contingent* taken for *possible* in them are converted in the same way as those that are assertoric and with *necessary* in them are. The result is that a universal affirmative is converted by limitation and a particular

16 Aristotle *Prior Analytics* 1.3.25a35.

17 Latin adjectives can be taken as adjectives or nouns and, respectively, predicated or function as subjects.

18 Aristotle *Prior Analytics* 1.3.25a26.

19 For how these notions differ and their implications for conversion see 287–288. See also 376–377.

affirmative simply, and a universal negative simply and by limitation – according to Aristotle a particular negative is not converted except by conversion by contraposition[20] – as in 'It is contingent that every man is an animal; therefore it is contingent that some animal is a man', 'It is contingent that some man is an animal; therefore it is contingent that some animal is a man', and 'It is contingent that no horse is a man; therefore it is contingent that no man is a horse', whether *contingent* be taken for *necessary* or for *possible*. A particular negative is converted by contraposition in the same way as assertoric propositions are, as in 'It is contingent that some animal is not a man; therefore it is contingent that some nonman is not a nonanimal', rather than that it is an animal or lion. [3.61]

[287] With respect to propositions with *contingent* taken for *nonnecessary* in them one should know that, since *contingent* taken for *nonnecessary* has two senses, namely, *indefinitely contingent*, i.e., *indeterminately*, and *naturally contingent*, an affirmative proposition with *indefinitely contingent* in it is converted in the same way as the assertoric ones are, namely, a universal affirmative is converted by limitation in the same sense of *contingent*, and a particular affirmative proposition is converted simply in the same sense of *contingent*, as in 'It is contingent that every man is white; therefore it is contingent that something white is a man' and 'It is contingent that some man is black; therefore it is contingent that something black is a man'. But affirmative propositions with *naturally contingent* in them are converted in terms, but not in the same sense of *contingent*. More, they are converted into *contingent* taken for *possible*, as in 'It is contingent that every man becomes grayheaded in old age; therefore it is contingent that something becoming grayheaded in old age is a man'. The conclusion is verified of *contingent* taken for *possible* or for *necessary*, not for *indeterminate*, but in no way for *naturally contingent*. Likewise, a particular affirmative. [3.62–63]

[288] But a universal negative proposition, whether it is one with *indeterminately* or *naturally contingent* in it, is not converted with the same sense of *contingent*. Rather, it is converted with the sense of *commonly contingent*, i.e., taken for *possible*, as in 'It is contingent that no man is a white thing; therefore it is contingent that no white thing is a man' and 'It is contingent that no man becomes black in old age; therefore it is contingent that no [masculine] thing becoming black in old age is a man'. The conclusion is always one with *contingent* taken for *possible* and not with the same sense of *contingent*, as is clear, since then a universal affirmative would be converted simply. For if 'It is contingent that every *b* is an *a*', is asserted, then 'It is contingent that no *b* is an *a*' [would follow], because propositions with *contingent* taken for *nonnecessary* in them are converted

20 Aristotle *Prior Analytics* 1.3.25a35. See also 284, at end.

by opposite qualities. But if 'It is contingent that no *b* is an *a*' [is asserted], and it is converted with the same sense of *contingent*, then 'It is contingent that no *a* is a *b*' would follow, and if 'It is contingent that no *a* is a *b*', then 'It is contingent that every *a* is a *b*'. Therefore, from the beginning, if 'It is contingent that every *b* is an *a*', then 'It is contingent that every *a* is a b', which is impossible. Yet this follows from what was said, [namely], that a universal negative would be converted with respect to terms having the same sense of *contingent*, when a proposition is taken with *contingent* taken as *nonnecessary* in it. So, this is impossible. But a particular negative is legitimately converted with respect to terms when *contingent* taken for *nonnecessary* in it is taken, because it is convertible with a particular affirmative by opposite qualities, which is legitimately converted with respect to terms. Thus 'It is contingent that some man is not a white thing; therefore it is contingent that some white thing is not a man' legitimately follows with the same sense of *contingent*. So Aristotle says that a particular is converted, but a universal is not converted.[21] [3.64–66]

[289] A syllogism is either ostensive or *per impossible*. A *per impossible* syllogism involves taking the opposite of a conclusion to be proved (which opposite is called an hypothesis) along with another clearly true proposition in order to conclude something impossible from these two. Once the result is destroyed, it is necessary to destroy the hypothesis (which is the opposite of the [original] conclusion), and thus the opposite conclusion will be concluded. For example, let the conclusion to be proved be that Socrates is an animal, and let the opposite of this, 'Socrates is not an animal', be proposed by an adversary. Then let it be argued in this way: 'Socrates is not an animal, Socrates is a man; therefore some man is not an animal', which is impossible. Therefore that is impossible from which it follows. But this was the hypothesis: 'Socrates is not an animal'. So, this is impossible and therefore its opposite, 'Socrates is an animal', is necessary.[22] [3.67–68]

[290] An *ostensive* syllogism is one that arises from three terms and two propositions that conclude directly or indirectly.[23] One of these terms is called the major extremity, the second the minor extremity, and the third the middle term.[24] The *middle term* is the one that is taken twice before the conclusion. [The middle term] can be placed in different positions, for if it functions as a subject in the first proposition and is predicated in the

21 Aristotle *Prior Analytics* 1.3.25b18.

22 For additional statements on a syllogism *per impossible* see 296–297; Aristotle *Prior Analytics* 1.29.45a24–b10, and *Posterior Analytics* 1.26.87a1–30; and Kneale, *The Development of Logic*, pp. 76–77.

23 For the notions of directly and indirectly derived conclusions see 289.

24 The subject and predicate of the conclusion will normally be, respectively, the minor and major extremes. But see 291 and its notes.

second, it is called the first figure; if it is predicated in both it is called the second figure; and if it serves as a subject in both, it is called the third figure.[25] Hence, the verse:

A subject and a predicate in the first,
Twice a predicate in the second,
In the third twice a subject.

The *major extremity* is always asserted in the first proposition, which is called the major from that term. The *minor extremity* is always asserted in the second proposition, which is so-called from it and other causes – but I have no interest in them. The major extremity in the first figure is always the predicate of the major proposition; the minor extremity the subject of the minor. In the second figure the major extremity is the subject of the major; the minor extremity the subject of the minor. In the third figure the major extremity is the predicate of the major; the minor extremity the predicate of the minor. [3.69–77]

[291] To conclude *directly* is to predicate the major extremity of the minor extremity in the conclusion, and the conclusion is derived in this way in the third and second figures and in the first four moods of the first figure.[26] To conclude *indirectly* is to predicate the minor extremity of the major extremity, and the conclusion is derived in this way in the last five moods of the first figure.[27] [3.78–79]

[292] One should know, however, that nothing follows from exclusively negative propositions. Nor does anything follow from only particular ones. Then again, if either of the premises is negative, the conclusion will be negative. If either is particular, the conclusion will be particular. A universal affirmative and particular negative can be concluded in the first figure because both the minor and major can be universal, particular, affir-

25 A syllogistic figure is simply the arrangement of the terms in a syllogism. The arrangement dictates the validity or invalidity of the inference. To be subordinated is to serve as a subject in a sentence. Thus the arrangement of the terms in the premises of the three figures of a syllogism are as follows:

S = subject of conclusion; P = predicate of conclusion; and M = middle term.

	First Figure	Second Figure	Third Figure
Major	M P	P M	M P
Minor	S M	S M	M S
Conclusion	S P	S P	S P

26 In direct inferences the subject of the conclusion appears in the minor and the predicate in the major.

27 In indirect inferences the subject of the conclusion appears in the major and the predicate in the minor. In 297–299 Bacon will show how to reduce indirect syllogisms to direct ones, namely, by conversion and transposition of the major and minor.

mative or negative. In the second figure the major is always universal and the conclusion negative. In the third figure the minor is always affirmative and the conclusion particular. [3.80–86]

[293] The *first figure* has nine moods. The first four conclude directly; the last five conclude indirectly.[28] The *first mood* consists of two universal affirmatives concluding to a universal affirmative, as in 'Every animal is a substance, every man is an animal; therefore every man is a substance'. The *second mood* consists of a preceding universal negative and a subsequent universal affirmative concluding to a universal negative. Thus, 'No stone is an ass, every pearl is a stone; therefore no pearl is an ass'. The *third mood* consists of a preceding universal affirmative and a subsequent particular affirmative concluding to a particular affirmative, as in 'Every man is an animal, some grammarian is a man; therefore some grammarian is an animal'. The *fourth mood* is [made up] of a preceding universal negative and a subsequent particular affirmative concluding to a negative particular. So, 'No man is a stone, something capable of laughing is a man; therefore something capable of laughing is not a stone'. The *fifth mood* consists of two universal affirmatives concluding to a particular affirmative. Thus, 'Every white thing is a colored thing, every thing that pierces sight is a white thing; therefore some colored thing is a thing that pierces sight'.[29] The *sixth mood* consists of a preceding universal negative and a subsequent universal affirmative concluding to a universal negative, as in 'Nothing capable of braying is a man, every ass is something capable of braying; therefore no man is an ass'. The *seventh mood* consists of a preceding universal affirmative and a subsequent particular affirmative concluding to a particular affirmative. E.g., 'Every whiteness is a color, some habit is a whiteness; therefore some color is a habit'. The *eighth mood* consists of a preceding universal affirmative and a subsequent universal negative concluding to a particular negative, as in 'Every natural power is a quality, no passion is a natural power; therefore some quality is not a passion'. The *ninth mood* consists of a preceding particular affirmative and a subsequent universal negative concluding to a particular negative. Thus, 'Some figure is a quality, no passive quality is a figure; therefore some quality is not a passive quality'. [3.87–96]

[294] The *second figure* contains four moods. The *first mood* consists of a preceding universal negative and a subsequent universal affirmative concluding to a universal negative, as in 'No natural power is a relation, every equivalency is a relation; therefore no equivalency is a natural

28 Existential import is to be assumed in all universal propositions.

29 For Bacon's reduction of this mood see 297. After the Middle Ages the five indirect moods of the first figure were grouped together in a fourth figure.

power'. The *second mood* consists of a preceding universal affirmative and a subsequent universal negative concluding to a universal negative, as in 'Every putting on of a tunic is a habit, no when is a habit; therefore no when is a putting on of a tunic'. The *third mood* consists of a preceding universal negative and a subsequent particular affirmative concluding to a particular negative. E.g., 'No horse is a man, something capable of laughing is a man; therefore something capable of laughing is not a horse'. The *fourth mood* consists of a preceding universal affirmative and a subsequent particular negative concluding to a particular negative, as in 'Every man is a substance, some quality is not a substance; therefore some quality is not a man'. In this figure one always concludes directly.[30] [3.97–102]

[295] The case is similar in *the third figure*, which arises when the middle term serves as the subject in both propositions. It contains six moods. In this figure the minor is always affirmative and the conclusion particular. The *first mood* consists of two universal affirmatives concluding to a particular affirmative, e.g., 'Every man is an animal, every man is a substance; therefore some substance is an animal'. The *second mood* consists of a preceding universal negative and a subsequent universal affirmative concluding to a negative particular, as in 'No stone is a man, every stone is a substance; therefore some substance is not a man'. The *third mood* consists of a preceding particular affirmative and a subsequent universal affirmative concluding to a particular affirmative, e.g., 'Some pearl is a substance, every pearl is a stone; therefore some stone is a substance'. The *fourth mood* consists of a preceding universal affirmative and a subsequent particular affirmative concluding to a particular affirmative, e.g., 'Every ass is an animal, some ass is a thing capable of braying; therefore some thing capable of braying is an animal'. The *fifth mood* consists of a preceding particular negative and a subsequent universal affirmative concluding to a particular negative. So, 'Some stone is not an animal, every stone is a substance; therefore some substance is not an animal'. The *sixth mood* consists of a preceding universal negative and a subsequent particular affirmative concluding to a particular negative, e.g., 'No lion is a stone, some lion is a thing that roars; therefore some thing that roars is not a stone'.

Barbara, Celarent, Darii, Ferio, Baralipton
Celantes, Dabitis, Fapesmo, Frisesomorum
Cesare, Campestres, Festino, Baroco, Darapti
Felapton, Disamis, Datisi, Bocardo, Ferison[31] [3.103–111]

30 For the notion of concluding directly see 291.

31 In 296 this mnemonic is explained; its purpose is to facilitate one's ability to remember all the nineteen valid moods and how the last fifteen are reduced to the first four.

[296] One should know about reduction that all moods of the third and second figures and the five moods of the first that conclude indirectly are reduced to the first four moods of the first figure.[32] Note too that any mood that begins with 'B' ought to be reduced to Barbara; any beginning with 'C' is reduced to Celarent; any by 'D' to Darii; and any by 'F' to Ferio. Also, it should be known that 's', wherever placed, signifies that the preceding vowel is converted simply, i.e., the proposition that is designated by that vowel. And wherever 'p' is placed, it signifies that the proposition that is understood by the preceding vowel is wont to be converted by limitation. Wherever 'm' is placed, it signifies a transposition of the premises. And where 'c' is placed, it signifies a reduction *per impossible*. Because the first four moods of the first figure are perfect, all the other moods are imperfect, and so are reduced to them, because everything imperfect is reduced to something perfect.[33] [3.112–118]

[297] The fifth mood, therefore, of *the first figure* is reduced to the first mood by conversion by limitation of the conclusion. But this seems to be against conversion, because it has already been said that a particular affirmative is only converted simply. One should reply that, although a particular of its nature and in as much as it is considered by itself and absolutely might not be able to be converted to a universal, nevertheless it can legitimately be so converted by its comparison and relation to the preceding universal propositions, which [latter] can be led to a universal and a particular conclusion.[34] The sixth mood is reduced by simple conversion of the conclusion. The seventh mood is reduced in a similar manner. The eighth mood is reduced by conversion by limitation of the major and by simple conversion of the minor, and by transposition of the minor into the major, and vice versa.[35] The ninth mood is reduced by simple conversion of the major and the minor and by transposition of the major and minor. [3.119–125]

[298] The first mood of *the second figure* is reduced to the second mood of the first figure by simple conversion of the major. The second

32 For the notions of direct and indirect inference see 291.

33 For the notions of perfect and imperfect syllogisms see 276.

34 To call an 'A' proposition the converse of an 'I' is to focus simply on the mechanics of conversion by limitation – exchange the positions of the terms and change the quantity – with no dependence on the inclusion/exclusion of the terms themselves. Hence, it would be more accurate to say in these kinds of cases that the premises of themselves yield the desired 'A' proposition whose converse by limitation is the 'I' proposition given as the stated conclusion.

35 As Kretzmann notes apropos of William's and Peter's (and I would add, Lambert's) identical claim, "this is not a genuine reduction because conversion by limitation is not reversible." The mistake, he adds, is Aristotle's. *Introductiones*, trans. Kretzmann, p. 64 and n. 30; *Tractatus* 4.6; *Logica*, p. 116.27–30; Aristotle *Prior Analytics* 1.6.28a17–29.

mood is reduced to the second mood of the first figure by simple conversion of the minor and conclusion and by transposition of the major into the minor, and vice versa. The third mood is reduced to the fourth mood of the first figure by simple conversion of the major. The fourth mood is reduced to the first mood of the first figure by a syllogism *ad impossible* that must consist of the contradictory of the conclusion, [the former] given by hypothesis. From [the contradictory of the conclusion] taken along with the major the contradictory of the minor (which is an impossible one) ought to be concluded and, once it is destroyed, that is destroyed from which it followed.[36] But this was the contradictory of the proposed conclusion because one of the premises is necessary, and hence, it is impossible. So, the conclusion was incorrectly said not to follow from the premises because, whenever the opposite of the conclusion of any argumentation taken with one of the premises implies the opposite of the other premise, that argumentation is valid. [3.126–129]

[299] The first mood of *the third figure* is reduced to the third mood of the first figure by conversion by limitation of the minor. The second mood is reduced to the fourth mood likewise by conversion of the minor by limitation. The third mood is reduced to the third mood [of the first figure] by simple conversion of the major, by transposition of the major into the minor, and by simple conversion of the conclusion. The fourth mood is reduced to the third mood by simple conversion of the minor. The fifth mood is reduced to the first mood of the first figure by a syllogism *ad impossible* that must consist of the contradictory of the conclusion together with the minor to imply the contradictory of the major and the opposite of the major asserted in the position of the conclusion.[37] The sixth mood is reduced to the fourth mood of the first figure by simple conversion of the minor. [3.130–135]

[300] An *enthymeme* is an imperfect syllogism, for it argues from one proposition actually posited and the other implied. E.g., 'A man is an animal; therefore Socrates is an animal'. It is derived from '*en*', which means in, and '*mime*', which means mind, as it were, "retaining one proposition in the mind."[38] Enthymeme is found under *syllogism*. [3.136–138]

[301] *Induction* is a progression from singular things to universal ones, as in 'This man runs, and that man runs, (and so on for singulars); therefore every man runs'. With respect to it two things ought to be noted: that no counter-example may occur and that it arise through proper singu-

36 For the notion of a syllogism *ad* (*per*) *impossibile* see 289.

37 Once again, for the notion of a syllogism *ad* (*per*) *impossibile* see 289.

38 There is some confusion at this time about the etymology of the term. Bacon derives it from 'έν' and 'μίμος' whereas Lambert says it comes from 'έν' and 'τίμος' (*Logica*, p. 111.5). Actually it comes from 'έν' and 'θύμος'.

lars. So, if it is argued thus: 'Socrates is Socrates, Plato is Plato, (and so on); therefore every man is every man', there is no induction because the singulars chosen are not the singulars of a universal, since the singulars of a universal proposition must communicate in a universal predicate, as in 'This man is every man, etc.'. [3.139–140]

[302] *Example* occurs when one particular is proved by another, as in 'In school a doctor is to be chosen not by lot but by art; therefore on ship a governor is to be chosen not by lot but by art'. [3.141]

[303] Since the form of a syllogism has been treated in general, we must now treat it with respect to its species. This form can be applied to necessary matter, and in this way a *demonstrative syllogism* arises. But it can also be applied to probable matter and in two senses: either to what is only superficially probable, and then we have a *sophistical syllogism*, or superficially and throughout, and then we have a *dialectical one*, in the sense in which we say something is wet that is wet on the surface and throughout, and something is wet that is wet only on the surface. Besides these there is a fourth way of syllogizing – the *falsigraphic syllogism* – which is opposed to the demonstrative just as the sophistical is opposed to the dialectical, because the dialectical syllogism consists of probables, the sophistical of apparently probables, the demonstrative of things true and necessary and derived from the principles of science, whereas the falsigraphic from the opposites of principles and from impossibles and principles incorrectly understood and adapted to what is false. [3.142–145]

[304] One sort of demonstrative syllogism is *quia*, the other *propter quid*.[39] A demonstration *propter quid* is that by which an effect is made known through a cause. This syllogism is defined by Aristotle in this way: "A demonstration is a syllogism causing one to know." "We are of the opinion," [he continues], "that we know each thing when we think we know the cause because of which it is and that of which it is a cause and that it is not possible for the case to be otherwise."[40] To know in this way is solely had by the demonstrative syllogism *propter quid* because such demonstration is "from things that are primary, true, and immediate, and are prior to, better known than, and the causes of a conclusion."[41] In this

39 For Bacon's treatment of a demonstration *quia* see 323. His treatment of the theory of demonstration is unique and for support of this claim see de Libera's comments in *Sd* 1–2, pp. 174–177.

40 For the first part of the definition see Aristotle *Posterior Analytics* 1.2.71b17–19; for the second part see ibid., 1.2.71b9–12.

41 "... [I]t is necessary for demonstrative understanding in particular to depend on things which are true and primitive and immediate and more familiar than and prior to and explanatory of the conclusion (for in this way the principles will also be appropriate to what is being proved)." Aristotle *Posterior Analytics* 1.2.71b20–22, trans. Jonathan Barnes, in *CWA*, vol. 1, p. 115.

sort of demonstration there must be propositions that are true and that are also necessary. Primary propositions are, according to what Algazel says in his *Logic*, "those that the intellect *per se* must naturally believe, e.g., these: 'Two is more than one', and 'Every whole is greater than any of its parts', and 'Whatever are equal to the same thing are equal to each other'."[42] True propositions are taken for necessary ones because no others occur in demonstrative syllogisms. An immediate proposition is one to which no other is prior in its class by which it can be demonstrated and between whose subject and predicate there is no middle by which the predicate could be demonstrated of the subject.[43] A proposition of this sort is a primary one. 'Prior' and 'better known' have two senses: with *respect to us* and with *respect to nature*. Things prior and better known *to us* are close to our senses, such as things that are more particular and singular, because every recognition (*agnitio*) of ours has its origin in a sensory faculty. Things prior *naturally* and absolutely are those that are farthest removed from a sensory faculty, as are those that are more universal. A demonstration of this sort arises from things prior naturally and absolutely. But it is necessary that those propositions be the causes of a conclusion. [3.146–158]

[305] One should know that there are three sorts of causes: a cause only of *implying a conclusion*, a cause of *implying and proving it*, and a cause of *implying it, of proving it, and of its being*. In every syllogism the premises or the middle are the cause of implying the conclusion, but in a syllogism arising from general matter – as in 'Every *a* is *b*, every *c* is *a*; therefore every *c* is *b*' – the premises are the cause only of implying the conclusion. In a dialectical syllogism the premises are the cause of implying and proving the conclusion. In a demonstrative one they are the cause of implying, of proving, and of the being of the conclusion. But in others – for example, in a sophistical syllogism, in one defective in matter, and in a falsigraphic one – the premises are neither the cause of the being of, nor of proving, nor of only implying the conclusion.[44] Although something false follows from false premises, yet the false is not proved by the false; the former appears true and probable but only because of the foolishness of a respondent, as in the case of a falsigraphic syllogism, or because of some fallacy, as in the case of a sophistic syllogism defective in matter. In a syl-

42 Algazel *Logica* 4, ed. Lohr, 274.539–541.

43 To say that these propositions need no middle to know their truth is to say they need nothing else in order for their truth to be known, which, also, is to say they are self-evident.

44 A defective syllogism is one defective either because it employs propositions only apparently probable which result in a fallacy – defective in matter (453–456) – or because of a defect in its mood, figure, or the way the premises are joined to imply the conclusion – defective in form (380–381).

logism defective in form the premises are in no way the cause of the conclusion; they only appear to be such causes. [3.159–163]

[306] One should know that there are four kinds of causes of the being of something, namely, *material*, *formal*, *final*, and *efficient*. Every caused thing has these four causes in some way. For example, the formal cause of a man is a soul, the material cause a body, the efficient cause is God, and eternal happiness the final cause, and so on. The premises in a demonstration, moreover, include such a cause of the conclusion, because the middle is necessarily one of these causes with respect to the conclusion. [3.164–166]

[307] So, one should know that a conclusion in a demonstration arises from a proper attribute and the latter's subject.[45] A *proper attribute* is always predicated of a subject in a conclusion, as in 'A triangle has three angles equal to two right [angles]': this is the conclusion of a demonstration. An attribute can be defined through a formal, material, final, or efficient cause. Then this definition must become the middle for proving the attribute. Nevertheless, not only the definition of an attribute is to be taken as the middle but also the principles of the *subject*, i.e., the definition of the subject ought to be taken along with the definition of the attribute because the complete definition of an attribute is not through its own principles. Indeed, the principles of the subject must be added, because Aristotle says in Book Seven of the *Metaphysics* that the definition of an attribute must arise by way of addition, namely, of the principles of a subject to its own definition constituted from its own proper principles.[46] For there is a definition that is only of an attribute itself, as one that is comprised of [the attribute's] own genus and differentia, i.e., [the attribute's] own principles.[47] This is not the middle in a demonstration. Another kind of definition is comprised of that definition plus the definition of [the attribute's] subject, and this kind is called '*propter quid*'. This is the middle in a demonstration. For example, the definition of "having three" is "being a plane figure bounded by three straight lines, having an outside angle equal to its two opposing inside angles." The definition of the subject is "plane figure bounded by three straight lines." "Having an [outside] angle [equal to its two opposing inside angles]" is the definition of the attribute, stating only the *quid* and not the *propter quid*. Therefore, let the demonstration be as follows: 'Every plane figure bounded by three straight lines and having an outside angle equivalent to the two inside angles opposite it has three angles equal to two right

45 A proper attribute is a proprium, for which see above, 16 and 20. For an example see 307.

46 Aristotle *Metaphysics* 7.5.1031a1–3.

47 E.g., "having three straight lines" is the definition of an attribute of a certain plane figure; but without mention of its subject (the plane figure) it cannot be used as the middle in the syllogism about triangles in the next paragraph.

ones; every triangle is like that; therefore every triangle has three angles equal to two right angles'. Likewise, examples of the other causes could be posited, but let these suffice for the present. [3.167–172]

[308] But one should note that not every attribute is wont to be demonstrated by the four causes, because mathematical attributes are only demonstrated by a formal cause, joined, however, to the matter in which [the attribute] is present, which is a subject or the principles of a subject, as was clear in the example just mentioned. For the formal definition of an attribute was joined to the definition of the subject in the middle, which definition of the subject signifies the matter in which the attribute is present, but not from which it is. So, in mathematics neither the matter from which nor the efficient cause nor the final cause is considered in order to demonstrate a conclusion, because these things are not present there. Nor does a mathematician consider the matter in which there is an attribute, which is true matter. For a subject and its principles are not true matter, but matter only analogically so-called. In mathematical things there occurs an abstraction of things from matter, and so a mathematician does not consider matter. He does not consider a line in so far as it exists in something bronze, or gold, or wood, or in some other such matter, but abstracts it from any sort of matter and considers it not in so far as it is present in some sort of matter. Because of this, matter does not pertain to his consideration. By the same line of reasoning neither does an efficient cause, because a mathematician abstracts his subjects likewise from movement and change, and so, since an efficient cause is a principle of movement and change, he does not concern himself with an efficient cause. Then too, because in mathematical things there is no good or goal, as Aristotle says in Book Three of the *Metaphysics*, so a mathematician does not concern himself with a final cause.[48] Because of this, mathematical attributes are not demonstrated by means of a material, efficient, or final cause, but only by a formal cause. But natural attributes can be demonstrated by means of all the causes. They are demonstrated by matter because all natural things are joined to matter, as Aristotle says in Book One of the *Metaphysics*.[49] They have a form in that matter, so there can be a demonstration there by means of a formal cause. Because form is educed from the potency of matter by an efficient cause, so there can be a demonstration by means of an efficient cause in natural things. And because all natural things have been placed in an order toward a good end, so can a demonstration by means of a final cause occur in them. [3.173–179]

[309] Yet one should note that there are conditions other than the preceding for demonstrative propositions, for it is necessary that they be about all, be *per se*, and be in accord with what the subject is. [3.180]

48 Aristotle *Metaphysics* 3.2.996a35–b1.

49 Aristotle *Metaphysics* 1.3.983b6, *ad sensum*.

[310] I call "*about all,*" not what is in one thing and not in another, nor sometimes is the case and sometimes is not, but what is in all and always.[50] So, let it be stated that, in the case of demonstrative propositions, for a proposition to be about all there must be a universality as to subjects in it and a universality as to time, as in 'Every man is an animal'. "About all" adds in the case of demonstrative propositions the universality of time over "said of all" in the absolute sense, which we have already treated (277). [3.181–183]

[311] A proposition is said to be *per se* in four ways. The first way occurs when the whole definition or some part of the definition is predicated of what is defined, as in 'Thunder is the extinction of fire in a cloud'.[51] The second way occurs when a proper attribute is predicated of a subject or of its definition, as in 'A triangle has three angles equal to two right angles', 'A plane figure bounded by three straight lines, etc.', 'A number is either even or odd', and 'A line is either straight or curved'. The third way of speaking *per se* is not a way of inherence but of being, according to which we say that something is *per se*, something else is *per accidens*. For example, a substance is *per se* – and especially a first substance – whereas accidents are *per accidens*, i.e., through another, namely, through a first substance. For Aristotle says this in Book Five of the *Metaphysics*, namely, that the third way of speaking *per se* pertains to what has place and position *per se*, and such is an individual in [the category] Substance.[52] In another translation in the chapter "*On Per Se*" in the *Posterior Analytics* it is said that something essential is in the third way, just as a first substance and a singular is said to be *per se*.[53] Hence, it is placed among the ways of speaking *per se* so that the number of ways might be completed and also to indicate that a subject in a demonstration has that way with respect to the attribute to be demonstrated. For otherwise it would not contribute to the nature of a demonstration. The fourth way occurs when the cause of a predicate is in a subject of which the predicate cannot be demonstrated.[54] Hence, it differs in name from the second way because there the

50 "About all" in this context is the condition that obtains when what is said in the predicate of a proposition applies to every individual named by the subject. When this condition obtains one has an 'A' proposition. The condition "according to what [the subject] is" obtains when what is said of the subject is said in virtue of its whole notion.

51 The example is from Aristotle's *Posterior Analytics* 2.11.94b32–34. For this paragraph see Aristotle's *Posterior Analytics* 1.4.73a35–b15.

52 Aristotle *Metaphysics* 5.18.1022a23.

53 Cf. Aristotle *Posterior Analytics* 1.4.73b5–9.

54 I.e., the predicate in 'The one who was killed has perished' is analytically (*per se*) contained in the subject, but the cause of perishing (by being slain) is not so contained. This assumes that the example (which follows in the same paragraph) is to be taken as representative of the fourth kind of *per se* and not the second.

cause of the predicate is in a subject of which [the predicate] can be demonstrated. [An example of the fourth way is] 'The one who was killed has perished'. Nor is it necessary to express the cause, as is claimed by many, i.e., that it ought to be said this way: 'The one who was killed has perished by a slaying', because the implicit and explicit create no essential difference anywhere. For were it to be asked of them whether the proposition 'The one who was killed has perished' were *per se* true, they necessarily would have to concede this. But, nevertheless, [this represents] neither the first way nor the second or third, and therefore the fourth is present there. And Aristotle sufficiently proposes in Book Five of the *Metaphysics* without mentioning a cause that 'Man is man' represents the fourth way.[55] So, the fourth way occurs when the same thing is predicated of itself, for the cause of which the predicate cannot be demonstrated is in the subject. [3.184–191]

[312] But one should know that the second way of speaking *per se* occurs in the conclusion, not in the premises. The third way in a demonstration denominates neither a proposition nor a conclusion. But the first way can occur in a conclusion when a material definition is demonstrated, as Aristotle teaches in Book Two of the *Posterior Analytics*;[56] it always occurs in the minor proposition of a demonstration in the strictest sense and in the first figure with respect to the principles and definition of a subject, which are taken in the middle. With respect to the principles of an attribute and its definition, which latter likewise is taken in the middle: if it is the formal definition of an attribute, then it is the fourth way, because it cannot be demonstrated of a subject. If it is a material definition, perhaps it is the second way, because it can be demonstrated of a subject by a formal definition.[57] The fourth way always occurs in the first proposition however it is considered, because the cause of the predicate is in the subject of which it cannot be demonstrated. The premises as well as the conclusion are about all.[58] [3.192–196]

[313] A proposition is said to be "*in accord with what the subject is*" when the subject taken as a whole is the cause of the predicate and a precise one and when the predicate principally inheres in it, as in the proposition 'A triangle has three [angles], etc.' For *triangle* is wholly the cause of this attribute, but *isosceles* or some other species of triangle is not. For an isosceles triangle is an equilateral triangle: in as much as it is a triangle it is the cause of this attribute, not in as much as it is equilateral.[59] And so it is

55 Aristotle *Metaphysics* 5.18.1022a33–35.

56 Aristotle *Posterior Analytics* 2.11.94a25–35.

57 For the difference between a formal and material definition see 306–307.

58 For the notion of "about all" see 309.

59 'Equilateral' is to be understood in the etymological sense of "equal sides," a notion which is meant to exclude the consideration of the base of the triangle.

a cause [of having three angles, etc.] according to a part of itself, not according to the whole. Because of this, the attribute ["having three angles"] does not inhere principally in it, nor "in accord with what the subject is." Likewise, this is "in accord with what the subject is": 'Man is something able to laugh', because man is the precise cause of this attribute, but not Socrates. Therefore, the condition "in accord with what the subject is" is a reduplication because man as man or man in as much as man is something able to laugh. Socrates, however, is able to laugh, not as Socrates, but as man. [3.197–199]

[314] From these three conditions – "about all," "*per se*," and "in accord with what the subject is" – there results one condition for demonstrative propositions, which condition is called *universality*. A predicate is universal with respect to a subject – this is always the case in demonstrative propositions – when the predicate inheres in it universally for all that it supposits and at all times, and when the predicate inheres in it *per se*, and when it inheres in a subject in accord with what the subject is. [3.200–201]

[315] In connection with this one should know that a proposition is said to be true *per accidens*. But this occurs in two ways: It is said to be true *per accidens* whenever the predicate is *per accidens* an accident, as in 'A man is white', or is an inseparable accident (which only is inseparable), as in 'A raven is black'.[60] A proposition is also said to be true *per accidens* when the opposite of the predicate inhering *per se* in the subject is removed from that very subject, as in 'A man is not an ass', for this is true *per accidens* with respect to 'A man is a man'; likewise in 'A man is not a stone' because, if it is an animal, it is not a stone. These ways of speaking *per accidens* are said to be against the *per se* way. Another way of speaking *per accidens* is when a proposition is true *per se*, but the predicate is not in the subject in a primary sense, but in a secondary sense and as a consequence, namely, because [the predicate] is understood in such a subject in which such a predicate inheres in a primary sense. For example, in 'An isosceles has three [angles] etc.'. In 'isosceles' there is understood 'triangle', in which [latter] such a predicate [as "having three angles", etc.] inheres in a primary sense, and so it inheres in 'isosceles' *per accidens*. This [sense of] *per accidens* is in contrast to "in accord with what the subject is," not in contrast to *per se*, because the proposition 'An isosceles has three angles, etc.', is true *per se*, and likewise 'Socrates is an animal', because animal inheres in Socrates in the first sense of speaking *per se* and in accord with what Aristotle says in Book Five of the *Metaphysics*, that Callias is alive in the first way of speaking *per se*, and 'a living thing' is asserted [in 'Socrates is an animal'] in place of 'animal'. For he says there that the predicate falls under the definition of the subject.[61] [3.202–209]

60 For a discussion of the notion of separable/inseparable accidents see 21–22.

61 Aristotle *Metaphysics* 5.18.1022a25.

[316] But this seems to be false since Callias is an individual and an individual does not have a definition. One should reply that an individual does not have a definition in a primary sense, yet as a consequence it does have one, namely, the definition of its species. So the definition of a species and all its parts, granted they are not in a primary sense in their individuals, yet are in them *per se* and in the first way of speaking *per se*. [3.210–211]

[317] But this way [of speaking *per accidens*] does not occur in a demonstration – at least not in the strictest sense – nor likewise when a part of a definition is predicated of what is defined, just as were 'A triangle is a figure' to be said, for it is necessary that the whole definition be predicated or serve as the subject, if a proposition of a demonstration in the strictest sense is to come about. [3.212]

[318] Along these lines one should know that a proposition is said to be true *secundum se* and true *per se*, and true *secundum accidens* and true *per accidens*; and these are not the same. What is true *per se* has already been explained (311–312), and what is true *per accidens* is already clear.[62] But a proposition is said to be true *secundum se* when what is naturally predicated is predicated and what naturally serves as a subject functions as the subject. This occurs when something higher is predicated of something lower, and a proprium or accident is predicated of a subject, as in 'A man is an animal', 'A man is something able to laugh', and 'A man is something white'. A proposition is said to be true *secundum accidens* when what is naturally predicated serves as the subject, and when what naturally serves as a subject is predicated. This occurs when something lower is predicated of something higher, as in 'An animal is a man', or when a subject is predicated of its proprium or accident, as in 'A thing able to laugh is a man', and 'Something white is a swan'. Aristotle proposes this in his *Posterior Analytics* and Boethius concurs in his second commentary *On Porphyry*, namely, that there are two sorts of predications: the one is oblique, the other direct: direct when it is *secundum se*, oblique when it is *secundum accidens*.[63] But since it is the same road from Thebes to Athens and vice versa, it seems that it would be the same way of speaking *per se* when one says 'A man is an animal' and 'An animal is a man' and 'A man is something able to laugh' and 'Something able to laugh is a man'. If one is permitted to call a way *per se* when it is not *secundum se*, the proposition will be reduced to the first way when the lower is predicated of the higher, and to the second when the subject [is predicated] of an accident or proprium.

62 For the notions of true *per se* and true *per accidens* see, respectively, 311–312 and 315–317.

63 Cf. Aristotle *Posterior Analytics* 1.4.73b26–74a3, and Boethius *In Isagogen Porphyrii Commenta* 2.5, ed. Brandt, p. 186.12–19.

But this will occur when taking 'ways *per se*' broadly and not strictly. [3.213–220]

[319] One should know, moreover, as Aristotle says in his *Posterior Analytics*, that whatever predicates inhere *per se* inhere necessarily, that is, that a proposition is necessary when the predicate inheres in the subject necessarily.[64] So it seems that the proposition 'A man is an animal' is true when no man exists, because it is a necessary proposition since it is *per se* true. To this I reply that the necessity of the proposition is not extended beyond the existence of the subject. So, as long as there is a man, the proposition 'A man is' is necessary because true, and 'A man is an animal', but not longer.[65] [3.221–224]

[320] But then it seems that every necessity would be relative, because, from what has already been said, a man is an animal only so long as he is, which is against what has previously been said when any necessity was said to be absolute. One should reply to this that the necessity of a proposition is not said to be relative because it has to do with the existence of the subject, but because it pertains to the determinate time in which the predicate applies to the subject, which predicate does not inhere in the subject at all times. This is clear: the proposition 'Socrates runs while he runs' is necessary by relative necessity, but not 'Socrates runs while he is'. But some contingent proposition might make a statement about an inseparable accident of a subject, and such a proposition has its truth in accord with an extension of the existence of its subject, because 'A raven is black' is true while there is a raven; but it is not a necessary proposition because the accident could be thought to be absent even though the subject remains. But this is not the case with a necessary proposition, for the predicate cannot be absent from the subject while the subject remains. A contingent proposition makes a statement about a separable accident, and its truth is not extended in accord with the extension of the existence of its subject, as in 'A man is white', because it can well be false while a man exists. From these things it is clear what sort of propositions are *per se* and what sort *per accidens*. [3.225–230]

[321] One should know that whatever inheres *per se* in a superior inheres *per se* in its inferior. Hence, just as when I say 'A man is an animal' the first way occurs, so when I say 'Socrates is an animal' and 'Socrates is able to laugh', each is true in the second way. [3.231–232]

[322] Then one should know that some demonstrations are universal, others particular. With respect to a universal one it has already been said

64 Cf. Aristotle *Posterior Analytics* 1.4.73b26–30.

65 This claim is stressed in the "*De signis*" (110–120) and *Compendium of the Study of Theology* (2.128).

(307) that it exhibits an attribute of a universal and primary subject. A demonstration is *particular* when it exhibits an attribute of a nonprimary subject, a lower and particular subject. Hence, a universal demonstration displays the attribute "having three [angles]" of a triangle, whereas a particular demonstration displays the same of an isosceles or of a quadratus triangle.[66] [3.233–236]

[323] With respect to a demonstration *quia* it should be known that there are two kinds: either it makes a cause known through an effect or an effect through a remote, nonproximate cause.[67] "*A cause through an effect*": e.g., let it be proved that a triangle is a plane figure, etc., by the fact that it has three angles equal to two right angles; or if one shows that the earth is interposed between the moon and sun by the fact that the moon is eclipsed and that the moon is interposed between us and the sun by the fact that the sun is eclipsed; or if one shows that the planets are near because they do not twinkle. For in all these cases a cause is made known through an effect. Should one argue from the converse a demonstration *propter quid* occurs. A demonstration [*quia*] *through a remote cause* occurs when one says: 'A wall does not breathe because it is not an animal'. Not to be an animal is a remote cause of why it does not breathe. These sorts of propositions can be formed into a syllogism in this way: 'Every thing that breathes is an animal, no wall is an animal; therefore no wall is a thing that breathes'. Likewise for others. [3.237–240]

[324] With respect to the *falsigraphic syllogism* one should know that it argues from a science's proper terms and principles, but as poorly understood and falsely applied, and from the opposites of principles. For example, someone wishing to square the circle, i.e., to show that a circle is equal to a square (and vice versa), squares by crescents in this way: 'Every line drawn from the same point to the same point is equal, an arc and a chord are of this sort; therefore they are equal; therefore any portion of a circle is equal to three sides of a square; therefore the whole is equal to the whole'. This syllogism is falsigraphic because it falsely applies the major proposition. For a geometrician or demonstrator understands it of straight lines, but [the one who attempts to square the circle] applies it to straight and curved ones. Or, they construct an impossible proposition (the major) in the proper terms of geometry. [3.241]

[325] We have spoken of demonstrative and falsigraphic syllogisms (304–323, 324), [and so now] we must speak of dialectical and sophistical ones. But first we must treat dialectical syllogisms because knowledge of

66 Reading at *Sd* 3, p. 218, 236.3, '*quadrato*' for '*gradato*' in MSS. O. and S. and the text.

For a comment on the term 'quadratus' see above, Part One, n. 108.

67 See 304.

something oblique depends on something direct.[68] A *dialectical syllogism* arises from probable propositions because it does not seek necessary things, but things that have the appearance of truth. For if it sometimes argues from necessary things, this is not in as much as they are necessary, but in as much as they are probable and have the appearance of truth.[69] The *probable* is what seems [to be true] to all or to many or to the most notable.[70] What is *probable to all* is that about which neither the crowd nor the wise hold a contrary opinion. What is *probable to many* is that about which the wise hold a contrary opinion. In this way one should understand with respect to the remaining: for example, those who move in the circle of the common and vulgar intellect are called "the many"; those who move in the circle of the private and certain [intellect are called] "the wise." So, the latter are called "the few" on the basis of what Aristotle says: "One must speak as the many, but think as the few," namely, the wise.[71] But because a dialectical syllogism requires a Topical relationship, one must understand Topics, because the force of such a syllogism depends on a Topic.[72] [3.242–249]

TOPICS[73]

[326] There are two kinds of Topics, namely, maxims and differentiae of maxims.[74] A *maximal proposition* is one that is known *per se* and these

68 The study of dialectical syllogisms is a focus on something oblique in the sense that such syllogisms are defined in contrast to demonstrative syllogisms. (See 325.) For the definition of 'dialectical syllogism' see Aristotle *Sophistical Refutations* 2, 165b2–4.

69 Later (373) the "probable things" to which dialectical syllogisms conclude will be called "absolutely probable" to distinguish them from the merely "apparently probable" things which are proper to sophistical syllogisms.

70 Aristotle speaks of opinions generally accepted by everyone, by the majority, or by philosophers, i.e., the most notable and illustrious. Aristotle *Topics* 1.1.100b21–22.

71 Aristotle *Topics* 2.2.110a15–19.

72 For the (promised) discussion of sophistical syllogisms see sections beginning 369 and 380. For comment on the term 'Topic' see the next note.

73 For general studies of this part of Logic see Aristotle *Topics*. Cf. Boethius *De differentiis topicis libri quattuor*, PL 64; and Kneale, pp. 33–44 (Aristotle), pp. 178–181 (Cicero), pp. 193–194 (Boethius), pp. 216–220 (Abelard), and p. 233 (William of Sherwood). See also the following works by Eleonore Stump: "Boethius's Works on the Topics," *Vivarium* 12 (1974): 77–93; *Boethius' De differentiis topicis*, trans. with notes and essays on the text (Ithaca and London: Cornell University Press, 1978); "Boethius's Theory of Topics and Its Place in Early Scholastic Logic" in *Atti del congresso internazionale di studi Boeziani*, ed. L. Obertello (Rome: Herder, 1981); "Peter of Spain on the Topics," in *Boethius and the Liberal Arts*, ed. Michael Masi (E. Bern and Las Vegas: Verlag Peter Lang, 1981), pp. 35–50; "Topics: Their Development and Absorption into Consequences,"

are primary and directly known propositions,[75] e.g., 'Of whatever a definition is predicated the thing defined is also predicated', 'Of whatever a species is said the genus is also said', and 'Whatever applies to a whole as a whole is also applied to each of its parts', and the like, as will be known later.[76] The *differentiae of maxims* are the terms placed in maxims by which maxims differ, e.g., *definition* and *thing defined*, *species* and *genus*, *whole* and *part*, and the like. A Topic that is a maxim is the foundation of an argument. For just as a foundation surrounds something in a place and gives it stability and makes it firm, so also a maximal proposition surrounds an argument and confirms it. A Topic that is a differentia of a maxim is that from which a suitable argument is drawn because an argument is given its name either from a definition or a description or a whole or a part, as will be known. [3.250–255]

[327] Some Topics are intrinsic, others extrinsic, still others intermediate. To understand this one should note that every argumentation ought to resolve a question.[77] A question, however, is a proposition about a matter in doubt, e.g., 'Does Socrates run or not'? Every question, moreover, has two terms, namely, a predicate and a subject. One must, therefore, discover a middle between the two terms placed in the question in order to compose or divide those terms. We discover that middle in some Topic, for example, in one that is the differentia of a maxim, and if this Topic pertains especially greatly to either of the terms placed in the question in such a way that it indicates its whole nature or a part, then it is called an intrinsic Topic because it pertains to the intrinsic nature of the term placed in the ques-

---

CHLMP, pp. 273–299; *Boethius's In Ciceronis Topica* (Ithaca: Cornell University Press, 1988); and "Logic in the Early Twelfth Century," in *Meaning and Inference in Medieval Philosophy*, pp. 31–55. '*Locus*' is Cicero's translation of Aristotle's term 'τόπος' and it is the Latin term that names the subject of this section, variously translated into English by 'Topic' or 'ground'. I have chosen the former and shall capitalize it to underscore that it is being used in a technical sense.

74 Apropos of the distinction between Topics and maxims Kretzmann writes: "The ground [Topic] of the dialectical argument is the necessary (or probable) connection supporting the inference, while the maxim is the formula expressing that connection in general terms." (*Introductiones*, trans. Kretzmann, p. 70, n. 7.) Note from what follows that 'differentia' here does not have the same meaning as it had in 14, where it was the name of one of the predicables.

75 Cf. Boethius *De differentiis topicis libri quattuor* 1, PL 64.1176C, trans. Stump, p. 33.18–25.

76 The reference is to all the different kinds of Topics treated in this section.

77 Cf. Aristotle *Topics* 1.10.104a3–105a9, where dialectical propositions and dialectical problems are distinguished.

tion.[78] If it pertains in no way to the nature of the terms placed in the question and is entirely alien, it is called an extrinsic Topic. But if it maintains a sort of middle status and is neither entirely alien nor entirely consonant and internal, it is called an intermediate Topic.[79] Examples of these will appear later. [3.256–262]

[328] *Intrinsic Topics* are divided into Topics from substance and from the concomitants of substance. The *Topic from substance* is a middle indicating the whole nature of either extreme of a conclusion to be proved, and there are six kinds of these: from definition, [from the thing defined], from description, from the thing described, from the explanation of a name, and from the name explained.[80] What a definition is, and what a description is, and how they come about have already been explained (28). An explanation of a name is a definition asserting other names, i.e., the exposition of one word by means of others, as in 'Philosophy is the love of wisdom' and 'A philosopher is a lover of wisdom', from '*philos*', which means love, and '*sophos*', which means wisdom.[81] [3.263–266]

[329] One argues from any one of these Topics in accord with four maxims. First, when affirming in this way: 'A mortal rational animal runs; therefore a man runs'. If it is asked where the Topic comes from, one should reply *from definition* because, if it is reduced to a syllogism, the middle term is the definition of 'man'. So it is clear that an argumentation of this sort is drawn from the differentia of a maxim. If the maxim is sought by which the argumentation is confirmed, this should be selected: Whatever is predicated of a definition is also predicated of the thing defined. Second, one argues when denying in this way: 'No mortal rational animal runs; therefore no man runs'. The Topic is from definition; the maxim: Whatever is removed from a definition is also removed from the thing defined. One argues a third way when affirming in this way: 'Socrates is still a sensitive animate substance; therefore Socrates is an animal'. The Topic is from definition; the maxim: Of whatever a definition is predicated the thing defined is also predicated. One argues a fourth way when denying in this way: 'A stone is not a sensitive animate substance; therefore a stone is not an animal'. The Topic is from definition; the maxim: From whatever

78 In 327 Bacon makes it clear that the relationship of the middle term to both terms in the conclusion is at issue, and confirms this by examples wherein the middle term serves at one time to define the subject of the conclusion and at another time the predicate (329).

79 Reading at *Sd* 3, p. 221, 261.1, *nec* with MS. O. against *sed* in MS. S. and the text.

80 The Topic from the thing defined is treated in 329; its name is inadvertently left out here by Bacon.

81 To be accurate '*sophos*' here should be '*sophia*' for the "explanation" of the first example. For an exposition of the Topic see 331.

a definition is removed the thing defined is also removed. If, however, the thing defined is used as the middle and the definition is placed in the question or the conclusion, the Topic will be from the thing defined. The maxims are the same, only the terms have been exchanged, as in 'A man runs; therefore a mortal rational animal runs'. The Topic is from the thing defined; the maxim: Whatever is predicated of the thing defined is also predicated of the definition. And likewise for the other examples and maxims. [3.267–272]

[330] The Topic *from description* arises in similar fashion in four ways. For example, 'A naturally domestic animal runs; therefore a man runs'. The Topic is from description; the maxim: Whatever is predicated of a description is also predicated of the thing described. It also arises when denying, as in 'That which is able to lie beneath accidents is not a relation; therefore a substance is not a relation'. The maxim: Whatever is removed from a description is also removed from the thing described. Similarly it arises when affirming in connection with a predicate: 'Whiteness is that because of which we are called qualified; therefore whiteness is a quality'. The maxim: Of whatever a description is predicated the thing described is also predicated. It arises when denying in this way: 'Blackness is not a movement on the basis of which it would be related to an agent; therefore blackness is not an action'.[82] The maxim: From whatever a description is removed the thing described is also removed. But if one argues vice versa, the Topic from the thing described will arise and the same maxims, only with the order of the terms transposed. [3.273–278]

[331] The Topic *from the explanation of a name* likewise arises in four ways. First, in this way: 'Love of wisdom is good; therefore philosophy is good'. The Topic is from the explanation of a name. The maxim: Whatever is predicated of the explanation of a name is also predicated of the name explained. In a similar way are the other [argumentations] and maxims made clear by what has already been said. An example: 'A *homo* (man) is an animal made *ab humo* (from the earth)', and 'A philosopher is a lover of wisdom'. One should know that, if every definition indicating what a name means is called an explanation, then this Topic will be constructive and destructive, just as in the previously given examples.[83] But if we include in it every etymology, i.e., every exposition of a name, the Topic will not be necessary but only probable, because Peter Helias says that some expositions provide more than the thing exposed, some less. For example, '*ledens pedem*' (foot-wounder) provides more [exposition] than '*lapis*' (stone) does,

82 Reading at *Sd* 3, p. 223, 277.1, '*quem*' against '*quod*' in MSS. O. and S. and the text.

83 'Constructive' and 'destructive' here are synonyms for 'affirmative' and 'negative'. But see n. 96.

and 'comprehension of letters' provides less than 'syllable' does.[84] The Topic from the name explained arises vice versa. [3.279–283]

[332] The Topic *from concomitants of substance* is a middle indicating part of the nature of either extreme of a conclusion to be proved. It is divided into seven kinds.[85] One is the Topic *from the whole*, another *from the parts*, another *from the cause*, another *from generation*, another *from destruction*, another *from uses*, and another *from associated accidents*. There are six Topics from the whole because 'whole' is spoken of in six ways. [3.284–286]

[333] One is a *universal whole*, like a genus with respect to a species, a species with respect to an individual, to which species an individual corresponds as a subjective part, as does an individual with respect to a species and a species with respect to a genus, and any particular differentia with respect to its higher differentia, and a proper particular with respect to what is a proprium and superior, and an accident and something inferior with respect to its superior. But the argumentation holds from this sort of whole to its part only when denying, as in 'A stone is not an animal; therefore it is not a man', 'Socrates is not something rational; therefore he is not this rational thing', 'He is not something able to laugh; therefore he is not this thing that is able to laugh', and 'He is not a white thing; therefore he is not this white thing'. If it is asked where the Topic comes from, one should reply that it comes from a universal whole. The maxim: From whatever a universal whole is removed each of its parts is also removed. [The Topic] from a universal whole can arise in the same way in connection with a subject when denying: 'No animal runs; therefore no man runs', 'No thing able to laugh runs; therefore no man runs', 'A man is not running; therefore this thing able to laugh is not running', and so on. The maxim: Whatever is removed from a universal whole is also removed from any part of it. But one should know that it is necessary that one always proceed from this sort of whole to a part in a universal negation in such a way that the negation is always placed before the whole, because, if it is placed after the whole and a negation of the particular arises, [the inference] does not hold. Neither 'An animal is not

84 Peter Helias, *Summa super Priscianum*, ed. Leo Reilly, vol. 1 (Toronto: Pontifical Institute of Mediaeval Studies, 1993), p. 70: "Etymology is the exposition of a word by another word, whether by one or several better known because of the property of the thing and the likeness of the letters, like '*lapis quasi ledens pedem*'." Kretzmann points out that '*lapis*' was mistakenly thought to be derived from '*laedens pedem*' and then notes that Peter simply speaks of the latter as the interpretation of the former. See *Introductiones*, trans. Kretzmann, p. 74, n. 24; for Peter see *Tractatus* 5.9, trans. Kretzmann and Stump, *CTMPT*, p. 231.

85 As the text (and supplied headings) will indicate Bacon discusses more than "seven kinds."

running; therefore a man is not running' holds, nor 'A man is not running; therefore Socrates is not running'. [3.287–289]

[334] The Topic *from a subjective part* arises when a part is arranged to serve as the middle. But such a Topic is [only] constructive, as in 'Socrates runs; therefore a man runs'. The maxim: Whatever is predicated of a subjective part is also predicated of its whole. Likewise, it arises in connection with a predicate: 'Socrates is a man; therefore Socrates is an animal'. The maxim: Of whatever a subjective part is predicated its whole is also predicated. [3.290–291]

[335] One should know, however, that these Topics are called by the common name 'Topic from a universal whole' and 'Topic from a subjective part'. But, when a genus is arranged to serve as the middle, the Topic is called *from a genus*, and this is only true of the Topic from a whole. When, however, a species is arranged to serve as the middle, it is called the Topic *from a species*. It is commonly said that it arises only when affirming, and so this is true only of the Topic from a part. Nothing special touches the others because, when a species is arranged to serve as the middle in a negative argumentation, then the Topic from a whole arises. When a proprium is arranged to serve as the middle, whether in an affirmative or negative argumentation, either the Topic from a whole arises or the Topic from a part. Likewise, with respect to a differentia and an accident, it is not said that in these cases the Topic from a universal whole arises or a subjective part. But, if use were to permit, it could be called the Topic from a species whenever a species is arranged to serve as the middle, whether in affirming or denying. Likewise [it could be called] the Topic *from a proprium* when a proprium is arranged to serve as the middle; and likewise the Topic *from a differentia* when a differentia is arranged to serve as the middle; and likewise the Topic *from an accident*, just as the Topic from a genus is spoken of in this way when a genus is arranged to serve as the middle. And thus are made clear the Topics, namely, from a universal whole and a subjective part. [3.292–293]

[336] Another [kind of whole] is an *integral whole*, which is one that is composed of more than one part, e.g., a house, Socrates, and the like, whose parts are integral, such as a wall, a roof, a foundation, and the like, and a hand, a foot, and the like. One argues in this way from a whole to a part only when affirming: 'There is a house; therefore there is a wall'. The maxim: If there is an integral whole, there is also its part.[86] One argues in this way from

86 Apropos of the use of the conditional form of the maxim one can note with Stump (*CHLMP*, p. 275) that it was Garlandus Compotista in the eleventh century who distinguished his treatment of Topics from Boethius' by using this form to provide and confirm the conditional premise of hypothetical syllogisms in the form of *modus ponens/tollens*.

an [integral] part to the [integral] whole, [but only] when denying: 'If there is no wall, there is no house'. Maxim: If there is no integral part, then there is no whole. Here one must diligently consider that an argumentation of this sort from an integral whole to a part, or vice versa, does not hold except when the whole and the part are referred to one another with respect to being, because 'Socrates runs; therefore his head (or his heart) runs' does not hold, not even vice versa or when denying. Nevertheless, in some cases an inference from a whole to a part (and vice versa) does seem to hold because of the terms, both when affirming and denying, just as when a part suffices to indicate a whole.[87] This happens in two ways. Sometimes an accident is found in one determinate part of a whole and only in it, e.g., curliness with respect to the head or monkeyness with respect to the nose. Then the argument holds because of the terms, as has been said, as in 'Socrates is curly; therefore his head is curly' and 'Socrates is not monkey-like; therefore his nose is not monkey-like', and vice versa, and when affirming or denying. Sometimes this inference also holds when the characteristic has no greater presence in one determinate part than another, namely, when the characteristic is present in one significant part which, consequently, gives a name to the whole, although it is not present in every part. For example, 'An Ethiopian is black except for his teeth; therefore what remains besides his teeth is black' follows well; and likewise when denying, and vice versa, both when denying and affirming. In such cases the consequence holds only because of the terms chosen, because, if other terms are chosen, it will not hold, as was just made clear. Also, one should know that this Topic does not hold unless principal parts are chosen, those which pertain to the being of a whole absolutely: once asserted, the whole is asserted; once removed, or any one of them destroyed, the thing is destroyed. Of this sort are the already mentioned parts of a whole, as the parts of Socrates are his heart, liver, stomach, head, lungs, and principal things like these. The inference does not hold with respect to the less principal things without which a whole can endure, such as a foot, a hand, etc. [3.294–299]

[337] Another whole exists with respect to *quantity*, namely, a common term taken with a universal sign, e.g., 'every man', 'every animal'. To these there corresponds a quantitative part, namely, its singulars, such as 'this man', 'that man', and a term without a sign, and one with a particular sign. They are similar with respect to a quantitative part. An argument holds *from a quantitative whole* only when affirming, as in 'Every man runs; therefore Socrates runs'.[88] The maxim: Whatever applies to a

87 'Because of the terms' is later (336) shown to mean that the soundness of these inferences depends on which terms are chosen: not just any will do.

88 In 447 this example will be given to illustrate the fallacy of Begging the Original Issue. Also, it is not clear why Bacon says this Topic holds only when affirming, for

quantitative whole also applies to its parts. Vice versa there is the Topic *from a quantitative part* when denying, as in 'Socrates is not running; therefore not every man runs' and 'Not a man (or not some man) runs; therefore not every man runs'.[89] The maxim: Whatever is removed from a [quantitative] part is also removed from its whole. If there is any difficulty about this Topic, it will be made clear in [the section] on fallacies (435, 438). [3.300–302]

[338] Next [is the Topic] *from a locational whole*. 'Everywhere' is a locational whole; 'somewhere', 'here', and the like are [locational] parts. The argument holds in this way when affirming: 'God is everywhere; therefore God is here'.[90] The maxim: To that which a locational whole applies its part also applies. Vice versa is the Topic *from a [locational] part* when denying: 'Socrates is not here, therefore Socrates is not everywhere'. [3.303–304]

[339] In the same way [when affirming] one argues by means of the Topic *from a temporal whole*. 'Always' is a temporal whole whose part is 'sometime', 'now', and 'then'. There arises an argument of this sort: 'God always is; therefore God is now'. The maxim: To whatever applies a temporal whole its part also applies. Vice versa there is the Topic *from a [temporal] part* when denying: 'Socrates is not now; therefore he is not always'. The maxim: From whatever is removed a temporal part its whole is also removed. [3.305]

[340] Next is the Topic *from a modal whole*. A modal whole is a completely unmodified word, e.g., 'he reads', 'he runs'. 'He runs well', 'he reads well', 'he argues well' are modal parts. One argues in accord with this Topic when denying, just as in connection with the Topic from a universal whole, as in 'Socrates is not running; therefore Socrates is not running well'. The maxim: From whatever is removed a modal whole its part is also removed. Vice versa there is the Topic *from a modal part* when affirming: 'Socrates runs well; therefore he runs'. The maxim: To whatever applies a modal part its whole also applies. [3.306–307]

'No man is running; therefore Socrates is not running' certainly holds, as William (*Introductiones*, trans. Kretzmann, p. 80), Peter (*Tractatus* 5.15, trans. Kretzmann and Stump, *CTMPT*, p. 234) and Lambert (*Logica*, p. 127.8–9) all acknowledge.

89 Peter and Lambert contend that the Topic from a quantitative part holds also when affirming: 'Socrates runs (and so on for the others); therefore every man runs'. (See, respectively, *Tractatus* 5.15, and *Logica*, p. 128.20–22.)

90 William states that the negative argument also holds and Peter provides one: 'Caesar is nowhere; therefore Caesar is not here' (See, respectively, *Introductiones*, trans. Kretzmann, p. 82, and *Tractatus* 5.17, trans. Kretzmann and Stump, *CTMPT*, p. 235.) Lambert is silent on the issue.

[341] Next is the Topic *from a cause*. There are four kinds of causes, as has already been said (306), namely, material, formal, final, and efficient. A *material cause* is that from which a thing comes to be; a *formal one* is that by which a thing is and from which it takes its name; an *efficient cause* is what moves and acts in such a way that a thing comes into being; a *final one* is the good that moves the efficient cause to prepare the matter for the induction of form. For example, a statue's matter is stone or wood or something else of which it might be made; form is the figure and the extension and composition of its parts and members; what brings it about is the craftsperson; and the goal is a memorial. An argument is formulated *from a material cause* in accord with this maxim: If a material cause is lacking, what is made from it is also lacking, as in 'He has no iron; therefore he has no iron weapons', and the like. But this argument does not hold universally unless one is discussing enduring matter, which does not undergo some sort of change in its substance when it appears in a composite, but maintains the same nature and properties both outside and inside a compound, as has just been said. For iron retains its characteristic of iron whether it is situated in the composition of weapons or not, and a stone, likewise, before it becomes a statue as well as afterwards, for it is always a stone.[91] So the Topic from a material cause holds in cases such as these. But if the matter is transformed and does not remain in its own nature, then [the argument] does not hold, just as 'These people have no flour and water; therefore they have no bread' does not follow because flour and water are the transient and nonenduring matter of bread. Because of this 'They have no milk; therefore they have no cheese' does not follow.[92] An argument is formulated *from a formal cause* in this way: 'If there is no figure, there is no statue' and 'If there is no soul, there is no animal'. The maxim: If there is no formal cause, there is also nothing having that form. Boethius presents the maxim and an example from a formal cause in a different way.[93] Thus: 'Daedalus had no wings; therefore he could not fly'. The maxim: Each thing can do only so much as its formal nature allows. An argument is formulated *from an efficient cause* in the same way. Thus: 'If the coming-together of people is natural, justice is also natural'. The maxim: That whose efficient cause is natural is itself natural.

91 An equally valid translation of '*semper enim est lapis*' in this context would be 'for a stone lasts forever'.

92 Bacon fails to mention the Topic from a material effect. William gives this example: "'The Moors have weapons; therefore the Moors have iron'. Maxim: *If what depends on the matter exists, then that matter exists.*" *Introductiones*, trans. Kretzmann, p. 85.

93 Boethius *De differentiis topicis libri quattuor* 2, PL 64.1189D–1190A, trans. Stump, p. 53.35–38.

One argues *from a final cause* in accord with this maxim: That whose end is good is itself as a whole also good, as in 'If happiness is good, justice is also good'. But note that in Topics of this sort one must conclude to properties of the cause with respect to what is caused in accord with what [the nature of the cause] permits and not universally. So, it does not follow that, if happiness is the highest good, virtue is the highest good.[94] [3.308–316]

[342] An argument *from generation* arises in this way: 'The generation of this person is good; therefore this person is good'. The maxim: That whose generation is good is itself good. [3.317]

[343] An argument *from uses* is formulated in this way according to the same maxim: 'The use of this horse is good; therefore this horse is good'. The maxim: That whose use is good is itself as a whole good. [3.318]

[344] An argument *from destruction* arises in this way: 'The destruction of a thief is good; therefore a thief is bad'. The maxim: That whose destruction is good is itself bad. 'The destruction of this is bad; therefore it itself is good'. The maxim: That whose destruction is bad is itself good. [3.319]

[345] The last Topic from the concomitants of substance is the Topic *from associated accidents*. One argues in accord with this maxim: Associated accidents are wont to be associated with one another. For example, 'If she is a mother, she loves', 'If he is elegantly dressed, he is an adulterer', 'If he is one who wanders about at night, he is a thief', and the like. These are probable and not necessary arguments because such accidents cannot or are not wont to separate themselves from each other. [3.320]

[346] There are seven extrinsic Topics: from a judgment of a thing, i.e., an authority, from a similar, from a greater, from a lesser, from proportion, from opposites, and from transumption.[95] [3.321]

[347] An argument is drawn *from authority* in accord with this maxim: What seems true to everyone, to several, or to wise men one ought not contradict. For example, 'Since all, or several, say the heaven is spherical, therefore it is the case that the heaven is spherical'. Under

94 The problem here seems to be that, were the inference sound, there would be two highest goods, and not just two highest in their respective categories, an end (happiness) and the means to that end (virtue). Nevertheless one can infer (with Lambert) that this follows: 'If beatitude (happiness) is good, so is virtue good'. (*Logica*, p. 132.4–5.) Neither Lambert nor Boethius treats this Topic, but William notes that the Topic is used when both affirming and denying, and indicates that the converse holds. William also mentions the objection that arguments from generation and destruction do not hold because these processes are not simultaneous with their end results. His response: "The end results are not taken simply to be supposita in a state of real being." *Introductiones*, trans. Kretzmann, p. 91 and n. 100.

95 For the notion of extrinsic Topics see 327.

this Topic is placed whatever is proven through testimony, i.e., through the authority of some person that either nature or time has approved, [i.e.], force of native talent, position, age, fortune, art, use, and necessity. [3.322–323]

[348] One argues *from a similar* in accord with this maxim: Judgments concerning similars are similar. For example, 'If grammar inheres in a man in a way similar to that by which whiteness inheres in snow, but whiteness is not a proprium of snow, then neither is grammar a proprium of a man'. [3.324]

[349] One argues *from a greater* in accord with this maxim: If what seems more to inhere does not inhere, then neither will what seems less to inhere also inhere. For example, 'If it seems more true that Socrates could more likely overcome Plato than he could Cicero, but he cannot overcome Plato, then neither is it likely that he could overcome Cicero'. [3.325]

[350] One argues *from a lesser* in accord with this maxim: If what seems less to inhere does inhere, what seems more to inhere also inheres. For example, 'If it seems less likely that a vowel would lose the force of a letter than a consonant would, but a vowel can lose this, then so also can a consonant'. [3.326]

[351] One argues by the Topic *from proportion* in accord with this maxim: That which applies to each and every thing must come about in that to which it stands in proportion. For example, 'As two stands to four, so also does three to six; but two is half of four; therefore three is half of six', for the Topic from proportion arises by possession; the Topic from a similar arises by inherence. [3.327]

[352] These four Topics can be multiplied in other ways, for the relation of greaters or lessers or equals sometimes is of one to two, and at other times of two to two. But the way of construction and destruction is always the same, for the Topic from a similar is constructive and destructive, the Topic from proportion likewise, whereas the Topic from a greater is always destructive, and the Topic from a lesser is always constructive. [3.328]

[353] The Topic *from opposites* is divided into four since there are four species of opposition: contrary, contradictory, privative, and relative. One argues from all of these except from contradictory opposition in accord with their different maxims. [3.329]

[354] In the first way one argues thus *from direct contraries*: 'Socrates is not healthy; therefore he is sick' and 'Plato is virtuous; therefore he is not lacking in virtue'. The maxim: When one of a pair of direct contraries is posited or destroyed, it is necessary that the other be destroyed or posited. [3.330]

[355] One argues *from indirect contraries* as in 'Socrates is white; therefore he is not black'. The maxim: When one of a pair of indirect contrary opposites is posited, it is necessary that the other be destroyed. Here it is fitting to argue when denying, just as in the case of direct con-

traries.[96] But if someone objects that the case is not similar to the preceding Topic because a denial posits nothing, it is clear by what has already been said how one should respond. [3.331–333]

[356] One argues *from privative opposites* in this way: 'Socrates has sight; therefore he is not blind' and 'Plato is not deaf; therefore he can hear'. The maxim: When one of a pair of privative opposites is asserted or destroyed, the other is destroyed or asserted. But the negative argument and maxim are to be understood only with respect to a subject susceptible of such opposites and not otherwise because 'A stone is not deaf; therefore it can hear', does not hold.[97] [3.334–335]

[357] One argues *from relative opposites* [in this way]: 'If there is a father, there is a child' and 'If there is no lord, there is no servant'. The maxim: When one of a pair of relative opposites is asserted or destroyed, it is necessary that the other be asserted or destroyed, because relatives affirm one another and things destroyed destroy themselves. [3.336]

[358] Although it is not customary, one could also argue in this way *from contradictory opposites*, for example: 'Socrates runs; therefore he is

96 Throughout their treatments of the Topics William, Peter, and Lambert classify the quality of the arguments as either constructive or destructive, whereas Bacon (for the most part) has accomplished the same purpose by saying, respectively, "when affirming" and "when denying." No problem up to here has arisen because the arguments so described have all consisted in propositions where the premise and conclusion were both affirmative or both negative. In the case of indirect and direct contraries and contradictories, however, one always finds these two situations: (A) a premise in the affirmative followed by a conclusion in the negative, or (B), a premise in the negative followed by a conclusion in the affirmative. Attention is called to this because it is clear that William and Peter disagree on how to classify these arguments. For William (A) is "destructive" and (B) is "constructive," whereas for Peter the case is the opposite. (Respectively, *Introductiones*, trans. Kretzmann, p. 97, and Peter *Tractatus* 5.29, trans. Kretzmann and Stump, *CTMPT*, p. 240.) Lambert avoids the problem by not characterizing these inferences. What Bacon says in 355 and 356 indicates he adopts the same convention as William. Thus William's and Bacon's characterization can be seen to derive from the quality of the conclusion whereas Peter's is derived from that of the premise.

97 William and Peter (as above), but not Lambert, note this and say that it does not hold (William constructively, Peter destructively) unless, as Peter says, "the sameness of the subject and a naturally determined period of time are given," or as William puts it, "the subject continues to be and is one of those existing things in which the other privative opposite ought to be." By way of examples Peter adds that "a kitten [dog, Lambert] is not said to be blind or to have sight before it is nine days old; and a child is not said to have teeth or be toothless before a determined time." (See William, *Introductiones*, trans. Kretzmann, p. 97; Peter, *Tractatus* 5.30; and Lambert, *Logica*, p. 135.13.) These remarks trade on the notion that the difference between just any quality and a privative one is that the latter is one which by nature ought to be present in the subject.

not not-running' and, vice versa, 'Socrates is not not-running; therefore he runs'. Their maxims are the same as before, namely, When one of a pair of contradictory opposites is asserted or destroyed, it is necessary that the other be destroyed or asserted.[98] But it is not so acceptable to argue in this way from contradictories as it is from the other [kinds of opposites]. So, one argues in another way thus: 'A man is an animal; therefore a nonanimal is a nonman'. The maxim: If one of a pair of contradictory opposites is predicated of another contradictory opposite, the opposite of the first is also predicated of the opposite of the second.[99] [3.337–339]

[359] One argues by the Topic *from contrary opposites* in this way: 'If it pertains to virtue to be praised, then it pertains to vice to be blamed'. [3.340]

[360] One argues *from privative opposites* in this way: 'If vision is a sensory ability, then blindness is a lack of a sensory ability'. [3.341]

[361] One argues *from relative opposites* in this way: 'If double is a multiple, then less than double is less than a multiple'.[100] [3.342]

[362] The same general maxim, which has already been stated, is in all these: If one opposite, etc.[101] Nevertheless, each [Topic] has its special maxim, for in contradictory opposites there is this maxim: If a finite is under a finite, then the infinite of the superior is under the infinite of the inferior.[102] In the case of contraries: Contraries apply to contraries. In the case of privative opposites this: If possession is in a possession, then privation is in a privation. In the case of relative opposites, this: Relatives apply to relatives. But one should know that the general maxim – If one opposite is predicated of another opposite, etc. – is to be understood differently in the case of contradictories and the others. In the case of contradictories [the maxim] is to be understood inversely (*e contrario*) and not directly (*in ipso*); in the case of the others [it is to be understood] directly, except when in the case of contraries sometimes the opposite consequence holds, namely, the inverse one. But [this happens only] rarely. To understand this, note that there are two sorts of consequences: the one inverse, the other

98 For a different version of this maxim see 362.

99 The Latin expression of the maxim is very enigmatic, but the '*pro*' prefix is used to distinguish the pairs of opposites: "Si oppositum de opposito, et propositum de proposito." (*Sd* 3, p. 231, 339.3–4.) It is curious that the maxim does not explicitly refer to *contradictory* opposites, but this later (362) allows Bacon to speak of it as a general maxim. For another maxim that covers the example more precisely see 360.

100 For the notions of double/multiple and subdouble/submultiple see above, respectively, 73 and 78–79.

101 There is no one maxim that is appropriate for all the Topics from contraries, as Bacon later acknowledges in this paragraph.

102 For an argument to which the maxim is applied see 358 and 362.

direct. A consequence is *direct* when the opposite of the predicate applies to the opposite of the subject, just as the predicate applies to the subject, as in 'As justice is useful, so also injustice is useless'. A consequence is *inverse* when the opposite of the subject applies to the opposite of the predicate as the predicate applies to the subject, as in 'If a man is an animal, a nonanimal is a nonman'. In contradictories, therefore, only inverse consequences arise; in relative and privative opposites only direct ones. But in contraries, for the most part, direct consequences arise, though in a few cases inverse ones also arise, as Aristotle says, and as an example of which he proposes the following: 'If vigor is health, then sickness is debility'.[103] [3.343–353]

[363] One argues by the Topic *from transumption* when the argument is changed from an obscure word to one better known in accord with this maxim: The same thing applies to synonyms. For example, if anyone doubts whether a philosopher is envious because the former is ignorant of the meaning of 'philosopher', the answer would be shown to him through a more recognized name. Thus: 'A wise man is not envious; therefore a philosopher is not envious'. And so on. [3.354]

[364] There are three intermediate Topics: from cases, from coordinates, and from division.[104] [3.355]

[365] A *case* is the inflection of a name to form an adverb, as from 'just' one derives 'justly' and from 'brave' one derives 'bravely'. One argues, therefore, in this way in accord with these maxims: If one principal [name is predicated] of [another] principal [name grammatically related to the former], so also is one case [predicated] of [another grammatically related] case, and vice versa.[105] [Also], if it is not true that one principal [name is predicated] of [another] principal [name grammatically related to the former], so also neither is it true that one case [is predicated] of [another grammatically related] case, but not vice versa. An example: 'If justice is good, what happens justly also happens well'. [3.356]

[366] When mobile names are derived from a substantival name, they are called coordinates, for the inflection of a name into a name is a conjugation. An argument [*from coordinates*] arises in accord with this maxim: If one principal [name is predicated] of [another] principal [name], so also what is derived [from the first is predicated] of what is derived [from the

103 Aristotle *Topics* 2.8.113b35.

104 For the notion of an intermediate Topic see 327.

105 Bacon's use of '*principale*' (principal) is very curious here, though appropriate for the next Topic, from conjugates, where the movement is from a principal name to one derived or denominated from it, like 'just' from 'justice' and 'good' from 'goodness'. (For the distinction see 30.) But here he has clearly told us (and the example illustrates) the move is from a name (noun or adjective) to an adverb. If Bacon is using 'principal name' in its technical sense, the maxim is far too restrictive to cover the (standard) example he gives.

second], and vice versa, when destroying as well as when constructing, as in 'If justice is good, a just man is good', and 'If whiteness is a color, a white man is someone colored'. [3.357]

[367] An argument *from division* is drawn in accord with this maxim: If one part of any disjunction is destroyed, the other remains, and vice versa, If one remains, the other is destroyed. For example, 'If Socrates is either healthy or sick, but is not healthy, then he is sick', or 'If he is sick, then he is not healthy'. [3.358]

[368] Let this division of Topics, given by Themistius, suffice for you for the present.[106] We do not intend to touch on Tullius's division.[107] And now we move on to sophistical Topics. [3.359–361]

DISPUTATIONS[108]

[369] Let us begin a new chapter on the species of disputation. We have already spoken of dialectical syllogism (325) and so now we must speak of sophistical syllogism. [3.362–3]

[370] *Sophistical syllogism* gives the appearance of being dialectical syllogism, but it is not, just as in the case of things: objects made of litharge and tin look like silver things, and objects made of brass and things painted

106 The reference is to Themistius (ca. 317–387 AD), a commentator on Aristotle. For the reference see Boethius *De differentiis topicis libri quattuor* 3, PL 64.1200CD, trans. Stump, p. 71.25–29. In *Ut dicit* we find the following: "These are called intermediate Topics by the same [Themistius]. Marcus Tullius offers no intermediate Topics, only intrinsic and extrinsic ones. Whether one division is better than another must be determined elsewhere. But in truth the division 'some are intrinsic, others extrinsic' is more artificial." (Ed. de Rijk, *LM*, vol. 2, pt. 2, p. 408.21–24.) Themistius is also mentioned in the *Introductio Parisiensis*: "As Themistius says, a Topic is the seat of an argument, i.e., its strength, because it communicates powers to an argument." (Ed. de Rijk, *LM*, vol. 2, pt. 2, p. 365.8–9.)

107 On Cicero's division see Boethius *De differentiis topicis libri quattuor* 3, PL 64.1195C–1200C, trans. Stump, pp. 63.23–71.20, and *In topica Ciceronis commentariorum libri sex* 1, PL 64.1054B, trans. Stump, *Boethius' In Ciceronis Topica* (Ithaca: Cornell University Press, 1988).

108 For a study of disputations see Ignaccio Angelelli, "The Techniques of Disputation in the History of Logic," *The Journal of Philosophy* 67 (1970): 800–815. For the medieval discussion of Aristotle's fallacies see de Rijk, *LM*, vol. 1: *On the Twelfth-Century Theories of Fallacy*, and Sten Ebbesen, "The Way Fallacies Were Treated in Scholastic Logic," *Cahiers de l'Institut du Moyen Age grec et latin* 55 (1987): 107–134, and *Commentators and Commentaries on Aristotle's* Sophistici Elenchi: *A Study of Post-Aristotelian Ancient and Medieval Writings on Fallacies* (Leiden: E. J. Brill, 1981). See also Irène Rosier, "L'un et le multiple: probleme sémantique de la tradition médiévale des commentaires sur les *Réfutations Sophistiques* d'Aristote," *Modèles Linguistiques* 5 (1983): 39–68.

with bull-bile seem to be golden, when they are not.[109] Some seek this sort of syllogism more than any other, but such people are only seeming seekers [of truth], not real ones. Such are sophists, who more wish to seem [to be wise] and not be than to be [wise] and not [merely] seem [to be so]. Because sophistical syllogism is something more properly directed to another person than is any other sort of syllogism, and [because] disputation is always something directed to another, the act of disputing is more suited to it than to the other sorts of syllogisms. [3.364–366]

[371] Because of this one should know that there are four kinds of disputation: didactic, dialectical, one that examines, and sophistical.[110] A *didactic* disputation is one that syllogizes from the proper principles of each discipline and not from those that [only] appear [to be proper] to a respondent, for the one who demonstrates is not concerned with the response given by the one who disputes with him. Whether the latter concedes or denies the things proposed by the former, [the one who demonstrates] proceeds nonetheless, because his inference cannot be blocked since it is based on principles primary and true, etc. A *dialectical* disputation is one that syllogizes from probable principles and has the ability to syllogize on both sides of a contradiction. A disputation *that examines* is one that syllogizes from things that seem [true] to a respondent, [from things] that it is necessary for him to know who feigns the possession of knowledge. And such things are things that are commonly accepted in every science. They are the things that nothing prevents the knower of the art [of examining] from being ignorant of, but which the one who is ignorant [of the theory of a science] must be unaware of.[111] A *sophis-*

109 See Aristotle *Sophistical Refutations* 1.164b23–24. De Libera uses the simile of bull bile here to support a claim that Bacon has a certain *modus operandi* and a way of commenting that are not found among his contemporaries. (*Sd* 3, p. 173.) Sten Ebbesen, however, informs me that the allusion to bull bile is found in virtually all commentaries on this point and in many glossed manuscripts of the Aristotelian text. (*On Sophistical Refutations* 4.164b23–25.) He refers to (among others) *Anonymous Aurelianensis* I and *Anonymous Bodleianus*, both of which, he says, antedate Bacon's *Summulae dialectices* by several decades. (*Cahiers de l'Institut du Moyen-Age grec et latin*, vol. 34, pp. 19 and 184.) Hence, Bacon's mention of bull bile does not serve to support any special interest in literature not focused on linguistics or chemistry, however well that may be supported on other grounds.

110 See Aristotle *Sophistical Refutations* 2.165a37–b12.

111 "*Et haec sunt, quae scientem nihil prohibet nescire artem, nescientem autem necesse est ignorare.*" (*Sd* 3, p. 234, 370.3–5.) Aristotle writes: "For it is possible even for one without knowledge to hold an examination of one who is without knowledge, if the latter grants him points taken not from the things that he knows or from the proper principles but from the consequences which a man may know without knowing the art in question (but which if he does not know, he is bound to be ignorant of the art)." *Sophistical Refutations* 11.172a24–27, trans. Pickard-Cambridge, in *CWA*, vol. 1, p. 292.

tical (contentious) disputation is one that proceeds from things that seem to be probable but are not. [3.367–371]

[372] Since every disputation arises by means of some sort of syllogism, to every sort of disputation there will correspond some sort of syllogism. So one could wonder why there is no syllogism that examines corresponding to disputations that examine, since there is sophistical syllogism for sophistical disputation, and so on for the others. One should say that a disputation that examines is one that is [directed] to something else, namely, to examining the ignorance of another. So, whereas disputation properly pertains to one person in relation to something else, syllogism does not do this, because *per se* one person can syllogize, but he cannot properly carry on a disputation, nor can he examine. Disputation and examination necessarily are directed to something else, and so "that examines" is a differentia of disputation, but not of syllogism.[112] [3.372–373]

[373] Hence, there is no syllogism that examines, although the opposite is claimed by many.[113] But sometimes an examiner uses a dialectical syllogism as his instrument, namely, when he examines someone in the latter's special science.[114] He proceeds from common propositions pertaining to a proper conclusion, just as the reasoning of Bryson with respect to squaring a circle was this: "In whatever one can find a greater and a lesser

112 In 370 disputation and sophistical syllogism (at least more so than any other kind of syllogism) are said to be directed to another person (*ad alterum*). In 372 disputation that examines is said to be directed to something else (*ad aliud*) and in the first part of its three occurrences the "something else" is said to be the ignorance of another. In its second occurrence the "something else" seems to be another person, as in 370. In the third occurrence "something else" has the meaning of its first occurrence here. In the Prologue (5) disputation that examines as well as disputation in general are both said to be directed "to something else." Peter and Lambert clearly define "disputation" as a syllogistic act of one *person* in reference to another person (*unius ad alterum*). See, respectively, *Tractatus* 7.1, and *Logica*, p. 142.32–34.

113 For example, Peter. Peter traces the origin of the problem to Aristotle's failure to discuss the probative syllogism in the *Topics* (1.1.101a1–2) and says that it is what others call a syllogism defective in matter. While, he says, they see the defect in the fact that it contains a false premise, he sees the problem in its acceptance of premises that seem probable to the respondent. (*Tractatus* 7.8.) At the end of this work Bacon will discuss what he calls the sophistical syllogism defective in matter, and focus on the significance of premises that are probable absolutely as opposed to those simply probable to the respondent (3.715–25).

114 I suspect (and the translation assumes) that "*in sua scientia speciali*" should read '*in eius scientia speciali*' because it is the respondent's knowledge that is at issue. This is substantiated by the correct use of '*sua*' in the second to last line of this paragraph in the Latin text. (See *Sd* 3, p. 234, 374.3–4.) See also ibid., p. 235, 378.1–2: "*respondens ... ignorans suam scientiam.*"

one can also find an equal, but one can find a greater and a lesser square in a circle; therefore one can find a square equal to a circle."[115] The conclusion is geometrical but the premises are dialectical, and the implication is dialectical. The syllogism, however, is sophistical, not absolutely, but in a certain respect, because it appears to produce knowledge in the conclusion, when it really does not, but only opinion. Since this appears not because of a fallacy but only because of the fatuity of the respondent (because he did not know his own science), it can be a dialectical syllogism, granted it is sophistical in a certain respect. One cannot examine with respect to a proper conclusion of some special science by means of common and probable principles, unless by means of those that are probable absolutely, from which a dialectical syllogism proceeds.[116] Nor by means of apparently probable principles, from which a sophistical syllogism proceeds, because those principles do not appear probable because of the fatuity of the respondent alone, but rather because of the cause of the semblance [of soundness] and the deception that is in them, i.e., because of some fallacy that is involved in the premises. Since the examiner must examine the ignorance of the respondent, the latter's ignorance is not revealed even though he does not know how to judge fallacies since it does not pertain to the specialized philosopher as it does to a geometrician and an arithmetician to reveal these, but only to the dialectician – I say this speaking *per se* and strictly. But while in a certain sense it happens that one examines by means of these principles, this will not be because they involve fallacies, but because they are common principles and neither necessary nor proper to a proper and specialized conclusion in such a science. So, should a respondent choose these principles for the proper premises of such a conclusion, he would be ignorant of his own science. [3.374–378]

[374] Sometimes the examiner uses a falsigraphic syllogism, [i.e.], when he proceeds from the proper principles in a science toward a proper conclusion in it and those principles are not the cause of the conclusion. For example, if one were to say he knew geometry and knew how to square a circle, the examiner could assume the opposite of those principles or he could assume poorly understood principles to prove a conclusion in geometry like the squaring of a circle or some other, just as occurs in the case of the proof of squaring a circle by crescents, which has already been touched on (324), for this is [a procedure] that examines and a falsigraphic one. [3.379]

115 Cf. Robert Kilwardby, *De ortu scientiarum* 512, ed. Albert G. Judy, Auctores Britannici Medii Aevi, vol. 4 (Toronto: Pontifical Institute of Mediaeval Studies, 1976), pp. 174.29–175.5, and see Aristotle *Sophistical Refutations* 11.171b17–18.

116 Here and in the ensuing discussion Bacon speaks of *communia* and *probabilia*. That he is thinking of common and probable *principles* is clear from 374, and so the translation supplies 'principles'.

[375] Sometimes the examiner proceeds from common [principles as premises] toward common [principles as conclusions], and then he examines the dialectician because common principles come under the consideration of the dialectician. These are either common principles that are improbable absolutely, that only appear probable because of the fatuity of the respondent and not because of some fallacy[117] – then his instrument is not a dialectical syllogism but rather that sophistical one which is touched on in Book Eight of the *Topics* and in the *Prior Analytics*, namely, that which is constructed from false (improbable) principles and which is only oblique and deficient in comparison to a dialectical syllogism.[118] [Such a sophistical syllogism] neither has nor appears to have the character and quality (*positio et habitus*) of a dialectical syllogism but only its privation, as if one were to say: 'Every ass is a mule, Burnellus is an ass; therefore Burnellus is a mule'. Or, the examiner takes principles that are improbable absolutely, but which appear to be probable not only because of the fatuity of the respondent but also because of a fallacy implicit in the premises. Then we have a sophistical syllogism as the instrument of this examiner, [a syllogism] defective as much in matter as in form. Having seen these, and omitting all others, we should now take up for consideration the sophistical disputation. [3.380–383]

[376] There are five goals of such a disputation because, besides the fact that the sophist intends to acquire glory and apparent wisdom for himself, he also intends victory over a respondent, which he achieves by leading him into some absurdity, on the basis of which a goal is so-called.[119] These goals are Refutation, Falsity, Paradox, Solecism, and Babbling. *Refutation* is the concession and denial of the same thing by the force of an argumentation. One is led into *Falsity* when the opponent causes the respondent to concede something obviously false or deny something obviously true, which is the same thing.[120] One is led into *Paradox* when one concedes a conclusion that contradicts the commonly accepted opinion of the many or of the wise. One is led into *Solecism* when one concedes an incongruous conclusion.[121] One

117 The second half of the disjunction appears several lines below.

118 Cf. Aristotle *Topics* 9.6.159b35–160a16.

119 '*Metae*' means limits or boundaries. The notion here is that someone seeks to force his opponent into some error which then is the limit of the disputation.

120 Peter: 'An Ethiopian is white'; Lambert: 'A man is an ass'. Peter reminds that the opponent does not achieve his goal (Falsity) if he pushes the respondent to utter something false but not *obviously* false. Respectively, *Tractatus* 7.15, and *Logica*, p. 144.33.

121 The incongruity relates to grammar, as in 'Men runs' or '*vir alba*', but, as Lambert notes, whereas the grammarian sees the incongruity in the lack of a well-formed sentence, the sophist sees it as something which impedes the apprehension of the truth of a proposition. *Logica*, p. 145.21–38.

is led into *Babbling* when one is forced to concede something in a way that pointlessly repeats the same thing in the same part of an expression.[122] Since, therefore, sophistical argumentation leads to these goals, one should know that there are special sophistical principles, i.e., special sophistical Topics, that lead to each of these goals. It is sufficient for the present to consider the Topics that lead to Refutation, because they are the most important in the sophistical art and those that the sophist prefers over all others. And they are more common than the others because they lead not only to Refutation but also to Falsity and Paradox. [3.384–391]

[377] Now we must open the question of what a sophistical Topic is, what a fallacy is, and how they differ; what a sophistical syllogism is; what a paralogical syllogism is; what a paraelenchus is; and what an elenchus is, because there is no true refutation without a true elenchus, nor is there an apparent refutation without an apparent elenchus. A *sophistical Topic* is the characteristic of a word or thing [signified] that is involved and implicated in an argumentation and provides the occasion for deceiving. A *fallacy* is the deception arising from the nature of a thing [signified] or a word. So, a sophistical Topic is the cause of a fallacy. A *sophistical syllogism* is an expression having within it a Topic that deceives. This is the same as a *paralogical syllogism*. An *elenchus* is a syllogism with a contradicting conclusion. A *paraelenchus* is an argumentation having a defect in the nature of the syllogism or in the contradiction or both, as will immediately be clear. [3.392–399]

[378] [Aristotle says], "A contradiction is the opposition of one and the same [attribute], about the same thing, not of the name alone but of the reality together with the name, and not of a synonym but of the very same [name], on the basis of those things that were given, and [following] necessarily, without including what was [stated] at the beginning, in the same relation, in the same respect, in the same way, and at the same time."[123]

122 E.g., 'A man man runs', 'A rational man'. Lambert says a respondent is "forced to concede the same thing stated frequently, immediately, without any cause." Peter cautions that the goal is not achieved in cases like 'A man is a man' or 'A man is rational' or even where repetition is used for emphasis as in 'God, my God'. Respectively, *Logica*, pp.145.40–146.2, and *Tractatus* 7.18.

123 What follows is a definition of 'refutation' given by Aristotle in Boethius' translation: "*nam elenchus est contradictio eiusdem et unius, non nominis sed rei, et nominis non sinonimi sed eiusdem, ex his quae data sunt ex necessitate, non connumerato quod erat in principio, secundum idem et ad idem et similiter et in eodem tempore.*" (*Sophistical Refutations* 5.167a23–27; *Aristoteles Latinus*, ed. Lorenzo Minio-Paluello, vol. 6, pts. 1–3, *De Sophisticis Elenchis*, ed. Bernard Dod [Leiden: E. J. Brill; Bruxelles: Desclée de Brouwer, 1975], pp. 80.40–81.4.) Apropos of this and the way it appears (and is translated) in the texts of Bacon, William, Peter, and Lambert, note the following:

When one truly contradicts something asserted by a respondent, it is necessary that the same subject and the same predicate in thing [signified] and word asserted by the respondent and concluded by the opponent be present, because 'Socrates is running, Plato is not running' and 'Cicero is running, Cicero is not arguing' are not contradictions, and likewise here: 'Marcus is running, Tullius is not running'.[124] By "the same thing" one understands the whole [definition] "A contradiction is the opposition of one and the same [attribute] about the same thing, etc." Besides this it is necessary that the conclusion occur by necessity of the premises, namely, by force of the syllogism, which implies by necessity. For example, if the respondent has said that an animal is running, the opponent may argue in

---

The term 'attribute' in the translation of Bacon's text is supplied in conformity with W. A. Pickard-Cambridge's translation which reads: "For to refute is to contradict one and the same attribute – not the name, but the object and one that is not synonymous but the same ... ." In contrast Kretzmann supplies 'predicate' and Peter expressly explains that "of the same" (*eiusdem*) refers to the same subject and predicate, and Lambert says that "of one and the same" (*unius et eiusdem*) has to refer separately and respectively to a subject and to a predicate in order to avoid Babbling. See, respectively, *Sophistical Refutations*, 167a23–27, trans. Pickard-Cambridge, in *CWA*, vol. 1, p. 282; *Introductiones*, trans. Kretzmann, p. 155; *Tractatus* 7.132; and *Logica* p. 189.30–37.

For the second occurrence of "of the same" (*eiusdem*) Pickard-Cambridge adds 'name', Kretzmann supplies 'name' (without brackets), and Lambert gives us (without a blush) 'of the same name' (*eiusdem nominis*). Lambert betrays the fact that we are dealing with his own addition to the text when, later, commenting on the occurrence of 'synonym' in the definition, he speaks only of "not of a synonym but of the same" (*non synonimi sed eiusdem*), and then adds by way of explanation, "namely, name" (*scilicet nominis*). *Logica*, p. 189.37–43.

Finally, Bacon alone inserts the phrase 'about the same [thing]' (*de eodem*), and for the justification of the bracketed addition see 444.

William, Peter, and Lambert are in agreement that parts of this definition are there only because one is talking about a syllogism, that other parts are there because a contradiction is at issue, and that still others are present in virtue of both. See, respectively, *Introductiones*, trans. Kretzmann, p. 155; *Tractatus* 7.132; and *Logica*, pp. 188.8–189.21.

124 Reading at *Sd*, p. 238, 401.5 '*similiter*' with MS. O. against '*sed*' in MS. S. and the text. The MSS. pose a problem here for the translator. Does Bacon want to say that 'Marcus is running', 'Tullius is not running' are contradictory propositions? To answer this note the following: (1) MS. S. (adopted here by de Libera) introduces the last of the three examples in this sentence with "but neither here" (*sed nec hic*) whereas MS. O. introduces them with "and likewise here" (*similiter nec hic*). The use of 'but' in MS. O. suggests a contrast, and when joined with 'and not' (*nec*) the combined meaning becomes confused. Hence, the reading in MS. S. could signal that Bacon wants us to take the Cicero example as one of contradiction (in contrast with the preceding two examples) since the same subject is maintained in both

this way: 'No man is running; therefore no animal is running': the conclusion does not follow by necessity from the premises. This is what [he means when] he says, "on the basis of those things that were given, and [following] necessarily." Besides this it is necessary that [the opponent's] conclusion not have been the same as one of the premises – neither in thing [signified] nor in word – because a syllogism always concludes to something other and not the same. This is what [Aristotle means when] he says, "without including what was [stated] at the beginning." For example, if one says 'Marcus is running; therefore Tullius is running', he begs the original issue. It is also necessary that the contradiction be "in the same relation," because it is not a contradiction if I say 'A is twice B' and 'A is not twice C', because they are not related to the same thing. It is necessary that the contradiction be [of two attributes] "in the same respect." So, 'A is twice B in length and is not twice B in width' is not a contradiction. It is necessary that the contradiction be [of two attributes] "in the same way." Hence, 'Socrates dines with Plato and he does not dine with Cicero' and 'Socrates is healthy when awake and he is not healthy when sleeping' are not contradictions. It is also necessary that one be true and the other false "at the same time." Therefore, 'Socrates is running at [time] "a" and he is not running at [time] "b"' are not contradictory. Therefore, all these conditions must be fulfilled for there to be

---

propositions. (2) One of the features of a contradiction is that the two propositions must use the same names and no synonyms. But here, while we have the same subject, the subject has two different names and the names are in some sense analogous to synonyms. This could suggest that the contrast allowed in MS. S. but disallowed in MS. O. is intended. (3) A little later in this paragraph Bacon says that 'Marcus is running; therefore Tullius is running' commits the fallacy of Begging the Original Issue, because the subject and predicate in the premise and conclusion are the same, and Bacon does not pause to remind that, nevertheless, it violates the requirement about same name and no synonym. The reminder would support the lack of contrast in MS. O., but then Bacon is under no obligation to offer such a reminder since the inference is intended to address the issue of same subject. In consequence the text there is silent with respect to offering support for or against a contrast in the prior and problematic example. (4) If one were to ignore the 'but' in MS. S. and the 'likewise' in MS. O. Bacon would clearly be taken to be saying that the propositions were not contradictory, because the names of the subject are not the same, and no contrast with the preceding two examples is intended. And (5) Peter maintains this same example avoids contradiction (because, curiously, the names are not the same but synonyms!). *Tractatus* 7.132. Reflection on the preceding has led me to understand Bacon as wanting to be understood more in the way clearly stated in MS. O., i.e., without contrast to the preceding examples, than in the muddled way found in MS. S., and hence the translation supports the reading of the former over de Libera's choice of the latter.

a true contradiction. If, therefore, one of these is lacking, we have a paraelenchus and not a true elenchus. [3.400–411]

[379] Finally, one should know that there are two sorts of sophistical syllogism: the one is defective in the matter of a dialectical syllogism and is called a sophistical syllogism defective in matter; the other is lacking with respect to the form of a dialectical syllogism and is called one defective in form. Therefore, one must first speak about the one defective in form. [3.412–413]

Sophistical Syllogisms Defective in Form: Fallacies

[380] One should know that sophistical syllogism is defective first and *per se* with respect to dialectical syllogism and *per accidens* with respect to syllogism taken absolutely, because the form of a dialectical syllogism is the necessity of implying a conclusion from premises when they have been endowed with the quality of a Topic, namely, with the quality of the differentiae of the maxims. [3.414]

[381] There are three forms of syllogism absolutely: *mood*, *figure*, and *complexion*, that is, the necessity of implying.[125] Sophistical syllogism defective in form first and *per se* is defective with respect to the already mentioned form of dialectical syllogism, and consequently with respect to the form of syllogism absolutely. I speak of the third form, which is the necessity of implying, because this is the form which perfects syllogism absolutely. For it is not necessary that [sophistical syllogism] be lacking in the other respects, namely, in mood and figure, and especially in mood, because perhaps every paralogism could be reduced to the disposition of a syllogism in mood. But not every syllogism could have the characteristic called figure, as will be clear later on in the case of the paralogism of equivocation and others: since figure is the correct arrangement of the three and only three terms, sometimes there are four terms in a paralogism, and then the characteristic called figure is lacking. From these things it is clear that syllogism defective in form is neither dialectical syllogism nor syllogism absolutely, and so is not any sort of syllogism. [3.415–418]

[382] Sophistical Topics are divided into thirteen sophistical Topics, i.e., fallacies. One arises because of equivocation, another because of amphiboly, another because of composition and division, another because of accent, and another because of the figure of a word. These fallacies are called *verbal* because the principle of deception in them comes from a

125 For the notions of mood and figure see 293. For that of complexion (*complexio*) see 381 where it is said to be what "perfects syllogism taken absolutely." This notion does not seem to have been treated as a third and separate quality of syllogism when mood and figure were discussed.

word.[126] But another fallacy arises because of accident, another because of [taking the meaning of a word] in a certain respect as well as absolutely, another because of ignorance regarding refutation, another because of begging the original issue, another because of a consequent, another because of treating what is not a cause as a cause, and another because of treating more than one question as one. These fallacies occur *extra-verbally* because they derive their source of deception from the thing [signified] and not from the words. [3.419–423]

[383] First we must speak of *Equivocation*. Equivocation is the designation of diverse things by one word.[127] These can be significata, but sometimes are other things, as will be clear later (386). [3.424–426]

[384] One could object: Since signification is the perfection of a word, and each thing has only one perfection; therefore each word will have only one signification; therefore equivocation does not arise with respect to significata. One should reply to this that a word has two sorts of perfection: substantial and accidental, as is clear in the case of things.[128] For the substantial perfection of a man is his soul; his accidental perfections are his powers and knowledge. The case is similar with respect to expressions and words. The substantial perfection of a word is the way it is pronounced, i.e., its pronunciation, whereas its accidental perfection is its signification and its consignification.[129] Therefore, just as in the case of things there is only one substantial perfection yet many accidental ones, so also in the case of words. So, there is only one way to pronounce a word, though there can be many accidental ways. [3.427–432]

[385] The fallacy of Equivocation is the deception arising from a sameness in matter and form with the ability to signify [different things]. There are two things to consider in every fallacy, namely, the cause of the semblance and the cause of the nonexistence. The cause of the semblance in this fallacy is the sameness of a word in matter and form with the ability to signify [different things]. The matter is the word itself; the form is its

126 For the distinction between verbal and extra-verbal fallacies see Aristotle *Sophistical Refutations* 4.165b23ff. For a thorough study of Bacon's presentation of the verbal fallacies see Paola Müller, "La dottrina delle *fallaciae in dictione* in Ruggero Bacone," *Documenti e studi sulla tradizione filosofica medievale* 3 (1992): 453–490.

127 For additional texts on equivocation see Sten Ebbesen, "Texts on Equivocation. Part I. Ca. 1130–ca. 1270," *Cahiers de l'Institut du Moyen Age grec et latin* 67 (1997): 127–199, and "Texts on Equivocation. Part II. Ca. 1250–1310," ibid., 68 (1998): 99–307. See also Thomas S. Maloney, "Roger Bacon on Equivocation," *Vivarium* 22 (1984): 85–112.

128 For this distinction see 41.

129 For the notions of signification and consignification see, respectively, 116–118, 121, and 250, 256.

utterance. The cause of the nonexistence is the difference between the significata. There are three modes of this fallacy.[130] [3.433–438]

[386] The *first* [mode] occurs when a word principally and equally is related to more than one thing, either in signifying or in consignifying or in exercising functions or in suppositing or in referring.[131] An example of the first [submode] is 'A dog runs, one of the heavenly constellations is a dog; therefore one of the heavenly constellations runs'. One must say that the conclusion does not follow because of the fallacy of Equivocation in the premises. The major has two senses: 'dog' asserted there can signify something that can bark, and in this sense the major is true, or one of the heavenly constellations, and then it is false. The minor, moreover, similarly has two senses, but, vice versa, it is true and false. A similar example of the first [submode]: 'Whatever comes from Montmartre is earth or a stone, this man comes from Montmartre; therefore he is earth or a stone'. It must be said that because of equivocation the conclusion does not follow, because the major is ambiguous in that the preposition 'from' can indicate the circumstance of a material cause – and in this sense the major is true and the minor false – or a local circumstance, i.e., that of a formal or efficient cause – and in this sense the major is false and the minor true. For a place, in as much as it preserves and contains what is located in it, has the sense of a formal cause. But in as much as it is a principle of movement of what is located [in it] toward itself by a power of attraction that is actually in [the place] and complete, but that is incomplete in what is located, i.e., in what can be moved to [the place], it has the sense of an efficient cause, like a magnet with respect to iron. An example of the second [submode]: '*Episcopi* (the bishops) are priests, these asses are *episcopi* (the bishop's); therefore these asses are priests'. The conclusion does not follow because, in order for the first proposition to be true, '*episcopi*' must be in the nominative case, but for the second, in the genitive.[132] An example of the third

130 The three modes are defined in 358, 387, and 388, with additional clarification in 389. Each of the three is said to be a *modus* of Equivocation and, given what is said in 462, each has five additional *modi*.

131 Reading at *Sd* 3, p. 241, 439.2, '*exercendo*' with MS. S. against '*excludendo*' in MS. O. and the text. I am indebted to Sten Ebbesen for calling my attention to the need for this correction. See 389.

132 The deception arises in the English translation only when spoken aloud, as Kretzmann notes. (*Introductiones*, trans. Kretzmann, p. 136, n. 23.) Note also that since the problem lies with a difference in case ending, the equivocation arises from consignification and this tells us what (at least part of) the second submode of Equivocation is about. William points out that the fallacy here can also be taken to be that of The Figure of a Word because the sameness of the ending of the word '*episcopi*' in the two cases causes the deception. (*Introductiones*, trans. Kretzmann, p. 137.) But Lambert uses it to exemplify his third mode of equivocation (in con-

[submode] can occur if I say 'Nothing is true unless in this example', since 'unless' can bring about either an exception or a consequence.[133] In the first sense it is true, in the second, false. The case is similar with respect to a negation because it can make a term infinite or bring about a pure negation, as when I say '*Non homo currit*', and so on for the other words that exercise a function.[134] An example of the fourth [submode] is '(A) man is a species'. It is ambiguous because 'man' can have simple or personal supposition.[135] In the first sense it is true, in the second, false. An example of the last [submode] is '(The) woman who damned has saved'. If 'who' involves a simple relation it is true; if a personal relation, it is false.[136] [3.439–447]

[387] The *second* mode [of Equivocation] occurs when a word signifies one thing properly and *per se* and another metaphorically and less properly, as in 'Whatever runs has feet, the Seine runs; therefore the Seine has feet'. 'To run' signifies properly a swift movement of the feet, and this is transferred to signify the same as 'to flow'.[137] Likewise 'Every entity stands under accidents, whiteness is an entity; therefore it stands under accidents'. 'Entity' signifies strictly a substance and broadly an accident. [3.448–449]

[388] The *third* mode [of Equivocation] occurs when a word signifies by itself one thing, but signifies more than one thing when joined to

---

signification), but then says that it could involve the fallacy of Amphiboly, noting also that Aristotle himself acknowledges that the same expression can give rise to more than one fallacy. (*Logica*, p. 152.7–33.)

133 For a study of medieval attempts to analyze expressions containing exceptive terms in them see Norman Kretzmann, "Syncategoremata, Exponibilia, Sophismata," in *CHLMP*, pp. 216–230.

134 Stated explicitly, the two readings would be, respectively, 'A nonman is running' and 'It is not the case that a man is running'. Cf. 151 where how this (Latin) expression is to be read is clear in at least one context.

135 For the notions of simple and personal supposition see 213 and 214.

136 If '*mulier*' is rendered by 'the woman' or 'a woman' it will supposit personally for Eve and 'who' will refer personally to Eve, and the proposition will be false on the supposition that Mary, not Eve, saved us. If, however, '*mulier*' is rendered by something like 'womankind' or 'woman' or 'the female sex', the supposition will be simple and the proposition true. For more analysis of this form of ambiguity see C. H. Kneepkens, "*Mulier quae damnavit, salvavit*: A Note on the Early Development of the *Relatio Simplex*," *Vivarium* 14 (1976): 1–25. See also 230 and cf. William *Introductiones*, trans. Kretzmann, pp. 114–115, n.43, and Lambert *Logica*, p. 236.8–18.

137 See Aristotle *Sophistical Refutations* 4.166a14ff, and de Rijk, *LM*, vol. 1, pp. 135–139 and 499.

another.[138] An example (having indicated a black man): 'Whoever is white has a white color, this man is a white monk; therefore he has a white color'. 'White' by itself signifies what is colored with whiteness, but joined to the word 'monk', it can signify either whiteness in color or the whiteness of a monk's habit. Likewise, 'The white one was going to engage in disputation' is ambiguous in that it can appellate men present or past.[139] The case is similar for every expression about the past or the future or having the power to ampliate whenever a term not restricted to present men serves as a subject.[140] The equivocation here is not from signification or from any other of the previously stated [sub]modes, but from appellation. Equivocal appellation pertains to entities and nonentities, for by its nature a term is a name only of things present, as has already been said (248). But in virtue of the nature of an adjoined verb it becomes the name of nonexistent things.[141] If such a paralogism as this arises: 'Whoever was getting up is standing, one sitting was getting up; therefore one sitting is standing', it can be said that equivocation in the first [sub]mode is present here because the participle 'sitting' principally and equally signifies present and past time, as Priscian says in Book One of *Constructions*.[142] Or, perhaps it is better said here that [the equivocation] is in the second [sub]mode because ['sitting'] consignifies present time properly and past time less properly. [The latter signification] is lacking because we do not have in our Latin language a past participle in the active voice. But this could be here the third mode because 'one sitting' is a name, since a participle can be changed into a

138. Alain de Libera suggests that the third mode gives evidence of Bacon's reliance on the *Fallaciae ad modum Oxoniae*. (See, respectively, *Sd* 3, "*Introduction*," pp. 181–182, and "*Fallaciae ad modum Oxoniae*," in *Die Fallaciae ad modum Oxoniae: Ein Fehlschlusstraktat aus dem 13. Jahrhundert*, ed. Clemens Reiner Kopp, p. 21.1–5, Dissertation, Faculty of Philosophy, University of Cologne [Cologne, 1985].) And this is confirmed, de Libera says, by the fact that Robertus Anglicus (an English contemporary of Bacon) underscores the specifically English character of the definition of the third mode when he remarks that the *English* are accustomed to presenting the mode described here. On this point see also Sten Ebbesen and Irène Rosier-Catach, "Robertus Anglicus on Peter of Spain," in *Medieval and Renaissance Logic in Spain*, pp. 61–95.

139. From this point to 388 Bacon focuses on equivocation that arises because of different appellations, for which notion see 238–265, esp. 248–257 and 264–265. De Libera notes that this notion of equivocation draws on what the English tradition of the School of Petit-Point presented in the twelfth century in terms of univocation: a simple variation in reference. (*Sd* 3, "*Introduction*," pp. 181–182.)

140. For the notion of ampliation see 2, nn.132 and 187.

141. See 248.

142. For the reference see Priscian *Institutiones grammaticae* 17.180, *GL*, vol. 3, p. 199.23–24.

noun.[143] But then there will be a case of equivocation from different appellations, as was said earlier (248), because, when '*sedens*' is a name, it appellates only present men, just as other names do. In virtue of the nature of what it is joined to, however, it can appellate nonentities. [3.450–459]

[389] One should know that the second and third modes can be subdivided just as the first, i.e., with respect to significata that exercise a function and the like. So, 'All the apostles are twelve' reflects the third mode, because 'all' can bring about a collection or a distribution. If a collection, it is true, if a distribution, then false. Now the words 'every' and 'all' by their nature are only distributive, but in virtue of the nature of the predicate joined to them they are taken collectively. [3.460–461]

[390] Next is *Amphiboly*. Amphiboly is the designation of more than one judgment by one expression. Its name comes from '*amphi*', which means doubt, and '*logos*', which means expression: thus "doubtful expression." The fallacy of Amphiboly is the deception arising from the sameness of an expression in matter and form. The cause of the semblance in this fallacy is the sameness of the expression in matter and form, i.e., in word and the way of pronouncing it, with the ability to signify. The cause of the nonexistence is the difference between the significata. [3.462–467]

[391] There are three modes of Amphiboly. The *first* occurs when an expression principally signifies more than one thing, as in 'Whomever I would want myself to accept I would want them to accept me, those fighting I would want me to accept; therefore I would want them to accept me'. It must be said that the minor is ambiguous because 'me' can be taken to precede the verb 'to accept' and to follow 'those fighting', and in this sense it is true, whereas, vice versa, it is false.[144] Likewise this: 'What someone sees this sees, someone sees a column; therefore a column sees'. The major is ambiguous because 'this' can be taken as a subject of what follows, and in this sense [the major] is false, or as a predicate of what follows it, and in this sense it is true.[145] The *second* mode occurs when an expression signifies one thing principally and strictly and signifies another metaphorically and broadly. For example: 'Whoever is plowing is doing something worthwhile, this man is plowing the seashore (indicating a person doing some-

143 In the example in 388 the participle '*sedens*' was used as a noun. The change comes about by its use with other words.

144 The two readings of the minor are: 'I would want me to accept those fighting' and 'I would want those fighting to accept me'.

145 If 'this' (*hoc*) in the major is taken as the subject of what follows it, we get: 'What someone sees, this sees' which is false, given the minor, but then forms part of a valid but unsound syllogism. If, however, 'this' is construed as the direct object of what follows it we have: 'What someone sees, he sees this', which, while true, cannot be used to construct a valid syllogism here.

thing in vain); therefore he is doing something worthwhile'. The minor is ambiguous because it can signify strictly and broadly. Likewise, 'to wash a brick' signifies strictly to pour water on a brick, but broadly the same as 'to fail a task' does. Similarly, 'They are beating the air' and 'The wolf is in the fable' signify strictly and broadly when joined to another. The *third* mode occurs when an expression signifies one thing of itself but signifies more than one thing when joined to another. For example, the expression 'Knows the world' signifies one thing because it is proper to take 'the world' as preceding the verb because otherwise there is no subject there, and so it cannot be taken as following the verb. But should something be added to it, like 'an animal', it would signify more than one thing: either 'an animal' would be taken as following the verb, and then it would be false, or as preceding the verb, and then it would be true. [3.468–473]

[392] Next is the fallacy of *Composition*. Composition is the joining of things that ought to be disjoined, i.e., of things that are appropriately divided.[146] According to some the fallacy of Composition is the deception arising from the material sameness of an expression when [it is true] in the

146 In most places the text will speak of *things* to be compounded and divided, but in others it is made clear that these things are *terms*. (See, e.g., 393 and 396.) Interestingly, William defines Composition as "the connection of things that are more disposed to be *compounded*" (emphasis mine), on which see Kretzmann's comment. Peter states the issue this way: "When the words in the expression are arranged in accordance with the more appropriate place, then the expression is said to be compounded. But if the words are separated from that place and put in a less appropriate place, then the expression is divided." Lambert says that Composition arises when what ought to be divided is composed, and Division, vice versa. Thus, these fallacies arise, respectively, because of inappropriate composition and division. (See, respectively, *Introductiones*, trans. Kretzmann, p. 140 and n. 48; *Tractatus* 7.61, and trans. Kretzmann and Stump, *CTMPT*, p. 248; and *Logica*, p. 155.24–30.) For an older definition of Composition see 413. See Georgette Sinkler, "Roger Bacon on the Compounded and Divided Sense," in *The Rise of British Logic*, ed. Osmund Lewry, Acts of the Sixth European Symposium on Medieval Logic and Semantics, Balliol College, Oxford, 19–24 June 1983, Papers in Mediaeval Studies, vol. 7 (Toronto: Pontifical Institute of Mediaeval Studies, [1985]), pp. 145–171, and Maria-Luisa Rivero, "Early Scholastic Views on Ambiguity: Composition and Division," *Historiographia Linguistica* 2 (1975): 25–47. See also Sten Ebbesen, who offers an analysis of ambiguous statements like 'Whatever lives always is' (see 402) to illustrate the development of medieval justifications for distinguishing between Amphiboly, Composition and Division, Equivocation, and Accent and to illustrate the history of discussions on *pausatio* – pauses expressed by commas today to indicate how words are to be grouped when ambiguity is present – and other suprasegmental phonemes. See his "Suprasegmental Phonemes in Ancient and Medieval Logic," in *English Logic and Semantics*, pp. 331–359.

divided sense with its aptitude for the compounded sense.[147] But the cause of the semblance in this fallacy is the material sameness of the word when it is true in the divided sense with its aptitude for the compounded sense. For, because we see that it is true in the divided sense, and the expression is materially the same in the compounded sense, we think that it would be true in the compounded sense. Because of this we are deceived in the way just stated. So, it is always false in the compounded sense.[148] [3.474–477]

[393] The Topic has two modes. The *first* occurs when something is compounded with one thing and, when it is divided, it is not compounded with another, as in 'It is possible that a sitting man walks'.[149] [The expression] is ambiguous because 'a sitting man' can be divided from 'walks' and in this sense [the expression] is true, or 'a sitting man' can be compounded with 'walks' and in this sense it is false.[150] Likewise: 'That one who is not writing writes is possible'. Without exception every expression that has a modal name in it is said to be such on the basis of it being [an expression] *de re* and *de dicto*. The compounded sense is always present when it is a divided statement *de dicto* – *de dicto* is said to occur when the whole dictum functions as the subject; *de re*, when the [verbal] action serves as the subject. The *second* mode occurs when a word is compounded with one thing and, when it is divided, can be compounded with another, as in 'Whoever knows the alphabet now has learned it, this man knows the alphabet (indicating a

147 In 395 Bacon will add to this that the cause of the deception is a division that is either explicit or implicit (*voce vel intellectu facta*). The reference to an aptitude is brought out more clearly by Peter when he says: "... if a paralogism was made on the basis of composition, the solution will come from division, and if the paralogism was made on the basis of the fallacy of Division, the solution will come from composition." (*Tractatus* 7.63, and trans. Kretzmann and Stump, *CTMPT*, p. 250.)

148 I.e., it is always false when it contains the fallacy of Composition. Apropos of this claim, however, Peter writes: "Notice also that whenever composition or division or accent occurs, it is not necessary that the expression is always true in one way and false in another, because it can happen that it is false in both senses or true in both senses." (*Tractatus* 7.63, and trans. Kretzmann and Stump, *CTMPT*, p. 250.) For the cause of the fallacy of Composition see 395.

149 To say that the disjoined term is not re-compounded is a bit imprecise, since every word in an expression must be construed with some other word, at least as subject of a predicate and vice versa. Here the claim is that in this mode the disjoined word is not re-compounded in an improper or ambiguous way such as to give rise to another fallacy of Composition.

150 The dictum 'that a sitting man walks' has two notions: a sitting man and the act of walking. If these are taken in the compounded sense, then the meaning is that someone while sitting is walking, which is false and not possible. If taken in the divided sense, however, as two disjoined notions, then the meaning is that someone, now sitting, in the future is walking, and this is true and possible.

man who learned it ten years ago); therefore he now has learned the alphabet'. The major is ambiguous because the determination 'now' can determine 'has learned', i.e., can be compounded with it, and in this sense [the major] is false, or ['now' can] be divided from it and be compounded with 'knows', and in this sense [the major] is true. 'With what you saw this man struck he was struck, you saw him struck with an eye; therefore he was struck with an eye'. The major is ambiguous because 'with which' can be compounded with 'you saw', and in this sense it is false, or ['with which'] can be divided from ['you saw'] and compounded with 'struck', and in this sense it is true. Likewise, the minor can be distinguished in the same way with respect to 'with an eye'.[151] And 'What can carry one thing only can carry more than one' is ambiguous because 'only' can be compounded with 'one', and in this sense it is false, or be divided from it and compounded with the participle 'being' that is implicit there, and then it is true in the sense of 'What can carry one thing (being) a sole thing can carry more than one'. In this sense 'sole thing' is taken as a categorematical [term], whereas in the first sense as a syncategorematical one.[152] [3.478–487]

[394] According to some the [last] is an example of a third mode.[153] Hence, they say that a third mode occurs when a determination is com-

151 See 410.

152 The paralogism reads: "*Quod unum solum potest ferre plura potest ferre.*" One of the problems here is to understand the deception to arise from division and not equivocation, since '*solum*' can be translated by 'only', 'alone' or 'sole item'. A person, thinking of a boat and uttering the proposition 'What can carry one thing only can carry more than one thing', and taking 'only' with what precedes it, could have two meanings in mind: (a) that the boat can carry *just* one thing and only one thing, and in that sense the proposition is false, or (b) that it can carry more than one thing, but at the moment is carrying only one thing, and in that sense it is true. Bacon, however, proposes a different sense in which, for the saying to be true, '*solum*' becomes a categorematical term and is construed with the implied participle 'being'. He seems to have in mind something like 'What can carry one thing being a sole item can carry more than one thing', assuming an example like the boat just described in (b). Here '*solum*' is taken as a substantive adjective to fit the requirement of its being taken as a categorematical term. For the notion of categorematical and syncategorematical terms see 128–129. But note that Bacon rejects this solution and proposes another in 394 which requires that 'only' in the utterance be divided from what precedes it, but then fails to indicate with what, if anything, it is to be construed if the saying is to be true.

153 Both William and Peter present only two modes of Composition (and Division). Bacon will be seen to agree in 394. But de Libera notes that, while the three-fold division is found in the Oxford tradition, it is also used by Albert the Great and Lambert of Auxerre. (See, respectively, ed. August Borgnet, *Opera omnia*, vol. 3 [Paris, 1890], p. 548a, and *Logica*, p. 158.10–24). In the Oxford tradition see the commentary on *Sophistical Refutations* by Robert Kilwardby (MS. Paris Nat. lat. 16619), as noted by de Libera, *Sd* 3, p. 180.

pounded with one thing and, when it is divided, it is compounded with another implicit thing. But, because an expression in the compounded and divided senses is materially the same and unchanged in substance or the order of parts, it is necessary that the same letters, syllables, and words be present in expressions in the compounded and divided senses. So, since the participle 'being' is neither an implicit nor explicit part of the expression in the compounded sense, it will not be a part of the expression in the divided sense.[154] For this reason the expression 'What can carry one thing only can carry more than one' is ambiguous because 'only' can be compounded with 'one', and in this sense it is false, or be divided from ['one'], and then it is true, without being compounded with something implicit.[155] [3.488–491]

[395] Next is the fallacy of *Division*. The fallacy of Division is the deception arising from an explicit or implicit division of things that ought to be joined together, as the fallacy of Composition is the deception arising from an explicit or implicit joining of things that ought to be disjoined.[156] But the cause of the semblance is the material sameness of the expression when it is true in the compounded sense with its aptitude for the divided sense. Because we see an expression to be true in the compounded sense we think it to be true in the divided sense, and vice versa; and so we are deceived. The cause of the nonexistence in both fallacies is the difference in utterances along with the difference in significata. The fallacy of Division, therefore, is the deception arising from the already mentioned cause of the semblance. But, when it is said here that "the division is a separation of things that ought to be joined," 'of things that ought to be joined' is to be understood to be said of those things that are naturally suited to be joined.[157] [3.492–497]

[396] The *first* mode occurs when something is divided from one thing and is not compounded with another thing, as in 'Whatever are two and three are even and odd, five are two and three; therefore five are even and odd'. The minor is ambiguous because 'two' can be divided from 'three', and so [the minor] is false [when read] in the sense of 'Five are two and five are three'. Or, ['two'] can be compounded with ['three'], and then [the

154 But see 395.

155 Bacon's analysis leaves unclear with what 'only' is to be construed for there to be a true sense of the expression. Not, he says, to 'one thing' or to something implicit. That leaves only 'can' and 'carry'. If 'only' is compounded with 'can' we get 'What only *can* carry one thing can carry more than one thing' and this is false. If it is compounded with 'carry' we get 'What can only *carry* (as opposed to eat, sing, manufacture) one thing can carry more than one thing', but this fails to focus on the problem of the one and the many that is the crux of the paradox.

156 In 394 implicit terms were said to violate the principle of sameness in matter in Composition and Division.

157 See 413.

minor] is true. The major is true and false, vice versa. So, the fallacy of Composition is present in the major and the fallacy of Division in the minor because, generally speaking, in that sense in which it is false, it is false because of what has already been explained. This mode occurs in all expressions where a conjunction between terms or between propositions can occur. [158] Likewise, a disjunction, as in ‘Every proposition or its contradictory is true’. Also, where a proposition can be conditional or have a conditioned predicate or subject, as in ‘The false is true if the Antichrist is’. The *second* mode arises when a determination is divided falsely from one thing and compounded with another thing placed in the expression, as in ‘God ceases now to exist’. It is ambiguous because ‘now’ can be divided from ‘to exist’ and be compounded with ‘ceases’, and in this sense it is false, or it can be compounded with ‘to exist’, and then it is true.[159] Other similar examples can be posited: ‘Forty of men one hundred divine Achilles left’. If the term ‘one hundred’ is divided from ‘men’ it is false; if it is compounded it is true. Likewise, ‘I made you a slave being a free man’. If the expression is directed to ‘slave’ and the participle ‘being’ is divided from ‘slave’, it is false; if the expression is compounded, then it is true.[160] [3.498–506][161]

[397] But in this paralogism a third mode of Division is said to be present because, although the determination is divided from something actually asserted in the expression, it is compounded with something else [implicitly] understood.[162] But perhaps this does not constitute Composi-

158 For a comment on the negation of these (and the following) links see 408.

159 William provides the full syllogism: ‘Whatever ceases now to exist will not exist hereafter, but God ceases now to exist; therefore God will not exist hereafter’. (*Introductiones*, trans. Kretzmann, p. 143.) In the divided sense that is false the minor would read: ‘God now ceases to exist’, implying immediately hereafter there is no God. In the compounded sense that is true it would read: ‘God ceases to exist now’, i.e., at t^1 because this passes away, but will continue to exist at t^2, which reading, of course, would render the syllogism unsound.

160 In the compounded (and true) sense the expression would read: ‘I made you, being a slave, a free man’, whereas in the divided and false sense it would read: ‘I made you, being a free man, a slave’. Bacon gives no reason why the first reading is true and the second false, but Peter provides one based on the notion that signs (words) should be joined in ways that reflect what they signify: to pass from slavery to freedom is “more joined to human nature” than the opposite. (*Tractatus* 7.62, and trans. Kretzmann and Stump, *CTMPT*, p. 249.)

161 Reading at *Sd* 3, p. 247, last line, ‘506’ against ‘596’ in the text.

162 Reading at *Sd* 3, p. 248, 507.3, ‘*<cum alio sub>intellecto*’ against ‘*intellecto*’ in MSS. O. and S. and the text.

This is to say that, while division actually occurs in the expression in 396, so does compounding, though implicitly. Neither William nor Peter present a third mode of Division, though Lambert does. (*Logica*, pp. 164.20–165.5.) See also *Sd* 392.

tion as we speak of it here, and because of this the first mode is there.[163] [3.507–508]

[398] One should carefully note that, either there is only one determination and only one determined thing – and then the expression is said to be compounded because of the continuous utterance of those with respect to each other and divided because of the discontinuous utterance, as in the first mode – or there is [only] one determination but more than one determinable thing.[164] Then one must consider whether the two determined things are actually asserted in the expression, because, if they are, then one must take further note of whether [the determination] is positioned between the determinables or not. [3.509–511]

[399] [Rule 1] If it is positioned between them, the determination either applies to [one of] the determinable things in some specialized natural sense or not. If it does, then the expression is said to be compounded because of the composition of the determination with that determinable thing, and divided because of the division of that [determination] from that [determinable thing]. For example, 'truly', 'falsely', and the like, and all adverbs of affirming and denying are more naturally suited to the indicative mood than to the other moods because 'truly' indicates an affirmation in a certain sense and 'falsely' a negation. Those things that have the nature of an affirmation and negation are more suited to the indicative [mood] than to any other, as is clear from Priscian in his book *Constructions*.[165] From this is it clear how the following expression is compounded and divided: 'You cannot truthfully deny you are not an ass'. For it is compounded if the adverb 'truthfully' is compounded with

163 If there is no compounding after the division, then the example fits first and not second mode Division.

164 Bacon inserts here a series of rules for determining how to interpret certain kinds of ambiguous statements. While I suspect that 'one *determined* thing' should read 'one *determinable* thing', in its present state the reference is to the determinable term once it has been determined by being linked with the determining term through a determination resulting in a compounded or a divided sense. For two excellent studies of these rules, their origins and their significance, see Alain de Libera, "De la logique à la grammaire: Remarques sur la théorie de la *determinatio* chez Roger Bacon et Lambert d'Auxerre (Lambert de Lagny)," in *De Ortu Grammaticae: Studies in Medieval Grammar and Linguistic Theory in Memory of Jan Pinborg*, ed. G. L. Bursill-Hall, Sten Ebbesen, and Konrad Koerner, Amsterdam Studies in the Theory and History of Linguistic Science, vol. 43 (Amsterdam, Philadelphia: John Benjamins, 1990), pp. 209–226, and Paola Müller, "La dottrina delle *Fallaciae in dictione* in Ruggero Bacone," pp. 453–490, esp. pp. 476–482. (On p. 490 she presents a schematic outline of all the possibilities covered by the rules.) For Lambert's presentation of such rules see *Logica*, p. 165.6–43.

165 Cf. Priscian, *Institutiones grammaticae* 15.39, *GL*, vol. 3, p. 89.14–17.

'you cannot', and divided if it is divided from that and compounded with 'deny'.[166] But if [the determination] does not apply [in some specialized natural sense] to one of the determinable things, then one must take note of the nature of the determinable thing or the determination. If in the second way, either the determination is a pure determination or it is an adjectival determination. [3.512–517]

[400] [Rule 2] If it is a pure determination, then it is more naturally suited to be compounded with the determinable thing before it than with the one after it, because a determination absolutely is posterior and depends on the determinable thing.[167] For example, if I say 'You saw with a stick this man who was struck', [the expression] is [taken in] the compounded sense when 'with a stick' is compounded with 'you saw'. But if the determination is one having the nature of an adjective, then one must take note of the nature of the determinable thing as to whether both determinable things are substantives, or one a substantive and the other an adjective, or both adjectives. If the first way, then two possibilities arise: Either one is more finite, independent, and stands more on its own than the other does, or not. [3.518–521]

[401] [Rule 3] If it has these characteristics, the expression is said to be compounded because of the composition of the determination with something of that sort, because a determination is something dependent and inclining toward something else, needing that other that terminates its dependency. Such is the infinitive mood with respect to the other moods because it indicates the thing [signified] by the verb as something standing on its own and stable, although its inclination (which is a mood) is infinitive, as in 'God ceases now to be'.[168] [3.522]

[402] [Rule 4] But if the one [determinable thing] is not more finite or stable than the other, then the expression is always said to be compounded because of the continuation of the determination with the substantive that follows, because, as Priscian says, adjectives are more suitably placed before substantives than after them.[169] This is the case with all adjectives, and also adverbs (which are things adjoined to verbs),[170] although they can

166 In the compounded sense the claim is that one never has the *ability* to deny one is not an ass, whereas in the divided sense it is granted one can make the claim, but, if one does, the claim will be false.

167 Do adjectives (adverbs) appropriately precede or follow the terms they modify? Paragraphs 400–404 are a discussion that illustrates the significance of this issue.

168 Reading at *Sd* 3, p. 249, 522.4, and 522.6, respectively, '*infinit<iv>us*' and '*infinit<iv>a*' against '*infinitus*', and '*infinita*' in MSS. O. and S. and the text, for which see 404.

169 Priscian, *Institutiones grammaticae* 15.39, *GL*, vol. 3, p. 89.14–17.

170 Ibid.

well be placed before and after [verbs], except those that make a determination of the sort that 'not' does – these always have to be placed before the verb and never after it. This can be confirmed because accidents greatly contribute to the knowledge of a subject, as Aristotle says.[171] But knowledge and the manifestation of anything derive more from the beginning than from the end, and more from the apparent than from the hidden, and so adjectives ought to be placed before [those terms to which they are adjoined]. An example of this is 'Whatever lives always is'. The expression is a compounded one if the adverb is compounded with the last verb.[172] Likewise: 'Whoever knows the alphabet now has learned it'.[173] [3.523–527]

[403] [Rule 5] But if the one is an adjective and the other a substantive, whether the adjective be pure or a substantival [adjective], the expression is always said to be compounded because of the composition of [the adjective] with the substantive, since a substantive is more naturally suited to terminate the dependency of an adjective than a pure adjective is. For example, 'I see a good man knowledgeable about music' is compounded when 'good' is uttered along with 'man'.[174] [3.528]

[404] [Rules 6–7] But if both [determinable terms] are adjectives, then either it is the case that one is a substantival [adjective], and then [the expression] is said to be compounded because of the composition of the determination with it,[175] or both are pure adjectives, and then [the expres-

171 Aristotle *On the Soul* 1.1.402b21–22

172 To remove ambiguity one can place a comma before or after 'always'. Peter compounds 'always' with 'is' because "the adverb will more correctly determine the verb that is more rather than less principal ... ." (*Tractatus* 7.61, and trans. Kretzmann and Stump, *CTMPT*, p. 249.) For additional comment on the example see above, n. 146, at the end. For analysis of an analogous example see 393.

173 One can remove the ambiguity by placing a comma before or after 'now'. For an analysis of this example see 393.

174 The ambiguity appears only in the Latin: "*Video hominem bonum musicum.*" In the compounded sense it reads: 'I see a good man knowledgeable about music'; in the divided sense it could read: 'I see a man very knowledgeable about music' (or, less likely, but grammatically more illustrative of the point expressed in Latin: 'I see a man, a good man knowledgeable about music'). Presumably one of the latter would be the compounded reading if '*musicum*' were taken as a substantive, since the determining adjective '*bonum*' precedes it (see 402). However, there may also be an unstated rule that says that, when the determining term stands between two determinable substantive terms, one of which is a pure substantive (like '*homo*') and the other a substantive adjective (like '*musicus*'), the determination is to be compounded with the pure substantive, which would then construe 'good' with 'man'. Note that the divided sense here becomes the compounded sense in 404 because a different rule is operating.

175 E.g., in a context of talking about various kinds of good things that can happen one says: 'A beautiful good happened' (*Pulcrum bonum accidit*).

sion] is said to be compounded because of the composition of the one with the last adjective, since [the latter] is more of a substantive in that it follows an adjective.[176] [3.529]

[405] But if the determination is not positioned between [determinable terms], either it is positioned before them or it is positioned after them. [3.530]

[406] [Rule 8] If it is placed before them, then either [the determination] applies more naturally to one than the other – and then [the expression] is said to be composed when the determination determines that one, unless a stronger reason precludes this. For example, if I say 'It is not the case that "Every man runs" follows from "Any man runs,"' the expression is compounded if 'not' determines the word 'follows', which is in the indicative mood, the reason for which has already been touched on (399). [The expression is said to be] divided if ['not'] determines the word 'runs', unless perhaps several reasons cancel one: the infinitive is more stable and independent than the indicative is and also more immediately ordered to the negation. But let the resolution of this be left to disputation. [3.531]

[407] [Rule 9] Or [the determination] is indifferent to both [the determinable terms].[177] Then one must take note of the determinable things as to which of them is the more determinable. The requirements of determinability are that a thing stand [on its own], be stable, and be independent so that it can terminate the dependence and inclination of the determination. If the determination determines such a determinable thing, the expression will be compounded. A whole is always like this with respect to its part, a substantive to an adjective, and an infinitive verb to any other one.[178] [3.532–534]

[408] [Rule 10] But if the determinable things are equal with respect to each other, i.e., if one is no more naturally suited to determine the inclination of the determination than the other of its nature is, then one must take note of distance and proximity. It is to be asserted that an expression is compounded if the determination is compounded with the determinable thing from which it is the least distant because, since the dependence of [the determination] ought to be terminated, it is, as it were, more quickly terminated by what is closer, since its inclination seeks this. For example, 'With an eye or a stick you saw this man struck' is a compounded expression, if 'with an eye' or 'with a stick' is compounded with 'you saw'.[179] There are examples of a second sort when negation occurs with respect to

176 See "good ... knowledgeable about music (*bonum musicum*) in 403.

177 This is the second half of the disjunction announced in 406.

178 Reading at *Sd* 3 p. 251, 534.5, '*infinit<iv>um*' against '*infinitum*' in MSS. O. and S. and the text, for which see 401 and 406.

179 I.e., instead of with 'struck'. Cf. 393 and 400.

a whole dictum or a part of a dictum, for example, where a negation can negate a whole conjunctive expression or a part, or a whole disjunctive one or a part, or a whole conditional one or a part, and so on for similar cases.[180] [3.535–537]

[409] [Rule 11] But if the determination is asserted after [the determinable terms], one should reply in the same way as in the case where it was asserted before them. For if the determination applies more to one in some specialized natural sense, then [the expression] is compounded when the determination determines that one. For example, if I say 'I want you to make a book truly', the expression is compounded when 'truly' is compounded with 'I want', and it is divided when it is divided from ['I want'] and compounded with 'you to make'. [3.538–539]

[410] [Rule 12] But if the determination applies no more to one thing than to the other, one must take note whether one [of the terms] is more stable and independent, and then the expression is said to be compounded if the determination is compounded with that one.[181] For example, 'He struck the one looking with an eye' is compounded if the determination ['with an eye'] is compounded with 'the one looking', because a participle is more stable and independent than a verb is. If the determination 'with an eye' is more applicable to the participle than to the verb (since [an eye] is the proper instrument of seeing and not striking), then there are two reasons why the expression is said to be compounded, [the second derived] from the continued pronunciation of the determination with the participle.[182] The case is similar when a relation refers to a whole or a part, as in 'Every thing other than an animal which along with Socrates constitutes two things differs from Socrates'.[183] Similarly when a relative refers to an antecedent with or without distribution, and likewise for the others. [3.540–542]

[411] [Rule 13] For if the determination is not more applicable to one thing than to the other, and if one determinable thing is not more stable and standing on its own than the other, then one must take note of the proximity and distance [of the terms], as previously (408) an expression was said to be compounded from the continuous pronunciation of the determi-

180 Cf. 396.

181 Reading at *Sd* 3, p. 251, 540.1, '*determinatio*' with MS. S. against '*determinato*' in MS. O. and the text.

182 Reading at *Sd* 3, p. 252, 540.4, '*haec determinatio*' against '*hoc determinato*' in MS. O., an omission in MS. S., and '*determinato*' in the text.

183 For the statement to be true one must recognize that Socrates is an animal, and that anything not he, added to him, makes two. The statement would be false if the animal were that which constitutes the generic part of Socrates' nature, for then there would not be two distinct things. (I am indebted to Paul Spade for assistance in wording the translation here and in numerous other places in the text.)

nation with that thing from which it was less distant. It belongs to the diligence of one who weighs these questions to make the inquiry. [3.543]

[412] [Rule 14] But if the determination is related to two determinable things of which one is actually asserted in the expression and the other not, but is implicitly present, it could probably be said that the expression is compounded because of the composition of the determination with what is actually asserted in the expression, since what absolutely is in act has more the sense of a determinable thing than what is in a certain sense in potency – I say this if the third mode ought to be assigned.[184] [3.544]

[413] According to the earlier writers it is said that composition is the connection of things that ought to be disjoined, i.e., of those things that later are divided, not of those that are naturally suited to be divided.[185] In connection with this the paralogism [of Composition] arises whenever one proceeds from something true by composition to something false by division. For example, in 'Five are two and three; therefore five are two and five are three' the first is true because of composition and false because of division, and the conclusion is false because of division. The fallacy of Composition is likewise present here: 'An animal is a body and a soul; therefore an animal is a body and an animal is a soul'. But the fallacy of Division is present when one proceeds from something true by division to something false by composition. So, this division is the disjoining of things that ought to be compounded, that later are compounded, not [of those] that are naturally suited to be compounded, as in 'Whatever you know now you learned, you know the alphabet; therefore you learned the alphabet now': from what is true by division one infers what is false by composition.[186] Likewise: 'With what this man was struck, you saw him struck, you saw him struck with an eye; therefore with an eye, etc.' And so on. [3.545–549]

[414] If by chance it seems reprehensible that according to Aristotle paralogisms of Composition are placed in [the treatment of] Division, and vice versa, we reply that an expression is compounded or divided in two ways: either by composition in the conclusion, and it is taken in this way by Aristotle, or by a composition that is in the premises, and it is taken in this way here – and this is more proper. For no one is said to doubt that the fallacy of Composition runs along this line: If jointly [in the premises], then dividedly [in the conclusion], and Division on this maxim: If dividedly [in

184 For previous comment on a third mode of Composition and Division see 394 and 397.

185 De Libera suggests James of Venice. (See *Sd* 3, pp. 180–181.) For the initial definition see 392.

186 Reading at *Sd* 3, p. 253, 548.3, '*non <eorum> quae*' against '*non quae*' in MSS. O. and S. and the text. For the original definition of 'Division' see 395.

the premises], then jointly [in the conclusion]. Therefore, composition is granted in the fallacy of Composition and division is proved, and vice versa in the fallacy of Division. [3.550–551]

[415] But one should know that 'Composition' and 'Division' are names of fallacies, as has already been said, but in addition to this they are names of things an expression undergoes: when the fallacy of Composition is present in an expression, then there is present a division that is something an expression undergoes but not a fallacy, and when the fallacy of Division is present in an expression, then there is present there a composition that is something an expression undergoes but not a fallacy. These are said to be things something undergoes because an expression suffers division or composition in its parts that have been joined together or separated from one another. [3.552–553]

[416] Next is the fallacy of *Accent*. Accent here is the lack of distinction between words signifying different things, or between words and expressions that fall under the same word.[187] The fallacy of Accent is the deception arising from such a lack of distinction. The cause of the semblance in this fallacy is the sameness of a word only in matter, along with its aptitude for different pronunciations, i.e., accents. The cause of the nonexistence is the difference between the significata accompanying the difference in pronunciation. [3.554–558]

[417] This Topic has two modes because sometimes the lack of distinction is between words signifying different things, and sometimes it is between words and expressions. In accord with this there are two modes: the first occurs when a word can have a grave or an acute accent; the second occurs when a word can have only one accent or more than one. [3.559–560]

[418] In connection with the *first* mode there occur paralogisms like this: 'It is necessary that just men *pendere* (hang), it is not necessary that just men *pendere* (suffer punishments); therefore it is necessary that they suffer and not suffer'. One should reply that it does not follow because the word '*pendere*' in the first proposition has a grave accent and in the second an acute one. It signifies something different in the first and in the second, and

187 An example in Latin of a word and an expression that "falls under the same word" is 'q-u-i-e-s': pronounced as one word it is '*quies*' (rest) and as two it is '*qui es*' (you who are). Technically speaking, Bacon's examples in 418 are not expressions. William defines 'Accent' as "the regular modulation of the voice with respect to raising and lowering it." (*Introductiones*, trans. Kretzmann, pp. 144–145.) Apropos of this Kretzmann remarks: "These descriptions of variations of pitch corresponding to the Greek accent marks are correct (as regards their original use), but scarcely relevant to a discussion of examples in Latin, where the differences at issue concern the 'quantity' of vowels and the degree of separation between words in speech. For a more appropriate medieval account of Accent see the twelfth-century *Fallacie parvipontane* (in de Rijk, *LM*, vol. 1, p. 583)." (*Introductiones*, trans. Kretzmann, p. 145, n. 75.)

hence the conclusion does not follow.[188] [Paralogisms occur] in connection with the *second* mode like this: 'Socrates is *in mundo* with Plato; therefore Plato is *non mundus*'. The first has two senses because '*in mundo*' can have only one accent or more than one: if only one, the conclusion follows well; if more than one, it does not follow.[189] Likewise, 'God has made nothing *invite*, but fruit and leaves are *in vite*; therefore God has not made fruit and leaves'. One should reply that the word '*invite*' can have only one accent, and then the major is true, but the conclusion does not follow, or two accents, and then it is false, but the conclusion follows.[190] [3.561–564]

[419] Next is the fallacy of *The Figure of a Word*. This figure is the resemblance of a word, or two words, or of one to itself.[191] The cause of the semblance is the resemblance of this sort. The cause of the nonexistence is the difference between things that have a resemblance. The fallacy of The Figure of a Word is the deception arising from the resemblance of words.[192] [3.565–569]

[420] Paralogisms of this sort occur [in the *first* mode] in this Topic: '"Margarita" is feminine in gender; therefore so is "Catilina"', and '"*Secare*" signifies to do something; therefore so does "*exsecare*"'.[193] Like-

188 In the major the word is '*pendere*' (where the penultimate 'e' is short) and the word means to be suspended, i.e., to hang; in the second proposition the word is '*pendere*' (where the penultimate 'e' is long) and the word means to inflict punishment as would a judge. See Lambert *Logica*, p. 167.4–15.

189 The fallacy of Accent arises because the sounds 'i-n-m-u-n-d-u-s' can be heard with one accent to form the one word '*inmundus*' (unclean), or with two accents to form (mutatis mutandis) the two words '*in mundo*' (in the world).

190 The sounds 'i-n-v-i-t-e' with one accent form '*invite*' (unwillingly), but with two '*in vite*' (on a vine).

191 E.g., respectively, '*Catilina*' (masculine gender with feminine ending) (see 420); '*Plato*' and '*homo*' (426); and any common term suppositing for different things in different modes of supposition, e.g., 'a sort' (*quale quid*) and 'a particular thing' (*hoc aliquid*) (428). For comments on this fallacy see Reinhard Huelsen, "Concrete Accidental Terms and the Fallacy of Speech," in *Meaning and Inference in Medieval Philosophy*, pp. 175–185.

192 For comment on sameness in the matter and form of the words see 428–429.

193 See 422 for the description of this mode. 'Margarita' is the name of a woman, whereas 'Catilina' (in Latin) is that of a man, a Roman citizen against whom Cicero wrote near the end of the Republic. '*Secare*' means to cut and the addition of the prefix '*ex*' suggests a cutting *out* or *from* something. Given the differences in spelling, one is led to think that the two verbs mean different things, but, says Bacon, they both mean the performance of some action (*facere*). If this is what we are to get out of the example, surely it is a poor one to illustrate this fallacy: it would lead to the conclusion that all verbs (in the active voice) that are spelled differently are examples of The Figure of a Word since they all signify the same thing, i.e., actions (*facere*). In 422 Bacon distinguishes three modes of this fallacy, but later (423 and 427) he will concede that they really are not specifically different after all.

wise [in the *second* mode], 'Whatever you saw yesterday you see today, yesterday you saw *album* (something white); therefore today you saw *album* (white)'. Here The Figure of a Word is present because a what is transformed into a quality. 'Whatever' distributes for those things that indicate a what, whereas 'white' does not indicate a what but a quality.[194] Something similar happens when a what is transformed into a quantity, as in 'Whatever [you saw yesterday you saw today], but yesterday you saw something two cubits long; therefore [today you saw two cubits long]'. Another example: 'This one gives one sole denarius and he does not have one sole denarius; therefore he gives what he does not have'. Here a reciprocation or a quality is transformed into a what. For example, they say that to give one sole denarius is to give a what, but to give what one does not have is to give a quality.[195] Likewise, all the ten categories can be transformed into one another, as in 'Whatever sort of thing you saw yesterday, etc., but yesterday you saw a man; therefore, etc.'. Here a quality is transformed into a what, i.e., a substance. Again, 'However much you saw yesterday, today, etc., but yesterday you saw a lion; therefore today, etc.': a quantity is transformed into a substance, for 'however much' distributes for those things that indicate quantity or a quantity, whereas 'lion' indicates a what. [In the second mode] a species of one category can similarly be converted into another species of the same [category], as in 'Whenever you ate you were [already] born, you ate twice; therefore, etc.' Here a continuous quantity is transformed into a discrete one. And, vice versa, as in 'However much fingers you had in your youth you now have, but you had short ones in your youth; therefore you have short ones [now]'.[196] [3.570–576]

[421] One should note that in none of these paralogisms is The Figure of a Word present as in the first subject, but [each] must be resolved in the way the first [example] was.[197] Thus '*dare equum*' (to give a horse) and

194 See 422 for a description of this mode. This fallacy arises because there is a transition from one Aristotelian category in the major to a different one in the minor. Bacon's example here is given extended analysis in the article by Huelsen mentioned in n. 191.

195 The analysis of this example is unclear and the latter is not employed by William, Peter, or Lambert. Possibly Bacon has something like this in mind: to give a denarius is to give some thing (a what); to fail to have something is a quality. Hence, to give what one does not have is to give a quality, however strange the locution. Therefore, the syllogism in question commits the fallacy of The Figure of a Word when gives-a-what in the first premise is used as evidence for gives-a-Quality in the conclusion. With this understanding, the phrase "a Quality into a what" should be changed to "a what into a Quality." Finally, see 421 where 'to give one sole thing' (*dare unum solum*) is again addressed.

196 Here the move is within the category of Quantity from number to length.

197 This remark will be repeated several times (see 423, 425, 426, 427) and seems to mean that, whereas the fallacy involved in the examples of 'Margarita' and '*secare*'

'*dare unum solum*' (to give only one) are similarly formulated, but to give a horse is to give a what. Therefore, who gives only one, [but does not have only one], gives what he does not have.[198] The others must be reduced as occurred in the first example: '*Album*' (white) and '*pomum*' (apple) or something like these have similar endings, but '*pomum*' indicates a what or can be subsumed under 'whatever'; therefore [one is led to believe that so can] '*album*' (white). And so on.[199] [3.577–578]

[422] The *first* mode of this fallacy is indicated when the masculine gender is transformed into the others, or vice versa; and the case is similar with respect to the other accidents [of words]. The *second* mode occurs when one category is transformed into another, or a species of one into another [species of the same category]. But the *third* mode is indicated when a sort (*quale quid*) is transformed into a particular thing. [3.579–581]

[423] If, however, that fallacy is reduced to the first subject, it is clear that there is no difference between the paralogisms in form but only in matter and number. They are indicated and formed in the same way and so do not differ except as several individuals do of one species. [3.582]

[424] But one should know that every singular name indicates a particular thing, whereas every common name indicates a sort. So, there arises a paralogism in this way: 'Socrates is a man, Plato is a man; therefore Socrates is Plato'. One should reply that 'man' in the first proposition designates a sort; in the conclusion it is removed and 'Plato' is put in its place, which latter indicates a particular thing. Vice versa, there is this: 'Socrates is someone other than Plato, Plato is a man; therefore Socrates is someone other than a man'. [3.583–584]

[425] The fallacy of The Figure of a Word occurs, moreover, from changes in the supposition of a term.[200] For example: 'Any man's ass runs; therefore (an) ass of any man runs'.[201] [This happens] in all cases [of infer-

---

at the very beginning of 420 is not the same sort as those represented in the other examples in that paragraph – there the inference was from a what to a quality. Nevertheless, the latter represent analogous fallacious moves because they proceed from one category to another or from one species of a category to another of the same category, and hence are to be analyzed using the same principles indicated in the analysis of the first examples.

198 See 420.

199 Bacon, of course, is not proposing this as a sound syllogism, but presents it to show how we are deceived in the fallacy. The point, again, is that colors are qualities and as such are not things in the same sense as a substance is.

200 In 432 and 434 Bacon will become more precise and say that changes in *supposita* must accompany changes in modes of supposition if the fallacy is to occur, and he gives there an example in support of his claim.

201 425 seems to tell us that we are to understand the inference here to be one from merely confused supposition to determinate supposition. If this is so, then the term

ences] from (1) merely confused to determinate supposition, as was just said, [and] from (2) the same supposition, [i.e., from merely confused supposition], to confused and distributive supposition, and all the way to discrete supposition. An example of the first is 'Every man is an animal; therefore every animal is a man'.[202] An example of the second is 'Every man is an animal; therefore every man is this animal'. Although these examples of merely confused supposition are to be proved, as was previously signified (236–237), thanks to the common way of speaking, it is permissible to propose them. In all of them there comes about a transition from a sort to a particular thing, as they say, because, when a common term supposits merely confusedly, it always designates a sort, whereas when determinately or discretely or confusedly and distributively, it designates a particular thing. If one proceeds from (3) one of these [latter] to [merely] confused supposition, the process is from a particular thing to a sort. Likewise, The Figure of a Word occurs when one proceeds from (4) more than one determinate thing to one determinate thing, as in 'Some man is Socrates, some man is Plato (and so on for the others); therefore some man is every man'. This is a process from a sort to a particular thing because the many determinate things in the premises are equivalent to one merely confused thing. So the transition is, as it were, from one merely confused thing to one determinate thing. [3.585–593]

[426] But one should know that the fallacy of The Figure of a Word is present in all these by reduction to the first subject, but not as it was in the first subject, as is clear when one says in one [example standing] for all: 'Every man is an animal; therefore an animal is every man'. This must be reduced in this way: 'animal' in the one and in the other is spoken similarly. It supposits merely confusedly in the first; therefore [one is led to believe it supposits in the same way] in the second. Likewise, in the first example 'Plato' and '*homo*' (man) are similarly formulated because, just as the word 'Plato' consists of detectable letters and syllables, so also the word '*homo*'. Thus it seems that they are spoken similarly precisely because they have a similar ending. On the basis of this one proceeds further: just as one signi-

---

at issue must be 'ass' and not 'man', and we have an example like the one used by Lambert and mentioned in the preceding note. (See also 220.) The fallacious inference can be recognized if we state the premise as 'Every human has some ass (or other) and each ass runs' and the conclusion as 'Therefore, there is one ass which every human owns jointly, and it runs'.

From here to the end of the discussion of this fallacy Bacon investigates how a resemblance between words – same word used twice in a syllogism – occurs with changes in supposition and therefore leads to a deception. For the notions of the various kinds of supposition see 213–220.

202 The term in question here and in 425 is 'animal'.

fies a particular thing, so [we are led to believe does] the other. These things need further inquiry. [3.594–596]

[427] Because, therefore, all paralogisms are reduced in this way to the first subject in which the deception is rooted, it is clear that the formation of all the paralogisms are the same as that given in the first proposition: the similar figure of the words causes a deception. So one cannnot properly distinguish paralogisms of The Figure [of a Word] into modes.[203] It is clear in this way how the resemblance is discovered that is the cause of the semblance. [3.597]

[428] When, however, a consignified genus is transformed into another, a resemblance is present between two different things. Likewise when one genus of a category is transformed into another [genus], or a species of one [category] into another [species of the same genus]. But when a sort is transformed into a particular thing by a change in supposition, then it is commonly said that a resemblance is present of one and the same word to itself. But because resemblance is a relation and a relation requires different extremes, it must be the case that there is a difference between the extremes of the relation. This is true because a word suppositing in different ways in different expressions is numerically multiplied and is not numerically the same word, because, once it is uttered or written, it is impossible for numerically the same thing to be written or uttered again.[204] This is what Aristotle says: "What has been spoken can no longer be taken back," and Horace: "Once sent forth, a word flies away, irrevocable."[205] By this it is clear that resemblance in this fallacy is always between different words, at least as regards their number. But when a term supposits in different ways in two different expressions, the resemblance is nothing other than the identity of a word in matter and form, which causes the deception and is the cause of the semblance. [3.598–603]

[429] This, however, is the same thing as the cause of the semblance in the fallacy of Equivocation (385); therefore, here and there the cause of the semblance is the same thing, which is obviously false. One should reply that in the fallacy of Equivocation the total sameness of a word in matter and form is noted first and *per se* for the cause of the semblance. But this occurs in The Figure of a Word, but is not required *per se* because the cause of the semblance in The Figure of a Word is the similar configuration of the words themselves whether in their initial part or the endings or whether the

203 See 423, and cf. 422.

204 This seems to clarify some of the talk about resemblance of "a word" or "of one to itself" in 419. See also 428.

205 Aristotle *Categories* 6.5a34–35, and Horace *Epistulae* 1.18.71, in *Horace: Satires, Epistles, and Ars poetica*, trans. H. Rushton Fairclough, Loeb Classical Library, 1947, p. 374.

words are totally identical, and the form of the word (its pronunciation) is not considered, just as in the fallacy of Equivocation.[206] Other causes will be assigned by others. [3.604–606]

[430] But one should know that every common term, in whatever way it supposits, signifies a sort. But it does not signify a sort, i.e., it is not related in the manner of that which is a sort to supposition, because, although 'confused and distributive' and 'determinate' are terms signifying a sort, these terms supposit a particular thing, a singular thing, because terms suppositing in this way stand for singular things and not for their significata, which are sorts; and likewise discrete supposition occurs for a particular thing. But because of this they stand for and supposit for something by distributing and dividing and not in a confused and common way. Confusion and commonality are the proper conditions of a sort and are properly repugnant to a particular thing because every [sort] is something common and confused. So with respect to their way of suppositing, [common terms] do not indicate a sort, but a particular thing. Although merely confused supposition occurs for singular things and for a particular thing, nevertheless it occurs in a confused and common way without distributing and dividing, because one may not descend to anything in a divided way, nor can a locution be rendered true of some distinct thing by such supposition. In confused and distributive supposition one may descend to anything in a divided way. In the other [modes of supposition] a locution is rendered true of one thing in a divided way. And this suffices. So, the notion of a sort is more attributed to a term suppositing merely confusedly than to one suppositing confusedly and distributively, or determinately, or discretely.[207] When, therefore, one proceeds from this [merely confused supposition] to those others (or vice versa), one proceeds from a sort to a particular thing (or vice versa), because merely confused supposition has the characteristic of a sort with respect to a term's significatum and mode of suppositing. [3.607–611]

[431] Besides this one should know that a term with simple supposition also genuinely has the characteristic of a sort and supposits for a sort because [it supposits] for its significatum, as in 'Man is a species'. So, The Figure of a Word occurs, if one proceeds from that [simple supposition] to confused and distributive, or determinate, or discrete, as in 'Man is a species; therefore every man is a species', or '[therefore] this man is a species', or '[therefore] man is a species', [understood] in the sense in which

206 But in 385 sameness in pronunciation (form) was said to be one of the causes of deception in Equivocation.

207 Reading at *Sd* 3, p. 259, 610.1, '*termino*' with MS. O. against '*termini*' in MS. S. and the text.

'man' has personal supposition, because [the original proposition] is ambiguous, as has already been stated (222–226). [3.612–613]

[432] One should know that The Figure of a Word does not always arise from a change in supposition but when a term supposits in different ways and stands for different things in one supposition and another, as, for example, when one says 'Any man's ass runs; therefore (an) ass [of any man runs]'.[208] [3.614]

[433] One should know that the resemblance in this fallacy is sometimes spoken of with respect to a term, sometimes with respect to an expression. And there is confusion here when one speaks of the fallacy of The Figure of a Word – I mean with respect to the reference to a term and an expression – as will be made clear in [the treatise] *Sophisms*.[209] [3.615]

[434] If one objects that in the argument 'Every man is something able to laugh; therefore every thing able to laugh is a man' (and in similar ones) the fallacy of The Figure of a Word does not seem to be present and yet there is a change from merely confused to confused and distributive supposition (and vice versa), one can reply, if one pleases, that a change in supposition does not cause The Figure of a Word unless along with it that for which the supposition occurs is changed, as was just touched on (432), and so [the fallacy] is not present in these [arguments]. Perhaps better: although there is no actual deception arising here from the terms, nevertheless an aptitude for deceiving remains in that way of arguing. So, once [the suppositions of] the terms are changed, the fallacy will arise, although it would hold thanks to the terms, just as an argumentation with affirmative [premises] in the second figure holds in the case of convertible terms, granted not absolutely, since the fallacy of the Consequent might arise. [3.616–617]

[435] Next is the fallacy of *Accident*.[210] This fallacy is the deception arising from an apparent sameness between the middle and the extremities.

208 For the distinction between changes in supposition and changes in supposita see 434. See also 425 and n. 203.

209 In volume 14 of the *Opera hactenus inedita Rogeri Bacon* Robert Steele presents a work entitled *Summa de sophismatibus et distinctionibus*, attributes it to Bacon, and suggests it "dates possibly from his early years as a Regent Master in the University of Paris, though it might well have been part of an Oxford course" (p. iii). So far as I know no one has published a detailed study of it and the attribution is as yet unconfirmed. A cursory reading does not reveal any discussion of the fallacy of The Figure of a Word, and hence it does not seem likely that Bacon's reference here in 431 to *Sophisms* is to this work. Indeed, the words he uses here could equally well be translated "as will be made clear in [almost any discussion about] sophisms."

210 For comment by de Libera on the source of Bacon's treatment of this fallacy see *Sd* 3, pp. 182–184. For a study of the treatment of this fallacy principally by William of Sherwood, Peter of Spain, and Lambert of Auxerre see José Miguel Gambra,

So, the cause of the semblance is an apparent sameness. The cause of the nonexistence is the difference the middle makes when it is joined to the extremities. One should know that the sameness of the middle is based on a substance whereas the difference is a multiplicity in concepts. Ordinarily the fallacy occurs because something is attributed similarly to a subject and an accident although it inheres dissimilarly, i.e., although it inheres only in one of them and not in the other. [3.618–623]

[436] There are three things to consider in this fallacy, namely, an attribute, an accident, and a subject. The *attribute* is always the major extremity; the *subject* is the minor extremity; and the *accident* is the middle term. I say "always" if the paralogism of Accident is reduced to the arrangement of the first figure. One ought to reduce it in this way so that the defect may be clearer.[211] Since the accident in this fallacy is an alien predicate, as can be had from Aristotle,[212] it will be more the middle than any other would be because the middle relates differently and extraneously

---

"The Fallacy of the Accident in Peter of Spain's 'Tractatus' and in Other Thirteenth-Century Works," in *Medieval and Renaissance Logic in Spain*, pp. 21–60. And for comment on the function of the middle in this fallacy see L. M. de Rijk, "Die Streit über das *medium demonstrationis*: die Frucht eines Missverständnisses?" in *Argumentationstheorie: scholastische Forschungen zu den logischen und semantischen Regeln Korrekten Folgerns*, edited by Klaus Jacobi, Studien und Texte zur Geistesgeschichte des Mittelalters, vol. 38 (Leiden, Cologne: E. J. Brill, 1993), pp. 451–463. Apropos of the notion of Accident Peter calls attention to the fact that the accident at issue here is not that which is distinguished from Substance and comprises the nine categories called Accidents, nor is it one of the four predicates discussed by Aristotle in the *Topics* (1.5.102b4–7), nor even Porphyry's predicable called Accident. Rather, he says, it is "the accident that is the same as what does not necessarily follow" (*idem quod 'non-necessarium in consequendum'*). *Tractatus* 7.103.

211 In a syllogism in the first figure the middle term is the subject in the major and the predicate in the minor. It will be helpful in what follows to keep the following arrangement in mind:

Major:	accident	attribute
Minor:	subject	accident
Conclusion:	subject	attribute

But not all agree that one should reduce all examples of this fallacy to the first figure. De Libera refers to the author of the *Fallaciae ad modum Oxoniae* as an example. It is also opposed by Peter because, as he says, "... granted the middle is taken in different accidental relations, this is not because it accrues to the others but because the others accrue to it, just as to be a species accrues to man and in a different way Socrates accrues to it, as has been said." See, respectively, *Sd* 3, p. 182; *Fallaciae ad modum Oxoniae*, ed. Kopp, pp. 117.1–5 and 120.1–6; and *Tractatus* 7.107.

212 The reference to Aristotle is uncertain.

to the extremes in this fallacy: in as much as it is united to one extreme it is alien to the other. [3.624–626]

[437] There can be paralogisms of this sort on the basis of this fallacy: 'Man is a species, Socrates is a man; therefore Socrates is a species'. Likewise this: 'Animal is a genus, man is an animal; therefore man is a genus'. One should reply that this does not follow because something, [namely, to be a species], is attributed as inhering in the accident [(man)] in the first proposition, but in the subject [(Socrates)] in the conclusion. But this is not true because the middle is changed: 'man' is taken for an individual in the first proposition but not so in the second where it is something truly universal and common. Likewise for 'animal'.[213] Or ['man'] is taken for a concept in the first proposition and for a thing in the second. So, in as much as the middle is joined to the major extremity it is something accidental and alien to the minor [extreme]. Similar paralogisms arise in this way: 'All bronze is natural, this statue is bronze; therefore this statue is natural'. One should reply as before that here [to be natural] is attributed [as inhering in bronze and a statue], etc., and this does not follow, because the middle [(bronze)] is alien and accidental to the minor [extreme (statue)] in the sense in which it agrees with the major [extreme (being natural)]. Again, 'All water is natural, water is a bath; therefore a bath is natural'.[214] Likewise this: 'Coriscus is known by you, the one who is coming is Coriscus; therefore [the one who is coming is known by you]'. Also this: 'Yours is your Father, this dog is yours; therefore [this dog is your father]'.[215] [And this]: 'A good is a good cleric, this man is good; therefore he is a good cleric'. In all these [paralogisms] something [(the attribute)] is attributed as inhering in the accident and afterwards in the subject. Likewise, when the [attribute] inheres in dissimilar ways the middle is joined to the extremes in different ways in all these, and [the middle] is not predicated of the minor [extreme] in the same sense it has when it serves as the subject in the major. The case is similar in [paralogisms] of the sort where the middle is changed with respect to what is supposited, as in 'An animal is something white, a man is an animal; therefore a man is something white'. In the first something [(something white)] is attributed as inhering in the accident [(animal)] and in the conclusion as inhering in the subject [(a man)]. The middle is changed because 'animal' in the first proposition can stand for something other than a man but not in the minor. Likewise

213 Bacon misspeaks himself here: what is said of the first proposition is true of the second, and vice versa. In the next sentence he gets it right, but shows no awareness he has reversed himself.

214 For this example to be in the first figure the minor should read: 'A bath is water'.

215 For various versions of this example and its significance for the present work see de Libera, *Sd* 3, p. 183.

this: 'Something red is honey, bile is something red; therefore honey is bile'.[216] [3.627–637]

[438] In the way this last [paralogism] is uttered the fallacy of the *Consequent* is always present. So, because of it, let us look at consequences, i.e., the fallacy of Consequent. Consequent is part of Accident, and so the one will be made clearer after the other. The cause of the semblance in this fallacy is the apparent conversion of an antecedent and a consequence with respect to the consequent: we are deceived because we believe that a good consequence is converted when it is not converted.[217] The cause of the nonexistence is a defective conversion. There is only one mode of this fallacy and in it the procedure is always from the assertion of a consequence to the assertion of an antecedent.[218] But one should know that everything higher in the categorical line is a consequent with respect to what is lower, which latter are called antecedents. [219] [3.638–643]

[439] So, here is the fallacy of Consequent: 'It is a substance; therefore it is a body'. Again: 'It is a quantity; therefore it is a continuous quantity'. And again: 'It is a quality; therefore it is a habit'. And again, and so on: 'He is elegantly dressed; therefore he is an adulterer', 'He wanders about by night; therefore he is a thief', and 'The ground is wet; therefore it has rained'.[220] But if one proceeds vice versa when denying – e.g., 'Socrates is

216 To be in proper syllogistic form the conclusion should read 'Bile is honey'; but see 438.

217 One could state the point more clearly by saying that the cause of semblance is the fact that we sometimes take a proposition to be convertible when it is not and hence draw an invalid inference from it. Hence, when Bacon speaks of a "good consequence" he refers to a proposition that, while true in fact, does not follow necessarily from a proposition stated (or implied) as its antecedent.

218 There is some dispute on how to divide this fallacy. Peter divides it into three modes occurring when (1) a consequence is converted in accord with a Topical relation ('If it is a man, it is an animal; therefore if it is an animal, it is a man'); (2) when people think a consequence is convertible because of the circumstances of a person (as happens in rhetoric, he says) ('If he is an adulterer, he is elegantly dressed'); and (3) when people think a consequence is convertible on the basis of opposition ('If it is made, it has a source; therefore if it is not made, it has no source', thinking of the beginning of the world). (*Tractatus* 7.157–159.) Lambert, however, distinguishes two modes, the first includes Peter's first and second modes, and the second is based on opposition, Peter's third mode. (*Logica*, pp. 195.39–197.2.) William simply speaks of various species (Kretzmann, "varieties") but does not enumerate them. (*Introductiones*, trans. Kretzmann, p. 160.)

219 E.g., 'animal' is the name of a genus whereas 'man' that of a species, which is the relation of something higher to something lower on the Porphyrean Tree.

220 Bacon's examples – see here and below – are stated as syllogisms (enthymemes) but there is nothing significant in this as can be seen in those of William, Peter and Lambert who express the fallacy both in argument form as well as conditional

not a body; therefore he is not a substance' and so on in others – the mode is the same, namely, from the assertion of a consequent, because, just as Substance is something consequent to Body, so Nonbody is something consequent to Nonsubstance. Yet it is said that there is a procedure there from the destruction of an antecedent, and this is not anything different because it is the same thing to destroy what is antecedent to a substance and to assert what is consequent to a nonsubstance.[221] [3.644–646]

[440] But if someone says that, if the fallacy of Consequent is present in 'He is elegantly dressed; therefore, etc.', then, vice versa, 'He is an adulterer; therefore he is elegantly dressed' follows (which seems to be false), one should reply that the inference, vice versa, does follow and the consequence is probable, but it is not necessary. Such a consequence, however, suffices for a dialectician. [3.647]

[441] Next is the fallacy *In a Certain Respect and Absolutely.* What is uttered with a determination is "in a certain respect," and to be "absolutely" is to be uttered without a determination.[222] The cause of the semblance is the apparent identity of what is in a certain respect with what is absolutely. The cause of the nonexistence is their difference. One proceeds in accord with this Topic from something taken [in a certain respect] to that taken absolutely, or vice versa. [3.648–652]

[442] In the *first* mode are these sorts of paralogisms, and first, one with an accidental determination, e.g., 'Socrates is a good player of the zither; therefore he is good'. In the *second* mode it occurs with an alienating determination, e.g., 'A cadaver is a dead man; therefore a man is a cadaver' and 'A chimera is thinkable; therefore there is a chimera'. In the *third* mode it occurs with respect to a universal part: 'Socrates is not a rational animal; therefore he is not an animal'. Here there is also the fallacy of Consequent, but for another reason. In the *fourth* mode it occurs with respect to an integral part, e.g., 'An Ethiopian is white with respect to his teeth; therefore he is white'. In the *fifth* mode it occurs with respect to a determination pertaining to place, as in 'It is good to honor one's father in Troisvaux; therefore it is good to honor one's father'. In the *sixth* mode it occurs with respect to a determination of time, e.g., 'It is good to eat cold and moist things in the summer; therefore it is good to eat them' and 'It is

---

propositions. What is important to note is that for the medievals a consequence can involve implication, entailment, or inference, on which point see Ivan Boh, "Consequence," in *CHLMP*, pp. 300–301.

221 See 411–413 where Bacon discusses consequences *e contrario* and *in ipso*.

222 On the distinction between kinds of determination Kretzmann refers one to de Rijk's *LM*, vol. 1, pp. 130–131, 372–373, and 528–529, and then provides various examples of inferences involving strict, unstrict, and a third ("miscellaneous") determination. See *Introductiones*, trans. Kretzmann, p. 153, n. 124.

good to fast during Lent; therefore it is good to fast'. In the *seventh* mode it occurs with respect to a determination in mode, as in 'This man is naturally chaste; therefore he is chaste' and 'An egg is potentially an animal; therefore it is an animal'. In the *eighth* mode it occurs by means of a determination pertaining to a respect, e.g., 'This man is the most handsome of the Greeks; therefore he is the most handsome'. Likewise: 'This is good for a sick person; therefore it is good', 'This man is wise compared to those; therefore he is wise', and 'This man is richer than that man in silver; therefore he is richer than that man'.[223] One proceeds, vice versa, from "absolutely" to "in a certain respect" in each of these modes, but sometimes by affirming, at other times by denying, as the examples show. [3.653–661]

[443] Next is the fallacy of *Ignorance Regarding Refutation*. One should know that, as is clear from what has already been said (376), a refutation is a syllogism with a conclusion contradicting [some other proposition]. For example, if a respondent says that Socrates is not something white and an opponent constructs a syllogism such as 'Every man is something white, Socrates is a man; therefore Socrates is something white', this is a syllogism with a conclusion that contradicts that previously given by the respondent, and it is a refutation. Thus the nature of a syllogism and the nature of a contradiction are required for the nature of a refutation. A syllogism is an expression, etc. (275). A contradiction is the opposition of one and the same [attribute], not of the name alone, and not of a synonym, but of the same [name], on the basis of things that were given, and [following] necessarily, without including what was [stated] at the beginning, in the same respect, in the same relation, in the same way, and at the same time.[224] One should know, therefore, that ignorance regarding refutation or a weakening of a refutation can be accompanied in all cases by means of a defect in both the syllogism and the contradiction, and then we have a general fallacy to which all other fallacies are reduced.[225] In another way

223 Reading at *Sd* 3, p. 264, 660.4, *ditior illo* with MS. O. against *ditior* and an omission in MS. S. and the text.

224 For lengthy comment on this definition see 378 and n. 125.

225 In 443 Bacon distinguishes a general kind of ignorance regarding refutation from a more specific kind, the latter the fallacy that bears that name, one of the thirteen. The former, he says, is that which one finds in any fallacy, namely, a failure to observe that there is something wrong with both the syllogism and the way what is said stands to the opposite of the claim in the conclusion. Lambert also speaks of such a general and specific ignorance, but he distinguishes the two on a basis different from Bacon's. Such ignorance can occur, he says, (1) whenever *any* of the elements of the definition of 'refutation' are violated, and in this sense there occurs the general fallacy to which all other fallacies are subordinated, or (2) whenever one of the *last four* parts is not honored, and this gives rise to the fallacy under discussion. Peter refers at some length to these two kinds of refutation. See, respectively, *Logica*, p. 190.14–19, and *Tractatus* 7.179–181.

it can be accompanied by a lack of contradiction and a lack of the parts included in its definition, and then we have the special fallacy that is one of the thirteen.[226] [3.662–667]

[444] Paralogisms on the basis of this Topic arise in this way: 'A is twice B in length and not twice B in width; therefore it is twice and not twice'. The conclusion does not follow because the part "in the same respect" is omitted. Likewise this: 'A is twice as great as B and is not twice as great as C; therefore it is twice as great and not twice as great'. This does not follow because the part "in the same relation" is ignored. Similarly: 'Socrates sits at time A and does not sit at time B; therefore he sits and does not sit'. Here the part "at the same time" is ignored. Similarly: 'Socrates carries a rock with Plato and does not carry a rock with Cicero; therefore he carries a rock and does not carry a rock'. Here the part "in the same way" (*similiter*) is ignored.[227] Then again: 'Socrates runs and Plato does not run; therefore who runs does not run'. Here the part "about the same

226 Bacon fails to state the cause of semblance and nonexistence of this fallacy; ordinarily it would be treated at this point in his presentation of the fallacy. Peter says that the cause of semblance is "the agreement of two things taken in a certain respect (*secundum quid*) with two things taken absolutely (*simpliciter*); the cause of falsity [nonexistence] is their difference." (*Tractatus* 7.134.) Lambert says the cause of semblance is the apparent contradiction in the things concluded, whereas the cause of falsity (nonexistence) is a defect in the contradiction which is followed by a defect in a true refutation. (*Logica*, p. 190.10–14.) And William says this of them: "[The source of] the semblance of paralogisms of this kind is our ignorance, because we are ignorant regarding contradiction. Since there are so many little parts to a contradiction we believe that the omission of one little part does not impair the whole contradiction. Thus the difference between the semblance of this ground and the semblance of [the extra-verbal grounds] preceding it is obvious: the semblance of the preceding [extra-verbal grounds] has to do either with a thing or with a concept, while the semblance of this one has to do with us, because it results from our ignorance. Nevertheless, *some* of the semblance has to do with a thing, as said above." (*Introductiones*, trans. Kretzmann, pp. 156–157.) (The preceding extra-verbal grounds alluded to by William are Accident and In a Certain Respect and Absolutely.)

227 It is hard to see how this example differs from that given above where the issue is "the same relation" (*ad idem*). Both William's and Peter's examples more clearly illustrate the notion of "in the same way" (*similiter*). William: "'Socrates is naturally pious (*castus*) but he is not pious absolutely; therefore he is both pious and not pious'"; and Peter: "'Man is a species, no man is a species; therefore the same thing is both a species and not a species'." Respectively, *Introductiones*, trans. Kretzmann, p. 156, and *Tractatus* 7.137.

[thing]" is ignored.[228] And so on for the other parts, as is clear from what has just been said.[229] [3.668–673]

[445] Next is the fallacy of *Begging the Original Issue*. The cause of the semblance according to some is the broader knowledge expressed in the premise than in the conclusion. The cause of the nonexistence is the equal knowledge expressed in the premise with respect to the conclusion – or more narrow according to others. This fallacy arises, moreover, in as many ways as one can beg the original issue. [3.674–677]

[446] A *first* mode occurs when the same thing proves itself either in name and thing [signified] or in thing [signified] alone and not in name. An example of the first is 'Socrates runs; therefore Socrates runs'; an example of the second is 'Marcus runs; therefore Tullius runs'.[230] A *second* mode occurs when the same universal is begged in what is singular, e.g., 'Socrates is an animal, Plato is an animal, and so on for other singulars; therefore every man is an animal'.[231] A *third* mode is vice versa, e.g., 'Every man

228 Neither William, Peter, nor Lambert presents a fifth mode to deal with failures to treat that element of the definition of 'refutation' called "the same thing," for the simple reason that the phrase "about the same [thing]" (*de eodem*) does not appear either in Aristotle's text or in their own. Bacon inserts the phrase in the definition presented in 378, but does not repeat it in 443. See also next note.

229 It is not clear how literally to take this remark. William and Lambert explicitly and Peter implicitly remark that this fallacy arises by failure to honor only the *last four* parts of the definition of 'refutation'. If Bacon intends to be taken here to mean that the fallacy occurs where any one of the elements of the definition of 'refutation' is not met, then such would tend to evacuate the significance of the distinction he makes in 441. See, respectively, *Introductiones*, trans. Kretzmann, p. 155; *Logica*, p. 190.14–19; and *Tractatus* 7.134–138.

230 This mode occurs when the same is inferred from itself (as in Bacon's example) or when a thing defined is sought in its definition, as in 'A rational mortal animal is running; therefore a man is running'. Peter explicitly rejects as "ridiculous" the claim that this fallacy occurs when the same is predicated of itself on the ground that the conclusion assumes something identical to the original issue and not something *in* the original, and because there is no semblance of diversity. Thus he offers the following as an example of the first mode of the fallacy: 'A mortal rational animal runs; therefore, a man runs'. (Note that Kretzmann, in referring to Peter's example and using Bochenski's edition of Peter's work, presents a syllogism with the premise and conclusion reversed with respect to Bacon and with de Rijk's edition of the *Tractatus*.) See, respectively, *Tractatus* 7.143, and *Introductiones*, p. 157, n. 139.

231 This mode occurs when a universal is sought in a particular. Apropos of it Kretzmann writes: "As Sherwood puts it, this third way of Begging the Original Issue seems to be the same as an induction by exhaustive enumeration. Aristotle's

runs; therefore Socrates runs, etc.'.[232] And in these there is said to be a begging of the original issue because a substantial predicate like 'animal' is better known to inhere in a species than in an individual, and vice versa of an accidental predicate. A *fourth* mode occurs when something convertible is begged in its own convertible, e.g., 'Socrates is equal to Plato; therefore Plato is equal to Socrates'. A *fifth* mode occurs when what is joined is begged in what are distinct, as in 'Medicine pertains to the healthy, medicine pertains to the sick; therefore medicine pertains to the healthy and the sick'. [3.678–684]

[447] Others say (more modestly) that the cause of the semblance in this fallacy is the apparent difference between the premises and the conclusion along with an apparent more narrow knowledge [expressed in the premises]. The cause of the nonexistence is the absolute identity [between the premises and the conclusion along] with equal or more narrow knowledge [in the premises]. But according to them there is no fallacy except when the original issue is genuinely begged. The truth of these judgments will be aired in disputations. [3.685–688]

[448] Next is the fallacy of *Treating What Is Not a Cause as a Cause*. A cause is a proposition *per se* necessary for a conclusion (as in enthymemes and examples), or leading with another premise to a conclusion (as in syllogisms) or with other premises (as in inductions). What is not a cause is clear by opposition since a noncause is a proposition that does not lead to a conclusion, neither by itself nor with another premise. Therefore, to assert a noncause as a cause is to demolish sophistically a proposition that is not a cause along with those necessary to the inference of the conclusion, without which [premise that is a noncause], nevertheless, a conclusion occurs. The cause of the semblance is the apparent necessity of some proposition for a conclusion. The cause of the nonexistence is the lack of such a necessity. The fallacy of Treating What Is Not a Cause as a Cause is the deception arising from demolishing a proposition that is not a cause along with the others that are causes of the conclusion. There is only one mode of arguing fallaciously on the basis of this Topic. [3.689–696]

---

description of it does not give this impression: 'A third way is if anyone were to beg in particular cases what he undertakes to show universally: e.g., if he undertakes to show that the knowledge of contraries is always one, and begged it of certain pairs of contraries: for he also is generally considered to be begging independently and by itself what, together with a number of other things, he ought to have shown' (*Topics*, 8.13, 163a4ff)." (William *Introductiones*, trans. Kretzmann, p. 157, n. 140.) For Bacon's analysis see 447.

232 This mode occurs when a particular is sought in a universal. In 337 Bacon used this example to illustrate the Topic from a quantitative whole.

[449] Let it be posited that someone has said that a soul and life are the same thing and that an opponent wishes to take this as an hypothesis, constructing an argument from this. There will be a paralogism on the basis of this Topic in this way: 'A soul and life are the same thing, everything contrary to corruption is a generation, life is something contrary to corruption; therefore life is generation'. One should reply that an enthymeme does not hold that is made up of the denial of a conclusion and the denial of the proposition that is a noncause because the proposition that is a noncause is not part of the argumentation from which that enthymeme draws its necessity. [3.697–698]

[450] Next is the fallacy of *Treating More Than One Question as One*. The cause of the semblance is the apparent unity of a proposition when there is none. The cause of the nonexistence is the plurality [of the questions]. The fallacy of Treating More Than One Question as One is the deception deriving from the apparent unity. [3.699–702]

[451] In this Topic arise paralogisms of this sort: "Do you have a church; do you want a church?" If one says, "No," then one argues: 'Therefore, you do not want a church'. If one says, "Yes," [then one infers]: 'Therefore, you have a church'. Likewise: "Are you crazy; do you want to be a bishop?" If one says, "Yes," 'Therefore, you are crazy' is implied. If one says, "No," 'Therefore, you do not want to be a bishop' [is implied]. Similarly: "Do you think this one and this one is a man?" If you say, "Yes," then 'Therefore, who struck this one and this one struck a man and not [two] men' [is implied]. If you say, "No," then 'Therefore, neither this is a man nor that one' [is implied]. Likewise: presented with two things of which one is good and the other is bad, one is asked, "Are these good or not good?" If [you say], "Good," 'Therefore, bad is good' [is implied]. If [you respond], "Not good," 'Therefore, good is bad' [is implied]. One must solve all such by means of two responses and not by one. When one asks, "Are these things good?" one must reply that one of these is good and one bad. Similarly, with respect to the first "Do you have a church; do you want a church?" one must reply, "I have no church, but I want a church." And so on.[233] [3.703–709]

233 Peter says there are two modes of this fallacy: the first occurs when several things are under a term in the singular, as, when presented with Brunellus (the ass) and Socrates, one asks, "Is this one and that one a man?" The second occurs when several things are spoken of under a term in the plural, as, when presented with one good thing and one bad, one asks, "Are these things good?" (*Tractatus* 7.177–178.) Lambert speaks of a third mode in this way: "... [G]iven that there are two men, one asks: 'Do you think this one and this one is a man?' If the answer is Yes, then who strikes this one and this one strikes a man and not men, which is false." (*Logica*, pp. 203.7–10.)

[452] Since the syllogism defective in form in its complete division into thirteen fallacies has already been discussed and a solution provided for each, one must now speak of [the syllogism] defective in matter. [3.710]

Sophistical Syllogisms Defective in Matter

[453] One should know, therefore, that, while a word and a proposition are material things with respect to a syllogism, no defect is said to occur in the matter [of a syllogism] because of a defect in a word with respect to its syllables and letters (which are matter). Rather, a defect is said to arise in the proposition because a proposition is a material part *per se* of a syllogism, whereas a word only *per accidens* and by consequence. One should know that the defect is not said to arise in the substance of a proposition but only in the quality of a proposition. A syllogism is not said to have a defect in its matter because of the omission of words and terms in a proposition – such pertain to the substance of a proposition – but because some due quality is not observed. [3.711–713]

[454] Some say that that quality is truth. So, they concur with Aristotle who proposes in Book Two of *On Sophistical Refutations* (where he gives a judgment on the correct solution) that the solution by demolishing is fitting for a syllogism defective in matter.[234] But this solution is not given except with respect to a false proposition. Consequently, it seems that one defective in matter is such by having a false proposition. Truth will in this way be the quality apropos of which it is defective. But that that is not true is shown from things apparently probable, as Aristotle proposes in the beginning of the *Topics*, that is, from things that are improbable that appear to be probable.[235] Since, therefore, what is improbable falls within its definition and not what is false, its quality will be improbability and not falsity. So, if it will be defective with respect to the quality of a proposition, it will be defective with respect to probability and not to truth. The same thing is clear based on the fact that a sophistical syllogism defective in matter is said to be defective with respect to the matter of a dialectical syllogism, just as a syllogism defective in form is said to be defective with respect to the form of a dialectical syllogism, because a sophistical syllogism is the oblique of a dialectical one and not of another. Therefore, since the matter of a dialectical one is a probable proposition and not a true one, what is defective with respect to the matter of a dialectical one will be defective because it does not take its proposition as probable. Which is to be conceded. [3.714–716]

234 "Thus it comes about that one solves arguments that are properly deduced by demolishing them, whereas one solves merely apparent arguments by drawing distinctions." Aristotle *On Sophistical Refutations* 18.176b35, trans. Pickard-Cambridge, in *CWA*, vol. 1, p. 301.

235 Aristotle *Topics* 1.1.100b25–101a5.

[455] To the opposed opinion one should reply that solutions by demolishing and by speaking *per se* and in accord with the truth of a thing pertain to improbability, but *per accidens* to falsity: what is improbable absolutely is false absolutely, and what is improbable to someone is false to someone. In this way the practice [arises] of claiming syllogisms defective in matter are solved only by demolishing, i.e., by saying that one of the propositions is false, while, however, sometimes it is true, although improbable. Thus one ought not say there is a defect in the matter because the proposition is false but because it is improbable.[236] [3.717]

[456] In truth, however, one should know that not just anything improbable brings about a sophistical syllogism defective in matter in the sense in which we are speaking here, but what appears to be probable because of a fallacy that is involved. For if I were to say 'Every man is an ass, Socrates is a man; therefore Socrates is an ass', there would be no sophistical syllogism defective in matter, although someone would concede the conclusion because of the premises, being ignorant of what was signified by the term 'ass'. I say "sophistical syllogism absolutely," granted the syllogism would be sophistical in a certain respect since it would not cause deception because of a cause of semblance existing in it but only because of the fatuity of the respondent. This sort of syllogism is only oblique with respect to a dialectical one, and so its knowledge depends on the knowledge of a dialectical syllogism according to what Aristotle says in *On the Soul*, [namely,] that "the straight is the judge of itself and the oblique," as if to say, "by knowledge of the straight the oblique is known," because the knowledge of opposites is the same.[237] So, such a syllogism – one that arises from improbable things that do not appear to be improbable because of a fallacy but because of the fatuity of the respondent – is known through knowledge passed on in the *Topics*. But the sophistical syllogism absolutely, which has a semblance because of a fallacy involved in it, cannot be known by theories in the *Topics* with respect to the principles and causes of its semblance. And so there is a necessary treatise on it entirely separate from the *Topics*, namely, *On Sophistical Refutations*. [3.718–720]

[457] But one should note that, although a sophistical syllogism that includes something improbable that appears probable only because of the fatuity of the respondent is not, commonly speaking, called one defective in matter – because it is not distinguished from one defective in form, since it is not a sophistical syllogism absolutely but only in a certain respect, since it does not cause a fallacy nor is it deceptive because of something in it nor is it naturally [deceptive] – nevertheless, in truth it is defective in the

236 See 461 for further comment on this point.
237 Aristotle *On the Soul* 1.5.411a5–7.

matter of a dialectical [syllogism] since it includes an improbable proposition. It is not commonly said to be defective in matter because of the difference it has with what truly is defective, since of its nature it appears not to be defective and also because it does not by itself lead to a defect or error in the mind of the listener. But the other that is sophistical absolutely does lead [to a defect or error]. Therefore, what is sophistical absolutely more merits the name of being defective from its effect. [3.721]

[458] But one should know that, although matter and form are needed for the existence of something composed – and so a composite would remain under them – a syllogism defective in matter is a true syllogism, although one defective in form is not.[238] But note that [the sophistical syllogism] defective in matter is not the syllogism with respect to whose matter it is defective, just as [the syllogism] defective in form is not that with respect to whose form it is defective – such is the dialectical syllogism. Yet, a syllogism defective in matter can be a syllogism absolutely, although it [could] not be a dialectical one because it is not defective with respect to its matter: the matter [under discussion] is the two propositions correctly positioned in mood and figure with respect to the composition construed from three terms, namely, the major, the minor, and the middle. Neither is it defective with respect to its form since it has the power to imply necessarily, which is the perfect form of a syllogism absolutely. But one defective in form, although it is defective first and *per se* with respect to a dialectical syllogism, nevertheless is defective by consequence with respect to syllogism absolutely because it has the form of neither, as was just said, though it appears to have [such]. And so a syllogism defective in form is not entirely a syllogism, although one defective in matter is a syllogism. [3.722–723]

[459] Given this, one should know that a syllogism defective in matter is multiplied in almost the same way as one defective in form is, namely, through sophistical Topics. Aristotle proposes these in Chapter Seven of *On Sophistical Refutations* [when he says], "Since we know, etc."[239] Almost every sophistical Topic that causes an argumentation to seem to be good when it is not can cause a proposition to seem to be true and probable when it is not. I say "almost" because of Begging the Original Issue and Treating What Is Not a Cause as a Cause, for these can cause an argumentation to seem to be true when it is not, but never a proposition to seem

238 The theory that materially defective syllogisms were not really syllogisms at all was condemned (Proposition 2) in 1277 by Robert Kilwardby at Oxford.

239 "Since we know on how many points apparent deductions depend, we know also on how many sophistical deductions and refutations may depend." Aristotle *On Sophistical Refutations* 8.169b18ff, trans. Pickard-Cambridge, in *CWA*, vol. 1, p. 287.

to be true or probable when it is not. That a syllogism defective in matter does not arise in all the fallacies is clear from Aristotle when he says in the chapter just recalled, "Therefore, there will be false syllogisms in all or some of them."[240] He says "some" because of the Topics mentioned, whose confirmation may be left to disputation. [3.724–726]

[460] Paralogisms that are defective because of fallacies in matter can be formed in this way in connection with Equivocation: 'Every thing named with the name "dog" is a dog (indicating a sea creature and what barks), both of these are named with the name "dog"; therefore both are dogs'. The first premise is false and improbable absolutely, though it appears to be true and probable because of the semblance in Equivocation. Since the vocal sound of the name 'dog' is one and the same when referred to the things they name, it is thought that its signification is one, which is false, for no one signification is applicable to them all. So, whether the term stands for what barks or for the sea creature or for the heavenly constellation, in every sense [the premise] is false and improbable absolutely. Likewise, an example can be given in connection with The Figure of a Word: 'Every name ending in "a" (like the name "*musa*") is feminine in gender, but the name "Catilina" is such; therefore it is feminine in gender'.[241] The fallacy of The Figure of a Word occurs in the first proposition because of the cause of semblance in The Figure of a Word, which is the similar ending in the feminine gender: it seems that the major is true and probable when it is not. Let examples in connection with the other fallacies be sought in which it is possible that a syllogism defective in matter occurs. [3.727–729]

[461] Since, therefore, the method of constructing such paralogisms is this way, one should know that the method of solving them is one only, namely, by demolishing.[242] For one should respond to a proposition that is false or improbable when it is false absolutely or at least false to a respondent. So, a respondent can say, as it seems to him, namely, that it is false. But it is to be demolished first and *per se* because of its improbability and secondarily because of the falsity that is there or that seems to be there, because sometimes a proposition is improbable that is not false, although it seems to a respondent that it is false. [3.730–731]

240 Aristotle *On Sophistical Refutations* 8.169b32.

241 '*Musa*' (muse) is grammatically feminine in gender in Latin and refers to one of the (*female*) Muses; '*Catilina*', while also ending in "a", is the Latin name of a man. For the fallacy of The Figure of a Word see 419 and 420.

242 What is said here and in 461 must be taken with what has been said in 455–456.

Appendix

Paragraph correlations between de Libera's Latin text (in left-hand columns) and Maloney's English translation (bold numbers in the right-hand columns) of Roger Bacon's *Summulae dialectices*

Prologue		1.2.9	**29**	1.2.115	**60**
1–4	**1**	1.2.10–14	**30**	1.2.116–118	**61**
5–10	**2**	1.2.15–19	**31**	1.2.119	**62**
11–12	**3**	1.2.20–27	**32**	1.2.120	**63**
13–17	**4**	1.2.28	**33**	1.2.121–123	**64**
18	**5**	1.2.29–35	**34**	1.2.124	**65**
19–27	**6**	1.2.36–42	**35**	1.2.125–132	**66**
28–29	**7**	1.2.43–44	**36**	1.2.133–137	**67**
30	**8**	1.2.45	**37**	1.2.138–140	**68**
		1.2.46–51	**38**	1.2.141	**69**
Part One		1.2.52–60	**39**	1.2.142–148	**70**
1.1.1	**9**	1.2.61–65	**40**	1.2.149	**71**
1.1.2–5	**10**	1.2.66–67	**41**	1.2.150	**72**
1.1.6	**11**	1.2.68–72	**42**	1.2.151–152	**73**
1.1.7	**12**	1.2.73	**43**	1.2.153–154	**74**
1.1.8–12	**13**	1.2.74–75	**44**	1.2.155–162	**75**
1.1.13	**14**	1.2.76	**45**	1.2.163–169	**76**
1.1.14–20	**15**	1.2.77–81	**46**	1.2.170–182	**77**
1.1.21–27	**16**	1.2.82–84	**47**	1.2.183	**78**
1.1.28	**17**	1.2.85–87	**48**	1.2.184–185	**79**
1.1.29–30	**18**	1.2.88–90	**49**	1.2.186	**80**
1.1.31–32	**19**	1.2.91–92	**50**	1.2.187–188	**81**
1.1.33–34	**20**	1.2.93	**51**	1.2.189–191	**82**
1.1.35–36	**21**	1.2.94	**52**	1.2.192–194	**83**
1.1.37–39	**22**	1.2.95	**53**	1.2.195–198	**84**
1.1.40–43	**23**	1.2.96	**54**	1.2.199–200	**85**
1.1.44–47	**24**	1.2.96	**55**	1.2.201	**86**
1.1.48	**25**	1.2.97	**56**	1.2.202–210	**87**
1.2.1–2	**26**	1.2.98	**57**	1.2.211–217	**88**
1.2.3–5	**27**	1.2.99	**58**	1.2.218–222	**89**
1.2.6–8	**28**	1.2.100–114	**59**	1.2.223	**90**

1.2.224	91
1.2.225–226	92
1.2.227	93
1.2.228	94
1.2.229	95
1.2.230	96
1.2.231–232	97
1.2.233–234	98
1.2.235	99
1.2.236	100
1.2.237–238	101
1.2.239	102
1.2.240	103
1.2.241	104
1.2.242–246	105
1.2.247	106
1.2.248–249	107
1.2.250	108
1.2.251	109

Part Two

2.1–3	110
2.4–6	111
2.7	112
2.8	113
2.9–13	114
2.14–18	115
2.19	116
2.20	117
2.21–23	118
2.24	119
2.25	120
2.26–28	121
2.29–30	122
2.31–33	123
2.34–36	124
2.37–41	125
2.42	126
2.43–46	127
2.47–54	128
2.55–56	129
2.57–58	130
2.59–60	131
2.60a–63	132
2.64–70	133
2.71–72	134
2.73–78	135
2.79–81	136
2.82–85	137
2.86–93	138
2.94–97	139
2.98–100	140
2.101–104	141
2.105	142
2.106–115	143
2.116–118	144
2.119–120	145
2.121	146
2.122	147
2.123	148
2.124	149
2.125–128	150
2.129–133	151
2.134–137	152
2.138–146	153
2.147–149	154
2.150–153	155
2.154–157	156
2.158–159	157
2.160–162	158
2.163–166b	159
2.167–169	160
2.170–172	161
2.173–176	162
2.177–179	163
2.180–183	164
2.184–187	165
2.188–195	166
2.196–200	167
2.201–202	168
2.203–207	169
2.208–216	170
2.217–219	171
2.220–224	172
2.225–229	173
2.230–235	174
2.236–242	175
2.243–244	176
2.245–249	177
2.250–251	178
2.252–263	179
2.264	180
2.265–268	181
2.269–271	182
2.272–277	183
2.278–279	184
2.280–284	185
2.285–286	186
2.287–293	187
2.294–301	188
2.302–303	189
2.304–310	190
2.311–316	191
2.317–318	192
2.319	193
2.320–321	194
2.322–323	195
2.324–325	196
2.326–343	197
2.344	198
2.345	199
2.346–347	200
2.348–349	201
2.350–354	202
2.355–356	203
2.357–365	204
2.366–372	205
2.373–389	206
2.390–392	207
2.393–397	208
2.398–404	209
2.405–411	210
2.412–413	211
2.414–420	212
2.421–422	213
2.423–424	214
2.425–426	215
2.427–428	216
2.429	217

2.430–431	**218**	2.597–600	**261**	3.141	**302**
2.432–433	**219**	2.601–602	**262**	3.142–145	**303**
2.434–437	**220**	2.603–606	**263**	3.146–158	**304**
2.438–442	**221**	2.607–612	**264**	3.159–163	**305**
2.443–448	**222**	2.613–619	**265**	3.164–166	**306**
2.449–454	**223**	2.620–624	**266**	3.167–172	**307**
2.454–456	**224**	2.625	**267**	3.173–179	**308**
2.457	**225**	2.626–627	**268**	3.180	**309**
2.458–461	**226**	2.628–632	**269**	3.181–183	**310**
2.462–465	**227**	2.633–635	**270**	3.184–191	**311**
2.466	**228**			3.192–196	**312**
2.467–471	**229**	Part Three		3.197–199	**313**
2.472–481	**230**	3.1–2	**271**	3.200–201	**314**
2.482–496a	**231**	3.3–6	**272**	3.202–209	**315**
2.496b–498	**232**	3.7–9	**273**	3.210–211	**316**
2.499–501	**233**	3.9–13	**274**	3.212	**317**
2.502	**234**	3.14–18	**275**	3.213–220	**318**
2.503	**235**	3.19	**276**	3.221–224	**319**
2.504–505	**236**	3.20–21	**277**	3.225–230	**320**
2.506–510	**237**	3.22–26	**278**	3.231–232	**321**
2.511–520	**238**	3.27–30	**279**	3.233–236	**322**
2.521–525	**239**	3.31–32	**280**	3.237–240	**323**
2.526–528	**240**	3.33–36	**281**	3.241	**324**
2.529–538	**241**	3.37–40	**282**	3.242–249	**325**
2.539–541	**242**	3.41–45	**283**	3.250–255	**326**
2.542–543	**243**	3.46–50	**284**	3.256–262	**327**
2.544–548	**244**	3.51–60	**285**	3.263–266	**328**
2.549–550	**245**	3.61	**286**	3.267–272	**329**
2.551–552	**246**	3.62–63	**287**	3.273–278	**330**
2.553–555	**247**	3.64–66	**288**	3.279–283	**331**
2.556–559	**248**	3.67–68	**289**	3.284–286	**332**
2.560–561	**249**	3.69–77	**290**	3.287–289	**333**
2.562–565	**250**	3.78–79	**291**	3.290–291	**334**
2.566–568	**251**	3.80–86	**292**	3.292–293	**335**
2.569–575	**252**	3.87–96	**293**	3.294–299	**336**
2.576–580	**253**	3.97–102	**294**	3.300–302	**337**
2.581	**254**	3.103–111	**295**	3.303–304	**338**
2.582–583	**255**	3.112–118	**296**	3.305	**339**
2.584–586	**256**	3.119–125	**297**	3.306–307	**340**
2.587–588	**257**	3.126–129	**298**	3.308–316	**341**
2.589	**258**	3.130–135	**299**	3.317	**342**
2.590	**259**	3.136–138	**300**	3.318	**343**
2.591–596	**260**	3.139–140	**301**	3.319	**344**

3.320	**345**	3.427–432	**384**	3.582	**423**
3.321	**346**	3.433–438	**385**	3.583–584	**424**
3.322–323	**347**	3.439–447	**386**	3.585–593	**425**
3.324	**348**	3.448–449	**387**	3.594–596	**426**
3.325	**349**	3.450–459	**388**	3.597	**427**
3.326	**350**	3.460–461	**389**	3.598–603	**428**
3.327	**351**	3.462–467	**390**	3.604–606	**429**
3.328	**352**	3.468–473	**391**	3.607–611	**430**
3.329	**353**	3.474–477	**392**	3.612–613	**431**
3.330	**354**	3.478–487	**393**	3.614	**432**
3.331–333	**355**	3.488–491	**394**	3.615	**433**
3.334–335	**356**	3.492–497	**395**	3.616–617	**434**
3.336	**357**	3.498–506	**396**	3.618–623	**435**
3.337–339	**358**	3.507–508	**397**	3.624–626	**436**
3.340	**359**	3.509–511	**398**	3.627–637	**437**
3.341	**360**	3.512–517	**399**	3.638–643	**438**
3.342	**361**	3.518–521	**400**	3.644–646	**439**
3.343–353	**362**	3.522	**401**	3.647	**440**
3.354	**363**	3.523–527	**402**	3.648–652	**441**
3.355	**364**	3.528	**403**	3.653–661	**442**
3.356	**365**	3.529	**404**	3.662–667	**443**
3.357	**366**	3.530	**405**	3.668–673	**444**
3.358	**367**	3.531	**406**	3.674–677	**445**
3.359–361	**368**	3.532–534	**407**	3.678–684	**446**
3.362–363	**369**	3.535–537	**408**	3.685–688	**447**
3.364–366	**370**	3.538–539	**409**	3.689–696	**448**
3.367–371	**371**	3.540–542	**410**	3.697–698	**449**
3.372–373	**372**	3.543	**411**	3.699–702	**450**
3.374–378	**373**	3.544	**412**	3.703–709	**451**
3.379	**374**	3.545–549	**413**	3.710	**452**
3.380–383	**375**	3.550–551	**414**	3.711–713	**453**
3.384–391	**376**	3.552–553	**415**	3.714–716	**454**
3.392–399	**377**	3.554–558	**416**	3.717	**455**
3.400–411	**378**	3.559–560	**417**	3.718–720	**456**
3.412–413	**379**	3.561–564	**418**	3.721	**457**
3.414	**380**	3.565–569	**419**	3.722–723	**458**
3.415–418	**381**	3.570–576	**420**	3.724–726	**459**
3.419–423	**382**	3.577–578	**421**	3.727–729	**460**
3.424–426	**383**	3.579–581	**422**	3.730–731	**461**

Works Cited

1. WORKS BY BACON

Brewer, J. S., ed. *Fr. Rogeri Bacon opera quaedam hactenus inedita.* Rerum Britannicorum Medii Aevi Scriptores (Rolls Series). Vol. 15. London, 1859. Nendeln: Kraus Reprint, 1965.

Bridges, John Henry, ed. *The 'Opus Maius' of Roger Bacon.* 3 vols. Oxford, 1897. Reprint, Frankfurt am Main: Minerva, 1964.

Burke, Robert Belle, trans. *The Opus Maius of Roger Bacon.* 2 vols. Philadelphia: University of Pennsylvania Press; London: Humphrey Milford; Oxford: University Press, 1928.

Fredborg, Margareta, Lauge Nielsen, and Jan Pinborg, eds. "An Unedited Part of Roger Bacon's *Opus Maius*: '*De Signis*'." *Traditio* 34 (1978): 75–136.

Libera, Alain de, ed. *Summulae dialectices.* In "Les Summulae dialectices de Roger Bacon." Parts 1–2: *De termino, De enuntiatione*; Part 3: *De argumentatione.*" *Archives d'histoire doctrinale et littéraire du Moyen Age* 53 (1986): 139–289; 54 (1987): 171–278.

Maloney, Thomas S., ed. and trans. *Compendium studii theologiae. Roger Bacon: Compendium of the Study of Theology.* Studien und Texte zur Geistesgeschichte des Mittelalters, vol. 20. Leiden, New York, Copenhagen, Cologne: E. J. Brill, 1988.

_____, trans. *Three Treatments of Universals by Roger Bacon.* Medieval & Renaissance Texts & Studies, vol. 66. Binghamton, NY: Medieval & Renaissance Texts & Studies, 1989.

Steele, Robert, ed. *Opera hactenus inedita Rogeri Bacon.* 16 vols. Oxford: Clarendon Press, 1905?–1941.

- fasc. 2: *Liber primus Communium naturalium Fratris Rogeri* (Parts 1–2), 1905?
- fasc. 11: *Questiones altere supra libros prime philosophie Aristotelis* (*Metaphysica* I–IV) and *Questiones supra Librum de plantis.* With Ferdinand Delorme. *Metaphysica vetus Aristotelis e cod. Vetustissimis.* 1932, respectively, pp. 1–170, 173–252, and 255–312.
- fasc. 12: *Questiones supra Librum de causis.* 1935, pp. 1–158.
- fasc. 13: *Questiones supra octo Physicorum Aristotelis.* Edited by Ferdinand-M. Delorme, with Robert Steele, 1935.
- fasc. 14: *Summa de sophismatibus et distinctionibus.* 1937, pp. 135–208.
- fasc. 15: *Summa grammatica* necnon *Sumule dialectices.* 1941, respectively, pp. 1–190 and 193–359.

2. OTHER PRIMARY SOURCES

Accessus philosophorum VII artium liberalium. See Lafleur, ed.

Albert the Great. *B. Alberti Magni Opera Omnia*. Edited by August Borgnet. Paris: Louis Vives, 1890.

Algazel. *Logica*. In "*Logica Algazalis*: *Introduction and Critical Text*." Edited by C. H. Lohr. *Traditio* 21 (1965): 221–291.

_____. *Metaphysica*. *Algazel's Metaphysics*: *A Medieval Translation*. Edited and translated by J. T. Muckle. Toronto: St. Michaels College, 1933.

Anonymus magister artium (c. 1245–1250). *Lectura in librum de anima a quodam disciplulo reportata*. Edited by René Antoine Gauthier. Spicilegium Bonaventurianum, vol. 24. Grottaferrata: College of St. Bonaventure, 1985.

Aristoteles Latinus. Edited by G. Verbeke. Leiden: E. J. Brill; Brussels: Desclée de Brouwer, 1957–.

Vol. 1, pts. 1–5: *Categoriae vel Praedicamenta*. Translatio Boethii – Editio Composita, Translatio Guillelmi de Moerbeka, Lemmata e Simplici Commentario Decerpta, Pseudo-Augustini Paraphrasis Themistiana. Edited by Lorenzo Minio-Paluello. Bruges and Paris: Desclée de Brouwer, 1961.

Vol. 1, Pts. 6–7: *Categoriarum Supplementa*. Porphyrii Isagoge, Translatio Boethii. Anonymi Fragmentum Vulgo Vocatum "Liber sex principiorum." Isagoge Fragmenta M. Victorino interprete et Specimina Translationum Recentiorum Categoriarum. Edited by Lorenzo Minio-Paluello with Bernard G. Dod. Bruges and Paris: Desclée de Brouwer, 1966.

Aristotle. *The Complete Works of Aristotle: The Revised Oxford Translation*. Edited by Jonathan Barnes. Bollingen Series, vol. 71, pt. 2. Princeton, N.J.: Princeton University Press, 1984.

Ars emmerana. In *Logica Modernorum*, ed. Rijk, vol. 2, pt. 2, pp. 143–174.

Ars meliduna. In *Logica Modernorum*, ed. Rijk, vol. 2, pt. 1, pp. 292–390.

Augustine. *The City of God*. Translated by Gerald G. Walsh, Demetrius B. Zema, Grace Monahan, and Donald J. Honan. Garden City: Doubleday, 1958.

_____. *De dialectica*. Edited by Jan Pinborg. Translated by B. Darrell Jackson. Synthese Historical Library, vol. 16. Dordrecht, Boston: D. Reidel, 1975.

_____. *De doctrina Christiana*. Edited by Joseph Martin. Corpus Christianorum Series Latina, vol. 32. Turnhout: Brepols, 1962.

_____. *De ordine*. Edited by R. P. H. Green. Corpus Christianorum Series Latina, vol. 29. Turnhout: Brepols, 1953.

_____. *De trinitate*. In *The Trinity*. Translated by Stephen McKenna. Washington: The Catholic University of America, [1963].

Averroes. *De coelo. Aristotelis opera cum Averrois commentariis*. Vol. 5. 1562–1574. Reprint, Frankfurt am Main: Minerva Press, 1962.

_____. *Metaphysica. Aristotelis opera cum Averrois commentariis*. Vol. 8. 1562–1574. Reprint, Frankfurt am Main: Minerva, 1962.

_____. *Metaphysica. Averrois in librum V metaphysicarum Aristotelis commentarius*. Edited by Ruggero Ponzalli. Bern: Francke, 1971.

Bernardus Silvestris. *De mundi universitate libri duo* (*Megacosmus et Microcosmus*). Edited by Carl Sigmund Barach and Johann Wrobel. Biblioteca Philosophorum Mediae Aetatis, vol. 1. Innsbruck: Verlag der Wagnerischen Universitäts Buchhandlung, 1876.

Boethius. *De arithmetica libri duo*. PL 63.1079–1166.

_____. *De differentiis topicis libri quattuor*. PL 64.1173–1216.

_____. *Boethius's De differentiis topicis* Translated by Eleonore Stump. Ithaca: Cornell University Press, 1978.

_____. *De syllogismo categorico libri duo*. PL 64.793–832.

_____. *De syllogismo hypothetico libri duo*. PL 64.831–876.

_____. *De trinitate*. In *Boethius: The Theological Tractates*. Translated by H. F. Stewart and E. K. Rand. Loeb Classical Library. 1918.

_____. *In categorias Aristotelis libri quattuor*. PL 64.159–294.

_____. *In Isagogen Porphyrii Commenta*. 2nd ed. Edited by Samuel Brandt. Corpus Scriptorum Ecclesiasticorum Latinorum, vol. 48. Vienna: Tempsky; Leipzig: Freytag, 1906.

_____. *In librum Aristotelis Peri hermeneias*. 1st ed. *Anicii Manlii Severini Boetii Commentarii in librum Aristotelis Περι ερμενειασ*. Pars prior. Edited by Karl Meiser. Leipzig: Teubner, 1877.

_____. *In librum Aristotelis Peri hermeneias*. 2nd ed. *Anicii Manlii Severini Boetii Commentarii in librum Aristotelis Περι ερμενειασ*. Pars posterior. Edited by Karl Meiser. Leipzig: Teubner, 1880.

_____. *In Topica Ciceronis commentariorum libri sex*. PL 64.1039–1174.

_____. *Boethius's In Ciceronis Topica*. Translated by Eleonore Stump. Ithaca: Cornell University, 1988.

Braakhuis, H. A. G., ed. *De 13de Eeuwse Tractaten over Syncategorematische Termen*. Deel 1. *Inleidende studie*. Deel 2. *Uitgave van Nicholaas van Parijs Sincategoremata*. Meppel: Krips Repro, 1979.

Cicero. *De natura deorum*. Edited and translated by H. Rackham. Loeb Classical Library. 1956.

Cum sit nostra. In *Logica Modernorum*, ed. Rijk, vol. 2, pt. 2, pp. 413–451.

Dialectica Monacensis. In *Logica Modernorum*, ed. Rijk, vol. 2, pt. 2, pp. 453–638.

Donatus. *De arte grammatica libri*. Edited by Heinrich Keil. In *Gram-*

matici latini. Vol. 4. Edited by Heinrich Keil. Hildesheim: Georg Olms, 1961.

Ebbesen, Sten, ed. "Texts on Equivocation. Part I. Ca. 1130–ca. 1270." *Cahiers de l'Institut du Moyen Age grec et latin* 67 (1997): 127–199.

_____. "Texts on Equivocation. Part II. Ca. 1250–1310." *Cahiers de l'Institut du Moyen Age grec et latin* 68 (1998): 99–307.

Fallaciae ad modum Oxoniae. In *Die Fallaciae ad modum Oxoniae: Ein Fehlschlusstraktat aus dem 13. Jahrhundert*. Edited by Clemens Reiner Kopp. Dissertation, Faculty of Philosophy, University of Cologne, 1985.

Fallacie Parvipontane. In *Logica Modernorum*, ed. Rijk, vol. 1, pp. 551–609.

Garlandus Compotista. *Dialectica*. Edited by L. M. de Rijk. Assen: Van Gorcum, 1959.

Hamesse, Jacqueline, ed. *Les Auctoritates Aristotelis: Un florilège médiévale, étude historique et édition critique*. Philosophes Medievaux, vol. 17. Louvain: Publications Universitaires; Paris: Béatrice Nauwelaerts, 1974.

Horace. *Epistulae*. In *Horace: Satires, Epistles, and Ars poetica*. Edited and translated by H. Rushton Fairclough. Loeb Classical Library. 1947.

Isidore of Seville. *Etymologiae*. In *Etymologiarum sive originum libri xx*. Edited by W. M. Lindsay. Oxford: Clarendon Press, 1911.

Keil, Heinrich, ed. *Grammatici Latini*. 8 vols. Vols. 2–3: Priscian. *Institutiones grammaticae*. Edited by Martin Hertz. Vol. 4: Donatus. *De arte grammatica libri*. Edited by Martin Hertz. 1855–1880. Reprint, Hildesheim: Georg Olms, 1961.

Kretzmann, Norman, and Eleonore Stump, trans. *The Cambridge Translations of Medieval Philosophical Texts*. Vol. 1: *Logic and the Philosophy of Language*. New York: Cambridge University Press, 1988.

Lafleur, Claude, ed. *Accessus philosophorum VII artium liberalium*. In *Quatre introductions à la philosophie au XIIIe siècle: Textes critiques et étude historique*. Edited by Claude Lafleur, pp. 179–253. Publications de l'Institut d'études médiévales de Université de Montréal, vol. 23. Montréal: Institut d'études médiévales, Université de Montréal; Paris: Librairie philosophique J. Vrin, 1988.

Lambert of Auxerre. *Logica* (*Summa Lamberti*). Edited by F. Alessio. Pubblicazioni della facoltà di lettere di filosofia dell'università di Milano, vol. 59. Florence: La Nuova Italia Editrice, 1971.

_____. *Logica*. (*De appellatione*). Edited by Alain de Libera. "Le traité *De appellatione* de Lambert de Lagny (Lambert d'Auxerre)." *Archives d'histoire doctrinale et littéraire du Moyen Age* 48 (1981): 227–285.

_____. *Logica*. (Chapter Eight: "*De suppositionibus et de significationi-*

bus"). In *Cambridge Translations of Medieval Philosophical Texts*, trans. Kretzmann and Stump, pp. 102–162.

Liber de causis. In *Le Liber de causis*. Edited by Adriaan Pattin. Louvain: Éditions du Tidjschrift voor Filosofie, [1966].

Liber sex principiorum. See *Aristoteles Latinus*, vol. 1, pts. 6–7.

Nicholas of Damas. *De plantis*. Edited by E. H. F. Meyer. *De plantis libri II Aristotelis vulgo adscripti*. Leipzig, 1841.

Nicholas of Paris. *Syncategoremata*. See *De 13de Eeuwse Tractaten*, ed. Braakhuis.

Peter Abelard. *Super perihermenias*. In *Abaelardiana inedita*. Edited by Lorenzo Minio-Paluello. In *Twelfth Century Logic: Texts and Studies*, vol. 1. Rome: Edizioni di Storia e Letteratura, 1958.

Peter Helias. *Summa super Priscianum*. 2 vols. Edited by Leo Reilly. Toronto: Pontifical Institute of Mediaeval Studies, 1993.

Peter of Spain (Petrus Hispanus Portugalensis). *Peter of Spain on Composition and Negation*. Translated by Joke Spruyt. Artistarium Supplementa, vol. 5. Nijmegen: Ingenium, 1989, pp. 119–123.

_____. *Syncategoreumata*. Edited by L. M. de Rijk and translated into English by Joke Spruyt. Studien und Texte zur Geistesgeschichte des Mittelalters, vol. 30. Leiden: E. J. Brill, 1992.

_____. *Tractatus*. Edited by Joseph P. Mullally. In *The Summulae logicales of Peter of Spain*. (Only the treatises on supposition, relatives, ampliation, appellation, restriction, distribution, and exponibles.) Notre Dame, IN: Notre Dame University Press, 1945.

_____. *Tractatus*. Edited by L. M. de Rijk. *Peter of Spain (Petrus Hispanus Portugalensis): Tractatus, Called Afterwards Summule logicales*. Assen: Van Gorcum, 1972.

_____. *Tractatus*. Translated into English by Francis P. Dinneen. *Peter of Spain: Language in Dispute*. Amsterdam Studies in the Theory and History of Linguistic Studies. Series III: Studies in the History of the Language Sciences, vol. 39. Amsterdam and Philadelphia: John Benjamins, 1990.

_____. *Tractatus*. (Selections.) Translated by Norman Kretzmann and Eleonore Stump. *The Cambridge Translations of Medieval Philosophical Texts*. Vol. 1: *Logic and the Philosophy of Language*, pp. 216–261. Cambridge, New York, New Rochelle, Melbourne, Sydney: Cambridge University Press, 1988.

Porphyry. *Isagoge*. In *Aristoteles latinus*, vol. 1, pts. 6–7. Translated by Boethius. Edited by Lorenzo Minio-Paluello. Bruges and Paris: Desclée de Brouwer, 1966.

_____. *Isagoge*. *Porphyry the Phoenician. Isagoge*. Translated by Edward W. Warren. Mediaeval Sources in Translation, vol. 6. Toronto: Pontifical Institute of Mediaeval Studies, 1975.

Priscian. *Institutiones grammaticae*. Vols. 1–2. Edited by Martin Hertz. In *Grammatici latini*. Edited by Heinrich Keil. Vols. 2–3. Hildesheim: Georg Olms, 1961.

Pseudo-Boethius. *De disciplina scholarium*. Edited by Olga Weijers. Studien und Geistesgeschichte des Mittelalters, vol. 12. Leiden and Cologne: E. J. Brill, 1976.

Pseudo-Cicero. *Ad C. Herennium de ratione dicendi* [*Rhetorica ad Herennium*]. Edited and translated by Harry Caplan. Loeb Classical Library. 1954.

Pseudo-Hieronymus. *Epistulae*. PL 30.

Rijk, L. M. de, ed. *Logica Modernorum: A Contribution to the History of Early Terminist Logic*. 2 vols. Vol. 1: *On the Twelfth-Century Theories of Fallacy*. Vol. 2, pt. 1: *The Origin and Early Development of the Theory of Supposition*. Vol. 2, pt. 2: *The Origins and Early Development of the Theory of Supposition: Texts and Indices*. Assen: Van Gorcum, 1962 and 1967.

Robert Kilwardby. *De ortu scientiarum*. Edited by Albert G. Judy. Auctores Britannici Medii Aevi, vol. 4. Toronto: Pontifical Institute of Mediaeval Studies, 1976.

Robert Kilwardby (attr.). *Commentarium in Sophisticos elenchos*. MS. Cambridge Peterhouse 205; MS. Paris Bibl. nat. lat. 16619. In Alain de Libera, "Les *Abstractiones* d'Hervé le Sophiste (Hervaeus Sophista)." *Archives d'histoire doctrinale et littéraire du Moyen Age* 53 (1986): 180–183.

Terence. *Eunuchus*. Vol. 1. Edited and translated by John Sargeaunt. Loeb Classical Library. 1931.

Tractatus Anagnini. In *Logica Modernorum*, ed. Rijk, vol. 2, pt. 2, pp. 215–332.

Ut dicit. In *Logica Modernorum*, ed. Rijk, vol. 2, pt. 2, pp. 375–411.

Virgil. *Aeneis*. In *Virgil: Eclogues, Georgics, Aeneid I–IV*. Vol. 1. Edited and translated by H. Rushton Fairclough. Loeb Classical Library. 1950.

William of Sherwood. *Introductiones in logicam*. Edited and translated into German by Hartmut Brands and Christoph Kann. Philosophische Bibliothek, vol. 469. Hamburg: Felix Meiner Verlag, 1995.

_____. *Introductiones in logicam*. Translated by Norman Kretzmann. *William of Sherwood's Introduction to Logic*. [Based on Grabmann's emended text.] Westport, CT: Greenwood Press, 1966.

_____. *Syncategoremata*. Edited by J. R. O'Donnell. "The *Syncategoremata* of William of Sherwood." *Mediaeval Studies* 3 (1941): 46–93.

3. SECONDARY SOURCES

Angelelli, Ignaccio. "The Techniques of Disputation in the History of Logic." *The Journal of Philosophy* 67 (1970): 800–815.

_____, and Paloma Pérez-Ilzarbe, ed. *Medieval and Renaissance Logic in Spain.* Acts of the 12th European Symposium on Medieval Logic and Semantics, held at the University of Navarre, Pamplona, 26–30 May 1997. Philosophische Texte und Studien, vol. 54. Hildesheim, Zurich, and New York: Georg Olms, 2000.

Bäck, Alan. "The Structure of Scotus' Formal Distinction." In Angelelli (2), pp. 411–438.

Boh, Ivan. "Consequences." In *Cambridge History of Later Medieval Philosophy*, ed. Kretzmann et al., pp. 300–314.

Braakhuis, H. A. G. "The Views of William of Sherwood on Some Semantical Topics and Their Relation to Those of Roger Bacon." *Vivarium* 15 (1977): 111–142.

_____, Kneepkens, C. H., and L. M. Rijk, ed. *English Logic and Semantics: From the End of the Twelfth Century to the Time of Ockham and Burleigh.* Acts of the Fourth European Symposium on Medieval Logic and Semantics, Leiden-Nijmegen, 23–27 April 1979. Artistarium Supplementa, vol. 1. Nijmegen: Ingenium Press, 1981.

_____. *See also under* "Other Primary Sources"

Broadie, Alexander. *Introduction to Medieval Logic.* 2nd ed. Oxford: Clarendon Press, 1993.

Bursill-Hall, G. L., Sten Ebbesen, and Konrad Koerner, ed. *De Ortu Grammaticae: Studies in Medieval Grammar and Linguistic Theory in Memory of Jan Pinborg.* Amsterdam Studies in the Theory and History of Linguistic Science, vol. 43. Amsterdam and Philadelphia: John Benjamins, 1990.

Crowley, Theodore. "Roger Bacon and Avicenna." *Philosophical Studies* (Ireland) 2 (1952): 82–88.

_____. *Roger Bacon: The Problem of the Soul in His Philosophical Commentaries.* Louvain: Editions de l'Institut supérieur de philosophie. Dublin: James Duffy, 1950.

Easton, Stewart C. *Roger Bacon and His Search for a Universal Science: A Reconsideration of the Life and Work of Roger Bacon in the Light of His Own Stated Purposes.* New York: Russell & Russell, 1952. Reprint, 1971.

Ebbesen, Sten. *Commentators and Commentaries on Aristotle's* Sophistici Elenchi: *A Study of Post Aristotelian Ancient and Medieval Writings on Fallacies.* Leiden: E. J. Brill, 1981.

_____. "Concrete Accidental Terms: Late Thirteenth-Century Debates about Problems Relating to Such Terms as '*Album*'." In *Meaning and Inference in Medieval Philosophy*, ed. Kretzmann, pp. 107–174.

_____. "Early Supposition Theory (12th and 13th Century)." *Histoire, épistémologie, langage* 3 (1981): 35–48.

_____. "Suprasegmental Phonemes in Ancient and Mediaeval Logic." In *English Logic and Semantics*, ed. Braakhuis et al., pp. 331–359.

_____. "The Way Fallacies Were Treated in Scholastic Logic." *Cahiers de l'Institut du Moyen Age grec et latin* 55 (1987): 107–134.

_____, and Irène Rosier-Catach. "Robertus Anglicus and Peter of Spain." In Angelelli (2), pp. 61–95.

_____. *See also under* "Other Primary Sources"

Engels, J. "La doctrine du signe chez saint Augustin." Edited by F. Cross, pp. 366–373. *Studia Patristica*, vol. 6. Texte und Untersuchungen, vol. 81. Berlin: Akademie-Verlag, 1962.

_____. "Origine, sens et survie du term boécien '*secundum placitum*'." *Vivarium* 1 (1963): 87–113.

Fredborg, Karin Margareta. "Roger Bacon on '*impositio vocis ad significandum*'." In *English Logic and Semantics*, ed. Braakhuis et al., pp. 167–192.

Gambra, José Miguel. "The Fallacy of the Accident in Peter of Spain's 'Tractatus' and in Other Thirteenth-Century Works." In Angelelli (2), pp. 21–60.

Henry, Desmond Paul. *The* De grammatico *of St. Anselm: The Theory of Paronomy*. [Notre Dame, IN]: University of Notre Dame Press, 1964.

_____. "Suppositio and Significatio in English Logic." In *English Logic and Semantics*, ed. Braakhuis et al., pp. 361–387.

Huelsen, Reinhard. "Concrete Accidental Terms and the Fallacy of Figure of Speech." In *Meaning and Inference in Medieval Philosophy*, ed. Kretzmann, pp. 175–185.

Kneale, William, and Mary Kneale. *The Development of Logic*. Oxford: Clarendon Press, 1962.

Kneepkens, C. H. "*Mulier quae damnavit, salvavit*: A Note on the Early Development of the *Relatio Simplex*." *Vivarium* 14 (1976): 1–25.

Knuuttila, Simo. "Modal Logic." In *Cambridge History of Later Medieval Philosophy*, ed. Kretzmann et al., pp. 342–357.

Kretzmann, Norman. "Aristotle on Spoken Sound Significant by Convention." In *Ancient Logic and Its Modern Interpretations*, edited by John Corcoran, pp. 3–21. Dordrecht: Reidel, 1974.

_____, ed. *Meaning and Inference in Medieval Philosophy: Studies in Memory of Jan Pinborg*. Synthese Historical Library, vol. 32. Dordrecht and Boston: Kluwer Academic Publishers, 1988.

_____, Anthony Kenny and Jan Pinborg, eds. *The Cambridge History of Later Medieval Philosophy: From the Rediscovery of Aristotle to the Disintegration of Scholasticism 1100–1600*. Cambridge, London, New York, New Rochelle, Melbourne, Sydney: Cambridge University Press, 1982.

_____. *See also under* "Other Primary Sources"

Libera, Alain de. "De la logique à la grammaire: Remarques sur la théorie de la *determinatio* chez Roger Bacon et Lambert d'Auxerre (Lambert de Lagny)." In Bursill-Hall, pp. 209–226.

_____. *See also under* "Works by Bacon"; "Other Primary Sources"

Little, Andrew G. "The Franciscan School at Oxford in the Thirteenth Century." *Archivum Franciscanum Historicum* 19 (1926): 803–874.

_____. *The Grey Friars in Oxford.* Oxford: Clarendon Press, 1892.

Longpré, E. "La *Summula dialectica* de Roger Bacon." *Archivum Franciscanum Historicum* 31 (1938): 204–205.

Malcolm, John. "A No Nonsense Approach to St. Anselm." *Franciscan Studies* 41 (1981): 336–345.

Maloney, Thomas S. "Is the *De doctrina christiana* the Source for Bacon's Semiotics?" In *Reading and Wisdom: The* De doctrina christiana *of Augustine in the Middle Ages*, edited by Edward D. English, pp. 126–142. Notre Dame, IN, and London: Notre Dame University Press, 1995.

_____. "Roger Bacon on the Division of Statements into Single/Multiple and Simple/Composed." *The Review of Metaphysics* 56 (2002): 321–356.

_____. "Roger Bacon on Equivocation." *Vivarium* 22 (1984): 85–112.

_____. "Roger Bacon on the *Significatum* of Words." In *Archéologie du signe*, edited by Lucie Brind'Amour and Eugène Vance, pp. 187–211. Recueils d'études médiévales/Papers in Mediaeval Studies, vol. 3. Toronto: Pontifical Institute of Mediaeval Studies, 1983.

_____. *See also under* "Works by Bacon"

Michaud-Quantin, Pierre. "L'Emploi des termes *logica* et *dialectica* au Moyen Age." In *Artes libéraux et philosophie au Moyen Age.* Actes du quatrième congrès international de philosophie médiévale, Université de Montréal, Canada, 27 August – 2 September 1967. Montréal: Institut d'études médiévales; Paris: Librairie philosophique J. Vrin, 1969.

Müller, Paola. "La dottrina delle *fallaciae in dictione* in Ruggero Bacone." *Documenti e studi sulla tradizione filosofica medievale* 3 (1992): 453–490.

Nuchelmans, Gabriel. "The Distinction *Actus Exercitus/Actus Significatus* in Medieval Semantics." In *Meaning and Inference in Medieval Philosophy*, ed. Kretzmann, pp. 57–90.

Pelster, Franz. "Der Oxforder Theologe Richardus Rufus O.F.M. über die Frage: '*Utrum Christus in triduo mortis fuerit homo*'." *Recherches de théologie ancienne et médiévale* 16 (1949): 258–280.

Perreiah, Alan R. "Supposition Theory: A New Approach." *The New Scholasticism* 60 (1986): 213–231.

Pinborg, Jan. "Roger Bacon on Signs: A Newly Recovered Part of the *Opus maius*." *Miscellanea Mediaevalia* 13, no. 1 (1981): 403–412.

_____. *See also under* "Works by Bacon"; "Other Primary Sources"

Rijk, L. M. de. "The Development of *suppositio naturalis* in Medieval Logic." *Vivarium* 9 (1971): 71–107.

_____. "The Origins of the Theory of the Properties of Terms." In *Cambridge History of Later Medieval Philosophy*, ed. Kretzmann et al., pp. 161–173.

_____. "Die Streit über das *medium demonstrationis*: die Frucht eines Missverständnisses?" In *Argumentationstheorie: scholastische Forschungen zu den logischen und semantischen Regeln Korrekten Folgerns*, edited by Klaus Jacobi, pp. 451–463. Studien und Texte zur Geistesgeschichte des Mittelalters, vol. 38. Leiden, Cologne: E. J. Brill, 1993.

_____. *See also under* "Other Primary Sources"

Rivero, Maria-Luisa. "Early Scholastic Views on Ambiguity: Composition and Division." *Historiographia Linguistica* 2 (1975): 25–47.

Rosier, Irène. "L'un et le multiple: probleme sémantique de la tradition médiévale des commentaires sur les *Réfutations Sophistiques* d'Aristote." *Modèles Linguistiques* 5 (1983): 39–68.

_____. "Variations médiévales sur l'opposition entre signification 'ad placitum' et signification naturelle." In *Aristotle's Peri hermeneias in the Latin Middle Ages*, edited by H. A. G. Braakhuis and C. H. Kneepkens, pp. 165–205. Artistarium Supplementa, vol. 10. Groningen-Haren: Ingenium, 2003.

_____. *See also under* Ebbesen.

Schlüter, D. "*Actus exercitus/actus signatus*." In *Historisches Wörterbuch der Philosophie*. Vol 1. Basel and Stuttgart: Schwabe, 1971.

Sharp, Dorothea. *Franciscan Philosophy at Oxford in the Thirteenth Century*. New York: Russell & Russell, 1964.

Sinkler, Georgette. "Roger Bacon on the Compounded and Divided Sense." In *The Rise of British Logic*, edited by Osmund Lewry, pp. 145–171. Acts of the Sixth European Symposium on Medieval Logic and Semantics, Balliol College, Oxford, 19–24 June 1983. Papers in Mediaeval Studies, vol. 7. Toronto: Pontifical Institute of Mediaeval Studies, [1985].

Spade, Paul Vincent. "The Logic of the Categorical: The Medieval Theory of Descent and Ascent." In *Meaning and Inference in Medieval Philosophy*, ed. Kretzmann, pp. 187–224.

_____. "Recent Research on Medieval Logic." *Synthese* 40 (1979): 3–18.

_____. "The Semantics of Terms." In *Cambridge History of Later Medieval Philosophy*, ed. Kretzmann et al., pp. 188–196.

Spruyt, Joke. "Thirteenth-Century Discussions on Modal Terms." *Vivarium* 32 (1994): 196–226.
_____. *See also under* "Other Primary Sources"
Stump, Eleonore. "Boethius's Theory of Topics and Its Place in Early Scholastic Logic." In *Atti del congresso internazionale di studi Boeziani,* edited by Luca Obertello, pp. 249–262. Rome: Herder, 1981.
_____. "Boethius's Works on the Topics." *Vivarium* 12 (1974): 77–93.
_____. "Logic in the Early Twelfth Century." In *Meaning and Inference in Medieval Philosophy*, ed. Kretzmann, pp. 31–55.
_____. "Peter of Spain on the Topics." In *Boethius and the Liberal Arts,* edited by Michael Masi, pp. 35–50. E. Bern and Las Vegas: Verlag Peter Lang, 1981.
_____. "Topics: Their Development and Absorption into Consequences." In *Cambridge History of Later Medieval Philosophy*, ed. Kretzmann et al., pp. 273–299.
_____. *See also under* "Other Primary Sources"

Index of Names

I = Introduction   P = Prologue   1, 2, 3 = Sections in the Text

General Index

I = Introduction P = Prologue 1, 2, 3 = Sections of the text